SEX AND SEXUALITY

SEX AND SEXUALITY

Volume 3
SEXUAL DEVIATION AND
SEXUAL OFFENSES

Edited by Richard D. McAnulty and M. Michele Burnette

PRAEGER PERSPECTIVES

PRAEGER

Westport, Connecticut
London

Library of Congress Cataloging-in-Publication Data

Sex and sexuality / edited by Richard D. McAnulty and M. Michele Burnette.
    v. cm.
   Includes bibliographical references and index.
   Contents: v. 1. Sexuality today : trends and controversies—v. 2. Sexual function and dysfunction—v. 3. Sexual deviation and sexual offenses.
   ISBN 0–275–98581–4 (set : alk. paper)—ISBN 0–275–98582–2 (v. 1 : alk. paper)—ISBN 0–275–98583–0 (v. 2 : alk. paper)—ISBN 0–275–98584–9 (v. 3 : alk. paper)
   1. Sex.   2. Sex customs.   3. Sexual disorders.   4. Sexual deviation.
I. McAnulty, Richard D.   II. Burnette, M. Michele.
HQ21.S4716   2006
306.77—dc22   2006001233

British Library Cataloguing in Publication Data is available.

Library of Congress Catalog Card Number: 2006001233
ISBN: 0–275–98581–4 (set)
      0–275–98582–2 (vol. 1)
      0–275–98583–0 (vol. 2)
      0–275–98584–9 (vol. 3)

First published in 2006

Praeger Publishers, 88 Post Road West, Westport, CT 06881
An imprint of Greenwood Publishing Group, Inc.
www.praeger.com

Printed in the United States of America

The paper used in this book complies with the
Permanent Paper Standard issued by the National
Information Standards Organization (Z39.48–1984).

10 9 8 7 6 5 4 3 2 1

Contents

Preface

We have had many opportunities to teach and interact with both college students and professional audiences about some very important topics and issues in human sexuality in our roles as authors and college professors. When we were approached to write this three-volume set on sex and sexuality, we were intrigued with the idea of having a forum in which to reach a broader audience. That is our goal for this work. With that in mind, we encouraged our contributors to "talk to" a general audience when writing about the topics that were most important to them. The authors we selected to write these chapters represent both established authorities and budding scholars on the various topics in human sexuality. We are confident that they have all helped us accomplish our goal.

To us, few, if any, other topics in the realm of human behavior are more interesting, exciting, or controversial than sex. And we hope that you will agree after reading the chapters from this set. Each chapter stands alone, and you can choose to read as many or as few as you would like—pick the ones that interest you. We hope that you will find this work to be of significant value to you, whether you are in pursuit of a better general understanding of sexuality or are looking for answers to specific questions.

One theme you will find throughout these texts is that human sexual function is affected by a whole host of factors. These factors are biological, sociocultural, and psychological in nature. The scientific study of sexuality is for all practical purposes a "young" field, and we have only touched the surface in an attempt to fully understand how these factors interact and impact sexuality.

Another theme or concern you will find throughout this work is the question whether "scientific" views of sex are biased by social judgments about normal versus abnormal and/or functional versus dysfunctional sexual behavior. U.S. culture, in particular, holds many strong values and prohibitions about sex. In this context, studying and interpreting research on sexuality in an unbiased manner can be a challenge. Many of our authors caution the reader about this concern.

We wish to thank all the researchers and clinicians, past and present, who have contributed to the science of sex. Many of them have contributed chapters to this set, and for that we are grateful. We also thank our colleagues, families, and friends who supported us during the writing and editing process. Finally, we thank "the team" at Praeger Publishers.

Introduction

Few topics inspire more curiosity than sexual practices deemed unusual, deviant, or deplorable. It is, however, very challenging to define deviance with respect to sexual preferences. Norms regarding sexual behavior vary over time and across cultures. Consider, for example, the changing perspective on homosexuality. Although we currently view homosexuality as a normal variation or alternative lifestyle, it was officially classified as a sexual deviation until fairly recently. It was not until 1973 that the American Psychiatric Association elected to drop homosexuality from its official list of mental disorders.

Modern culture has brought many previously taboo and forbidden topics out of the bedroom into the living room. Many sexual practices that were previously considered obscure and uncommon are discussed openly on the Internet. Bondage, domination, and fetishism, for example, are terms that are familiar to many people. The extent to which these represent deviant sexual practices is the subject of debate. There is little disagreement, however, that they qualify as atypical; these sexual practices are not considered mainstream in any culture.

Some sexual practices are unquestionably maladaptive and deviant, often even criminal. Sexual activity that involves force and coercion is deviant in every sense of the word. Rape is a legal term that can be applied to any form of sexual assault. Sexual activity with persons below the age of consent, such as children, is illicit and criminal. Child molestation therefore is another form of sexual coercion since children are incapable of providing consent. This volume offers an overview of research on the various forms of nonconsenting sexual practices, including findings of the causes, characteristics of perpetrators and victims, and interventions for addressing these problems. There is also discussion of some sexual practices that are deemed atypical although not necessarily maladaptive, such as sadomasochism.

In Chapter 1, Murphy and Page offer an overview of exhibitionism, better known as indecent exposure. They address the prevalence of this problem and such questions as whether these men are dangerous and if there are effective treatments. In Chapter 2, Santtila, Sandnabba, and Nordling explore the phenomenon of consensual sadomasochism. Flagellation and bondage are preferred activities in the sexual scripts of practitioners. However, their sexual practices are so diverse as to defy any simple description. In Chapter 3, Vandiver examines a problem that was ignored until recently: female sexual offending. The typical offender is a young adult who has psychological problems and was herself the victim of childhood sexual abuse. The sexual offense often involves an adult male co-offender. The recent disclosure of pedophilia in the clergy has drawn much attention to the problem. In Chapter 4, McAnulty offers an overview of the characteristics of pedophile, challenging popular stereotypes about the perpetrators. For example, not all pedophiles were themselves the victims of childhood sexual abuse. In Chapter 5, Calhoun, McCauley, and Crawfold explore the scope of the problem of sexual assault and the effects on victims. Sexual assault is an enormous problem that drastically impacts the lives of countless individuals. The consequences include emotional distress, short and long-term disruption in functioning, psychological and physical health problems, increase in suicide risk, increased vulnerability to additional forms of sexual and physical violence, and more. Not only are survivors affected, but others in their lives also suffer serious consequences. Kenyon-Jump's chapter (Chapter 6) on incest victims and offenders covers the effects of incest on male and female survivors at various developmental stages and in different victim-perpetrator relationships, such as mother-son incest. Incest is often unreported; early interventions have been shown to reduce the likelihood of long-term problems in victims.

In Chapter 7, Wright and Hatcher review the state of the art therapies for sex offenders. Contrary to popular belief, they find that treatment actually reduces rates of recidivism in this challenging population. In Chapter 8, Collie, Ward, and Gannon offer an innovative perspective on the treatment needs of sex offenders. They argue that the traditional approach to risk management is missing an important component: teaching offenders "to lead a better kind of life." Their *Good Lives* model intends to help an individual meet his needs in socially acceptable and personally satisfying ways. In Chapter 9, Alison and Ogan conclude that traditional approaches to offender profiling, in which offender attributes are directly inferred from crime scene evidence, are flawed. The media, however, perpetuate the public's fascination with the notion that behavioral experts or "profilers" have special insights into the minds of killers, allowing them to draw conclusions from the crime scene alone. A more sensible approach to profiling involves spelling out which claims are purely speculation and intuition and which are based on sound research. This approach discourages investigators from relying too heavily on information that may not be very accurate; it also recognizes that not all information generated by profilers is equally useful.

In Chapter 10, Marshall and Hucker address the various definitions of severe sexual sadism. Their review concludes that some features that are considered classic signs, such as torture, cruelty, and humiliation of victims, are not seen in every case. In Chapter 11, on sexual homicide, Wright, Hatcher, and Willerick explore this disturbing phenomenon. Sensational depictions in the media have fueled the public's fascination with murders that occur in the context of lust, power, and brutality. Interestingly, the authors conclude that there may be as many as 200 serial killers at large at any point in time.

Exhibitionism

William D. Murphy and I. Jacqueline Page ◆

INTRODUCTION

The term "exhibitionism" is attributed to the French physician Lasègue (cited in MacDonald, 1973), who in 1877 described a number of cases he had seen. Also during the late 1800s, Krafft-Ebing published his classic book, *Psychopathia Sexualis* (1965), describing a variety of deviant sexual behaviors including exhibitionism. These early scientists and clinicians described exhibitionism as exposure of one's genitals by males, generally to females, for sexual pleasure without any attempt at further sexual contact (MacDonald, 1973). They proposed that exhibitionism is related to some type of pathology, either some type of brain disease that interferes with behavioral control, or a mental disorder.

Over 125 years later, the clinical description of exhibitionism has changed little. Exhibitionism is considered a psychiatric disorder by the mental health field and is one of the paraphilias described in the *Diagnostic and Statistical Manual of Mental Disorders* of the American Psychiatric Association (1994). In this psychiatric nomenclature, exhibitionism is described as meeting the following two criteria: (1) recurrent, intense sexually arousing fantasies, sexual urges, or behaviors involving exposing one's genitals to an unsuspecting stranger, over a period of at least six months; (2) the fantasies, sexual urges, or behaviors caused clinically significant distress or impairment in social, occupational, or other important areas of functioning.

Mental health professionals and researchers may view exhibitionism as a disorder; others see it differently. For the criminal justice systems, exhibitionism is a crime, and in almost all jurisdictions it is considered a misdemeanor, with maximum sentencing being eleven months and twenty-nine days. Although those in the criminal justice system may feel that exhibitionists need treatment, they also view the behavior as requiring punishment.

When the lay public thinks of exhibitionism, they many times picture the frequent cartoons of an individual in a raincoat or a trench coat "flashing" an unsuspecting woman. Rather than using the somewhat sanitized term "paraphilia," many in the general public are likely to see the individual engaging in such behavior as a "pervert," who at the very least is a nuisance.

Regardless of view, clinicians, scientists, law enforcement personnel, and the public many times have the same questions:

1. Who are the victims and how often does this behavior occur?
2. Does exhibitionistic behavior cause harm to the victim?
3. Are exhibitionists dangerous?
4. Do exhibitionists share certain mental disorders or psychological problems that cause exhibitionism?
5. Can exhibitionists be "cured" or treated?

This chapter will provide some information on these questions, but as the reader will see, for many, we do not have a definitive answer.

HOW OFTEN DOES EXHIBITIONISM OCCUR?

Trying to determine how often any sexual behavior occurs is very difficult given the private nature of such behavior. This is compounded when trying to determine how frequently criminal sexual behavior, such as exhibitionism, occurs. Individuals who engage in such behavior are generally not forthcoming in admitting such behavior, and many victims never report the behavior to the police. For example, Cox and Maletsky (1980), in reviewing early studies, point out that only about 17 percent of women surveyed who had been exposed to exhibitionism report it to the police. A more recent study in the United Kingdom (Riordan, 1999) found that approximately 29 percent reported their offenses to the police.

There are a number of methods researchers use to try to determine the incidence or prevalence of sexual crimes. One way is to look at official criminal justice records; a second is to attempt to sample the general population to determine how many report exposing themselves or being exposed to. A third method is to ask identified exhibitionists how often they engage in the behavior, which is limited by their willingness to admit criminal behavior. Relying on criminal justice records will always underestimate the true frequency since there is significant underreporting. Interviewing individuals in the general population can also be problematic in that it is sometimes difficult to find a random sample and therefore one is never sure of whether the sample is representative of the population. Also, when surveying the general population, there will be people who refuse to participate, or are reluctant to admit being victimized or engaging in criminal behavior. Given these limitations, we will attempt to provide an overview of what we know.

One study by Abel and Rouleau (1990) interviewed 142 exhibitionists who were promised confidentiality. This group reported on the average that they had exposed themselves to 513 victims. Exhibitionists reported more victims per offender than any other paraphilia.

In terms of criminal justice records, Murphy (1990) reviewed a number of early studies which indicated that approximately one-third of sexual offenders coming into contact with the legal system were exhibitionists. Frenken, Gijs, and Van Beek (1999) found that between 1980 and 1994, one-third to one-half of all sex crimes registered by the Dutch police were for indecent exposure. This represents a rate of 24 per 100,000 to 37 per 100,000 in the population aged 12 to 79. This means that in a year, from 0.02 percent to approximately 0.04 percent of the population between the ages of 12 and 79 are arrested for exhibitionism. In Germany, Pfäfflin (1999) found that between 1981 and 1994 there were between 8,000 and 12,000 cases of exhibitionism reported to the police every year, and about 16 percent of all those who were sentenced for a sex offense were exhibitionists. Unfortunately, we do not have similar data for the United States. Although there are numerous sources from which to determine the number of rapes reported to the police or the number of official reports of children sexually abused, such data are usually not kept nationally for exhibitionism, which, as noted, is considered a misdemeanor.

There are two studies known to us that have attempted to look at the frequency with which individuals in the community report engaging in exhibitionistic behavior. The first of these sampled college students (Templeman & Stinnett, 1991) and found that one of sixty of the males sampled admitted to exhibitionistic behavior, which represents about 2 percent of the sample group. A much more extensive study has recently been conducted in Sweden by Långström and Seto (in press). This study was a random selection from 6.2 million 17- to 18-year-olds in the general Swedish population. Approximately 4,800 people were approached for participation and actual data was obtained from 2,800. This survey was a more general study on sexuality and health sponsored by the Swedish Public Health Institute. Subjects in this study were specifically asked, "Have you ever exposed your genitals to a stranger and become sexually aroused by this?" Overall, 3.1 percent of the sample admitted to exhibitionism. The rate for males was 4.3 percent and the rate for females was surprisingly 2.1 percent.

There have also been a number of surveys of women, questioning whether they have been exposed to exhibitionism. Most of these have not been random samples of the population, but they show surprising consistency across time and countries. Cox and MacMahon (1978) found that 32 percent of 405 female college students from four universities across the United States reported being victims of exhibitionism, while Cox, Tsang, and Lee (1982) found almost the same percentage in a sample of undergraduate students in Hong Kong. Gittelson, Eacott, and Mehta (1978) found that 44 percent of a sample of 100 British nurses with a mean age of 37 had been exposed to outside the work situation. Over twenty years later, a study by Riordan (1999) that involved both college students and women in the community in the United Kingdom found that 48.6 percent reported being exposed to, and a 2004 study in Germany of 309 female college students indicated that 39.5 percent reported being exposed to (Kury, Chouaf, Obergfell-Fuchs, & Woessner, 2004). A study conducted in the United States (Finkelhor, Ormrod, Turner, & Hamby, 2005) surveyed a national sample of children and youth between the ages of 2 and 17. Either the child or the parent was interviewed, depending on the child's age, regarding the child's exposure to a variety of victimization experiences. Of this group of children and youth, 2.8 percent indicated that they had been exposed to in the last year. This percentage would indicate that approximately 1.6 million children between the ages of 2 and 17 are exposed to each year.

Although none of the above studies are perfect, there is a very clear pattern across time, and a good deal of consistency across countries. Surveys are very consistent that 30 percent to over 40 percent of women have an experience of being exposed to, and so have a significant number of children and adolescents. This is a rather alarming number of individuals being subjected to an unwanted and intrusive sexual behavior.

WHAT IS THE IMPACT ON THE VICTIM?

There have been multiple studies of the impact of child sexual abuse and rape on the psychological functioning, interpersonal functioning, and health status of victims. There is, however, a tendency to view exhibitionistic behavior as a nuisance but not a behavior that causes harm. In reality, we have few studies that address this issue.

The first thing to consider is the high percentage of victims that are children and adolescents. Gittelson et al. (1978) found that 57 percent of their sample reported being exposed to before age 16, and twenty years later, the study by Riordan again found that 50 percent reported being exposed to by age 16. As we saw in the previous section, the national survey by Finkelhor et al. (2005) found that over one million children and youth were exposed to in any given year. A few early studies conducted before 1980 assessed the impact of exhibitionism on victims (see Cox & Maletsky, 1980, for a summary). Overall, 50–80 percent of victims describe the experience in negative terms. For example, Gittelson et al. (1978) indicated that 50 percent of their sample reported fear, 30 percent disgust, and 9 percent anger. Cox and MacMahon (1978) found that 14 percent of their sample indicated that the experience seriously or very seriously affected their attitude toward men. Riordan (1999) is the only study that could be located since the 1970s, and its findings were very similar, with about 49 percent reporting shock and about 26 percent fear, and 68 percent considering the exhibitionist dangerous.

It should be noted that in most cases, the negative reactions were not long lasting and tended to resolve within a month. However, another factor that was found across studies was that many women avoided places where the act occurred.

Although for most women exhibitionism does not lead to long-term negative sequelae, a small percentage experience more long-term negative effects, and a high percentage report initial negative reactions. In addition, being a victim does seem to impact a woman's (as most reported cases are female) feeling of safety in her own community. The fact that being exposed to does not lead to long-term trauma for most victims should not lead to seeing the behavior as only a nuisance. It is not appropriate to create short-term fear in women and to impact their feelings of safety in their own community. Nor is exhibitionism an appropriate way to introduce children to sexual behavior.

ARE EXHIBITIONISTS DANGEROUS?

As noted by Riordan (1999), 68 percent of women who have been exposed to perceive the exhibitionist as dangerous. In addition, as we also reviewed, over 50 percent of exhibitionists expose to children and youth. The question of dangerousness is usually framed as whether the exhibitionist is likely to reoffend and, probably more important to most people, whether they progress from hands-off offending to hands-on offending such as rape or child molestation.

Recidivism

Determining the true reoffense rate or recidivism rate for sex offenders is difficult. What is considered recidivism is usually based on individuals who have at least been charged for a new offense or who have been reconvicted for a new offense. However, as we have seen, many victims of exhibitionists never report the offense, and when the offense is reported, the police may not be able to arrest the suspect, or may not be able to charge the offender, or prosecutors may elect not to prosecute. Therefore, official recidivism rates generally underestimate true rates of reoffending.

Given these limitations, the research suggests that exhibitionists tend to have high recidivism rates as compared to other sex offenders. For example, in an early study, Frisbee and Dondis (1965), found that 40.7 percent of treated exhibitionists reoffended after five years as compared to 18.2 percent of pedophiles who targeted female children and 34.5 percent of pedophiles who targeted male children. It should be noted that although they were labeled treated offenders, the treatment program at that time would not meet current standards for effective treatment. It should also be noted that this was a population of individuals sentenced to a secure residential treatment program under what were at that time termed sexual psychopath laws. Today, exhibitionists would not be sent to such secure facilities.

More recent data also suggest fairly high rates of recidivism. Marshall, Barbaree, and Eccles (1991), in a small study of forty-four exhibitionists, found a 39 percent recidivism rate for treated offenders and a 57 percent rate for untreated offenders. Because of these high rates, Marshall et al. (1991) described a second study where they modified their treatment program to address a broader range of treatment issues. Their previous program had focused more on strategies directed toward the urges in exhibitionists to expose themselves, but the new program focused on factors such as the exhibitionists' perceived need to be perfect and assisted them in developing more intimate relationships. In this study, although there was no control group, the recidivism rate was down to 24 percent. These results, although still somewhat high for reoffending, are promising. Firestone, Kingston, Wexler, and Bradford (2005) followed over 200 exhibitionists for an average of thirteen years and found that 23.6 percent reoffended sexually.

It should also be noted that those who expose to children have higher recidivism rates than those who expose to adults (Frisbee & Dondis, 1965). In addition, those who have antisocial personalities, have higher scores on an alcohol measure, and are less educated (Firestone et al., 2005; Greenberg, Firestone, Bradford, Greenberg, 2002) have higher rates of reoffending.

Progression to More Serious Offending

One method researchers have used to answer this question is to study known exhibitionists to determine whether in the past they have had other sexual offenses. The most extensive data is provided by Freund (1990) and Abel and Osborn (1992). Freund found that among the 240 exhibitionists studied, 15 percent had histories of rape. Abel and Osborn's 1992 study is unique in that data was collected from outpatients who were promised confidentiality under a federal certificate of confidentiality. This federal certificate is provided to research programs to protect research subjects' confidentiality. They found that of 118 individuals whose primary diagnosis was exhibitionism, 39 percent self-reported previous molestation of children and 14 percent reported that they had previously raped. Rooth (1973) suggests that exhibitionists who exposed preferentially to children may be at increased risk for becoming hands-on sex offenders against children. Rooth's own data on a sample of thirty fairly chronic exhibitionists indicated that few had engaged in rape but that 25 percent had been involved in pedophilic activity and 40 percent in frottage (touching or rubbing up against another person). Firestone et al. (2005) found that 31.3 percent of their subjects had a violent and/or sexual reoffense. Of the 23.6 percent who reoffended sexually, about 38 percent reoffended with a hands-on sexual offense.

A second method is to study known rapists and child molesters and to determine how many had a past history of exhibitionism. A relatively large study (Longo & Groth, 1983) found that 28 percent of the child molesters and 15 percent of the rapists they studied had engaged in exhibitionistic behavior as juveniles. Abel et al. (2004) found that among 1,170 adolescents who molested children, 13 percent also reported histories of exhibitionism.

English, Jones, Pasini-Hill, Patrick, and Cooley-Towell (2000) studied a group of offenders on parole and probation who were presumably hands-on offenders. They were required to take a polygraph (lie detector) test as part of their parole and probation monitoring. Prior to their polygraph, 22 percent reported hands-on offenses, and after the polygraph, 67 percent indicated hands-off offenses. In this study, hands-off offenses were defined as exhibitionism, voyeurism, and stalking, so it is not possible to determine exactly the number of people who only exposed themselves.

Not all studies have found such high percentages. Marshall et al. (1991) found only a very small number of child molesters who had also engaged in exhibitionistic behavior. Rooth (1973) reviewed a number of early studies that suggested that 10–12 percent of exhibitionists had either raped in the past or were convicted of rape in the future. Sjöstedt, Långström, Sturidsson, and Grann (2004) present a prospective study where they followed a group of 1,303 offenders released from prison in Sweden between the years 1993 and 1997. They looked at offenses that occurred after release for an average follow-up of six years. Their finding was that those subjects whose index offense was a noncontact offense showed relatively stable recidivism histories and their most frequent reoffense was another noncontact offense. In this study, noncontact offenses were not broken down into subtypes such as exhibitionism or voyeurism, so it cannot be determined how many subjects were exhibitionists and how many were other noncontact offenders such as voyeurs.

A problem with the above studies is that they involve subjects primarily identified by the legal system. As we have reviewed, most exhibitionists are never reported and of those reported, many are never arrested or processed through the criminal justice system. Those who are arrested may represent the most chronic offenders and may differ from the majority of exhibitionists in a number of ways. The most extensive data by Sjöstedt et al. (2004) did not suggest that noncontact offenders were at high risk for progression to more serious offenses. However, there does seem to be a small group of exhibitionists, maybe between 10 percent and 30 percent, who are at risk to engage in hands-on offenses, and there is evidence that exhibitionists who expose to children may be at risk for molesting children.

CHARACTERISTICS OF THE OFFENDER AND THE OFFENSE

Exhibitionism, like many sex offenses, has an early onset. Abel and Rouleau (1990) report that 50 percent of the exhibitionists in their clinic reported that they had the onset of their interest in exhibitionism by age 18. In a small sample, Mohr, Turner, and Jerry (1964) found a bimodal distribution of onset. There seemed to be two peak times, one in the mid-teens and one in the mid-twenties, for onset of exhibitionism. Onset then tends to decrease over time, and a number of early studies with clinical and forensic populations found that between 6 percent and 27 percent of the exhibitionists began their behavior after age 40 (see Murphy, 1997).

In clinical and forensic situations, exhibitionists are almost exclusively males, with only a few cases of female exhibitionists reported in the literature. Most victims are female. However, it is of interest to note that in the Långström and Seto (in press) study a little over 2 percent of women in their national sample answered yes to the question, "Have you ever exposed your genitals to a stranger and became sexually aroused by this?" But it is always difficult to determine how the respondent has interpreted this question, and the overall data would suggest that few females engage in chronic exhibitionistic behavior. The national survey by Finkelhor et al. (2005) also suggests that among children, males and females appear to be equally at risk of being victims of an exhibitionist.

Exhibitionists are similar to the general population in factors such as socioeconomic status, education, intelligence, and marital status (Blair & Lanyon, 1981). For example, Mohr et al. (1964) found that the mean IQ for their sample was 104, which is fairly similar to the mean IQ of the general population. Blair and Lanyon (1981) report that across studies about 62 percent of their subjects were married or had been married, which, given that exhibitionists tend to be younger, would not differ significantly from the general population.

WHAT CAUSES EXHIBITIONISM?

Criminality

Before answering the question, "What is the cause of exhibitionism?" we need to ask, "Do exhibitionists differ from other criminals?" There has been a tendency when looking at the causes of sex offending to assume that somehow sex offenders are different in some ways from other criminal populations. As one will see in later parts of this chapter, there have been a number of attempts to explain the behavior of sex offenders in general and exhibitionists in particular as being related to specific psychiatric disorders or psychological problems.

However, in the general field of criminology, there is support for a general theory of crime (Gottfredson & Hirschi, 1990). Criminals tend to be diverse, rather than specialist, in their criminal behavior, and Gottfredson and Hirschi proposed that the underlying factor is low self-control which impairs the individual's ability to delay gratification and control impulses. They feel that poor parenting is the primary cause of this low self-control, although other factors such as birth complications, which impact brain functioning, may also contribute (Beaver & Wright, 2005).

Research on sex offenders has generally proceeded as if sex offenders are different from the general criminal population and as if their offenses are more specialized; but this has been recently questioned (Smallbone & Wortley, 2004). These authors suggest that sex offenders engage in a variety of criminal behaviors that might be best understood from a general criminal perspective rather than searching for specific sexual pathology.

For example, Berah and Myers (1983) found that of the forty subjects they studied, 69 percent had been convicted for crimes other than exhibitionism. Blair and Lanyon (1981), in their review, found that across studies, 17–30 percent of exhibitionistic subjects had committed nonsexual offenses. More recently, Greenberg et al. (2002) also found high rates of general criminal behavior in their sample of exhibitionists.

The issue of general criminal behavior is important because the extent to which an exhibitionist does or does not engage in other criminal behavior is related to their risk for continued offending and to the type of personality disturbance.

Childhood and Familial Factors

In research with sex offenders in general and exhibitionists in particular, there has been an attempt to identify childhood experiences or family factors that lead to sex offending. Histories of childhood abuse, specifically sexual abuse, have been posited as a cause of sex offending. However, exhibitionists tend to have fairly low rates of sexual abuse as compared to other types of sex offenders, specifically child molesters. Saunders and Awad (1991) found that 13 percent of their sample had been physically abused and 17 percent had been sexually abused. Fehrenbach, Smith, Monastersky, and Deisher (1986) found that 7.5 percent of their subjects had a history of sexual abuse while 9.4 percent had histories of being physically abused. Lee, Jackson, Pattison, and Ward (2002) found that exhibitionists in their sample did not differ significantly from a comparison group in terms of histories of sexual abuse or physical abuse. However, they did differ in terms of their history of childhood emotional abuse and general family dysfunction.

It should be recognized, however, that high rates of childhood abuse are also related to general criminal behavior, and that none of the above studies separated out those exhibitionists whose offenses were only exhibitionism versus those who had exhibitionistic and nonexhibitionistic offenses. In addition, histories of abuse and family dysfunction are found in the background of many individuals with psychological and psychiatric disturbances, and it does not appear that this is specific to sex offenders alone.

Personality Characteristics and Psychological Disturbance

In searching for a cause of exhibitionism, there have been many attempts to look at whether a certain type of psychopathology or certain types of personality characteristics place individuals at risk for sexual offending. If one asks the general population what they feel the personality characteristics of exhibitionists are, they would generally assume that the exhibitionist is someone who has poor skills relating to women, may feel sexually inadequate, and may be shy and inhibited. Early descriptive studies of exhibitionists tended to support this view (Blair & Lanyon, 1981).

However, when studies used more standardized psychological instruments, the results were much more mixed. For example, in a study with a large number of exhibitionists (Langevin et al., 1979), using a variety of standardized tests, researchers found few to no differences between exhibitionists and control subjects on measures of heterosocial skills or assertiveness. Other investigators have found that disturbances on psychological tests, such as the Minnesota Multiphasic Personality Inventory (Dahlstrom, Welsh, & Dahlstrom, 1972), correlated with previous convictions. That is, subjects with one or two convictions showed little psychological disturbance, while those with six arrests tended to have a number of psychological problems (McCreary, 1975). Later studies, however, indicated that this disturbance was more related to those who showed repeat nonexhibitionist criminal behavior than to those with exhibitionistic behavior (Forgac, Cassel, & Michaels, 1984; Forgac & Michaels, 1982), which is consistent with the findings of Firestone et al. (2005), who found those with antisocial personality traits to have the highest recidivism.

A more recent study by Lee et al. (2002) sheds further light on some of the above observations. This study compared exhibitionists not only to a comparison group but also to other sex offender groups, such as pedophiles and rapists. They studied two broad concepts labeled "anger and hostility" and "sexual maladjustment and heterosocial skills deficits" using multiple measures of each of these concepts. The results suggested that all of the paraphilias shared certain characteristics and that both anger and hostility and sexual maladjustment and heterosocial skills deficits separated sex offenders as a group from controls. Exhibitionists were somewhat lower on heterosocial skills as compared to the control group. It was found that both pedophiles and exhibitionists tended to suppress their anger and direct it toward themselves, while rapists tended to direct their anger outwardly. However, of the different paraphilic groups, exhibitionists seemed to show the least psychopathology and sexual maladjustment. The authors' conclusions were that exhibitionism in terms of psychopathology was the "least severe disorder among the group of paraphilias studied."

In summary, research has failed to find specific personality characteristics or types of psychological disturbances that would explain the onset of exhibitionism. What the literature does suggest is that exhibitionists vary on a number of factors such as degree of social competence, sexual adjustment, and their ability to manage emotions, such as anger. Some of this variation is probably due to the sample studied. Those who are more chronic may have more psychological disturbances as do those who engage in both exhibitionistic behavior and nonexhibitionistic criminal behavior.

Neurological Impairment

Krafft-Ebing (1965), in explaining exhibitionism, stated that there was a group that suffered from "acquired states of mental weakness," which were caused by "cerebral (or spinal) disease." He went on to describe a number of cases where there appeared to be some brain impairment. There has been a continued interest in this area, although there are limited studies with exhibitionists. Although case studies have appeared that describe exhibitionists having certain types of brain pathology (see Murphy, 1997, for review), there have been very few controlled studies. The most extensive data comes from Flor-Henry and Lang (1988) and Flor-Henry, Koles, Reddon, and Baker (1986). In studies that use both neuropsychological test data and EEGs (measures of brain electrical activity), they found deficits in the left hemisphere of the brain. The neuropsychological data suggested left frontal temporal lobe dysfunction. The temporal lobe is important because early animal studies have shown that temporal lobe injury in primates can lead to hypersexuality (Kluver & Bucy, 1939). However, as pointed out by O'Carroll (1989), subjects used in Flor-Henry's studies were recidivist, incarcerated offenders who averaged five to six convictions.

At this time, data is too limited to indicate whether there is any specific neurological impairment in exhibitionists. It is likely, based on the case reports that have appeared in the literature, that there are some individuals who expose themselves as a result of some type of brain pathology, although it is unlikely that this applies to the vast majority of people who expose themselves.

Deviant Sexual Interest

As we noted earlier, many studies of sex offenders and exhibitionists have examined early childhood experiences, sexual or psychological pathology, personality deficits, and, to a lesser extent, neurological problems as possible causes or factors that place individuals at risk for exhibitionistic behavior. As we have seen above, these studies have generally had mixed results, and we have been unable to identify any one specific factor. Beginning in the late 1960s and continuing from then, researchers in the field of sex offense began questioning whether such behavior occurred not because of psychopathology but because the individual had a specific interest in different forms of deviant sexual behavior. A technology was developed called penile plethysmography (also called phallometry) that used a gauge that directly measured changes in penis size while subjects were exposed to specific sexual stimuli. The stimuli could include slides depicting people of different ages, videotaped depictions of sexual behavior, or audiotaped descriptions of sexual behavior. Subjects' responses to deviant stimuli were compared to responses to nondeviant stimuli, and studies have compared a variety of sex offenders to non-sex offenders. The history of this research and the data related to it have been reviewed by Murphy and Barbaree (1994) and Marshall and Fernandez (2003).

There have been numerous studies investigating this assessment methodology with child molesters and rapists. Results have suggested that certain subtypes of child molesters, those who molest nonrelatives, have a tendency to respond more to child-type stimuli than normal.

Marshall and Fernandez (2003) reviewed approximately ten studies that have attempted to determine whether exhibitionists have specific sexual attraction to exhibitionistic behavior. None of the studies indicated that exhibitionists responded more to exhibitionistic stimuli than nonexhibitionistic stimuli; nor did any study indicate that exhibitionists differed in any meaningful way from nonexhibitionistic controls. These findings are fairly clear that exhibitionists' arousal patterns do not differ from what would be expected of men in the general population.

However, Firestone et al. (2005) and Greenberg et al. (2002) found that exhibitionists who reoffended showed more arousal to child stimuli than those who did not reoffend. This suggests that, although exhibitionists may not show arousal to exhibitionist stimuli, their arousal to other deviant stimuli may have value in predicting those more likely to reoffend.

EVALUATION AND TREATMENT

Does Treatment Work?

The reader of this chapter by now should recognize that exhibitionism impacts a large number of women and children (both male and female) in our society. Exhibitionists have victims, and a fairly high percentage of women report that they have been exposed to, many of them in childhood. It also should be clear that when apprehended exhibitionists have fairly high rates of reoffending, both sexually and nonsexually, and a small percentage of them progress to more serious sex offenses. The reader may, however, note that our review of the research and the characteristics of exhibitionists suggests that they are very diverse and heterogeneous in their functioning. They vary on criminality, social skills, psychological dysfunction, and deviant sexual interest. One may question how a treatment program should be designed for such a diverse population.

There is also the general public perception that treatment for sex offenders does not work. The question whether any treatment program works is rather complex. The most accepted scientific method for proving the effectiveness of treatment is termed the randomized clinical trial. In this type of study, subjects are randomized to receive the treatment of interest while the control group is randomized to receive either placebo treatment or some alternative treatment. These are common designs used in drug studies where the experimental group receives the investigative drug and the control group receives a placebo. The advantage of randomization is that there is an expectation that groups will be equal, because they are randomly assigned, on other variables that might impact treatment outcome such as severity of the disorder. Unfortunately, there are very few randomized clinical trials in the study of sex offenders in general and to our knowledge none in the study of exhibitionism.

A second type of study, which also provides some evidence for effectiveness of treatment, although not as strong as the randomized clinical trial, is where assignment to groups is incidental or where subjects are matched (Hanson et al., 2002). An example of these types of studies would be a prison system that establishes a treatment program for sex offenders. Individuals who completed this program are compared to people who were released from the prison prior to the onset of the program.

Another approach is to compare treated offenders to a comparison group of untreated men who match them on such important variables as history of previous offenses, type of sexual offense, and the like. As noted, these studies provide some evidence, but one can never be sure that the groups do not vary on some important variable unrelated to the treatment. There have been a number of these studies for sex offenders in general but fewer for exhibitionists.

Another research issue in determining whether treatment is effective is that no one study can provide a definitive answer. That is, to determine whether treatment is effective, one would like to see multiple studies. Because no one study in itself can be considered definitive, researchers use a method called meta-analysis to combine studies to look at the overall effects of treatment. In the general area of treatment of sexual offenders, there have been a number of these meta-analyses, with the two most recent and largest being reported by Hanson et al. (2002) and Lösel and Schmucker (2005). The Hanson et al. meta-analysis does not look specifically at exhibitionists, but some of the studies included did have exhibitionistic subjects. The data they reported summarized forty-three different studies. When the studies were combined, there were a total of 5,078 treated sex offenders and 4,376 untreated sex offenders. When the authors looked at only studies that were random or had incidental assignment (the most acceptable studies), they found a sexual recidivism rate of 9.9 percent for treated offenders and a 17.4 percent rate for untreated offenders, which is highly significant. The most recent Lösel study included many topics of the Hanson study, as well as those from studies published since that time, including a number of European studies. They were able to locate eighty independent comparisons between treated and untreated offenders that included over 22,000 offenders. Their findings were very similar to those of Hanson et al., with a recidivism rate of 12 percent for the treated groups and 24 percent for the comparison groups. Again, most of the studies reviewed in the Lösel and Schmucker meta-analysis were not on exhibitionists. However, these authors did separate out four studies that focused specifically on exhibitionists. Although this is only a small number of treatment studies, results did indicate that treated exhibitionists did significantly better than untreated exhibitionists, although they did not provide specific recidivism rates.

Although the area of sex offender treatment lacks studies that have used the strongest research designs, there have been multiple studies using relatively appropriate control groups. When such studies are combined, there seems to be an indication that sex offender treatment can be effective. Although we do not have the definitive answer to the effectiveness of treatment, the general public's view that sex offenders cannot be treated does not appear to be warranted, and the evidence does suggest that recidivism can be reduced by appropriate treatment. This also appears to apply to exhibitionists. However, it is also clear that although treatment may reduce recidivism, exhibitionists still have higher rates of reoffense as compared to other offenders.

What to Treat?

The above review suggests that sex offender treatment can be effective. However, the second question is what does one actually treat to reduce recidivism? This is another area where there have been significant advances in our research understanding of what kind of factors need to be targeted in treatment to actually reduce recidivism. Some of the public's skepticism of sex offender treatment is probably due to many early studies that provided treatment that was not highly effective. These studies provided treatment from a psychoanalytic model focusing on early childhood experiences and relationship with mother. There is little evidence that focusing on these types of factors will reduce recidivism.

What research has shown is that to reduce the recidivism of sex offenders in general, and we feel this applies to exhibitionists too, we must focus on what are termed dynamic risk factors. Research has identified approximately four broad areas related to recidivism (Beech, Fisher, & Thornton, 2003; Hanson & Harris, 2000; Hanson & Morton-Bourgon, 2004). Although different researchers use different terminology for each of the broad areas, we will try to summarize each below.

Sexual Self-Regulation or Sexual Interest

Research has indicated that sex offenders in general, and to some extent exhibitionists in theory, vary in their ability to regulate their sexual interest. Some offenders have specific deviant sexual interest, that is, they are sexually aroused by the act of exhibitionism. Also, offenders vary in the degree of sexual preoccupation, with some offenders being highly compulsive, not only in their exhibitionistic behavior but also in other aspects of their sexual behavior. They may frequently masturbate and view pornography. In addition, there is evidence that offenders use sex as a coping strategy. That is, when experiencing negative emotional states, rather than using coping strategies that would resolve stress, they turn to sex. As we noted earlier, most exhibitionists do not show deviant sexual interest at least as measured phallometrically, although some do. Many exhibitionists, however, are somewhat compulsive in their sexual behavior and may use sex as a coping strategy. There are a number of behavioral treatments available that assist individuals in controlling their deviant sexual interests. For example, one such technique is called covert sensitization, where the individual would be asked to imagine the act of exposing and then told to switch to imagining negative consequences such as being arrested, going to jail, or losing their family. There are also more aversive techniques where the thoughts of exhibitionism can be paired with an aversive odor such as sniffing ammonia. Also, there are medications such as antiandrogens, which reduce male testosterone and drive, and selective serotonin reuptake inhibitors, which are used for depression and obsessive compulsive disorders but also may reduce the sexual preoccupation (Hill, Briken, Kraus, Strohm, & Berner, 2003).

Attitudes Supportive of Offending

The second factor that contributes to sex offender recidivism is attitudes the offenders hold that they use to justify their behavior. These include feelings of sexual entitlement, perceiving women as deceitful, viewing relationships as adversarial, perceiving that women enjoy being exposed to, or that they are "asking for it" because of the way they dress. This may also include general hostility toward women. Exhibitionists, like other offenders, can vary on which of these types of attitudes they hold and the strength of the attitudes. The goal of treatment of this area is to help the offenders identify their attitudes and help them through what is termed cognitive restructuring, to examine these attitudes and learn to challenge the reality of their thinking.

Social-Emotional Functioning

Another broad area that relates to reoffending can be deficits in establishing relationships and in handling negative emotional states. These include such factors as inability to establish intimate relationships, feeling lonely and isolated, being underassertive, and feeling inadequate. As we noted before, many early studies pointed out a number of these traits for exhibitionists. However, literature also indicates that this is not true for all exhibitionists. Again, the purpose of an evaluation of an offender is to identify if the individual who exposes himself has deficits in these areas and to provide appropriate psychological intervention. Treatments for these areas are similar to treatment for a number of general psychological problems. They can involve assertiveness training, training to teach appropriate relationship skills, and again modifying beliefs that lead to feelings of inadequacy.

This area can also include a general lack of concern for other people and callous and unemotional traits. It should be noted that these types of attitudes are much more difficult to change and tend to be associated with offenders who engage in not only sex offending but general criminal behavior as well.

General Self-Regulation or Self-Management

A fourth general area related to recidivism is what we term general self-management. This includes issues such as general impulsivity, poor problem-solving skills, and poor emotional control with a tendency to explosive and angry outbursts. Exhibitionists, as in the other areas, vary considerably on this dimension. Some exhibitionists maintain steady employment, are married, and show no indications of difficulties in regulating their behavior outside the area of exhibitionism. However, there are a few who engage in general criminal behavior and who show instability in numerous aspects of their lives. There are a number of treatments, such as anger management training or what are termed cognitive skills programs. These types of programs focus on offenders learning skills to reduce their impulsivity, to problem solve more effectively, and to manage emotions more effectively.

Treatment Style

Another advance in the treatment of sex offenders, which also applies to exhibitionists, is the way in which treatment is delivered. Early treatment of sex offenders tended to be very confrontive in nature. It was felt that offenders were always lying, and that they had to be constantly challenged. Current treatment styles recognize that such an approach is probably not effective, and are very different compared to some of the early treatments. People specializing in sex offender treatment still believe offenders need to accept responsibility for their behavior but have begun to recognize that if one expects change, then one must collaboratively work with offenders. In addition to focusing on negative aspects of the offenders' behavior and functioning, therapists must help establish more positive goals to replace the inappropriate behavior and assist the offender to lead a more prosocial life (Marshall et al., 2005).

In summary, there has been an evolution in treatment for sex offenders in general, which also applies to exhibitionists. Even though we do not have the final answer, there appears to be accumulating evidence that treatment of sex offenders can be effective. The literature clearly indicates that treatments that are cognitive-behavioral in nature, that focus on learning skills, that directly address issues related to recidivism rather than general psychological deficits, and that are delivered in a style that allows the offender to change, can be effective.

CONCLUSIONS

Compared to other paraphilias, we have much less knowledge of this population. We do know that the behavior occurs frequently and impacts upward of 40 percent of women and up to 1.6 million children each year. We have learned that there is no one type of exhibitionist and that they vary across a number of characteristics. It is also clear that not all exhibitionists are "harmless" and that a significant minority goes on to commit more serious sex offenses and other violent offenses. We also have some limited evidence that treatment can be effective, although exhibitionists still seem to reoffend at higher rates than other paraphiliacs.

A prime area for the future is to focus on adolescents who expose. We know that up to 50 percent of exhibitionists begin in adolescence. It is also this population that authorities may not take seriously. We need to be able to identify those who are more at risk to continue the behavior or to escalate into more serious offenses, and to provide interventions earlier.

REFERENCES

Abel, G. G., Jordan, A., Rouleau, J.-L., Emerick, R., Barboza-Whitehead, S., & Osborn, C. (2004). Use of visual reaction time to assess male adolescents who molest children. *Sexual Abuse: A Journal of Research and Treatment, 16,* 255–265.

Abel, G. G., & Osborn, C. (1992). Stopping sexual violence. *Psychiatric Annals, 22,* 301–330.

Abel, G. G., & Rouleau, J.-L. (1990). The nature and extent of sexual assault. In W. L. Marshall, D. R. Laws, & H. E. Barbaree (Eds.), *Handbook of sexual assault: Issues, theories, and treatment of the offender* (pp. 9–21). New York: Plenum Press.

American Psychiatric Association. (1994). *Diagnostic and statistical manual of mental disorders* (4th ed.). Washington, DC: Author.

Beaver, K. M., & Wright, J. P. (2005). Evaluating the effects of birth complications on low self-control in a sample of twins. *International Journal of Offender Therapy and Comparative Criminology, 49,* 450–471.

Beech, A. R., Fisher, D. D., & Thornton, D. (2003). Risk assessment of sex offenders. *Professional Psychology: Research and Practice, 34,* 339–352.

Berah, E. F., & Myers, R. G. (1983). The offense records of a sample of convicted exhibitionists. *Bulletin of the American Academy of Psychiatry and Law, 11,* 365–369.

Blair, C. D., & Lanyon, R. I. (1981). Exhibitionism: Etiology and treatment. *Psychological Bulletin, 89,* 439–463.

Cox, D. J., & MacMahon, B. (1978). Incidence of male exhibitionism in the United States as reported by victimized female college students. *National Journal of Law and Psychiatry, 1,* 453–457.

Cox, D. J., & Maletsky, B. M. (1980). Victims of exhibitionism. In D. J. Cox & R. J. Daitzman (Eds.), *Exhibitionism: Description, assessment, and treatment* (pp. 289–293). New York: Garland.

Cox, D. J., Tsang, K., & Lee, A. (1982). A cross cultural comparison of the incidence and nature of male exhibitionism in college students. *Victimology, 7,* 231–234.

Dahlstrom, W. G., Welsh, G. S., & Dahlstrom, L. E. (1972). *An MMPI handbook: Vol. 1. Clinical interpretation.* Minneapolis: University of Minnesota Press.

English, K., Jones, L., Pasini-Hill, D., Patrick, D., & Cooley-Towell, S. (2000). *The value of polygraph testing in sex offender management.* Denver, CO: Colorado Department of Public Safety, Office of Research and Statistics.

Fehrenbach, P. A., Smith, W., Monastersky, C., & Deisher, R. W. (1986). Adolescent sexual offenders: Offender and offense characteristics. *American Journal of Orthopsychiatry, 56,* 225–233.

Finkelhor, D., Ormrod, R., Turner, H., & Hamby, S. L. (2005). The victimization of children and youth: A comprehensive, national survey. *Child Maltreatment, 10,* 5–25.

Firestone, P., Kingston, D. A., Wexler, A., & Bradford, J. M. (2005). *Long term follow-up of exhibitionists: Psychological, phallometric, and offence.* Unpublished manuscript.

Flor-Henry, P., Koles, Z. L., Reddon, J. R., & Baker, L. (1986). Neuropsychological studies (EEG) of exhibitionism. In M. C. Shagrasi, R. C. Josiassen, & R. A. Roemer (Eds.), *Brain electrical potentials and psychopathology* (pp. 279–306). Amsterdam: Elsevier Science.

Flor-Henry, P., & Lang, R. (1988). Quantitative EEG analysis in genital exhibitionists. *Annals of Sex Research, 1,* 49–62.

Forgac, G. E., Cassel, C. A., & Michaels, E. J. (1984). Chronicity of criminal behavior and psychopathology in male exhibitionists. *Journal of Clinical Psychology, 40,* 827–832.

Forgac, G. E., & Michaels, E. J. (1982). Personality characteristics of two types of male exhibitionists. *Journal of Abnormal Psychology, 91,* 287–293.

Frenken, J., Gijs, L., & Van Beek, D. (1999). Sexual offender research and treatment in the Netherlands. *Journal of Interpersonal Violence, 14,* 347–371.

Freund, K. (1990). Courtship disorder. In W. L. Marshall, D. R. Laws, & H. E. Barbaree (Eds.), *Handbook of sexual assault: Issues, theories, and treatment of the offender* (pp. 331–342). New York: Plenum.

Frisbee, L. V., & Dondis, E. H. (1965). *Recidivism among treated sex offenders* (California Mental Health Research Monograph No. 5). Sacramento, CA: Department of Mental Hygiene.

Gittelson, N. L., Eacott, S. E., & Mehta, B. M. (1978). Victims of indecent exposure. *British Journal of Psychiatry, 132,* 61–66.

Gottfredson, M., & Hirschi, T. (1990). *A general theory of crime.* Stanford, CA: Stanford University Press.

Greenberg, S. R., Firestone, P., Bradford, J. M., & Greenberg, D. M. (2002). Prediction of recidivism in exhibitionists: Psychological, phallometric, and offense factors. *Sexual Abuse: A Journal of Research and Treatment, 14,* 329–347.

Hanson, R. K., Gordon, A., Harris, A. J. R., Marques, J. K., Murphy, W., Quinsey, V. L., et al. (2002). First report of the collaborative outcome data project on the effectiveness of psychological treatment for sex offenders. *Sexual Abuse: A Journal of Research and Treatment, 14,* 169–194.

Hanson, R. K., & Harris, A. J. R. (2000). Where should we intervene? Dynamic predictors of sexual offense recidivism. *Criminal Justice and Behavior, 27,* 6–35.

Hanson, R. K., & Morton-Bourgon, K. (2004). *Predictors of sexual recidivism: An updated meta-analysis.* Ottawa, Canada: Public Works and Government Services.

Hill, A., Briken, P., Kraus, C., Strohm, K., & Berner, W. (2003). Differential pharmacological treatment of paraphilias and sex offenders. *International Journal of Offender Therapy and Comparative Criminology, 47,* 407–421.

Kluver, H., & Bucy, P. (1939). Preliminary analysis of functions of the temporal lobes in monkeys. *Archives of Neurological Psychiatry, 42,* 979–1000.

Krafft-Ebing, R. V. (1965). *Psychopathia sexualis.* New York: Bell.

Kury, H., Chouaf, S., Obergfell-Fuchs, J., & Woessner, G. (2004). The scope of sexual victimization in Germany. *Journal of Interpersonal Violence, 19,* 589–602.

Langevin, R., Paitich, D., Ramsey, G., Anderson, C., Kamrad, J., Pope, S., et al. (1979). Experimental studies of the etiology of genital exhibitionism. *Archives of Sexual Behavior, 8,* 307–331.

Långström, N., & Seto, M. C. (in press). Exhibitionistic and voyeuristic behavior in a Swedish national population survey. *Archives of Sexual Behavior.*

Lee, J. K. P., Jackson, H. J., Pattison, P., & Ward, T. (2002). Developmental risk factors for sexual offending. *Child Abuse and Neglect, 26,* 73–92.

Longo, R. F., & Groth, A. N. (1983). Juvenile sexual offenses in the histories of adult rapists and child molesters. *International Journal of Offender Therapy and Comparative Criminology, 27,* 150–155.

Lösel, F., & Schmucker, M. (2005). The effectiveness of treatment for sexual offenders: A comprehensive meta-analysis. *Journal of Experimental Criminology, 1,* 117–146.

MacDonald, J. M. (1973). *Indecent exposure.* Springfield, IL: Charles C. Thomas.

Marshall, W. L., Barbaree, H. E., & Eccles, A. (1991). Early onset and deviant sexuality in child molesters. *Journal of Interpersonal Violence, 6,* 323–336.

Marshall, W. L., & Fernandez, Y. M. (2003). *Phallometric testing with sexual offenders*. Brandon, VT: Safer Society.

Marshall, W. L., Ward, T., Mann, R. E., Moulden, H., Fernandez, Y. M., Serran, G., et al. (2005). Working positively with sexual offenders: Maximizing the effectiveness of treatment. *Journal of Interpersonal Violence, 20*, 1096–1114.

McCreary, C. P. (1975). Personality profiles of persons convicted of indecent exposure. *Journal of Clinical Psychology, 31*, 260–262.

Mohr, J. W., Turner, R. E., & Jerry, M. B. (1964). *Pedophilia and exhibitionism*. Toronto, Canada: University of Toronto Press.

Murphy, W. D. (1990). Assessment and medications of cognitive distortions in sex offenders. In W. L. Marshall, D. R. Laws, & H. E. Barbaree (Eds.), *Handbook of sexual assault: Issues, theories, and treatment of the offender* (pp. 331–342). New York: Plenum.

Murphy, W. D. (1997). Exhibitionism: Psychopathology and theory. In D. R. Laws & W. O'Donohue (Eds.), *Sexual deviance: Theory, assessment, and treatment* (pp. 22–39). New York: Guilford.

Murphy, W. D., & Barbaree, H. E. (1994). *Assessments of sexual offenders by measures of erectile response: Psychometric properties and decision making*. Brandon, VT: Safer Society Press.

O'Carroll, R. (1989). A neuropsychological study of sexual deviation. *Sexual and Marital Therapy, 4*, 59–63.

Pfäfflin, F. (1999). Issues, incidence, and treatment of sexual offenders in Germany. *Journal of Interpersonal Violence, 14*, 372–395.

Riordan, S. (1999). Indecent exposure: The impact upon the victim's fear of sexual crime. *Journal of Forensic Psychiatry, 10*, 309–316.

Rooth, G. (1973). Exhibitionism, sexual violence and paedophilia. *British Journal of Psychiatry, 122*, 705–710.

Saunders, E. B., & Awad, G. A. (1991). Male adolescent sexual offenders: Exhibitionism and obscene phone calls. *Child Psychiatry and Human Development, 21*, 169–178.

Sjöstedt, G., Långström, N., Sturidsson, K., & Grann, M. (2004). Stability of modus operandi in sexual offending. *Criminal Justice and Behavior, 31*, 609–623.

Smallbone, S. W., & Wortley, R. K. (2004). Criminal diversity and paraphilic interests among adult males convicted of sexual offenses against children. *International Journal of Offender Therapy and Comparative Criminology, 48*, 175–188.

Templeman, T. L., & Stinnett, R. D. (1991). Patterns of sexual arousal and history in a "normal" sample of young men. *Archives of Sexual Behavior, 20*, 137–150.

2

Sadomasochism

Pekka Santtila, N. Kenneth Sandnabba, and Niklas Nordling

The perspectives on sadomasochistic sexual behavior range from seeing it as a crime or a psychiatric disorder to seeing it as "a sophisticated erotic activity with several layers of meaning and significance" (Henkin, 1992). Modern popular culture and fashion contain stylized representations of fetishistic and sadomasochistic activity in, for example, mainstream music videos (chains and leather clothes have been popular features). You can also find an advertisement on the Internet for "a practical 4-day course to explore SM sex" that promises a practical and hands-on workshop with lots of demonstrations and useful tips about SM equipment, etiquette, and negotiation of safer sex in SM scenes (MetroM8, n.d.), and a description of the diagnostic criteria for sexual masochism (diagnosis number 302.83) and sexual sadism (diagnosis number 302.84), which include clinically significant distress or impairment in social, occupational, or other important areas of functioning in the *Diagnostic and Statistical Manual of Mental Disorders* (American Psychiatric Association, 2000). The question becomes, is sadomasochistic sexuality a more or less voluntary variant of human sexuality that does not necessarily imply psychiatric illness and need for treatment, or is it a deviant behavior with serious consequences (psychological distress and physical injury) both for the individual and the society? Also, it is open to question whether sadomasochistic sexuality can be viewed as a single, homogenous phenomenon or whether the different perspectives might be describing relatively independent phenomena that have been loosely labeled as sadomasochistic.

Regarding the prevalence of sadomasochistic sexual practices, Långström and Seto (in press) found that 2.2 percent of the respondents in a representative national sample of 18- to 60-year-old Swedish men and women reported having deliberately used physical pain and become sexually aroused by its use. In a nationally representative survey of the Finnish population with 2,188 participants, Kontula and Haavio-Mannila (1993) found that 0.5 percent reported using a whip, handcuffs, or chains in association with sexual interaction or masturbation, a clearly more restrictive definition of sadomasochistic sexuality. In a cross-sectional national American survey (Janus & Janus, 1993) with a total of 2,765 SM respondents, 16 percent of the males and 12 percent of the females agreed or strongly agreed with a statement claiming that pain and pleasure really go together in sex.

During the last two decades, a number of researchers (i.e., Baumeister, 1988; Falk & Weinberg, T. S., 1983; Moser & Levitt, 1987; Spengler, 1977) representing various areas of social science have started to examine sadomasochism as a social phenomenon dependent on the subcultural context and the developmental history of the people involved. For example, social well-being appears to be associated with levels of integration in sadomasochistic subcultures.

According to Moser (1988), there is no commonly accepted definition of what constitutes sadomasochistic sexual behavior (SM sex). A non-clinical definition of consensual SM sex by Townsend (1983) identifies six characteristic features in a sadomasochistic scene: a relation of dominance and submission, infliction of pain that is experienced as pleasurable by both partners, using fantasy or role-playing by one or both partners, deliberate humiliation of the other partner, fetishistic elements (clothes, devices, scenery), and one or more ritualistic activities (e.g., bondage, whipping). Other definitions have been offered by M. S. Weinberg, Williams, & Moser (1984) and by Kamel (1983).

Previous studies have not taken account of the potential preferences that may exist for individuals in engaging in a set of SM-sex behaviors (i.e., the administration or receiving of pain) over another set of behaviors (i.e., humiliation). One possibility is that individuals would only engage in a limited set of behaviors, and not in others, suggesting that sadomasochism is in fact a label for a variety of relatively independent phenomena. Another possibility is that individuals emphasize a particular set of behaviors but also engage in other activities to a more limited extent. Also, there have been no investigations exploring whether a preference for one facet over another is related to the gender and the sexual orientation of the SM practitioners, and whether there is a preference for the "sadistic" or the "masochistic" partner to engage in one facet more than any other. This is clearly an interesting set of research questions that can clarify the nature of SM sex.

Several studies exploring sexual behavior and social adaptation of SM-sex practitioners have shown them to be generally well adjusted (e.g., Moser & Levitt, 1987; Sandnabba, Santtila, & Nordling, 1999; Spengler, 1977; Weinberg, T. S., 1987). This suggests that childhood experiences of SM practitioners will not, in the large majority of cases, reveal pathological patterns of family inter-action, although a number of clinical case reports have suggested this to be the case (Blos, 1991; Blum, 1991; Coen, 1988; Rothstein, 1991). These reports have two flaws. On one hand, they are lacking in systematic empirical support, and on the other, they are exclusively based on people who have sought psychological help. So far, no studies have focused on exploring associations between child-hood experiences and the way in which a nonclinical sample of SM practitioners express their sexuality. For example, attachment theorists (e.g., Shaver, Hazan, & Bradshaw, 1988) have shown that attachment style affects the expression of sexuality in a number of areas including trust, desire for reciprocation, and fear of closeness. They also suggest that for every feature of adult love relationships, there is either a documented or a plausible infant parallel.

Likewise, the question of whether childhood abuse experiences have etiological significance for sadomasochistic behavior has largely been ignored. Due to the complexity of sadomasochistic sexual behavior (SM sex) and the significance of social influences on it, it is unlikely that any simple associations between childhood abuse experiences and later SM sex could be found. Nevertheless, it is important to ascertain empirically what the role of sexual abuse—if any—is for the development of sadomasochistic sexual interests and for the choice of either sadistic or masochistic position.

The empirical results reported in this chapter to clarify some of these questions mainly derive from a series of seven empirical articles describing different aspects of sadomasochistic sexual behavior based on a large number of SM practitioners (Alison, Santtila, Sandnabba, & Nordling, 2001; Nord-ling, Sandnabba, & Santtila, 2000; Nordling, Sandnabba, Santtila, & Alison, 2005; Sandnabba et al., 1999; Sandnabba, Santtila, Beetz, Nordling, & Alison, 2002; Santtila et al., 2000; Santtila, Sandnabba, Alison, & Nordling, 2002).

WHO ARE THE SADOMASOCHISTS?

Overall, many studies suggest that practitioners of SM sex are not psy-chologically disturbed or dysfunctional but are rather better educated and are in a generally higher-earning bracket than the general population (Baumeister, 1988; Spengler, 1977; T. S. Weinberg, 1987). This is also what was found in our series of empirical reports. Whereas one out of five men in the general population is single, almost half of the SM practitioners are. The SM practi-tioners also had on average fewer children than the general population, which is partly explained by the fact that many more of the study participants were gay male or lesbians. The SM practitioners that participated in our study were all older than 21 years, with less than 10 percent being over 50 years old.

Of the SM practitioners, 43 percent reported being mainly heterosexual, 5 percent bisexual, and 52 percent mainly homosexual in their sexual orien-tation. It should be noted that no conclusions can be drawn from these results concerning the proportion of SM practitioners who are gay male or lesbian as our study was aimed at getting about equal numbers of straight and gay SM practitioners by targeting different kinds of clubs. Of all the SM practitioners 27 percent identified themselves as mainly sadistic, 23 percent as both sadistic and masochistic, and 50 percent as mainly masochistic in their behavior.

On average, first awareness of sadomasochistic interest had taken place when the male SM practitioners had been between 18 to 20 years of age. Also, first experience with SM sex and onset of regular sadomasochistic behavior took place mostly between the ages of 21 and 25 years. The relatively late awareness of sadomasochistic interests and late start of behavior is noteworthy.

Most of the SM practitioners (88 percent) had practiced ordinary sex, that is, consensual heterosexual or gay male sexual activity without sadomasochistic elements, before engaging in sadomasochism. Some 5 percent of the SM practitioners no longer practiced ordinary sex. On average, they stopped having ordinary sex at 25 years of age. On the other hand, approximately a fourth (27 percent) of the male SM practitioners endorsed a statement suggesting that only sadomasochistic sex could satisfy them. These results suggest that the development of sadomasochistic sexual behavior starts after experience with more ordinary sexual behavior and the establishment of a sexual orientation.

These results relate to the relationship between sadomasochistic sexual practices and other sexual activities. The cue-response model of sexual arousal (Suppe, 1985) is a suitable model for analyzing this question, since it stresses inflexibility as a primary criterion for paraphilia. The model presents a classification of how specific cues stimulate or inhibit an individual's arousal. Cues interfering with sexual arousal are classified as inhibitory, while cues that neither inhibit nor intensify sexual arousal are seen as nonfacilitative. Facilitative cues, on their part, enhance but are not necessary for sexual arousal. Finally, cues that are necessary for sexual arousal are named paraphiliac. This differs from the definition of paraphilia in *DSM-IV*, where a clinically important distress or impairment of work, social, or personal functioning is required for diagnosis. According to Suppe's model, sadomasochism is paraphiliac if it is the *only* way for an individual to get sexually aroused and satisfied. This also means that if a person also engages in sex without sadomasochistic elements, sadomasochism should not be viewed as a paraphiliac cue for him or her. These results are also relevant for viewing sadomasochism as a sexual minority. This would not seem to be the case; instead, sadomasochistic sexuality is, for the most part, an additional feature of the sexuality of the SM practitioners who also engage in more ordinary sexual behavior.

It has been suggested that it would be a development from taking mostly the masochistic role in an SM scene toward taking mostly the sadistic position (Baumeister, 1988). This hypothesis of development has not been unequivocally supported, however. When exploring the changes in sadomasochistic preference, it was found that almost half of the male SM practitioners had not changed their preference at all. About a fifth had changed their behavior toward sadistic and another fifth toward masochistic preferences. Changes toward

Table 2.1. Feelings after the First Sadomasochistic Experience

Statements	Percent of SM Practitioners Who Completely or Partly Agreed
I wanted to do it again	97
I felt happy	86
I was glad	86
I felt safe	79
I was proud	59
I felt guilty	24
I was troubled	22
I was afraid about the future	20
I thought it was immoral	12
I was disgusted with myself	9

sadistic behavior were, therefore, no more prevalent than changes toward masochistic behavior. The hypothesis of development was also contradicted by the fact that many of the younger SM practitioners in the sample were sadists.

Central to the discussion of whether sadomasochistic sexual activity is a psychiatric disorder is its relationship to psychological distress, which is one of the diagnostic criteria for paraphilia. Although the majority of the SM practitioners had a positive emotional reaction after their first experience with SM sex (see Table 2.1), about one-fourth had at least some negative feelings. From the percentages of the statements "I wanted to do it again," which 97 percent were in agreement with, and "I was disgusted with myself," which 9 percent were in agreement with, it can be deduced that at least a majority of those feeling disgust, nevertheless, wanted to repeat the experience. This could be interpreted as a sign of compulsivity or nonvoluntary nature of the sexual interests. However, many individuals may experience negative feelings after their first experience of ordinary sexual interaction and still want to repeat the experience, which is not interpreted as compulsive.

WHAT DO SADOMASOCHISTS DO (IN BED AND ELSEWHERE)?

Most people have some kind of an image of what sadomasochistic sex involves. Still, there are no generally accepted definitions of what constitutes sadomasochistic sex, and such popular images may be more reflective of cultural and media influences than of the reality of sadomasochistic sex. Therefore, a good way of looking at the question is to ask individuals who consider themselves to be sadomasochists to report what they actually do. Table 2.2 presents the proportions of male participants who have engaged in different

Table 2.2. Frequencies with which Male SM Practitioners Participated in Different Sexual Behaviors and Role-Plays

Sexual Practice or Behavior/Role-Play	Proportion of All-Male SM Practitioners	Prevalence
1. Oral sex	95.2	E
2. Bondage	88.7	E
3. Flagellation	82.8	S
4. Anal intercourse	80.6	G
5. Handcuffs	74.7	E
6. Rimming	73.1	G
7. Dildos	72.6	G
8. Leather outfits	72.6	G
9. Chains	71.0	E
10. Verbal humiliation	69.9	S
11. Clothespins, clamps	66.6	E
12. Mask, blindfold	66.2	S
13. Spanking	65.5	E
14. Cockbinding	64.5	G
15. Gag	53.8	S
16. Biting	53.3	E
17. Rubber outfits	52.1	S
18. Cane whipping	50.6	S
19. Vaginal intercourse	47.3	S
20. Water sports	47.3	E
21. Wrestling	45.7	G
22. Body odors	42.5	E
23. Face slapping	40.3	E
24. Use of weights	39.3	E
25. Enema	39.3	E
26. Special equipment, e.g. slings, crosses, cages	38.1	G
27. Hot wax	35.0	E
28. Ice	33.9	E
29. Fist fucking	33.3	E
30. Cross-dressing	28.5	S
31. Piercing	21.0	E
32. Skin branding	17.3	E
33. Scat (coprophilia)	17.3	E
34. Hypoxyphilia	16.7	E
35. Straitjacket	15.6	S
36. Electric shocks	15.0	S
37. Knives, razor blades	13.4	E
38. Mummifying	12.9	E
39. Catheter	9.2	E
40. Zoophilia	6.4	E
Role-Plays		E
1. Master/Madame-slave	55.9	S
2. Uniform scenes	38.8	G
3. Teacher-student	29.1	S
4. Execution scenes	23.6	E
5. Hospital scenes	15.7	S
6. Rape scenes	13.5	E

E=equally prevalent among gay and straight males; G=more prevalent among gay males; S=more prevalent among straight males.

kinds of sexual behaviors and role-plays during the twelve months preceding our survey.

This information indicates that, in accordance with the results of the studies of Moser and Levitt (1987), flagellation and bondage were among the most popular activities. Additionally, some activities not specific to sadomasochism, for example, oral sex and anal intercourse, that these authors did not investigate, were also quite popular. The similarities between the percentages of some behaviors (bondage, verbal humiliation, gag, biting, cane-whipping, water sports, enema, face-slapping, hot wax, cross-dressing, piercing, skin branding, and zoophilia) in our study and that of Moser and Levitt were noteworthy.

Most SM practitioners had engaged in sadomasochistic sex during the preceding twelve months from two to five times overall. The analysis of the effect of sadomasochistic preference on the frequency of sadomasochistic sessions gave some indication of the sadistic males being more often engaged in sadomasochistic sex than the masochistic males. The average number of sadomasochistic sessions during a month that the SM practitioners would have liked to have was six. Sadomasochistic preference had no effect on this variable. It seems that sadomasochists are not able to have SM sex as often as they would have wanted. However, as pointed out above, most of them also engaged in ordinary sexual activity.

The discrepancy between how often the SM practitioners engaged in sessions, and how often they would have liked to, may depend on difficulties in finding a partner who would share the same sexual interests, because this in most cases requires involvement in the sadomasochistic subculture. Also, the high number of masochistic heterosexual men and the relative lack of women create difficulties, a result established earlier by researchers in the field (e.g., Moser & Levitt, 1987) and confirmed again. The difficulties experienced by the masochistic SM practitioners may also have been reflected in their expressed desire for having steady relationships.

ARE GAY AND STRAIGHT SM PRACTITIONERS DIFFERENT?

The relationship between sadomasochistic preferences and sexual orientation has not been thoroughly explored, although it has been suggested that sexual orientation issues are usually clarified prior to engagement in sadomasochistic sex (Falk & T. S. Weinberg, 1983; Moser & Levitt, 1987). Here we present some informative data on the relationship between sadomasochistic interests and sexual orientation issues, and review some of the earlier literature on the matter.

T. S. Weinberg (1987) emphasizes the importance of sadomasochistic clubs in developing attitudes supportive of the practice. These attitudes enable individuals who are integrated in the subculture to justify their sexual desires more easily. Previous studies (Kamel, 1983; Spengler, 1977) have shown gay men to be more integrated in the sadomasochistic subculture. However, during the last two decades, sadomasochism has become more visible and it may be that such differences no longer exist. To the extent that gay male sadomasochistic subculture still offers more role models and possibilities of engaging in sexual behavior than the straight sadomasochistic subculture (Kamel, 1983), it may be that gay male sadomasochists are more satisfied with their sex lives than straight male sadomasochists.

There was some indication that the gay male SM practitioners are better educated (43 percent had college education) compared to straight men (29 percent had college education). The gay male SM practitioners also had a higher income than the population in general. To the extent that educational attainment is viewed as a measure of social and psychological well-being, it seems that the gay male SM practitioners had succeeded well in this respect (Sandnabba et al., 1999).

Exclusively straight males became aware of their sadomasochistic preferences at a younger age than other groups of SM practitioners. Further, they also had their first experience at a younger age. In a similar manner, there was a tendency for them to differ from the other groups in terms of the onset of regular sadomasochistic activity (Sandnabba et al., 1999). This means that the gay male SM practitioners became aware and started practicing their sadomasochistic interests later.

One reason might be that the gay male SM practitioners only become interested in sadomasochistic activities after they have resolved issues related to sexual interest. This would agree with findings showing that gay male individuals establish their sexual orientation and start sexual activity later than heterosexual males (Coleman, 1982; Kontula & Haavio-Mannila, 1993). This is also consistent with Kamel's idea of sadomasochism as a reaction to dissatisfaction with the ordinary gay male scene (1983). These results also suggest that the development of sadomasochistic sexual behavior starts after experience with sexual behavior without sadomasochistic elements and the establishment of a sexual orientation.

Correlations between sexual orientation (rated on a five-point scale with anchors exclusively homosexual and exclusively heterosexual with the middle point being bisexual) and sadomasochistic preference (also rated on a five-point scale with anchors exclusively sadistic and exclusively masochistic with the middle point being equally sadistic and masochistic) were computed separately for male and female SM practitioners. Both male and female SM practitioners with a more heterosexual orientation were more likely to have a more masochistic preference while the more gay SM practitioners were more likely to be sadistically oriented. This association was stronger in females when compared to male SM practitioners.

As already reported above, 27 percent of all male SM practitioners endorsed a statement suggesting that only sadomasochistic sex could satisfy them.

The straight males were somewhat more likely to endorse this statement than the gay males (Sandnabba et al., 1999).

WHAT DO GAY AS OPPOSED TO STRAIGHT SADOMASOCHISTS DO IN TERMS OF SEX?

As evident from Table 2.2, clear differences in the frequencies of sexual and sadomasochistic behaviors and role-plays between the straight and gay male SM practitioners were found; for example, the gay male SM practitioners were more fond of leather outfits, anal intercourse, rimming, dildos, wrestling, special equipment, and uniform scenes, while the straight SM practitioners more often enjoyed verbal humiliation, mask and blindfold, gags, rubber outfits, cane whipping, vaginal intercourse, cross-dressing, and straitjackets. Different role plays, except for uniform scenes, were involved more often in the sexual repertoires of the straight male SM practitioners. In terms of the number of SM sessions, the straight male SM practitioners had fewer sessions than the gay male and bisexual SM practitioners.

Also, sadomasochistic activity did not seem to be associated with extensive substance abuse during or before sadomasochistic sex. However, the use of poppers and alcohol by the gay male SM practitioners was an exception to this pattern and could perhaps be understood as a distinctive pattern of the gay male subculture (Sandnabba et al., 1999).

Lesbian and straight female SM practitioners had engaged in different sexual behavior and role-plays. Most frequently reported behaviors among the lesbian SM practitioners were the use of leather outfits, flagellations, use of dildos, bondage, oral sex, as well as blindfolds, whereas, in contrast to the straight female participants, the lesbian SM practitioners did not participate in scenes including rubber outfits, use of weights, hypoxyphilia (sexual arousal produced while reducing the oxygen supply to the brain), mummifying (wrapping the body with tape or bandage), and straitjackets. Straitjackets and rubber outfits were especially preferred by the straight male participants, which could explain some of the differences.

Sadomasochism is a label of convenience for a set of related sexual activities of particular subcultures (Haeberle, 1978; Katchadourian & Lunde, 1975). Facets include physical restriction and bondage (Baumeister, 1988) and humiliation (Baumeister, 1988; Moser & Levitt, 1987; Weinberg, T. S., 1987), among others. M. S. Weinberg, et al. (1984), Lee (1979) and Kamel (1983) refer to a subset of behaviors commonly associated with the gay male "leather" scene that, to observers, appears to be sadomasochistic in origin. These behaviors include enemas, catheters, anal fisting, and scatological practices and are sometimes described by the subjects as displays of "masculinity and toughness" (Weinberg, M. S., et al., 1984, p. 387). Using a statistical analysis, we identified groups of behaviors that co-occurred in the sexual behavior of the SM practitioners. Four such groups were identified (Alison et al., 2001) and labeled: hypermasculinity; administration and receiving of pain; physical restriction and psychological humiliation. The behaviors making up the different groups are listed in Table 2.3.

There were significant differences between the gay and straight male SM practitioners in terms of their involvement in the hypermasculinity (involving rimming, water sports, cockbinding, fisting [inserting a hand and part of an arm into the anal cavity], scatologia, and the use of dildos, enemas, and catheters) and humiliation (involving faceslapping, flagellation, the use of a gag, the use of knives and razors, and verbal humiliation) regions. The gay male subjects were more likely to engage in a larger number of the behaviors of the hypermasculinity region compared to the straight male subjects, whereas the latter were more likely to engage in a larger number of humiliation behaviors.

One of the most striking differences between the gay male and straight male sadomasochists is the fact that more gay male sadomasochists are sadistically oriented and have a preference for masculinization of their sexual behavior. The gay male sadomasochistic subculture exaggerates the male aspects of sexual behavior while the straight men seem to play down these aspects and adopt more submissive roles with emphasis on pain and humiliation. However, it is important to remember that these differences were group differences: Many gay men preferred primarily the behaviors in the humiliation group and some straight men engaged in behaviors in the hypermasculinity group.

When drawing conclusions regarding the differences between gay and straight sadomasochists, it should be remembered that it cannot be totally excluded that these are just differences between gay and straight individuals in general or if the sadomasochism plays a specific part. Indeed, a single behavior

Table 2.3. Groups of Sadomasochistic Behaviors Formed on the Basis of Their Co-occurrence

Hypermasculinity		Administration of pain		Humiliation		Physical restriction	
Activity	%	Activity	%	Activity	%	Activity	%
Rimming	77.5	Clothespin	67.6	Flagellation	81.8	Bondage	88.4
Dildo	70.2	tortures		Verbal	70.1	Handcuffs	73.2
Cockbinding	68.3	Spanking	64.0	humiliation		Chains	70.8
Water sports	50.6	Caning	50.7	Gag	53.0	Wrestle	45.1
Enema	42.7	Use of weights	41.5	Face	37.2	Slings	39.0
Fisting	32.9	Hot wax	34.8	slapping		Ice	31.7
Scat	18.2	Electricity	16.4	Knives	10.9	Straitjacket	17.0
Catheter	10.4	Skin branding	15.8			Hypoxyphilia	16.5
						Mummifying	13.4

Source: Santilla et al., 2002.

can seldom be classified unambiguously as sadomasochistic or not without knowing the context of the behavior and the interpretation assigned by the individuals engaging in the behavior. Certainly, nonsadomasochistic gay men also can be interested in and engage in behaviors classified into the hypermasculinity group of sadomasochistic behavior.

The finding related to hypermasculinity is interesting as a major aspect of the stereotypes linked to gay and lesbian individuals has been that they do not fit the accepted stereotypes for their own gender (Lips, 2001, p. 27). Also, a common stereotype of gay men is that they are effeminate (Deaux & Lewis, 1984). However, the gay male SM participants accentuate their masculinity, contradicting the stereotype. This does not mean that the gay males engaged in SM are necessarily more masculine than other gay men. Also, previous research has indicated that a lot of gay men have antieffeminacy prejudice (Taywaditep, 2001). In light of these findings, the hypermasculinity of gay men within the sadomasochistic subculture could be understood as a reaction to these stereotypes and a coping strategy to handle the conflict between internalized aspects of such stereotypes and antieffeminacy attitudes held at the same time. Likewise, some gay men adopt an exaggerated feminine pose, probably in an attempt to handle the same conflict by internalizing the stereotype completely and denying any antieffeminacy attitudes. In the same way, the straight men who have sadomasochistic sexual interests may be escaping from the pressures of their narrow gender role demanding that they be strong, masculine, active, dominant, and successful. The masochistic role in a sadomasochistic sexual encounter is to some extent the exact opposite of such a role, and it is therefore interesting that many of the straight men in our sample were, in fact, masochistically oriented. Further, it can be speculated that the small numbers of women engaging in sadomasochistic sex could be related to the female gender role being broader in these respects.

HOW ARE SM SESSIONS SCRIPTED?

Interpersonal sexual scripts refer to social interactions of a sexual nature between individuals. The way in which people behave and act out their sexuality is influenced by their perceptions of what others expect of them. Script theory suggests that sexual interaction is hardly ever spontaneous, but rather, conforms to a premeditated sequence of intentional actions. Script theory has mainly been used for describing conventional heterosexual activities (DeLamater & MacCorquodale, 1979; Laumann, Gagnon, Michael, Michaels, 1994). However, little is known about the "scripting" of more unusual sexual activities, including sadomasochistic sexual behavior. Because sadomasochism tends to involve ritualistic patterns of behavior in which partners are often assigned roles (Sandnabba et al., 1999) and are expected to enact particular sequences of behavior, these patterns could be viewed as highly scripted. Thus, it could be hypothesized that members of the sadomasochistic subculture learn patterns that facilitate the enactment of complicated sadomasochistic sexual scenarios. No studies have so far empirically scrutinized the idea of sexual scripts in SM sex.

We wanted to discern whether particular SM behaviors are always preceded by others, thereby creating sequences of various SM scenes. The intention was, in other words, to examine the relationship that individual actions may have in the context of learned and developing sequences of behaviors in much the same way that studies of conventional heterosexual activity have examined the progression of kissing to intercourse. It could, for example, be hypothesized that people who use straitjackets (which have to be specially acquired, suggesting a more advanced type of restraint) in their SM scenarios would previously have engaged in bondage (for which it is not necessary to acquire specialized equipment, suggesting that it is a less extreme form of restraining a person).

Hypermasculinity

Among the 184 SM practitioners studied (see Table 2.3), only 57 of the 256 possible combinations of the 7 hypermasculinity behaviors (i.e., profiles) occurred, which suggests the existence of an underlying structure in how the behaviors are combined, that is, sexual scripts (Santtila et al., 2002). This means that the behaviors in this group combine in certain predictable ways and not randomly. Therefore, from knowing whether a subject has engaged in a particular behavior, for example fisting, it is possible to tell something about other behaviors he or she is likely to have engaged in as well.

SM practitioners who engaged in water sports were also engaged in rimming. Cockbinding, however, was a qualitatively different aspect of hypermasculinity. SM practitioners who engaged in fisting most certainly also had experienced scat, and those with experience of scat in turn had also experienced enema. Thus, the presence of these behaviors combined with either the rimming/water sports behaviors or the cockbinding behavior identify SM practitioners with the most experience. However, all of these behaviors seem more related to the rimming/water sports dimension, pointing to a script within the hypermasculinity theme starting with rimming and ending at fisting. Use of dildo together with catheter had no clear relationship with either sequence. This may have something to do with them being pieces of technical equipment. In conclusion, the use of dildos does not give information on the level of an SM practitioner's experience with respect to other hypermasculinity behaviors. The use of catheter was quite rare, which may explain why it was not a structured part of the hypermasculinity scripts.

Pain

Forty out of the 128 possible combinations of the presence of the behaviors in this group were observed, again suggesting the existence of a clear underlying structure in the combination of the different behaviors. SM practitioners who had practiced spanking had also practiced caning. Both of these behaviors are classical SM behaviors and appear to be similar with regard to their psychological meaning and physical sensation. The ordering of the structure where caning precedes spanking (without any aid) most likely represents differences in the psychological and physical distance between the sadist and the masochist, where this distance is shorter when they are practicing spanking. In the other major distinction revealed by the analysis of behaviors, electric stimulation, use of weights, and clothespin torture formed a sequence, with clothespin torture being the most common behavior and electric stimulation the rarest. This is an understandable structure as the rarer behaviors require the purchase of special equipment whereas the clothespins are to be found in every household. It can be suggested that these two sequences reflect potential differences in the intensity of the pain the behaviors cause as well as in the narrowness of their focus on erogenous zones with spanking and caning being less intense and less focused on erogenous zones than electric stimulation, use of weights, and clothespin torture. The rarely occurring skin branding could be a behavior emphasizing either one of these sequences. This may be explained by it being on the one hand intense but on the other hand less focused on erogenous zones, thereby sharing characteristics of both of these sequences. The use of hot wax did not belong clearly to either of these two major distinctions.

Humiliation

Of the thirty-two possible profiles, eighteen were identified, again suggesting the existence of a clear underlying structure. The major distinction could be drawn between flagellation and knives on one hand and face slapping on the other. SM practitioners who had used knives in their SM sessions had most certainly also been involved in sessions where flagellation had been enjoyed. The remaining two behaviors, verbal humiliation and gag did not clearly belong to any of these two major distinctions. However, when examining the results of the analysis further, it was noticed that gag was more associated with the flagellation/knives script. In contrast, there was some indication that verbal humiliation was more associated with a script involving face slapping. Verbal humiliation, which was a relatively common behavior, may, therefore, be seen to express similar intentions as face slapping, albeit in a milder form.

Restraint

Results concerning the nine restraint behaviors were somewhat less clear when compared to the above results. However, an interesting sequence was revealed. Six of the behaviors were ordered in a sequence of restraint behaviors starting from the less extreme bondage, and going through chains, handcuffs, slings, and straitjacket, and finally ending with the most extreme variation of hypoxyphilia. This is understandable since all of them (with the possible exception of hypoxyphilia) involve the use of some kind of equipment. Also, the roles of the sadist and the masochist are clearly defined in scripts involving these behaviors.

One of the behaviors, wrestling, represented a qualitatively different kind of restraint behavior. It differs from the above behaviors in that it does not require clearly defined dominant and submissive positions and also in that no equipment is necessary in order to engage in this behavior. The use of ice could not be associated to the other behaviors in a structured way. This can be explained because ice is not a restraint behavior per se, rather it is used for additional fun in an SM script involving restraint. Finally, mummifying represented an extreme form of both the group of six behaviors described above as well as an extreme form following wrestling. The association between mummifying and wrestling could be understood as two different ways to limit the freedom of movement.

Clearly, the sadomasochistic behaviors are not haphazardly combined with each other. Rather, evidence for structured patterns of co-occurrences was found. Further, the combining of the behaviors was also theoretically meaningful, indicating the existence of progressions of sadomasochistic behaviors which can be likened to sexual scripts for ordinary heterosexual sexual behavior (Gagnon, 1990; Gagnon & Simon, 1987).

These results have important implications for the understanding and conceptualization of sadomasochism as a sexual phenomenon. Some of the behaviors are observed in almost all participants, such as bondage, flagellation, rimming, and clothespin torture (Alison et al., 2001). However, in addition to these "core" behaviors, there are a number of less-common activities expressed in sadomasochistic sex that form specific and distinct scripts. Different persons, creating subgroups of individuals, differentially engage in these scripts. The existence of such emphases suggests that individual careers within the sadomasochistic subcultures are determined in an interplay between the individual's own developmental history, psychological characteristics (see Santtila, Sandnabba, & Nordling, 2000), and the subcultural context within which the individual faces information concerning possible pathways of expression and conformist group processes that make the development of certain scripts more likely than others (cf. social constructionist approaches to sexuality, e.g., Hart, 1985). This process may be more transparent in sadomasochism due to its highly ritualized nature, but the process itself is probably shared in most expressions of human sexuality.

Further, the SM practitioners' involvement in the subculture through sexual contacts and porn was positively associated with greater variability in their sexual behavior. Although the design of the study does not warrant any causal conclusions, the results nevertheless imply that sadomasochistic behavior is at least partly a product of adult socialization processes where real or imagined sexual contact leads the SM practitioners to adopt new behaviors and sexual scripts. This finding accords well with social constructionist explanations of sexual behavior (Weinberg, T. S., 1987; Weinberg, M. S., et al., 1984).

CAN SADOMASOCHISM BE PART OF SEXUAL EXPERIMENTATION? THE ASSOCIATION BETWEEN SADOMASOCHISM AND ZOOPHILIA

Though sexual contact with animals has occurred throughout history (Miletski, 1999) there is a paucity of research on this issue and, in particular, the ways in which individuals use animals for sexual gratification in the context of other forms of sexual behavior. We focused specifically on the ways in which male SM practitioners have incorporated the use of animals into their sexual, sadomasochistically oriented practices. There are some studies that suggest a connection between sadomasochism and bestiality (Karpman, 1962; Rosenberger, 1968).

Since none of the twenty-two female SM practitioners reported bestiality interests, the proportion of the participants who had engaged in sexual contact with an animal during the preceding twelve months was based on the 164 males only. This resulted in 7.3 percent (n = 12). Of the bestiality group, 50 percent (n = 6) had taken an active role in the sexual interaction with the animal, whereas 25 percent (n = 3) had taken a passive role and 25 percent (n = 3) had taken both roles. We compared these twelve participants with another twelve participants who had not engaged in sexual behavior with animals but were otherwise similar to them.

The participants with interest in bestiality were likely to have become aware of their sadomasochistic interests relatively late and to have started practicing sadomasochism late as well. The same pattern was also observed regarding starting practicing sadomasochistic sex. Also, in comparison with more general findings on bestiality, these individuals used animals for sexual pleasure at a later stage of their sexual development. Existing research on bestiality suggests that most of the experimental sexual contacts with animals occurs in adolescence (Kinsey, Pomeroy, & Martin, 1948; Miletski, 1999). Further, the majority of our sample (n = 11 out of 12) had their experience with bestiality after they started sadomasochistic sexual practices. Therefore, this group appears to have come to use animals at a much later stage than is usually the case. Similarly, they also experimented with SM practices relatively late and therefore appear to be "late developers" in acquiring their sadomasochistic preferences.

From Table 2.4 it can be seen that the SM practitioners with bestiality interests showed more experience with sexual practices that were rare in the total sadomasochistic population compared to the comparison group.

Table 2.4. Differences in Various Sexual and Sadomasochistic Behaviors and Role-Plays between SM Practitioners with Experience in Bestiality and Comparison Group Ordered According to the Magnitude of the Differences

Behavior/Role-Play	SM Practitioners with Experience in Bestiality	Comparison Group
Knives, razor blades	54.5	–
Skin branding	45.5	–
Scat (coprophilia)	54.5	8.3
Biting	81.8	33.3
Face slapping	72.7	25.0
Water sports	83.3	41.7
Use of weights	66.7	25.0
Ice	54.5	16.7
Spanking	90.9	58.3
Straitjacket	50.0	16.7
Cross-dressing	58.3	25.0
Piercing	58.3	25.0
Fist fucking	66.7	33.3
Catheter	36.4	8.3
Hospital scenes	45.5	8.3
Rape scenes	60.0	0.0

The SM practitioners with experience in bestiality were more prepared to employ a range of sexual and sadomasochistic behaviors in their repertoire as reported in Table 2.4. Indeed, on all but one behavior (special equipment), they were more inclined to try different sexual practices. Also, the behaviors they engaged in were not limited to one of the specific sadomasochistic scripts (hypermasculinity, psychological humiliation, administration and receiving of pain, and physical restriction) earlier identified (Alison et al., 2001). Therefore, they were more experimental than the control group as well as the whole sample.

Similarly, in contrast to other bestiality studies, the majority in this sample had a steady partner (with whom they had more often practiced SM) and over half had children. This suggests that this group represents a particular subset of individuals who use animals for sexual gratification, distinct from individuals who are more exclusively focused on animals. It appears that this group is generally more sexually experimental and that the use of animals, rather than being a specific preference, is part of a more general desire for sexual experimentation. The fact that they tried other, more unusual sex practices than the control group and also often involved the partner in the sadomasochistic activities also suggests that they may have partners with similar interests with whom they feel comfortable in a variety of experimental sexual practices. Overall, the behavior of the individuals here resembles an earlier described "sex-dominated personality" constellation where the individual is actively obsessed with the need for erotic release (Masters, 1966). It is also interesting that the SM practitioners were highly educated in accordance with Miletski's (1999) findings and the whole sample (Sandnabba et al., 1999).

WHAT HAS THE CHILDHOOD OF SADOMASOCHISTS BEEN LIKE?

We also wanted to explore the question of how, in a group of sado-masochistic males, different patterns of family interaction produce different attachment styles, and if these in their turn affect the SM practitioners' satisfaction with their sexuality and sadomasochistic preferences (Santtila et al., 2000). According to attachment theory (Ainsworth, Blehar, Waters, & Wall, 1978; Bowlby, 1969, 1973; Scharff, 1988), individuals construct mental models of themselves and their major social-interaction partners during childhood. These models regulate a person's social behaviors and feelings throughout life, also affecting their sexual behavior. Sensitive responsiveness by primary caretakers is the factor that produces secure attachment, which in turn enables a person to establish enduring, close relationships to significant others during adult years (Grossman & Grossman, 1995). Insecure attachments involve avoidant, ambivalent, and disorganized strategies of interaction (Matas, Arend & Sroufe, 1978; Waters, Wippman & Sroufe, 1979). Some evidence suggests that demanding, disrespectful, and critical maternal behavior, as well as unfair and threatening paternal behavior, lead to these kinds of attachment styles (Ainsworth et al., 1978; Shaver et al., 1988). Insecure attachment may lead to contradictory internal models of relating to others and to difficulties in identifying with the attachment figure. Earlier research has shown that the relationship between the maternal behavior and children's attachment is clearer and stronger than the relationship between the paternal behavior and children's attachment (Crowell & Feldman, 1988; Lamb, Pleck, Charnov, & Levine, 1985; Main, Kaplan, & Cassidy, 1985).

The classification of the male SM practitioners into different attachment groups in relation to the father was: 47 percent were securely attached, 28 percent had an avoidant attachment, and 10 percent an ambivalent attachment. The rest were nonclassifiable, or else the question was left unanswered. Corresponding results concerning attachment to the mother showed that 54 percent were securely attached, 13 percent had an avoidant attachment, and 19 percent an ambivalent attachment. The rest (14.6 percent) were, again, non-classifiable or the question was left unanswered. The distribution of different attachment styles among the male SM practitioners was almost identical to distributions obtained in previous studies with general adult samples using similar methods of measurement (Shaver et al., 1988). This again suggests that conclusions drawn from clinical case reports based on people who have sought psychological help cannot be generalized to the majority of men practicing SM sex. Also, there was considerable agreement in the participants' attachment to both their fathers and mothers across all attachment categories. This suggests that internal representations regarding mother and father in adult age may not be differentiated but rather describe parental behavior in general. This finding is in line with observations made by Kalmuss (1984) in a study of family violence.

The male SM practitioners' attachment to their fathers was related to paternal use of physical punishment and alcohol consumption. Their attachment to their mothers was related to her use of physical punishment and emotional closeness, but not to maternal alcohol consumption. The style of attachment to the mother was also found to be related to the sexual adjustment of the male SM practitioners, in that those with avoidant attachment to their mothers had higher levels of sexual neuroticism (a conflict between strong sex drives and conscience or some other factor holding back the person from indulgence) and lower levels of sexual satisfaction than the SM practitioners with secure or ambivalent attachment to their mothers. Securely and ambivalently attached SM practitioners were sexually better adjusted than avoidantly attached SM practitioners. But this was only true of the attachment to the mother. This finding is in accordance with earlier research that has shown that mothers' behavior is a more significant predictor of children's attachment style than fathers' behavior (Crowell & Feldman, 1988; Lamb et al., 1985; Main et al., 1985). The sadistic males were more likely to have an ambivalent attachment and less likely to have a secure attachment to their mothers. In an opposite manner, the masochistic males were less likely to have an ambivalent attachment and more likely to have a secure attachment to their mothers.

The sexual adjustment of the participants was correlated with different aspects of interaction in their primary families. The strongest connection was a positive correlation between participants' recollection of expression of opinion in the primary family and their current sexual satisfaction. Perception of the extent of family support was positively correlated with current sexual satisfaction. Also, the less the participants thought that they had had influence on decision making in their primary families, the more they reported current sexual neuroticism.

Interestingly, the family background of the more sadistically inclined participants could be described as a situation where the children expressed their opinions but were not listened to. Thus, it can be speculated that they are compensating for the lack of influence on decision making in their childhood by wanting to be controlling in the sexual arena.

It was also apparent that the overwhelming majority of the SM practitioners had grown up in traditional two-parent households. Further, structural aspects of the primary family did not predict later sadomasochistic preferences, a finding expected on the basis of earlier research.

A risk factor that has specifically been suggested to be associated with sadomasochism is childhood sexual abuse. It has been suggested that sexually abused girls are vulnerable to revictimization in adulthood (Messman & Hirschman, 1981). Messman and Long (1996) found that several studies on this topic indicate that these girls are at an elevated risk for reexperiencing sexual abuse as adults compared to nonabused children. One possible mechanism for this effect is that abused women may see violence and domination by their partners as a part of sexuality and this may lead them to seek out punitive relationships. On the other hand, in boys sexual abuse seems to be associated with sexual aggression in adulthood (Ferrenbach, Smith, Monastersky, & Deisher, 1986; Friedrich & Luecke, 1988). Thus, the coping mechanisms of boys and girls seem to differ. Consequently, it could be assumed that some sexually abused individuals would be drawn to sadomasochistic sexual relationships, with females being more likely to take masochistic and males, sadistic roles.

Sexual abuse had occurred for 8 percent of the male and 23 percent of the female SM practitioners (Nordling et al., 2000). The abuse had occurred once for two SM practitioners, from two to ten times for ten SM practitioners, and more than ten times for five SM practitioners. The rate of occurrence did not differ between male and female SM practitioners. Further, the perpetrator was a family member in 61 percent of the cases.

The abused SM practitioners experienced more psychological distress. Of the sexually abused SM practitioners, 39 percent had attempted suicide, compared to 4 percent of the nonabused. Similarly, 33 percent of the abused SM practitioners had been inpatients in a psychiatric hospital, compared to 5 percent of the nonabused. Visits to a physician due to injuries obtained during SM sex were significantly more common among the abused SM practitioners (11 percent) than among the nonabused (2 percent). This may suggest that they had difficulties in setting appropriate limits to their SM activities. It was also found that the sexually abused SM practitioners had a higher level of sexual neuroticism compared to the nonabused.

As expected, the sexually abused female SM practitioners were significantly more likely to engage in masochistic sexual behavior than the nonabused. However, the abused male SM practitioners did not engage in sadistic sexual behavior more often than the nonabused. This finding supports the notion of abused women seeking out punitive relationships involving violence and domination (Messman & Long, 1996). The findings suggest that sexual abuse does not play a major role in determining whether the male SM practitioners take the sadistic or masochistic role in their sexual behavior.

The results also showed that the sexually abused SM practitioners were more often single (61 percent) compared to their nonabused counterparts (38 percent). This relative isolation may have been reflected in that the sexually abused SM practitioners were more prone to participate in SM–club activities. Sexual abuse was associated with poorer social adjustment as measured by income level and ability to establish steady relationships.

In conclusion, childhood sexual abuse had clearly adverse consequences in some SM practitioners. Therefore, one should be aware that a small subgroup of SM practitioners seems to be both psychologically and socially maladjusted.

WHAT DO THESE RESULTS TELL US?

The results presented in this chapter indicate that for the majority of the (male) SM practitioners, their level of social functioning is not impaired on characteristics like income and education when compared to the general population. On the contrary, they have a high income level and are highly educated (Moser & Levitt, 1987; Spengler, 1977; Weinberg, T. S., 1987). In contrast, the SM practitioners seemed to have difficulties in finding partners. The high number of masochistic heterosexual men and the relative lack of women create difficulties, a result that was previously documented (e.g., Moser & Levitt, 1987). The difficulties experienced by the masochistic males were also reflected in their expressed desire for steady relationships. In spite of this, the males seemed to have a positive and ego-syntonic view of their sexual behavior; that is, they viewed it as acceptable and consistent with their total personality.

The development of sadomasochistic sexual behavior starts after experience with more ordinary sexual behavior and the establishment of a sexual orientation. Specifically, the exclusively gay male SM practitioners became aware and started practicing their sadomasochistic interests later, which accords well with findings showing that gay male individuals establish their sexual orientation later than heterosexual individuals (Coleman, 1982; Kontula & Haavio-Mannila, 1993). Further, about one-third indicated that only sadomasochistic sex could satisfy them, which can be interpreted as sadomasochistic sex involving paraphiliac cues for these SM practitioners (Suppe, 1985). Many masochists (who were more likely to be heterosexual) had not engaged in ordinary sex, that is, either heterosexual or gay consensual sexual activity without sadomasochistic elements, before starting to practice sadomasochism. In contrast, many SM practitioners seem to be flexible in their sadomasochistic preference in that the persons who described themselves as exclusively sadistic or masochistic could occasionally take the other position. This indicates that sadomasochistic behavior involved facilitative as opposed to necessary cues for most SM practitioners (Suppe, 1985).

The results also indicate clearly that the sadomasochistic behaviors in which the SM practitioners were engaged were not haphazardly combined with each other. Rather, there is evidence for structured patterns of co-occurrences. Further, the combining of the behaviors indicates the existence of sadomasochistic sexual scripts similar to the existence of sexual scripts for ordinary heterosexual sexual behavior (Gagnon, 1990; Gagnon & Simon, 1987). The existence of such sexual scripts suggests that individual solutions within the sadomasochistic subcultures are determined in an interplay between the individual's own developmental history, psychological characteristics (see Santtila et al., 2000), and the subcultural context within which the individual faces information concerning possible pathways of expression and conformist group processes that make the development of certain scripts more likely than others (cf. social constructionist approaches to sexuality, e.g., Hart, 1985). This process may be more transparent in sadomasochism due to its highly ritualized nature, but the process itself is probably shared in most expressions of human sexuality.

Although the results discussed here are informative, some concerns may be raised about the reliability of the results concerning reports about childhood experiences due to the retrospective nature of these data. However, the childhood background of sexual behavior in general and unusual sexuality in particular is almost impossible to study using longitudinal designs. On the other hand, Brewin, Andrews, and Gottlib (1993) have provided evidence suggesting that retrospective reports of childhood experiences are not as unreliable and invalid as previously assumed. If anything, research by Widom and Shepard (1996) indicates that individuals tend to understate rather than exaggerate when retrospectively recalling childhood experiences. Therefore, it can be assumed that despite methodological problems, the use of retrospective reports from people with unusual sexual interests can give important information concerning their development and family background.

While we should note that sexual sadism and masochism should be separated from sadistic and masochistic personality disorders (American Psychiatric Association, 2000), this does not exclude the possibility that some individuals suffering from these personality disorders may occasionally engage in sexual behavior with sadistic and masochistic elements. These persons should not automatically be equated with individuals engaging in consensual sadomasochistic activities.

The variability in the phenomenon of sadomasochism makes it easy to understand that no one description—let alone explanation—can do it justice. Our results suggest that a person's sadomasochistic interest may be influenced by a number of factors. Individual sadomasochistic behavioral repertoire is also most certainly influenced by social and cultural features, which may be one of the reasons why gay and straight SM practitioners show such different repertoires. It can be speculated that sadomasochism can be both a creative part of an individual's sexual life (as suggested by Foucault, 1999) or have a protective function as a neosexual (i.e., nonnormative hetero- or homosexual consensual activities) creation in order to prevent severe psychological disturbances from appearing (as suggested by McDougall, 2000). The conflicting perspectives on sadomasochism until now may, to a great extent, be dependent on different researchers looking at different aspects and various subgroups of a phenomenon that is multifaceted and not easily amenable to general descriptions or conclusions.

REFERENCES

Ainsworth, M. D., Blehar, M. C., Waters, E., & Wall, S. (1978). *Patterns of attachment: Assessed in the strange situation and at home.* Hillsdale, NJ: Lawrence Erlbaum.

Alison, L., Santtila, P., Sandnabba, N. K., & Nordling, N. (2001). Sadomasochistically-oriented behavior: Diversity in practice and meaning. *Archives of Sexual Behavior, 30,* 1–12.

American Psychiatric Association. (2000). *Diagnostic and statistical manual of mental disorders* (4th ed., Text Revision). Washington, DC: Author.

Baumeister, R. F. (1988). Masochism as escape from self. *Journal of Sex Research, 25,* 28–59.

Blos, P. (1991). Sadomasochism and the defense against recall of painful affect. *Journal of American Psychoanalytical Association, 39,* 417–430.

Blum, H. P. (1991). Sadomasochism in the psychoanalytic process, within and beyond the pleasure principle: Discussion. *Journal of American Psychoanalytical Association, 39,* 431–450.

Bowlby, J. (1969). *Attachment and loss: Vol. 1. Attachment.* London: Hogarth Press.

Bowlby, J. (1973). *Attachment and loss: Vol. 2. Separation: Anxiety and anger.* London: Hogarth Press.

Brewin, C. A., Andrews, B., & Gottlib, I. H. (1993). Psychopathology and early experience: Reappraisal of retrospective reports. *Psychological Bulletin, 113,* 82–98.

Coen, S. J. (1988). Sadomasochistic excitement: Character disorder and perversion. In R. A. Glick & D. I. Meyers (Eds.), *Masochism, current psychoanalytic perspectives* (pp. 43–59). London: Analytic Press.

Coleman, E. (1982). Developmental stages of the coming out process. *Journal of Homosexuality, 7,* 31–43.

Crowell, J. A., & Feldman, S. S. (1988). Mothers' internal models of relationships and children's behavioral and developmental status: A study of mother-child interaction. *Child Development, 59,* 1273–1285.

Deaux, K., & Lewis, L. L. (1984). Structure of gender stereotypes: Interrelationships among components and gender label. *Journal of Personality and Social Psychology, 46,* 991–1004.

DeLamater, J. D., & MacCorquodale, P. (1979). *Premarital sexuality: Attitudes, relationships, behavior.* Madison: University of Wisconsin Press.

Falk, G., & Weinberg, T. S. (1983). Sadomasochism and popular Western culture. In T. S. Weinberg & G. W. Kamel (Eds.), *S and M studies in sadomasochism* (pp. 137–146). New York: Prometheus Books.

Ferrenbach, P. A., Smith, W., Monastersky, C., & Deisher, R. W. (1986). Adolescent sexual offenders: Offender and offense characteristics. *American Journal of Orthopsychiatry, 56,* 225–233.

Foucault, M. (1999). Sexualitet, makt och identitetens politik [Sexuality, power, and the politics of identity]. *Lambda Nordica, 2,* 122–137.

Friedrich, W. N., & Luecke, W. J. (1988). Young school-age sexually aggressive children. *Professional Psychology and Practice, 19,* 155–164.

Gagnon, J. H. (1990). The explicit and implicit use of the scripting perspective in sex research. *Annual Review of Sex Research, 1,* 1–43.

Gagnon, J. H., & Simon, W. (1987). The sexual scripting of oral genital contacts. *Archives of Sexual Behavior, 16,* 1–25.

Grossman, K. E., & Grossman, K. (1995). Attachment quality as an organizer of emotional and behavioral responses in a longitudinal perspective. In C. M. Parkers, J. Stevenson-Hinde, & P. Marris (Eds.), *Attachment across the life cycle.* London: Routledge Press.

Haeberle, E. (1978). *The sex atlas.* New York: Seabury Press.

Hart, J. (1985). Therapeutic implications of viewing sexual identity in terms of essentialist and constructionist theories. In J. P. DeCecco (Ed.), *Gay personality and sexual labeling* (pp. 39–51). New York: Harrington Park Press.

Henkin, W. A. (1992). *Ask the therapist.* Retrieved June 6, 2005, from www.sexuality.org/authors/henkin/att11.html

Janus, S. S., & Janus, C. L. (1993). *The Janus Report on Sexual Behavior: The first broad-scale scientific national survey since Kinsey.* New York: Wiley.

Kalmuss, D. (1984). The intergenerational transmission of marital aggression. *Journal of Marriage and the Family, 46,* 11–19.

Kamel, G. W. (1983). Leathersex: Meaningful aspects of gay sadomasochism. In T. S. Weinberg & G. W. Kamel (Eds.), *S and M studies in sadomasochism* (pp. 162–174). New York: Prometheus Books.

Karpman, B. (1962). *The sexual offender and his offences* (7th ed.). New York: Julian Press.

Katchadourian, H., & Lunde, D. (1975). *Fundamentals of human sexuality* (2nd ed.). New York: Holt, Rinehart & Winston.

Kinsey, A. C., Pomeroy, W. B., and Martin, C. E. (1948). *Sexual behavior in the human male.* Philadelphia: Saunders.

Kontula, O., & Haavio-Mannila, E. (1993). *Suomalainen seksi* [Finnish sex]. Juva: WSOY.

Lamb, M. E., Pleck, J. H., Charnov, E., & Levine, J. A. (1985). Paternal behavior in humans. *American Psychologist, 25,* 883–894.

Långström, N., & Seto, M. C. (in press). Exhibitionistic and voyeuristic behavior in a Swedish national population survey. *Archives of Sexual Behavior.*

Laumann, E. O., Gagnon, J. H., Michael, R. T., & Michaels, S. (1994). *The social organization of sexuality: Sexual practices in the United States.* Chicago: Chicago University Press.

Lee, J. A. (1979). The social organization of sexual risk. *Alternative Lifestyles, 2,* 69–100.

Lips, H. M. (2001). *Sex and gender: An introduction.* London: Mayfield.

Main, M., Kaplan, N., & Cassidy, J. (1985). Security in infancy, childhood and adulthood: A move to the level of representation. *Monographs of the Society for Research in Child Development, 50* (1–2, Serial No. 209).

Masters, R. E. L. (1966). *Sex-driven people: An autobiographical approach to the problem of the sex-dominated personality.* Los Angeles: Sherbourne Press.

Matas, L., Arend, R. A., & Sroufe, L. A. (1978). Continuity of adaption in the second year: The relationship between quality of attachment and later competence. *Child Development, 49,* 547–556.

McDougall, J. (2000). Sexuality and the neosexual. *Modern Psychoanalysis, 25,* 155–166.

Messman, T. L., & Hirschman, L. (1981). Families at risk for father-daughter incest. *American Journal of Psychiatry, 138,* 967–970.

Messman, T. L., & Long, P. S. (1996). Child sexual abuse and its relationship to revictimization in adult women: A review. *Clinical Psychology Review, 16,* 397–420.

MetroM8. (n.d.). *Introduction to SM sex: A practical 4-day course to explore SM sex!* Retrieved June 6, 2005, from www.metromate.org.uk/info/gw/sm-sex.phtml

Miletski, H. (1999). *Bestiality—zoophilia: An exploratory study.* San Francisco: Institute for Advanced Study of Human Sexuality.

Moser, C. (1988). Sadomasochism. In D. M. Dailey (Ed.), *The sexually unusual* (pp. 43–56). New York: Harrington Park Press.

Moser, C., & Levitt, E. E. (1987). An explanatory-descriptive study of a sadomasochistically oriented sample. *Journal of Sex Research, 23,* 322–337.

Nordling, N., Sandnabba, N. K., & Santtila, P. (2000). The prevalence and effects of self-reported childhood sexual abuse among sadomasochistically oriented males and females. *Journal of Child Sex Abuse, 9,* 53–63.

Nordling, N., Sandnabba, N. K., Santtila, P., & Alison, L. (2005). Differences and similarities between gay and straight individuals involved in the sadomasochistic subcultures. *Journal of Homosexuality, 50,* 41–57.

Rosenberger, J. R. (1968). *Bestiality.* Los Angeles: Medco Books.

Rothstein, A. (1991). Sadomasochism in the neurosis conceived as a pathological compromise formation. *Journal of American Psychoanalytical Association, 39,* 363–375.

Sandnabba, N. K., Santtila, P., Beetz, A. M., Nordling, N., & Alison, L. (2002). Characteristics of a sample of sadomasochistically-oriented males with recent experience of sexual contact with animals. *Deviant Behavior, 23,* 511–529.

Sandnabba, N. K., Santtila, P., & Nordling, N. (1999). Sexual behavior and social adaptation among sadomasochistically oriented males. *Journal of Sex Research, 36,* 273–282.

Santtila, P., Sandnabba, N. K., Alison, L., & Nordling, N. (2002). Investigating the underlying structure in sadomasochistically-oriented behavior. *Archives of Sexual Behavior, 31,* 185–196.

Santtila, P., Sandnabba, N. K., & Nordling, N. (2000). Retrospective perceptions of family interaction in childhood as correlates of current sexual adaptation among sadomasochistic males. *Journal of Psychology and Human Sexuality, 12,* 69–87.

Scharff, D. E. (1988). *The sexual relationship: An object relations view of sex and the family*. London: Routledge Press.

Shaver, P., Hazan, C., & Bradshaw, D. (1988). Love as attachment: The integration of three behavioral systems. In R. J. Steinberg & M. L. Barnes (Eds.), *The psychology of love* (pp. 68–99). New York: Vail-Ballou Press.

Spengler, A. (1977). Manifest sadomasochism of males: Results of an empirical study. *Archives of Sexual Behavior, 6,* 441–456.

Suppe, F. (1985). Classifying sexual disorders: The diagnostic and statistical manual of the American Psychiatric Association. In J. P. DeCecco (Ed.), *Gay personality and sexual labeling* (pp. 9–28). New York: Harrington Park Press.

Taywaditep, K. J. (2001). *Marginalization among the marginalized: Gay men's negative attitudes toward effeminacy*. Unpublished doctoral dissertation. University of Chicago.

Townsend, L. (1983). *The leatherman's handbook*. New York: Modernismo.

Waters, E., Wippman, J., & Sroufe, L. A. (1979). Attachment, positive affect, and competence in the peer group: Two studies in construct validation. *Child Development, 50,* 821–829.

Weinberg, M. S., Williams, C. J., & Moser, C. (1984). The social constituents of sadomasochism. *Social Problems, 31,* 379–389.

Weinberg, T. S. (1987). Sadomasochism in the United States: A review of recent sociological literature. *Journal of Sex Research, 23,* 50–69.

Widom, C. S., & Shepard, R. L. (1996). Accuracy of adult recollections of childhood victimization: Part I. Childhood physical abuse. *Psychological Assessment, 8,* 412–421.

3

Female Sex Offenders

Donna M. Vandiver ◆

Recently, media attention has been drawn to females who have sexually assaulted young boys. One of the most highly publicized cases was a teacher from Seattle, Mary Kay LeTourneau, who had an affair with her sixth grade student, Vili Fualaau ("Le Tourneau says," 2004). She spent six months in jail for the offense. Despite being arrested on two occasions, she continued to see her former student. She had two children with him and later married him in March 2005 after he had turned 21 years of age. Despite extensive media coverage of Mary Kay LeTourneau's love affair with her student, few equated this type of behavior with a bona fide "sex offender." The majority of people had not even heard of females sexually offending; sex offenders are typically thought to be male.

Researchers have identified relationships such as the one Mary Kay LeTourneau established with her student as a specific category of female sex offense, *teacher/lover*. In fact, this is only one of the many types of female sex offenses. A high percentage of females who sexually offend do not offend alone; they often sexually abuse a child with a male, possibly their husband. High rates of incest have also been found among this population of offenders, with mothers often abusing a son or daughter. For some females who sexually offend, the stereotypical rapist is turned on its head—an adult woman rapes an adult man. Other females start out on the wrong side of the law; the women are criminals, committing nonsexual offenses and the sexual offense is just another offense. Usually this is for the purpose of economic gain; it includes offenses such as forcing young girls to prostitute or forcing children to pose nude for pornographic material. Many female sex offenders are psychologically impaired or act out on latent homosexual feelings.

Some sex offenders begin offending at an early age; it is not simply an adult crime. Even though the majority of juvenile sex offenders are male, a few are female. There is a paucity of information regarding juvenile female sex offenders; the studies that have been conducted, though, are reviewed in this chapter.

PREVALENCE OF FEMALE SEX OFFENDERS

Several sources are available to answer the question of how many sex offenders are female. The Uniform Crime Reports (UCR) includes arrest data compiled by the Federal Bureau of Investigation; the data are released on an annual basis. In 2003, female offenders were arrested for 1.3 percent (n = 247) of the 18,446 forcible rapes (U.S. Department of Justice, 2005b). For sex offenses other than rape and prostitution, females accounted for 8.5 percent of the 63,759 arrests. While this information does not fully capture the extent of female sexual abuse, it does provide an indicator; females make up only a small portion of sex offenders. Whether they make up approximately 8 percent of sex offenders is questionable; official arrest data are limited because many victims do not report sexual offenses.

Another source for the number of females who have sexually offended is the National Crime Victimization Survey (NCVS). Rather than relying on arrests data, the information is based on an annual household survey that asks participants who are over the age of 12 about their victimization experiences; thus, information not reported to law enforcement is captured. It should be noted, however, that not every person in the United States is surveyed. Instead, it relies on samples, and subsequently estimates the population rates.

The NCVS includes an estimate of how many people were sexually abused but failed to report the incident to law enforcement. Interestingly, only 39 percent of sexual assault incidents were reported to law enforcement in 2003 (U.S. Department of Justice, 2005a). Sexual assaults, therefore, are often not fully captured by official arrest reports.

Data from the NCVS indicate that 3.5 percent of the sexual assaults with a single offender involved a female offender. For sexual assault incidents involving multiple offenders, females and males acting together accounted for 8 percent of the sexual assaults. Thus, reports from the UCR and NCVS indicate females account for a small proportion of sexual offenses, and males make up the majority of sex offenders. Despite the low numbers of females who sexually offend, law enforcement and social service agencies need to be knowledgeable about the characteristics of female sex offenders. More information is needed for the detection and treatment of this group of offenders.

Table 3.1. Summary of the Number of Female Sex Offenders

Researchers	Percentage of Offenders Who Are Female	Sample Size and Source
Travin et al., 1990	1	515 sex offenders in a specialized sex offender treatment program
Finkelhor et al., 1990 (female respondents)	1	Telephone survey of 1,481 women about their sexual victimization experiences
Rowan et al., 1990	1.5	600 sex offenders from the New Hampshire judicial system and Vermont social service agencies and courts
Vandiver & Kercher, 2004	1.6	29,376 registered sex offenders in Texas
Vandiver & Walker, 2002	2.4	1,644 registered sex offenders in Arkansas
Vandiver, in press	3.1	7,385 adults arrested for a sex offense; All adults arrested for a sex offense in 2001 (NIBRS data, including 21 states)
Faller, 1987	14	Child Abuse and Neglect Treatment Center in Michigan
Finkelhor et al., 1990 (male respondents)	17	Telephone survey of 1,145 men about their sexual victimization experiences
Finkelhor et al., 1988	40	271 child sexual abuse cases occurring in a daycare, nationwide
Petrovich & Templer, 1984	59	83 incarcerated rapists report of their childhood sexual victimization

Additional data for determining the extent to which females sexually offend can be drawn from individual sexual abuse studies. The number of females who sexually offended ranged from 1 percent to 59 percent (see Table 3.1). The studies listed in the table include self-report information from studies relying on known sex offenders, official data of known sex offenders, and surveys of the general population.

Table 3.1 illustrates how few studies include female sex offenders and of those, the majority of the studies indicate that female sex offenders make up less than 20 percent of sex offenders. While two studies included rates of more than 20 percent, one study (Finkelhor, Williams, & Burns, 1988) included a daycare sample, which is made up of primarily female employees. The other study (Petrovich & Templer, 1984) relied upon self-report from incarcerated rapists who reported they were sexually abused as children by women. The validity of their reports may not be accurate.

PROBLEMS IN RECOGNIZING
FEMALE SEX OFFENDERS

Many researchers have speculated that sex offenses in general are largely underreported (Finkelhor, Hotaling, Lewis, & Smith, 1990), and data from the NCVS support this notion. Measurement problems are inherent in reporting sexual abuse. While the majority of people are willing to call the police if someone steals their wallet or purse or their car, not everyone is willing to report a sexual offense. Many times the offender is a friend, relative, or even a caretaker (Johnson, R., & Shrier, 1987), and in these cases the victim is even less likely to report the offense. When the victim is a young child, he or she may not recognize the behavior as something that is wrong (Groth & Birnbaum, 1979). Victims may feel the abuse is their fault (Johnson, R., & Shrier, 1987) or may fear additional abuse if they tell someone. Detection and prosecution of sexual abuse is also problematic. Sexual abuse is more difficult to detect than physical abuse (Farrell, 1988). Physical abuse results in bruises and broken bones whereas sexual abuse does not result in such obvious physical markings. The victim is not always encouraged to tell his/her story because of the difficulty associated with criminal prosecution. Some believe sexual abuse is a mental health problem rather than a criminal justice problem; thus, it is better handled by social service agencies rather than criminal courts (Berliner & Barbieri, 1984).

The problems associated with reporting sexual abuse are compounded when the offender is female. The thought of a woman sexually offending is a perplexing concept to most; in our society we are not geared toward thinking that a female is physically capable of "rape" or any other type of sexual assault (Denov, 2004). This obstacle in our thinking is conveyed well by the title of a book chapter, "What harm can be done without a penis?" (Hislop, 2001).[1] Males are typically associated with violent crimes, and there is often an inability to associate a "submissive and passive" woman with a violent offense (Scavo, 1989). The problem is perpetuated by organizational structures within agencies such as law enforcement departments and treatment centers that rely on traditional constructs of who can and cannot sexually offend (Denov, 2004).

Researchers have identified many reasons why females are underrepresented in official data. Sexual abuse by a woman is often considered harmless despite research findings indicating the effects are prominent for victims of female sexual abuse (Hetherton, 1999). Women sex offenders often go unnoticed because women are able to disguise sexual offenses when engaging in routine child-rearing activities such as bathing and dressing (Groth & Birnbaum, 1979). Females who act with a male co-offender may be seen as less culpable than their male partner (Mayer, 1992).

RESEARCH ON FEMALE SEX OFFENDERS

Only recently has research begun to emerge on female sex offenders. The majority of the empirical evidence is derived from four sources:

1. clinical sources (see Faller, 1987, 1995; Johnson, R., & Shrier, 1987; Peluso & Putnam, 1996; Rosencrans, 1997; Rudin, Zalewski, & Bodmer-Turner, 1995; Travin, Cullen, & Protter, 1990);

2. incarcerated samples (see Kaplan & Green, 1995; O'Connor, 1987; Syed & Williams, 1996);

3. medical samples (i.e., hospital) (see Duncan & Williams, 1998; Marvasti, 1986); and

4. sex offender registries (see Vandiver & Kercher, 2004; Vandiver & Walker, 2002).

Each of the above sources includes information from the female sex offender herself (or her records) and from victims of female sex abuse (Denov, 2004; Johnson, R., & Shrier, 1987; Krug, 1989; Peluso & Putnam, 1996; Rudin et al., 1995; Sarrel & Masters, 1982). Most of these sources are limited in that they include offenses known only to social service agencies, medical personnel, or law enforcement; thus, they provide only the narrowest view into the world of female sex offenders, given that many do not come to the attention of such agencies.

While the number of studies specifically focused on female sex offenders is growing and includes approximately thirty empirical studies, many are limited by small sample sizes. Only about ten studies include more than thirty female sex offenders (see Duncan & Williams, 1998; Faller, 1987, 1995; O'Connor, 1987; Pothast & Allen, 1994; Rosencrans, 1997; Rudin et al., 1995; Vandiver & Kercher, 2004; Vandiver & Walker, 2002). With the exception of Vandiver and Kercher's (2004; n = 471), no study included more than 100 subjects. Many studies included fewer than fifteen female sex offenders (see Chasnoff et al., 1986; Chow & Choy, 2002; Denov, 2003; Johnson, R., & Shrier, 1987; Kaplan & Green, 1995; Krug, 1989; Marvasti, 1986; Nathan & Ward, 2002; Peluso & Putnam, 1996; Rowan, Rowan, & Langelier, 1990; Sarrel & Masters, 1982; Travin et al., 1990; Wolfe, 1985).

Description of Female Sex Offenders

The typical female sex offender is young, usually in her twenties or thirties. Researchers have found the average age of female sex offenders in their studies to be 26 (Faller, 1987, 1988), 28 (Lewis & Stanley, 2000), 30 (Nathan & Ward, 2002; Vandiver & Walker, 2002), 32 (Vandiver & Kercher, 2004), 33 (Rowan et al., 1990), and 36 (Kaplan & Green, 1995). Most studies indicate that approximately 80–90 percent of the women are Caucasian

(Faller, 1987, 1995; Lewis & Stanley, 2000; Vandiver & Kercher, 2004; Vandiver & Walker, 2002).

High rates of mental illness are reported by various studies. For example, Lewis and Stanley (2000) found in a study of fifteen women, 66 percent had a psychotic disorder (n = 2), schizophrenia (n = 1), or depressive symptoms (n = 7). Nathan and Ward (2002) also found 66 percent of the twelve female sex offenders had either depression (n = 4), an eating disorder (n = 3), or experienced self-mutilation with suicidal ideations. In an assessment of eleven female sex offenders, Kaplan and Green (1995) found 72 percent experienced posttraumatic stress syndrome, 63 percent had experienced major depression, 63 percent had avoidant personality disorder, and 45 percent had dependent personality disorder. In O'Connor's (1987) study, 48 percent of eighty-one incarcerated female sex offenders had a history of some type of psychiatric disorder. Additionally, 40 percent of the eighty-one women had psychotic features. In a study of seventy-two female sex offenders, 32 percent had some type of mental illness (Faller, 1995). A study of sixteen female sex offenders included 31 percent who had either borderline personality disorder or psychotic features. In a study of forty female sex offenders, 18 percent had psychotic features (Faller, 1987).

Even though the rate of mental illness has been found to be high, caution is suggested in interpreting these findings. Many of the sources relied upon are clinical sources (Faller, 1995; Lewis & Stanley, 2000; Matthews, Hunter, & Vuz, 1997); thus, many of the women were likely being treated primarily for a mental illness and the sexual offending was then discovered. Relying on clinical sources is likely to yield high percentages of persons with a mental illness.

A moderate number of cases with mental retardation and borderline intellectual functioning have also been found among this population of offenders. Thirty-three percent of forty cases in one study were mentally retarded or had brain damage (Faller, 1987). Twenty-seven percent of the fifteen cases in Lewis and Stanley's (2000) research had mild mental retardation. Twenty-two percent of seventy-two cases in another study were mentally retarded (Faller, 1995). Rowan et al. (1990) reported one of nine cases had mental retardation.

A few studies reported many female sex offenders had a history of drug and/or alcohol abuse. Slightly more than half of the forty cases in Faller's 1987 study and seventy-two cases in Faller's 1995 study had a substance-abuse history. In Rosencrans's (1997) study of ninety-three female sex offenders, 32 percent had abused alcohol and 19 percent had a substance-abuse history. The drug or alcohol abuse for many women may be evidence of poor coping strategies in general.

Experiencing sexual abuse as a child is also a common characteristic of female sex offenders. Eighty percent of the fifteen cases in Lewis and Stanley's (2000) study were sexually abused by either someone they knew or a family member. Approximately three-quarters (76 percent) of the thirty-eight female sex offenders in one study (Pothast & Allen, 1994) were sexually abused as a child. Fifty-eight percent of the twelve female sex offenders in Wolfe's (1985) study had a history of sexual abuse. In Miccio-Fonseca's (2000) study, 56 percent of the eighteen female sex offenders were sexually abused as a child. Almost half of the forty female sex offenders in Faller's (1987) study reported experiencing sexual abuse. In another study, the victims of female sex offenders believed 20 percent of their abusers had been abused by their father and 20 percent were abused by their mother (Rosencrans, 1997). Many of the reports of sexual abuse, however, were self-reported.

Behaviors of Female Sex Offenders

Despite the misconception that a woman could not physically assault another person, women who have sexually offended have engaged in a broad range of sexual offenses. This behavior includes physical fondling, oral stimulation, putting fingers inside the body, putting objects inside the body, forcing victims to watch others engage in sexual activity, and forcing victims to touch/fondle the perpetrator. Objects such as enema equipment, sticks, candles, vibrators, and other objects were inserted into victims' bodily orifices also. Some of the "other" objects included scissors, knives, hair rollers, needles, religious medals, vacuum cleaner parts, and even a goldfish. The victims were also forced to touch or fondle the perpetrator's genitals. Other sexualized touching included oral sex and lying on top of or under the perpetrator (Rosencrans, 1997).

Some of the abusive behaviors included hands-off offenses such as simply watching victims inappropriately. This included watching the victim bathing, dressing/undressing, using the bathroom, masturbating, and having sex with her father. The victims were also forced to watch their perpetrators dress/undress, masturbate, have sex with their spouse, and change their feminine hygiene products (Rosencrans, 1997).

From these reports, it is evident that female perpetrated sexual abuse covers a wide range of behavior including both hands-on and hands-off offenses. When considering female sexual abuse, it is important to recognize that while female perpetrators do not always physically rape their victim(s) as a man is known to rape a woman, they are still capable of committing a range of assaults on their victims.

Victims of Female Sex Offenders

The most common characteristic of the victims of female sex offenders is that they knew their offender. In fact, many of them were related to their abuser. The percentage of intrafamilial abuse ranged from 37 percent to 94 percent (see Table 3.2). Additionally, a high percentage of those who engaged in intrafamilial abuse included mothers abusing their own children. For example, in Syed and Williams's (1996) study, it was reported that of those who were related to their abuser, 80 percent of the victims were the children of their abuser.

Table 3.2. Summary of Relationship of Victim to Offender

Researchers	Number of Victims	Relationship to Offender			
		Related (%)	Acquaintances (%)	Stranger (%)	Other (%)
Faller, 1987	63	90	10		
Faller, 1995	72	75			Nonfamilial: 25
Lewis & Stanley, 2000	22*	76	24		
Peluso & Putnam, 1996	2	50	50		
Rudin et al., 1995	87	56	22	3	Caretaker: 19
Vandiver & Kercher, 2004	471	37	46	7	Missing or not applicable: 10**
Vandiver & Walker, 2002	16*	94			Nonfamilial: 6
Syed & Williams, 1996	18*	76			Nonfamilial: 24

* The original data did not include information on all victims; the number reported here includes the number of victims with available information.
** Several offenders did not have a specific victim (i.e., possession of pornography).

The victims are typically young, with an average age of less than 12 years (Faller, 1987, 1995; Lewis & Stanley, 2000; Nathan & Ward, 2002; Vandiver & Kercher, 2004). With regard to the sex of the victim, the studies vary. Many researchers report a slightly higher number of female victims as compared to male victims (Faller, 1987, 1995; Rowan et al., 1990; Rudin et al., 1995). One study, however, included reports that all of the victims, or a majority, were male (Lewis & Stanley, 2000). Vandiver and Kercher (2004), relying on 471 subjects, found half of the victims were male and half were female. Subsequent research by Vandiver (in press) indicated that the sex of the victim varies depending on whether the woman was acting by herself or with a co-offender. Those acting alone are more likely to have male victims while co-offenders are more likely to have a combination of male and female victims.

TYPOLOGIES OF FEMALE SEX OFFENDERS

While the typologies for male sex offenders are well developed, the typologies created for female sex offenders have only recently emerged. Unfortunately, most of the typologies of female sex offenders are based on small sample sizes; thus, the information yielded from these data are not likely to be exhaustive. With the exception of one study, the typologies were based on samples of less than thirty (see Table 3.3).

Table 3.3. Description and Source of Female Sex Offender Typologies

Author	Classifications	Data Source; Sample Size
Sarrel & Masters, 1982	• Forced assault • Babysitter abuse • Incestuous abuse • Dominant woman abuse	Male victims of female sexual abuse; n = 11.
McCarty, 1981; 1986	• Independent offenders of males (1986) • Independent offenders of females (1986) • Co-offenders and accomplices (1986) • Severely psychologically disturbed abuser (1981)	Female sex offenders identified by child protective services who engaged in mother-child incest; n = 26.
Mathews, 1987; Mathews et al., 1989	• Teacher/lover • Predisposed • Male-coerced molester • Exploration/exploitation • Psychologically disturbed (McCarty, 1986)	Female sex offenders sentenced to community correctional center; n = 16.
Mayer, 1992	• Female rapist • Female sexual harassment • Mother molester • Triads • Homosexual molestation	Prior empirical reports of female sex offenders.
Syed & Williams, 1996 (building on Mathews et al.'s [1989] categories)	• Teacher/lover (Mathews et al., 1989) • Male-coerced (Mathews et al., 1989) • Angry-impulsive • Male-accompanied, familial • Male-accompanied, nonfamilial	Female sex offenders incarcerated in Canada; n = 19.

(continued)

Table 3.3. continued

Author	Classifications	Data Source; Sample Size
Nathan & Ward, 2002 (building on Mathews et al.'s [1989] categories)	• Male-accompanied, the rejected/revengeful	Female sex offenders incarcerated in Australia; n = 12.
Vandiver & Kercher, 2004	• Heterosexual nurturers • Noncriminal homosexual offenders • Female sexual predators • Young adult child exploiters • Homosexual criminals • Aggressive homosexual offenders	Registered adult female sex offenders in Texas; n = 471.

Many of the researchers who have proposed classification systems of female sex offenders included overlapping categories. The majority of the proposed typologies can be classified into seven categories: nurturer, co-offender, incestuous, adult on adult, criminal offenders, psychologically impaired, and homosexual molester (see Table 3.4).

Nurturer

Nurturing abuse typically involves an inappropriate relationship between a woman and someone she knows. Several researchers have described different types of female sex offenders who fit into this category; they are summarized as *heterosexual nurturer, teacher/lover,* and *babysitter abuse.* Each involves a woman in a position of authority who engages in a sexual relationship with (usually) a young boy, often a teenager, whom she is responsible for in some way. This type of sex offender is not "predatory" in terms of the woman specifically going to certain locations (i.e., school, parks, etc.), yet there does appear to be a grooming process where the woman becomes "friends" with the youth. Thus, there may be a grooming process where boundaries are slowly redefined over the period the relationship exists.

Heterosexual Nurturer

Vandiver and Kercher (2004) reported a broad category of inappropriate relationships, including any woman in a caretaking or nurturing role. For example, Vandiver (2003) described a woman who worked at a youth facility and "fell in love" with a young teenage boy; thus a mentor-mentee relationship existed. The woman had no history of sexual abuse. She was divorced with two children. She indicated the victim was a 14-year-old male whom she met through her work. She described the sexual act between her and the teenager as consensual, but followed up by stating that she knew it was wrong and did not want to make an excuse for what she had done. She indicated that the teenager came from a "bad family." He did not know his father and had been sexually abused by his grandfather.

The relationship began at the youth facility and the boy began to come over to her residence to talk and get something to eat. The relationship progressed into a sexual one after he kissed her once. She had sex with him approximately seven times over a six-month period. She stated, "When it happened it seemed natural—but I shouldn't say natural because it's not natural to have sex with a teenage boy. He kissed me and I didn't stop it."

The woman was with the boy when she had a car accident, which led to her arrest when law enforcement suspected the abuse. After she was arrested, she still tried to contact the young boy and was "taken in [by law enforcement] several times." At the time of the interview she had not seen the boy in several years.

Table 3.4. Summary of Female Sex Offender Typologies

Classification	Identified Categories of Female Sex Offenders and Researcher(s) Who Identified	Description
Nurturer	Heterosexual nurturer (Vandiver & Kercher, 2004)	Adult female molests young male (approximately 12 years old). Female has a mentorship role (i.e., teacher, caretaker, etc.) to the young male.
	Teacher/lover (Mathews et al., 1989)	A teacher who has a sexual relationship with a young boy, usually her student.
	Babysitter abuse (Sarrel & Masters, 1982)	Older woman or girl seducing a young boy whom she is not related to; abuse occurring while she is babysitting.
	Exploration/exploitation (Mathews et al., 1987)	Often abuse in a babysitting situation; young (14 to 16); typically no victimization history.
Co-offender	Triads (Mayer, 1992)	The female has a male partner.
	Male-coerced molester (Mathews et al., 1989)	The female has a male partner.
	Noncriminal homosexual offenders (Vandiver & Kercher, 2004)	No/few prior arrests, female victim, victim about 13 years old, co-offender likely.*
	Male-accompanied, familial (Syed & Williams, 1996)	The female has a male partner; victim is related.
	Co-offending mother & accomplices (McCarty, 1986)	Usually acting with dominant male; borderline intelligence, dependent personality, victim is mother's child.
	Male-accompanied, nonfamilial (Syed & Williams, 1996)	Female acting with a male; victim is not related.
	Male-accompanied, the rejected/revengeful (Nathan & Ward, 2001)	The female has a male partner; the motivation is revenge in response to feeling rejected.
Incestuous	Predisposed (Mathews et al., 1989)	History of sexual abuse in family; abuse family members, including their own children.
	Incestuous abuse (Sarrel & Masters, 1982)	Boys sexually abused by mother or older sister.

	Mother molesters (Mayer, 1992)	Mothers molesting their daughters or sons.
	Young-adult child exploiters (Vandiver & Kercher, 2004)	Mother molesting her own children (sons or daughters).
	Independent offenders of female/male children (McCarty, 1986)	Mother molesting alone either her female or male child.
	Mother molesters, mother-son incest (Mayer, 1992)	Mothers who molest their sons.
Adult on Adult	Female sexual harassment (Mayer, 1992)	On a continuum with female rapists; behaviors include sexual harassment, which may occur in the workplace.
	Female rapist (Mayer, 1992)	Similar to a male rapist; victim is male; typically the offenders knew their victim beforehand.
	Dominant woman abuse (Sarrel & Masters, 1982)	Traditional sex roles are reversed; overt female sexual aggression. Typically involves forced sexual intercourse.
	Forced assault (Sarrel & Masters, 1982)	Adult woman assaults adult male; physically constrains male; male is fearful.
	Angry-impulsive (Syed & Williams, 1996) Aggressive homosexual criminal (Vandiver & Kercher, 2004)	Female violently assaults an adult male; motivated by anger. Adult female molests adult female.
Criminal Offenders	Female sexual predator (Vandiver & Kercher, 2004) Homosexual criminals (Vandiver & Kercher, 2004).	Adult who molests young boys; high rate of rearrest. Adult who molests young girls; high rate of rearrest.
Psychologically Impaired	Severely psychologically disturbed abuser (McCarty, 1986)	Has a history of adolescent psychological problems.
Homosexual Molester	Homosexual molestation (Mayer, 1992)	Woman with homosexual tendencies; abuses child of same or opposite sex; may or may not have a co-offender; victim may or may not be her own child.

* The original research did not include whether the female acted alone or with someone. The characteristics of the women and victim were similar to latter research of co-offending women (see Vandiver, in press).

One of the interesting points to note about this situation is that the woman described the young boy as having nowhere else to go and no one else for support. In other words, he was "social junk."[2] She could not do anything to harm him—he was already damaged goods, so to speak. Similarly, Mary Kay LeTourneau also took a young boy under her wing who was in a similar situation.

The *heterosexual nurturer* category identified by Vandiver and Kercher (2004) was the most common category of female sex offenders. The largest percentage (31 percent, n = 146) of 471 adult women were classified in this category. This category of offenders would also include teachers who fall in love with their male students.

Teacher/Lover

As portrayed in the media, women in a position of authority (i.e., teacher) have engaged in a sexual relationship with a younger male, often a teenager (i.e., student). Mathews, Matthews, and Speltz (1989) found a case that fits the *teacher/lover* category. A teacher who "fell in love" with her adolescent student reported that she saw nothing wrong with the relationship. The teacher was not the victim of sexual abuse as a child; however, she was forced into prostitution as an adolescent. Turning to an adolescent male was described by Mathews et al. (1989) as the result of feeling fearful toward men.

Babysitter Abuse

Mathews et al. (1989) defined *exploration/exploitation* abusers who typically abuse in a babysitting situation. Sarrel and Masters (1982) also defined *babysitter abuse* as a category of female sex offense. Two cases of babysitter abuse were described by Sarrel and Masters (1982). In one case, a 25-year-old man reported he was sexually abused by his babysitter when he was only 10 years old. The young man described the event as pleasurable and reported it had occurred for approximately one year. The young man reported "she frequently manipulated his penis and that sometimes there was an erection, but he had no ejaculatory experience" (p. 122). The boy later told his family about the experience. His father whipped him severely. He then took his son to a priest and a psychiatrist. The father often referred to his son's "shameful conduct" and told his son that he should have reported the sexual activity sooner. He did not know what happened to the babysitter. The young boy reported that afterward he never masturbated and had overwhelming feelings of guilt. He did not date regularly and was not receptive to sexual advances made by women. The man, after establishing a platonic relationship with a young woman at the age of 24, discussed his fears regarding sex and the incidents that occurred with the babysitter. He then began psychiatric treatment.

In another case, an 11-year-old boy was sexually molested by his 16-year-old babysitter. The babysitter undressed the boy and put his penis inside her vagina. He was confused about the incident. Later, he did not masturbate and did not have sexual contact with anyone else. When he was 19, he married a young woman, but was not able to perform sexually on their wedding night. He had been in therapy for two years before he was married, but never mentioned the abuse to either his therapist or his future wife (Sarrel & Masters, 1982).

Both of these case studies indicate that the effects of such abuse are long term and profound. Many may think that babysitter abuse is not serious. In fact, it may even be interpreted (wrongly) as a pleasurable experience where a young boy is allowed to explore sex at an early age with someone who is more experienced than himself (see Hetherton, 1999).

Co-offender

Several of the typologies include a distinction between women who act alone (i.e., solo offenders) and those who act with another person (i.e., co-offenders) (Mathews et al., 1989; Mayer, 1992; McCarty, 1986; Nathan & Ward, 2001; Syed & Williams, 1996). The number of co-offenders in a given population is high, meaning it is not uncommon for women who have sexually offended to have a partner, usually male. In a recent study including a cross-national sample of 227 women arrested for a sexual offense, approximately half acted with another person (Vandiver, in press). This is indicative of high rates of coercion among this population of females who sexually offend.

Researchers reported co-offenders were significantly different than those who act alone. Co-offenders had more victims per incident. They were more likely to abuse a relative and to have both male and female victims. The type of behavior the women exhibit, however, includes a broad continuum from passive to active, with more cases of passive participation cited in the research (Vandiver, in press).

Characteristics that vary among co-offenders are the woman's relationship to the victim and the co-offender, her motivation (i.e., revengeful), whether she was coerced, and level of contact with the victim during abuse (i.e., hands-off or hands-on). Researchers have relied more on the relationship between the woman and the victim (related or not related) and her motivation for engaging in the sexual abuse (i.e., feeling of rejection and revenge) in developing classifications of co-offending women. For the purpose of this discussion, the following subcategories under male-accompanied are discussed: (1) male-accompanied, familial, (2) male-accompanied, nonfamilial, and (3) male-accompanied, rejected/revengeful.

Male-Accompanied

Mayer (1992) proposed a typology of five categories of female sex offenders, which includes a category of triads in which female offenders were not acting alone in the abuse. The typical combination includes a mother, father, and victim. The victim may include a child of the mother and father or a nonrelated child. The mother or the father may be the coercer. It has been speculated that when the mother is the initiator she may feel dependent or is seeking to nurture the child. She may be reenacting her own abuse. When the father is the initiator, the mother may be coerced.

Mathews et al. (1989) identified a category of women who acted with another male (*male-coerced*). This category depicts female offenders who were coerced into sexually abusing a victim, usually their daughters. After Mathews et al. proposed a male-coerced category, other researchers further developed this category by breaking it into those who were related to the victim (male-accompanied, familial), not related to the victim (male-accompanied, nonfamilial), and acting out of revenge (male-accompanied, the rejected/revengeful).

Male-Accompanied, Familial. Syed and Williams (1996), relying on the typology developed by Mathews et al. (1989), found in an examination of nineteen female sex offenders that not all of the cases could be classified within the proposed categories. Instead of relying on a male-coerced category, they found it more appropriate to create a new category: *male-accompanied, familial.* They found four of the offenders in their study fit into a male-accompanied, familial category. Likewise, McCarty (1986) identified a category of co-offending mothers who abused their own child/children.

An example of a mother abusing her children was described in Syed and Williams's (1996) research. A woman allowed her common-law husband to have sex with her daughter. The daughter was not biologically related to the common-law husband. The stepfather took the daughter's privileges away (i.e., telephone use) if she refused to participate in the sexual abuse. The mother assisted in the abuse by striking her daughter when she refused. The mother had a history of sexual victimization by her family members and nonfamily members. Her father was one of her abusers. Psychological tests were administered to the mother, which "indicated she had severe assertive and relationship deficits and, as a consequence, was a woman who did not possess the necessary skills to defend her rights" (n.p.).

Male-Accompanied, Nonfamilial. Syed and Williams (1996) also proposed a second category: *male-accompanied, nonfamilial.* Mathews et al. (1989) had also identified women who fit into this category. They described a husband and wife who molested a pair of 13-year-old twins who lived in the same apartment complex. The details are given below:

> [The woman] lived in an apartment building in an urban area. Her husband was unemployed, and she worked many hours to provide for their needs.

[The woman's] husband developed a friendship with a pair of 13-year-old twins. . . . He liked to have them come to the apartment to play video games, watch television, and talk. [The woman] was nervous about her husband's interest in these twins, very insecure and jealous of the attention he was showing them, and suspicious of his motive. . . . At a later date [the woman] returned home early from an outing with her sister. When she entered the living room, the male twin was watching television. She found his sister and her husband in the bedroom. The girl was on the bed, her husband was sitting on a chair, and both were nude. [The woman] . . . began screaming and crying . . . she again insisted that the children never come back . . . [her husband] blamed her for his actions . . . [he] "bugged" her about changing her mind and allowing the children to visit again . . . [she] finally relented, and the sexual abuse occurred almost as soon as the children started frequenting their home again . . . [the female victim] threatened to tell about her previous sexual contact with [the woman's] husband if [the woman] did not join in . . . she performed oral sex on [the female victim] . . . [the woman] and her husband also engaged in sexual behaviors in front of the children. . . . A few days later [her] husband was again involved with the girl. [The woman] reported that she felt sorry for the boy because he was left out, so she performed oral sex on him. The sexual contact was very stressful for her. (pp. 19–20)

The woman was arrested after the female victim's boyfriend reported the behavior. The woman was described as cooperative with law enforcement. She spent time in jail and participated in a sex offender treatment program.

This example of a *male-accompanied, nonfamilial* situation highlights the use of coercion by the dominant male. While not all male-accompanied cases include a male who coerces the female, it does show that women, even though they may actively participate in the sexual abuse, are highly vulnerable to coercion into sexual abuse. Additionally, the woman in this situation was the primary source of income for this family; thus, economic reliance on a dominant male was not a factor in her situation.

Male-Accompanied, the Rejected/Revengeful. Nathan and Ward (2002) suggested adding a category of female offenders who had a male partner, but were not coerced, *male-accompanied, the rejected/revengeful*. The authors noted that prior case studies included descriptions of female sex offenders who were motivated by feelings of rejection in their primary relationship; the sexual abuse appears to be out of revenge. One example included a woman who was a victim of chronic domestic violence and she reported that she was motivated by extreme jealousy.

Incestuous

Incestuous relationships with female offenders have been identified in many typologies of female sex offenders. Prior research has found that women have abused in the capacity of a relative, a mother, and an older sister (Mathews et al., 1989; Sarrel & Masters, 1982).

Mathews et al. (1989) identified a broad category of offenders, *predisposed,* who sexually abused their relatives; this was not limited to just their own children. Several cases were identified in which women acted alone in the abuse of daughters, sons, and nephews. Sexual abuse appeared to be prevalent in these families. While this type of female sex offender is a general incest category, other researchers have described the victim in more specific terms: mother-son incest, and mother-daughter incest.

Sister-Brother Incest

A case of sister-brother incest was discussed in Sarrel and Masters's (1982) research. A 14-year-old girl began molesting her 10-year-old brother, and the abuse occurred for two years. The researchers describe the abuse thus: "She stimulated him manually and orally and then inserted his penis into her vagina. At first he only felt frightened and did not understand what was happening. She usually threatened to beat him or attack him with a knife if he told anyone. He does not recall if he ejaculated. He was too frightened to tell his parents" (p. 125). Later, his sister went to psychiatric treatment; the victim subsequently became suicidal and he too was placed in psychiatric treatment. He entered treatment again when he married and was unable to consummate his marriage.

Mother-Son Incest

Several researchers have reported instances of mother-son incest (Lawson, 1993; Mayer, 1992). Two cases of incest were reported in Sarrel and Masters's (1982) research. A 30-year-old man reported to his therapist that his mother who had been divorced since he was 2 years old began playing with his genitals when he was 13 years old. The sexual activity later included her performing oral sex on him and having sex with him. They had sex two to three times a week until he left for college. When he went home, he continued having sex with his mother. His mother died during his senior year of college. He reported that he never approached his mother, but rather she always approached him. The researchers noted, "He felt strongly devoted to her, stating that he enjoyed her obvious pleasure during their sexual encounters far more than his own" (p. 124). After he left for college, he reported he was not able to achieve an erection when he attempted to have sex with a girl his own age. He felt guilty and felt he was not being faithful to his mother. Once he became so nauseated after having foreplay with a girl that he threw up. He resumed dating but was not able to have sex. He later married and entered therapy.

Mother-Daughter Incest

Accounts of mothers abusing their own daughters have been reported and identified by researchers as a salient category of female sex offenders. Mathews et al. (1989) identified a mother whose husband had passed away and she began first physically abusing her 4-year-old daughter and then sexually abusing her.

> When feeling alone and wanting to be close, "I would go into the bedroom and touch [her daughter]." The abuse consisted of kissing and fondling the child, usually over her pajamas or underwear. Initially the abuse occurred when her daughter was awake. As the child grew older, however, [the mother] would wait for [her daughter] to fall asleep before touching her. (p. 15)

The mother was abused by her own father when she was a child. After the mother entered substance abuse treatment, she reported the sexual abuse she had with her daughter. She was referred to sexual abuse treatment.

Adult on Adult

Several typologies include adult women who sexually assault another adult. Most of the categories describe (adult) women who sexually assault (adult) men. One category, however, includes an adult woman who sexually assaults another adult woman. This category of female sex offenders, therefore, is divided into two groups: female-on-male and female-on-female.

Female-on-Male

Several typologies have been proposed that include an adult woman specifically sexually assaulting an adult man: *female sexual harassment* and *female rapist* (Mayer, 1992), *dominant woman abuse*, *forced assault* (Sarrel & Masters, 1982), and *angry-impulsive* (Syed & Williams, 1996). Mayer (1992) described a continuum of this type of behavior that includes sexual harassment (a woman sexually harassing a man, possibly at the workplace) and female rape, in which she has sex with the man against his will.

Sarrel and Masters (1982) identified *dominant woman abuse* and used the term to describe cases where there was at least one episode of a woman engaging in overt sexual aggression—a complete role reversal where women behaved as men have in sexually aggressive incidents. Three cases were used to describe *dominant woman abuse*. In one of the cases, a man was sexually abused by his wife after they were legally separated. She aggressively approached him sexually and he reported feeling scared and not ejaculating as she had sex with him. She had an orgasm. It was confirmed by the wife that she did attack her husband and was "in a state of fury." She expressed wanting to hurt him and use sex as a way to express her rage.

In another case a 33-year-old woman who had only homosexual experiences forced a 35-year-old male to have sex with her. He reported being fearful and later suffered from sexual dysfunction. Another case involved a 17-year-old male, who was forced to have intercourse by a 23-year-old woman who was a friend of his family. He was a Mormon and expressed extreme guilt over the sexual incident because it was in conflict with his religious beliefs. No weapon was used, but he felt intimidated by her use of force (Sarrel & Masters, 1982).

Likewise, *forced assault* describes a woman who sexually assaults an adult male (Sarrel & Masters, 1982). The male is described as being fearful, not enjoying the experience. Four cases of forced assault were identified from eleven male victims of female sexual assault. One of the victims was a truck diver who was 27 years old. After meeting a woman whom he had known previously, he went to a motel with her and the following occurred:

> [H]e was given another drink and shortly thereafter fell asleep. He awoke to find himself naked, tied hand and foot to a bedstead, gagged, and blindfolded. As he listened to voices in the room, it was evident that several women were present . . . he was told that he had to "have sex with all of them." He thinks that during his period of captivity four different women used him sexually, some of them a number [of] times. Initially he was manipulated to erection and mounted. . . . He believes that the period of forcible, restrained and repeated sexual assaults continued for [more] than 24 hours. (Sarrel & Masters, 1982, pp. 120–121)

After the incident the man sought therapy. He never reported the incident to law enforcement. He suffered from psychological distress and was not able to complete sexual intercourse. He married later, but still was unable to engage in sexual intercourse. His wife was unaware of the rape that he endured (Sarrel & Masters, 1982).

Three other cases identified by these researchers included a 37-year-old married man who was forced at gunpoint to have sex and receive oral sex from several women. Another case involved a 23-year-old male medical student who was forced to have sex with his female aggressor. He was threatened with a scalpel. Another teenager who was 17 years old was forced by a group of five people (three women and two men) to have oral sex performed on him and was masturbated (Sarrel & Masters, 1982).

In all of the four cases, force or threatened use of force occurred. The men were constrained physically in some way and were fearful of the attackers. All were able to function sexually during the incident, yet none were able to adequately perform sexually after the incident (Sarrel & Masters, 1982).

A similar situation of a woman violently sexually assaulting a male (*angry-impulsive*) was described by Syed and Williams (1996). This type of female sex offender was motivated by anger. In one case, a woman violently assaulted her victim, an adult male. The researchers noted that none of the prior categories had addressed anger as the central feature of the sexual abuse.

Female-on-Female

One study yielded a unique category of sex offenders not identified in previous research. Vandiver and Kercher (2004) described *aggressive homosexual offenders,* which included women who were typically in their thirties with a victim also in her thirties. The offense of arrest was sexual assault. It was speculated that this group included domestic violence between homosexual couples. Furthermore, this type of female sex offender does not fit the typical female sex offender in that her motivations are different. Her motivations are likely to be similar to male sex offenders who sexually assault their spouse.

Criminal Offenders

Women who have a history of nonsexual arrests in conjunction with at least one sex offense have also been identified. Vandiver and Kercher (2004) identified two categories of such offenders, *female sexual predator* and *homosexual criminal*. The female sexual predator has male victims whereas the homosexual criminal has female victims. The women in the homosexual criminal category were arrested for "forcing behavior," including sexual performance on a child and compelling prostitution. An article appearing in the *Houston Chronicle* provides an example of such incidents.

> A woman and her boyfriend, convicted of making her 12-year-old daughter perform sexual favors for strangers for money, have each been sentenced to 40 years in prison . . . the mother arranged for men to have sex with the . . . daughter. The 12-year-old testified concerning two occasions. On one, she did [not] know how much money was given to her parents, she said, but they received $100 on the other. (Teachey, 2000, p. A, 40)

Reports such as these are not uncommon. The Associated Press ("Police rescue," 2001), for example, also reported of a 17-year-old girl from Milwaukee who was forced into a prostitution ring by a man and woman.

This category of offender can also include having children pose nude for photographs to be sold privately or made available on websites for the purpose of generating income. This type of offender, therefore, typically involves hands-off offenses. The offender is likely to already have a criminal record and uses the sexual abuse as another method for obtaining money. The payoff is economical rather than sexual. It should also be noted that these women are usually acting in concert with another person, usually a male. Sometimes they are part of a "ring" which involves many co-offenders. This category, therefore, overlaps with co-offenders.

Psychologically Impaired

A category of female sex offenders has been identified that includes psychologically impaired women. These women have been described as aggressive, impulsive, poorly socialized, depressed, and guilty (McCarty, 1981). Additionally, in many of the other identified categories of sex offenders, some form of mental illness has been found. For example, Mayer (1983) noted that mothers who abuse their daughters often exhibit psychotic behavior. As noted in the section titled "Description of Female Sex Offenders," many samples of female sex offenders included high rates of mental illness. Thus, mental illness may be a characteristic that occurs with many other identified characteristics of female sex offenders.

Homosexual Molester

Mayer (1992) identified a category of female sex offenders, *homosexual molesters*, that had many overlapping characteristics with other identified categories of female sex offenders. This type of offender has homosexual tendencies, possibly latent. She may molest a child who is the same sex or even the opposite sex. Additionally, she may act with a male offender or by herself. When she acts with a co-offender, she may assume a passive role to explore homosexual feelings. This category is unique from other categories of sex offenders in that she is motivated by her homosexual feelings; the abuse allows her the opportunity to explore such feelings.

Summary of Female Sex Offender Typologies

Based on prior research, a summary of seven categories of female sex offenders is identified (see Table 3.5). It should be noted that the typologies are based on small sample sizes, and the information about female sex offenders is evolving and developing as more research is conducted. Furthermore, many of the classifications overlap. For example, co-offenders may include relatives. Mental illness, particularly personality disorders and depression, may occur within any classification. Future research can further examine motivations of abuse in relationship to other characteristics to add more dimensions to the classification schemes that already exist.

Table 3.5. Summary of Female Sex Offender Typologies

1. Nurturer: Adult female in a position of authority having a sexual relationship with a younger boy.
   a. Teacher/lover
   b. Babysitter abuse
2. Co-offender: Adult female acting with a male in abusing a victim.
   a. Male-accompanied
   i. Male-accompanied, familial
   ii. Male-accompanied, nonfamilial
   iii. Male-accompanied, rejected/revengeful
3. Incestuous: Offender related to victim.
   a. Sister-brother incest
   b. Mother-son incest
   c. Mother-daughter incest
4. Adult on Adult: Adult sexually abusing another adult.
   a. Female-on-male
   b. Female-on-female
5. Criminal Offender: An offender who engages in many different types of crimes; the sexual offense is only one type.
6. Psychologically Impaired: The offender has marked psychological impairment.
7. Homosexual Molester: The offender has latent sexual feelings and chooses a victim based on those feelings.

MOTIVATIONS/EXPLANATIONS OF BEHAVIOR

Past research, specifically, has identified the following motivations for female sexual offending: reenactment of sexual abuse (Mayer, 1992; Saradjian & Hanks, 1996), emotional women acting out their feelings, narcissistic women abusing their own daughters (Mayer, 1992), extension of battered-woman syndrome, socialization to follow their male accomplices (Davin, Hislop, & Dunbar, 1999), desire for intimacy, economic gain, and domestic violence among homosexual couples (Vandiver & Kercher, 2004).

Reenactment of early trauma has been proposed as a primary explanation of females who sexually abuse (Mayer, 1992; Saradjian & Hanks, 1996). It is proposed that the victim experiences displaced anger and, thus, identifies with the aggressor. The victim later becomes an offender and acts out her experiences on another person. Typically, researchers will cite the high rates of abuse many sex offenders experienced themselves to support this notion; however, the extent to which one affects the other has not been fully supported. While there is a high rate of correlation between experiences of abuse and later abusing cited in studies (see Knopp, 1984), this does not necessarily translate into causation. In fact, as noted by Salter (2003), studies including more objective measures (i.e., polygraph) result in the number of victims–turned–victimizer decreasing by approximately 50 percent; thus, many sex offenders who report being sexually abused as a child had not been.

Narcissism was discussed by Mayer (1992) as a possible cause of female sexual offending. More specifically, she relied upon an example described by Forward and Buck (1979) of a mother who molested her daughter; she perceived the daughter as simply an extension of herself. The need to be nurtured coupled with the need to nurture resulted in a narcissistic mother with poor boundaries. Groth (1982) also described a similar situation of a woman with severe nurture deprivations.

While sexual gratification has been explored as a possible cause of women sexually offending, it does not appear to be a sole motivating factor (Davin et al., 1999). It is proposed that instead of a sexual motivation, a need exists to connect with another person; sexual abuse is just one avenue for meeting this need.

Several theories have been explored specifically for women who have co-offenders. For example, battered-woman syndrome may lead a woman to sexually abuse. Many women who were coerced into sexual abuse have a history of physical abuse by their male partner (Davin et al., 1999). Many women who are victims of abuse, however, do not sexually offend. Davin et al. also relied on sex-role theories in exploring other possible explanations. The authors note that these theories describe women as passive; thus, their male counterparts initiate the sexual abuse and the women follow the behavior.

In explaining the cause of adult women who "fall in love" with a younger boy (i.e., heterosexual nurturer and teacher/lover), a desire for intimacy has been proposed (Vandiver & Kercher, 2004). Many of these women describe their actions as the outcome of having feelings of "love" for the victim (see Vandiver, 2003). The behavior is not necessarily associated with criminal behavior. Additionally, economic gain has been proposed as a possible motivating factor for women who engage in hands-off offenses such as forcing a child into prostitution or to pose for pornographic pictures, which are later sold (Vandiver & Kercher, 2004).

COMPARISON OF FEMALE AND MALE SEX OFFENDERS

Several studies have included a comparison of female and male sex offenders. In some ways, men and women who sexually offended had similar characteristics. The abuse by male and female sex offenders did not differ in severity (Rudin et al., 1995). Additionally, both female and male sex offenders exhibited a lack of empathy toward their victims (Mayer, 1992), and male and female sex offenders did not significantly differ on self-reported reasons for therapy (i.e., anxiety, depression, relationship difficulty) (Miccio-Fonseca, 2000).

The two groups, however, had more differences than similarities. Women were more likely than men to be caretakers. Women were less likely than men to abuse strangers (Rudin et al., 1995). Female sex offenders were significantly less likely than male sex offenders to have legal problems (68 percent compared to 63 percent) (Miccio-Fonseca, 2000). The sexual offense arrest was likely to be the first arrest for women, but not the first arrest for the men (Vandiver & Walker, 2002). High rates of substance abuse exist among both populations of sex offenders (Faller, 1987). Female sex offenders reported fewer sexual partners when compared to male sex offenders. While both groups reported having experienced abuse as children (Mayer, 1992; Miccio-Fonseca, 2000), women were more likely to report being a victim of incest when compared to men (approximately 33 percent compared to 13 percent) and being a victim of rape (39 percent compared to 4 percent) (Miccio-Fonseca, 2000). Additionally, one study reported that 76 percent of the women, compared to 36 percent of the men, reported they had been sexually abused (Pothast & Allen, 1994). In another study, 54 percent of the women compared to 33 percent of the men were sexually abused by 6 years of age (Miccio-Fonseca, 2000).

JUVENILE FEMALE SEX OFFENDERS

Prevalence

In 2003, 59 of the 247 (23.8 percent) females arrested for forcible rape were juveniles according to the UCR (U.S. Department of Justice, 2005b). Additionally, juvenile females accounted for 21.9 percent of the females arrested for a sex offense other than forcible rape and prostitution. Although the number of juvenile females arrested for a sex offense is low, they make up a substantial portion (approximately 20 percent) of females arrested for a sex offense. Again, caution should be made in drawing conclusions from the numbers because law enforcement data do not fully capture the scope of this group of offenders.

Data from the NCVS regarding the number of juvenile females who sexually offended is not available.[3] NIBRS data indicates that juveniles were arrested for 172 of the 404 (42.6 percent) sexual offenses committed by females in 2001 (U.S. Department of Justice, 2004). Thus, information from UCR and NIBRS indicates that the number of female sex offenders is low, yet juvenile sex offenders make up a substantial portion of females who sexually offend.

Research on Juvenile Female Sex Offenders

The problems associated with the adult female sex offender population (i.e., few empirical studies and small sample sizes) are even more prevalent with the juvenile literature (Righthand & Welch, 2001). In fact, it was not until 1986 that empirical studies began to emerge in the literature. Since then, only a handful of studies have been conducted (Bumby & Bumby, 1997; Fehrenbach & Monastersky, 1988; Fehrenbach, Smith, Montastersky, & Deisher, 1986;

Fromuth & Conn, 1997; Johnson, T. C., 1989; LeTourneau, Schoenwald, & Sheidow, 2004). The number of juvenile females in the empirical studies ranges from eight to only sixty-one; thus, no study has been conducted on samples larger than sixty-one. The majority of the studies also rely on clinical sources. The source and the number of subjects limit the ability to fully describe this population of offenders.

Description of Juvenile Female Sex Offenders

The reported average age of juvenile females who have sexually offended includes 12 (Fromuth & Conn, 1997), 13.7 (Fehrenbach et al., 1986), and 15 (Hunter, Lexier, Goodwin, Browne, & Dennis, 1993). In regard to race, the juvenile population had a higher proportion of minorities as compared to the adult female population. For example, Hunter et al. (1993) reported 20 percent of a sample of 10 were African American and the other 80 percent were Caucasian. Again, the sample size is small and this finding may not fully represent the population of juvenile female sex offenders.

Psychological maladjustment was not more prevalent when compared to non-perpetrators (Fromuth & Conn, 1997). This study included a sample of 546 female college students in which 4 percent had sexually molested someone when they were younger. Hunter et al. (1993), however, reported that 80 percent of their sample had prior mental health treatment. It should be noted that the sample source included an inpatient clinical setting, which would likely include high rates of juveniles with emotional disturbances. Likewise, Bumby and Bumby (1997), relying on an inpatient sample, reported ten of the twelve females had a history of depression. High rates of depression, anxiety, and posttraumatic-stress syndrome have been found among this group of offenders (Mathews, Hunter, & Vuz, 1997).

Several studies included information regarding whether the juvenile female sex offenders had experienced sexual abuse. In fact, Vick, McRoy, and Matthews (2002) noted one of the strongest characteristics found among this population of offenders is physical and sexual abuse. Fehrenbach & Monastersky (1988) reported six of twenty-eight (21 percent) had been physically abused and fourteen (50 percent) had been sexually abused. Fromuth and Conn (1997) reported 70 percent of twenty-two females who had sexually offended had been sexually abused. Hunter et al. (1993) found all of the ten females had been molested, most with multiple molesters and beginning at a very young age. Sixty percent of the juveniles had been molested by a female.

Victims of Juvenile Female Sex Offenders

Juvenile female sex offenders were found to have more than one victim per offender. For example, Hunter et al. (1993) reported an average of three victims per offender whereas Bumby and Bumby (1997) reported an average of two. Fromuth and Conn (1997) found the average number of victims to be slightly more than one. The victims were very young, sometimes even in their infancy (Hunter et al., 1993). Few victims were older than 12 (Fehrenbach & Monastersky, 1988; Fromuth & Conn, 1997; Hunter et al., 1993; Vandiver & Teske, in press).

Most often, the victims knew or were related to their abuser. Only one study (Hunter et al., 1993) reported that strangers were molested. In this study, 39 percent of the thirty-three victims were strangers to their abuser. The sex of the victim appears to have no distinct pattern (see Table 3.6). Some studies reported a high proportion of juvenile female sex offenders choosing both males and females (see Hunter et al., 1993), while other studies report more male victims as compared to female victims (see Vandiver & Teske, in press). Still other studies report just the opposite: more female victims as compared to male victims (see Bumby & Bumby, 1997; Fehrenbach et al., 1986).

Motivations/Explanations of Behavior

Explanations of juvenile female sexual offending have been similar to the ones given for adult female sexual offending. For example, reenactment of abuse has been proposed (Johnson, T. C., 1989). One researcher noted that some young female sex offenders appear to act out their own sexual abuse experiences;[4] another suggests it to be the result of being sexually victimized (Araji, 1997). It has also been found in some cases that the child identifies with the aggressor (Turner & Turner, 1994).

It has also been reported that in many of the families of the juvenile female sex offender, sexual abuse is pervasive and the child may engage in the behavior on a younger sibling because it is inevitable he or she will be abused. If the juvenile female sex offender is the abuser, the abuse may be less severe as compared to being victimized by an older member of the family (Turner & Turner, 1994).

Table 3.6. Victim's Sex for Juvenile Female Sex Offenders

Researchers	Number of Victims of Juvenile Female Sex Offenders	Sex of Victim		
		Male only (%)	Female Only (%)	Male and Female (%)
Fehrenbach & Monastersky, 1988	28	35.7	57.1	0
Fromuth & Conn, 1997	24	70	30	0
Hunter et al., 1993	10	30	10	60
Bumby & Bumby, 1997	18	25	42	33
Vandiver & Teske, 2006	61	61	39	0

Poor family structure and support appear to be common denominators in many of the cases of young female sexual abuse. Many of the young females had families in which the caretakers had only a modicum of information about sexual issues; they had difficulty in expressing feelings associated with their sexual desire. In many instances the mother discussed her own sexual desires with her young daughter(s). The mother often had successive relationships with different males and sexually molested her daughter when no male was present. This type of behavior may be linked to the young female later sexually abusing (T. C. Johnson, 1989).

Similar to adult female sex offenders, sexual gratification has not been found to be a cause of juvenile female sexual abuse (T. C. Johnson, 1989). Sexual gratification was rarely noted to exist in many of the sexual abuse incidents. In fact, expressions of anger and jealousy were more commonly reported. Many of the young sex offenders abused a sibling who had not been abused previously and was described as the "favored" child in the family. This type of behavior may be explained as a way to get back at her parents. The sexual abuse, therefore, appears to be a way these young sex offenders express anger (T. C. Johnson, 1989).

Comparison of Juvenile Female and Juvenile Male Sex Offenders

Only a few studies have compared juvenile females to juvenile males. One of those studies compared eighteen females to eighteen male sex offenders; both groups were participants in an inpatient psychiatric facility who were being treated for emotional/behavior disorders (Bumby & Bumby, 1997). The females had an average age of 14.9 years, while the males had an average age of 13.2 years. An examination of school performance indicated that females were significantly more likely to be retained in at least one grade in school. Females also had a significantly higher rate of drug abuse and promiscuity than the males. Male and female juvenile sex offenders, however, did not significantly differ in regard to psychological symptoms, past delinquency, or physical and sexual victimization.

Another study, which employed a relatively large sample size, compared sixty-seven juvenile female sex offenders with seventy juvenile male sex offenders, and also found differences between these two groups (Mathews et al., 1997). The subjects were juveniles from sex offender treatment programs. The most notable differences included past victimization experiences. Females had a higher average number of molesters when compared to males (4.5 compared to 1.4) and a younger age at first victimization; 64 percent of the females compared to 26 percent of the males reported they were victimized before they reached 6 years of age. Additionally, females and males chose victims of the opposite sex proportionately (i.e., 45 percent of females chose male victims; 47 percent of males chose female victims). Also, while both groups were likely to choose young victims, females were more likely than males to choose those in the infancy to 5-years-of-age range (52 percent ccompared to 38 percent).

Kubik, Hecker, and Righthand (2002) found in a comparison of eleven juvenile female to eleven juvenile male sex offenders that females experienced more severe and pervasive abuse. They also found that the juvenile female and male sex offenders exhibited similar sex offender behaviors, criminal histories, and psychosocial characteristics.

SUMMARY AND CONCLUSION

Although the literature on female sex offenders is limited, it is growing. What is known about female sex offenders from available research is that the official reports are low; those numbers do not fully represent the extent of female sexual abuse. With that stated, it is likely that male sex offenders still outnumber female sex offenders. There are many barriers to acknowledging that a female can sexually offend—it is contrary to many fundamental beliefs we hold about gender roles. It is thought that a woman cannot physically rape a man; a man or young boy would not refuse an aggressive woman or one who is attacking; a woman who was trying to have sex with an unwilling participant cannot complete the act—he could not perform. Research has shown that these statements are myths (see Hetherton, 1999).

Research has found that female sex offenders are typically young and Caucasian. High rates of mental illness, particularly depression and anxiety, have been found among this population. Women engage in both hands-on and hands-off offenses. The female sexual offender typically knew or was related to her victim. Incidents of mother-child sexual abuse are prevalent. Her victims are usually very young, younger than 12 years.

Typologies of female sex offenders have been developed and the categories can be summarized into the following groups: nurturer, co-offender, incestuous, adult on adult, criminal offenders, psychologically impaired, and homosexual molester. The categories, however, are not mutually exclusive; many have overlapping characteristics. Women may be related to their victim (*incestuous*) and engage in the abuse with a male (*co-offender*) and have a history of depression (*psychologically impaired*). The last three categories, *criminal offenders, psychologically impaired,* and *homosexual molester,* appear to have features that could be present in the other categories. What the typologies do show is that women exhibit a variety of behaviors and characteristics; female sex offenders are a heterogeneous group of offenders. Many of their characteristics differ from male sex offenders as well.

Juvenile female sex offenders account for only a few of the arrests for sex offenses. They are also relatively young, approximately 13 years old. The majority are Caucasian, yet a higher percentage of minorities are among this population of sex offenders as compared to adult female sex offenders. Similar to the adult population, the juveniles exhibit high rates of mental illness, particularly depression. This group of offenders also reports a high rate of being sexually victimized. Their victims were very young, usually less than 12 years. The victims typically knew or were related to their abuser.

Female sex offenders, whether adult or juvenile, engage in a broad range of sexual behavior. The effects are long lasting and, many times, severe. The motivations appear to be complex and research has only recently emerged on this topic. As society becomes increasingly less tolerant of sex offenses in general, there may be a greater willingness to report, arrest, charge, and convict females who commit such offenses. It is likely in the future, as more law enforcement and social service agencies become knowledgeable about this type of abuse, that the numbers will increase and subsequent research will include increased sample sizes.

NOTES

1. The same statement was also made by J. L. Mathis (1972, p. 54).

2. "Social junk" is a term coined by Steven Spitzer. He applied Marxist theory in developing the term. It refers to those who make up a segment of society who are not in a position to acquire adequate resources for themselves, often falling between the cracks of social service agencies.

3. The NCVS publications do not include this information; however, the original data may contain such information.

4. T. C. Johnson's (1989) research focused on young juvenile sex offenders; many of the subjects were younger than 13 years. The term "young" sex offender rather than "juvenile" sex offender is used when discussing this research.

REFERENCES

Araji, S. (1997). *Sexually aggressive children: Coming to understand them.* Thousand Oaks, CA: Sage.

Berliner, L., & Barbieri, M. K. (1984). The testimony of the child victim of sexual assault. *Journal of Social Issues, 40*(2), 125–137.

Bumby, K. M., & Bumby, N. H. (1997). Adolescent sexual offenders. In B. K. Schwartz & H. R. Cellini (Eds.), *The sex offender: New insights, treatment, innovations, and legal developments* (Vol. 2, pp. 10.11–10.16). Kingston, NJ: Civic Research Institute.

Chasnoff, I. J., Burns, W. J., Schnoll, S. H., Burns, K., Chisum, G., & Kyle-Spore, L. (1986). Maternal-neonatal incest. *American Journal of Orthopsychiatry, 56*(4), 577–580.

Chow, E. W. C., & Choy, A. L. (2002). Clinical characteristics and treatment response to SSRI in a female pedophile. *Archives of Sexual Behavior, 31*(2), 211–215.

Davin, P. A., Hislop, J., & Dunbar, T. (1999). *Female sexual abusers: Three views.* Brandon, VT: Safer Society Press.

Denov, M. S. (2003). To a safer place? Victims of sexual abuse by females and their disclosures to professionals. *Child Abuse and Neglect, 27*, 47–61.

Denov, M. S. (2004). *Perspectives on female sex offending: A culture of denial.* Burlington, VT: Ashgate.

Duncan, L. E., & Williams, L. M. (1998). Gender role socialization and male-on-male vs. female-on-male child sexual abuse. *Sex Roles: A Journal of Research, 39*(9/10), 765–785.

Faller, K. C. (1987). Women who sexually abuse children. *Violence and Victims, 2*(4), 263–276.

Faller, K. C. (1988). The spectrum of sexual abuse in daycare: An exploratory study. *Journal of Family Violence, 3*(4), 283–298.

Faller, K. C. (1995). A clinical sample of women who have sexually abused children. *Journal of Child Sexual Abuse, 4*(3), 13–29.

Farrell, L. T. (1988). Factors that affect a victim's self-disclosure in father-daughter incest. *Child Welfare, 67*(5), 462–468.

Fehrenbach, P. A., & Monastersky, C. (1988). Characteristics of female adolescent sexual offenders. *American Journal of Orthopsychiatry, 58*(1), 148–151.

Fehrenbach, P. A., Smith, W., Montastersky, C., & Deisher, R. W. (1986). Adolescent sexual offenders: Offenders and offense characteristics. *American Journal of Orthopsychiatry, 56*(2), 225–231.

Finkelhor, D., Hotaling, G., Lewis, I. A., & Smith, C. (1990). Sexual abuse in a national survey of adult men and women: Prevalence, characteristics, and risk factors. *Child Abuse and Neglect, 14*, 19–28.

Finkelhor, D., Williams, L., & Burns, N. (1988). *Nursery crimes: Sexual abuse in day care.* Newbury Park, CA: Sage.

Forward, S., & Buck, C. (1979). *Betrayal of innocence: Incest and its devastation.* New York: Penguin Books.

Fromuth, M. E., & Conn, V. E. (1997). Hidden perpetrators: Sexual molestation in a nonclinical sample of college women. *Journal of Interpersonal Violence, 12*(3), 456–465.

Groth, A. N. (1982). The incest offender. In S. M. Sgroi (Ed.), *Handbook of clinical intervention in child sexual abuse* (pp. 215–239). Lexington, MA: D.C. Heath.

Groth, A. N., & Birnbaum, H. J. (1979). *Men who rape: The psychology of the offender.* New York: Plenum Press.

Hetherton, J. (1999). The idealization of women: Its role in the minimization of child sexual abuse by females. *Child Abuse and Neglect, 23*(2), 161–174.

Hislop, J. (2001). *Female sex offenders: What therapists, law enforcement and child protective services need to know.* Washington, DC: Issues Press.

Hunter, J. A., Lexier, L. J., Goodwin, D. W., Browne, P. A., & Dennis, C. (1993). Psychosexual, attitudinal, and developmental characteristics of juvenile female sexual perpetrators in a residential treatment setting. *Journal of Child and Family Studies, 2*, 317–326.

Johnson, R., & Shrier, D. (1987). Past sexual victimization by females of male patients in an adolescent medicine clinic population. *American Journal of Psychiatry, 144*(5), 650–652.

Johnson, T. C. (1989). Female child perpetrators: Children who molest other children. *Child Abuse and Neglect, 13*(4), 571–585.

Kaplan, M. S., & Green, A. (1995). Incarcerated female sexual offenders: A comparison of sexual histories with eleven female nonsexual offenders. *Sexual Abuse: A Journal of Research and Treatment, 7*(4), 287–300.

Knopp, F. H. (1984). *Retraining adult sex offenders: Methods and models.* Orwell, VT: Safer Society Press.

Krug, R. S. (1989). Adult male report of childhood sexual abuse by mothers: Case descriptions, motivations and long-term consequences. *Child Abuse and Neglect, 13*, 111–119.

Kubik, K. E., Hecker, E. J., & Righthand, S. (2002). Adolescent females who have sexually offended: Comparison with delinquent adolescent female offenders and adolescent males who sexually offend. *Journal of Child Sexual Abuse, 11*(3), 63–83.

Lawson, C. (1993). Mother-son sexual abuse: Rare or underreported? A critique of the research. *Child Abuse and Neglect, 17*, 261–269.

LeTourneau, E. J., Schoenwald, S. K., & Sheidow, A. J. (2004). Children and adolescents with sexual behavior problems. *Child Maltreatment, 9*(1), 49–61.

LeTourneau says she and former student are engaged. (2004; October 12). *CNN.com.* Retrieved August 15, 2005, from http://www.cnn.com/2004/US/10/12/letourneau.king/

Lewis, C. F., & Stanley, C. R. (2000). Women accused of sexual offenses. *Behavioral Sciences and the Law, 18*, 73–81.

Marvasti, J. (1986). Female sex offenders: Incestuous mothers. *American Journal of Forensic Psychiatry, 7*(4), 63–69.

Mathews, R. (1987). Preliminary typology of female sexual offenders. Minneapolis, MN: PHASE and Genesis II for Women.

Mathews, R., Hunter, J. A., Jr., & Vuz, J. (1997). Juvenile female sexual offenders: Clinical characteristics and treatment issues. *Sexual Abuse: A Journal of Research and Treatment, 9*(3), 187–199.

Mathews, R., Matthews, J. K., & Speltz, K. (1989). *Female sexual offenders: An exploratory study.* Orwell, VT: Safer Society Press.

Mathis, J. L. (1972). *Clear thinking about sexual deviations: A new look at an old problem.* Chicago: Nelson-Holt.

Mayer, A. (1983). *Incest: A treatment manual for therapy with victims, spouses and offenders.* Holmes Beach, FL: Learning.

Mayer, A. (1992). *Women sex offenders.* Holmes Beach, FL: Learning.

McCarty, L. M. (1981). Investigation of incest: Opportunity to motivate families to seek help. *Child Welfare, 60*, 679–689.

McCarty, L. M. (1986). Mother-child incest: Characteristics of the offender. *Child Welfare, 65*(5), 447–458.

Miccio-Fonseca, L. C. (2000). Adult and adolescent female sex offenders: Experiences compared to other female and male sex offenders. *Journal of Psychology and Human Sexuality, 11*(3), 75–88.

Nathan, P., & Ward, T. (2001). Females who sexually abused children: Assessment and treatment issues. *Psychiatry, Psychology and Law, 8*(1), 44–55.

Nathan, P., & Ward, T. (2002). Female sex offenders: Clinical and demographic features. *Journal of Sexual Aggression, 8*(1), 5–21.

O'Connor, A. A. (1987). Female sex offenders. *British Journal of Psychiatry, 150*, 615–620.

Peluso, E., & Putnam, N. (1996). Case study: Sexual abuse of boys by females. *Journal of the American Academy of Child and Adolescent Psychiatry, 35*(1), 51–54.

Petrovich, M., & Templer, D. I. (1984). Heterosexual molestation of children who later became rapists. *Psychological Reports, 54*, 810.

Police rescue kidnapping victim, suspects arrested in prostitution ring. (2001, June 29). *Associated Press.*

Pothast, H. L., & Allen, C. M. (1994). Masculinity and femininity in male and female perpetrators of child sexual abuse. *Child Abuse and Neglect, 18*(9), 763–767.

Righthand, S., & Welch, C. (2001). *Juveniles who have sexually offended: A review of the professional literature* (report). Washington, DC: Office of Juvenile Justice and Delinquency Prevention.

Rosencrans, B. (1997). *The last secret: Daughters sexually abused by mothers.* Orwell, VT: Safer Society Press.

Rowan, E. L., Rowan, J. B., & Langelier, P. (1990). Women who molest children. *Bulletin of the American Academy of Psychiatry and the Law, 18*(1), 79–83.

Rudin, M. M., Zalewski, C., & Bodmer-Turner, J. (1995). Characteristics of child sexual abuse victims according to perpetrator gender. *Child Abuse and Neglect, 19*(8), 963–973.

Salter, A. C. (2003). *Predators: Pedophiles, rapists, and other sex offenders.* New York: Basic Books.

Saradjian, J., & Hanks, H. (1996). *Women who sexually abuse children: From research to practice.* New York: John Wiley.

Sarrel, P. M., & Masters, W. H. (1982). Sexual molestation of men by women. *Archives of Sexual Behavior, 11*(2), 117–131.

Scavo, R. R. (1989). Female adolescent sex offenders: A neglected treatment group. *Journal of Contemporary Social Work, 70*, 114–139.

Syed, F., & Williams, S. (1996). *Case studies of female sex offenders.* Ottawa: Correctional Service of Canada.

Teachey, L. (2000, November 10). Mom, boyfriend gets 40 years for prostituting girls. *The Houston Chronicle,* p. A40.

Travin, S., Cullen, K., & Protter, B. (1990). Female sex offenders: Severe victims and victimizers. *Journal of Forensic Sciences, 35*(1), 140–150.

Turner, M., & Turner, T. (1994). *Female adolescent sexual abusers: An exploratory study of mother-daughter dynamics with implications for treatment.* Brandon, VT: Safer Society Press.

U.S. Department of Justice. (2004). Compiled by the U.S. Dept. of Justice, Federal Bureau of Investigation. ICPSR ed. Ann Arbor, MI: Inter-university

Consortium for Political and Social Research [producer and distributor], 2001. *Crime in the United States, 2001.* Washington, DC: U.S. Government Printing Office.

U.S. Department of Justice. (2005a). *Criminal victimization in the United States, 2003.* Washington, DC: U.S. Government Printing Office.

U.S. Department of Justice. (2005b). *Uniform crime reports, 2003.* Washington, DC: U.S. Government Printing Office.

Vandiver, D. M. (2003, March). *Female sex offenders: A case study approach.* Paper presented at the Academy of Criminal Justice Sciences, Las Vegas, NV.

Vandiver, D. M. (in press). Female sex offenders: A comparison of solo offenders and co-offenders. *Violence and Victims.*

Vandiver, D. M., & Kercher, G. (2004). Offender and victim characteristics of registered female sexual offenders in Texas: A proposed typology of female sexual offenders. *Sexual Abuse: A Journal of Research and Treatment, 16*(2), 121–137.

Vandiver, D. M., & Teske, R., Jr. (2006). Juvenile female and male sex offenders: A comparison of offender, victim, and judicial processing characteristics. *International Journal of Offender Therapy and Comparative Criminology, 50,* 148–165.

Vandiver, D. M., & Walker, J. T. (2002). Female sex offenders: An overview and analysis of 40 cases. *Criminal Justice Review, 27*(2), 284–300.

Vick, J., McRoy, R., & Matthews, B. M. (2002). Young female sex offenders: Assessment and treatment issues. *Journal of Child Sexual Abuse, 11,* 1–23.

Wolfe, F. A. (1985). *Twelve female sexual offenders.* Paper presented at the Next Steps in Research on the Assessment of Treatment of Sexually Aggressive Persons, St. Louis, MO.

4

Pedophilia

Richard D. McAnulty

INTRODUCTION

Sexuality has always been viewed as a force that must be tightly controlled and regulated. Sexual behavior has only been considered a legitimate topic of scientific inquiry for the past fifty years, beginning with Alfred Kinsey's landmark surveys. Before that time, sexuality and its problems were to be regulated by the church, the government, or medicine. Accordingly, sexual behavior that deviated from the established norm, however it was defined at the time, was declared sinful, criminal, or sick. Deviant sexual behavior, then, called for penitence, punishment, or a cure. This historical heritage still influences our thinking about sexual behavior. For example, do people who molest children suffer from an evil nature, a criminal mindset, or a mental illness?

I cannot answer such a question since it, like most questions relating to sexual behavior, hinges on personal values and beliefs. There are currently no universal and objective criteria for judging sexual attitudes and practices. Outside of sexual homicide, no sexual behavior is universally viewed as harmful or abnormal. Even sexual practices that would be condemned as child molestation in the United States took place openly and regularly in some cultures in the past (see Green, 2002). Although most definitions of sexual disorders emphasize that the associated patterns of sexual arousal deviate from normative patterns (hence the term *sexual deviations*), there are no clear criteria for defining normal sexual arousal or behavior. Definitions of what qualifies as *normal* vary over time and across cultures. Sexual norms do change, as illustrated by the shift in professional and societal attitudes toward homosexuality. Prior to 1973, homosexuality was classified as a sexual deviation by the American Psychiatric Association. It was dropped from the sexual deviation category after it was decided that homosexuality per se was not a harmful dysfunction or an abnormal sexual orientation (Wakefield, 1992). Curiously, the same line of reasoning has not been applied to other "disorders" such as fetishism and consensual sadomasochism. Several authors (Laws & O'Donohue, 1997) have argued that such conditions are not inherently harmful, and, like homosexuality, they are only variations in sexual lifestyles.

The topic of sexual deviation has the distinction of being one of the most controversial in psychology and related fields. Few disorders elicit as much curiosity and outrage as the sexual deviations, or *paraphilias* as they are officially known. Numerous cases of sexual offenses, and the ensuing sensational media coverage, have provoked alarm, outrage, and curiosity. Studies of victims and perpetrators suggest that these problems are not rare. Additionally, the Internet, with its sexually explicit sites, chat rooms, and special interest groups, has brought sexual deviations out of the closet and into cultural awareness. Sexual deviations themes are evident in several mainstream films, and they are regular features in televised talk shows, documentaries, and criminal justice media programs.

Unfortunately, there remains a great amount of undocumented information and often misinformation about sexual disorders. More than ever before, there is a need for sound research on sexual deviation. There are many unanswered questions about the features, causes, and effective treatments. The objective of this chapter is to provide an overview of pedophilia, or child molestation as it is popularly called. The overview begins with a discussion of definitions and classifications. The research findings on the characteristics common to pedophiles are reviewed, followed by a summary of leading theories. The coverage will be limited to male pedophiles since they are much more common, while female sex offenders are discussed elsewhere in this volume (see Chapter 3).

DEFINITIONS

The official definition of sexual deviation, including pedophilia, has changed considerably over time. According to the original definition by the American Psychiatric Association (1952), sexual deviations (or perversions as they were once called) were related to the "sociopathic personality disturbance." The sociopathic personality applied to individuals whose behavior failed to comply with social or cultural guidelines; in a sense, they were extreme nonconformists with respect to sexual practices. Pedophilia was formally introduced as a sexual deviation in 1968. The term "sexual deviation" was renamed *paraphilia* in 1980. Paraphilia was adopted because it was presumably more descriptive: *para-*, referring to an abnormality to which the person is attracted, *-philia*. According to the official description (American Psychiatric Association, 2000), the paraphilias involve recurrent and intense sexually arousing fantasies, sexual urges, or behaviors that typically involve (1) nonhuman objects (such as a shoe fetish), (2) the suffering or humiliation of oneself or of one's partner (as in sexual sadism), or (3) children or other nonconsenting persons (which would include exhibitionism and pedophilia).

For some individuals with paraphilias, their unusual urges or practices are necessary, even required, for sexual arousal. The person may not be able to perform sexually without the preferred item, situation, or partner. In other cases, they are not essential but desirable. In any case, the definition of a paraphilia requires that the urges or sexual practices are either distressing to the individual or cause impairments in one or more areas of life. The unusual sexual practices may cause problems in intimate relationships and lead to criminal arrest when they involve nonconsenting partners. Paraphilias entail sexual arousal that often interferes with "the capacity for reciprocal, affectionate sexual activity" (American Psychiatric Association, 1994, p. 524). In cases where the sexual urges and fantasies are essential for the person's sexual arousal, they may become a focus of the person's life. A man with a foot fetish, for example, may take a job as a salesperson in footwear. A man whose sexual urges involve immature children may coach youth sports teams to have access to potential victims.

Pedophilia (literally, *love of young children*) is officially described as involving recurrent, intense sexually arousing urges, fantasies, or behaviors involving sexual activity with a prepubescent child (usually 13 years old or younger). The person must be at least 16 years old and at least five years older than the victim. A relationship between an older adolescent and a 12- to 13-year-old would not qualify as pedophilia. Although the terms "pedophile" and "child molester" are often used interchangeably, there are important differences between them (Barbaree & Seto, 1997; McAnulty, Adams, & Dillon, 2001). Pedophilia is usually reserved for those individuals who show some degree of sexual preference for children: their urges and fantasies often focus on children, sometimes exclusively. Child molestation, however, is a broad term that can be applied to any person who engages in inappropriate sexual behavior with a child. Child molestation may be motivated by the unavailability of an adult partner (Freund, McKnight, Langevin, & Cibiri, 1972). It could be due to cognitive deficits such as mental retardation or dementia, or conditions related to lowered inhibitions, such as alcoholism or a psychopathic personality involving traits such as impulsiveness and thrill-seeking (Dorr, 1998). In these cases, the person's sexual actions with a child probably do not result from persistent and intense urges. In other words, pedophilia is but one of several possible motives for molesting a child. This distinction in terms is not simply a matter of semantics, because it has important implications for understanding offenders and making decisions about their treatment.

An important distinction should be made between sexual behavior and preference. Sexual activity is not always indicative of sexual preference; some gay men engage in heterosexual intercourse although they clearly prefer male sexual partners (and may resort to gay fantasy during encounters with a female). Sexual preferences, values, and behavior may be inconsistent, as evidenced by the observation that some pedophiles find their erotic interests despicable. Yet, they regularly engage in these "immoral" acts. In many cases, though, individuals enjoy their deviant urges and practices, and they resent interference from society.

CHARACTERISTICS OF PEDOPHILES

One consistent conclusion is that pedophiles represent a very diverse group of individuals. There is a high degree of variability in their personal characteristics, life experiences (including their family backgrounds), criminal histories, and reasons for molesting children. As Prentky, Knight, and Lee (1997) concluded, "there is no single 'profile' that accurately describes or accounts for all child molesters" (p. v). With this caution in mind, several consistent findings have emerged in studies of incarcerated pedophiles.

Sexual Preoccupation with Children

Pedophiles differ in the intensity and exclusivity of their sexual interests in children. Whether measured by the sexual histories, number of offenses, or sexual preferences, some offenders evidence an intense and exclusive sexual interest in children. These men have had multiple victims, have few experiences with adult partners, and their "sexual focus" is on children (Prentky et al., 1997). When tested in the lab using the penile plethysmograph, they show marked sexual arousal to pictures or videos of children, often with little arousal to adults of either gender. In one important study, Barbaree and Marshall (1989) discovered five separate sexual profiles among child molesters. Two profiles were indicative of pedophilia or a preference for children, one suggested a normal adult heterosexual orientation, one revealed a preference for adolescents, and the last involved indiscriminate arousal, or equal responsiveness to persons from all age groups. There is also evidence that nonfamilial child molesters are more sexually aroused by children than incestuous offenders are (Marshall, Barbaree, & Christophe, 1986; Quinsey, Chaplin, & Carrigan, 1979). Pedophiles who have a sexual preference for children are also higher risks for recidivism upon release from prison or treatment (see Seto, 2004).

Some research also suggests that offenders who have male victims, multiple victims, younger victims, and victims who are not related to them show more pedophilic sexual arousal than offenders who have female victims, few victims, older victims, and victims that are relatives (Seto, 2004). In other words, men who have sexually abused multiple young boys who are not relatives are more likely to be true pedophiles. As discussed in the next section, men who show a marked sexual preference for children with little to no arousal to adult partners are often labeled "preferential pedophiles." A consistent finding is that preferential pedophiles generally have deficits in their social and sexual relationships with adults. The majority of child molesters do not appear to be preferential pedophiles because they do not display an intense and exclusive focus on children.

Social Skills and Adjustment

It is well established that, as a group, pedophiles are described as deficient in their social skills (see Emmers-Sommer et al., 2004). As a group, pedophiles have been characterized as shy, unassertive, and passive (Langevin, 1983). Additionally, they have been described as introverted and socially withdrawn (Bard et al., 1987; Langevin, Hucker, Ben-Aron, Purins, & Hook, 1985). However, no single personality profile is consistently observed among pedophiles (Levin & Stava, 1987; Okami & Goldberg, 1992).

As a group, pedophiles are worried about negative evaluations by women, feel unassertive, and have very conservative stereotypes of women (Overholser & Beck, 1986). In interactions with adult females, they rate their performance more poorly than do rapists (Segal & Marshall, 1985). Because of these deficiencies and feelings of inadequacy, many pedophiles find children less threatening. These social skills deficits interfere with the offenders' capacity for developing normal sexual and social relationships, and, therefore, these deficits are believed to be important in the origins of perpetrators' deviant urges and fantasies (Prentky et al., 1997). It should be noted, though, that social skills deficits are only one of many factors in the development of pedophilia. Some offenders have relatively effective social skills; they are married and even respected members of their communities (prior to being charged with a sexual offense).

Antisocial Personality Traits

In some cases, men who molest children have a lengthy history of antisocial behavior. Individuals who molest younger children as adolescents are likely to have broken many rules, to have criminal histories, and to have had behavior problems at school and at home. Child molesters who committed their first sexual offense in adolescence usually acted out at school, often in the form of verbal and physical aggression. They were in trouble with the law as teenagers, a pattern that persisted into adulthood (Prentky et al., 1997). In these cases, the sexual offenses represent one part of a longer criminal history and antisocial lifestyle. As adults, these men persistently take advantage of others, often in the form of manipulation, deception, aggression, and impulsivity. Interpersonally, they are self-centered and insincere, and they seem to experience little remorse or guilt.

Recent studies suggest that a majority of incarcerated child molesters have committed nonsexual crimes. Criminal diversity, which refers to the range of criminal offenses in a person's past, is quite common among sex offenders in prison. Smallbone and Wortley (2004), who examined the criminal records of 362 convicted child molesters, reported that nearly two-thirds (64.4 percent) had prior criminal arrests, the majority of which were for nonsexual offenses such as theft, traffic violations, and drug offenses. In other words, this group of child molesters was criminally diverse. Nonsexual offenses accounted for 86 percent of all previous criminal offenses. These findings have led some re-searchers to question whether sex offenders are truly unique and different from incarcerated nonsex offenders (see Simon, 2000).

Studies suggest that 8–30 percent of child molesters have an antisocial or psychopathic personality disorder (Quinsey, Harris, & Rice, 1995; Serin, Malcolm, Khanna, & Barbaree, 1994; for a review see Dorr, 1998). Alcohol abuse is one of the most commonly reported problems among child molesters (Marshall, 1997). Antisocial traits, though, are not found in all cases. Para-doxically, some pedophiles are moralistic, conservative individuals in other aspects of their lives (Marshall & McKnight, 1975).

Troubled Childhoods

One final consistent finding is that pedophiles as a group are more likely to have had troubled childhoods. Their developmental histories often include being the victim of physical, emotional, or sexual abuse. Half or more of child molesters report having been the victims of sexual abuse during childhood (Bard et al., 1987; Marshall, 1997). Childhood emotional abuse is a devel-opmental risk factor for sexual deviation, including pedophilia (Lee, Jackson, Pattison, & Ward, 2002). Childhood sexual abuse is also related to the risk of becoming a perpetrator (Lee et al., 2002). Research shows that families that provide ineffective socialization, that are characterized by problematic parent-child relationships, and that involve high levels of parental conflict and vio-lence may place children at a higher risk of sexual offending later in life. Parental absence or inconsistency, as when a parent is emotionally unavailable to the child, increases the likelihood of later emotional and interpersonal problems, including anxiety, distrust, insecurity, excessive anger, and poor social skills (Prentky et al., 1997; Smallbone & Dadds, 1998). Parental in-sensitivity to a child's needs, in particular, is believed to compromise the child's ability to feel secure in adult relationships. Detrimental childhood ex-periences, such as having a severely dysfunctional family, can lead to social skills deficits and feelings of inadequacy, which can ultimately interfere with healthy adult relationships and intimacy.

Victim Preferences

Pedophiles often have very specific preferences for victims. They may differ in terms of preferred victim gender (male, female, or both), relationship to the victim (incestuous versus nonincestuous), and whether their sexual preference is exclusive (i.e., the pedophile is attracted only to children) or nonexclusive. The distinction between homosexual, bisexual, and heterosexual pedophilia is well established (Langevin, 1983; Lanyon, 1986). Heterosexual pedophiles (men who prefer immature girls) are apparently more common than homosexual pedophiles (men who prefer boys), whereas the bisexual subtype is uncommon. Homosexual pedophiles, however, tend to have a larger number of victims than the heterosexual pedophiles. For example, Abel et al. (1987) found that their sample of heterosexual child molesters (nonincestuous) reported an average of twenty victims, compared to 150 for the homosexual pedophiles (nonincestuous). Incestuous offenders in the same study admitted to an average of 1.8 female victims and 1.7 male victims. As with nonincestuous child molestation, most incestuous pedophiles chose female victims. In contrast to homosexual pedophilia, heterosexual child molesters are more likely to be married (Langevin, Hucker, Handy, et al., 1985).

Contrary to popular belief, pedophiles are not "dirty old men," as most incarcerated pedophiles are in their midtwenties to midthirties (Groth & Birnbaum, 1978; Langevin, Hucker, Handy, et al., 1985). By definition, the victims in both groups are prepubescent; average victim age is approximately 10 years (Groth & Birnbaum, 1978). Approximately 25 percent of victims are less than 6 years of age, another 25 percent are between 6 and 10 years of age, and roughly 50 percent are between 11 and 13 years of age (Erickson, Walbek, & Seely, 1988). Type of sexual activity with victims ranges from fondling to oral sex and actual penetration (Erickson et al., 1988). Among heterosexual pedophiles, fondling of the victim is by far the most common (54 percent), although vaginal contact (41.5 percent) and cunnilingus (19 percent) are not rare. For homosexual offenders, fondling of the victim is also most common (43 percent), followed by the performance of fellatio on the victim (41 percent). Anal contact in the latter group occurs in one-third of cases. In cases involving younger children, actual anal or vaginal penetration is uncommon; contact usually entails rubbing the penis against the orifice or between the thighs (Erickson et al., 1988; Langevin, Hucker, Handy, et al., 1985). In cases of intrafamilial incest, there tends to be a progression from masturbation and fondling to actual attempts at intercourse over time. Methods of obtaining victim compliance include enticement via bribery, seduction, appeal to curiosity, and intimidation and threats in some cases. The majority of pedophiles are at least acquainted with their victims. Incestuous pedophiles commonly molest biological, adoptive, or stepchildren, whereas the victims of nonincestuous offenders may include neighbors, relatives, and acquaintances.

Pedophiles typically have beliefs about sexual contact with children that facilitate acting out their deviant sexual urges (Hanson, Gizzarelli, & Scott, 1994; Ward, Hudson, Johnston, & Marshall, 1997). In general, the beliefs of pedophiles involve some degree of denial and minimization: they deny or minimize the actual harm suffered by their victims and they also minimize their own responsibility for the offenses. Specifically, they often claim that adult sexual contacts are beneficial to children ("it teaches them about sex"). Offenders not only deny or minimize their own responsibility for the offense, but also tend to view the victim as an instigator or willing participant (Stermac & Segal, 1989). Pedophiles often claim that a child's sexually provocative appearance or behavior actually invited the offense. These rationalizations are often used by offenders to justify their actions while reducing any sense of shame or remorse.

TYPES OF PEDOPHILES

One classification of pedophiles involves the distinction between preferential and situational pedophilia (Lanyon, 1986). This is similar to the exclusive-versus-nonexclusive (American Psychiatric Association, 2000) and fixated-versus-regressed classifications proposed by Cohen, Seghorn, and Calmas (1969) and Groth and Birnbaum (1978). *Preferential* or *fixated* pedophiles are primarily, and often exclusively, interested in children as sexual partners and tend to be unmarried. Homosexual pedophiles are usually preferential molesters. Their sexual experiences with adults tend to be very limited; they commonly have experienced lifelong difficulties in relating to adults, and their sexual development is described as fixated or blocked. For these offenders, encounters with children are usually premeditated rather than impulsive. These individuals tend to be more comfortable emotionally, socially, and sexually with children. The *situational* or *regressed* pedophiles tend to be primarily heterosexual child molesters. Incestuous offenders would generally be classified as situational offenders. These individuals are more likely to be married and to have more extensive sexual experience with adult partners than do preferential pedophiles. A common pattern is to have an apparently normal development with adequate social and heterosexual skills. As the person enters adulthood, however, his social, occupational, and marital adjustment become tenuous and marginal. The pedophilic acts are typically precipitated by direct confrontation with a female or a threat to the person's masculinity. These individuals' sexual encounters with children are more impulsive, usually with older but prepubescent females, and tend to occur intermittently rather than continuously (Lanyon, 1986). A major question is whether these individuals have always had some sexual arousal to children as well as adults. It is important to note that there is overlap between these categories. For example, Prentky et al. (1997) found that social skills problems could be found in cases of both preferential and situational pedophiles.

A final category includes the *aggressive* pedophile (Cohen et al., 1969) or sadistic child molester. Aggressive and sadistic sexual activity occurs in less than 20 percent of cases (Groth & Birnbaum, 1978). The victims are usually boys, and the sexual activity is clearly vicious and cruel. Sexual activity may include the mutilation of the victim's genitalia and the insertion of foreign objects into bodily orifices. In some cases, forcible anal intercourse (with resulting lacerations) may occur. Avery-Clark and Laws (1984) identified a group of aggressive pedophiles who were equally aroused by depictions of consenting intercourse with a child and graphic descriptions of aggressive assault of a child. Their measured sexual arousal suggested that these pedophiles were sexually aroused or at least not sexually inhibited by sexual aggression directed at children. Although these individuals are fairly rare, the results of their deviant sexual arousal are tragic; these offenders may be involved in the serial molestation and murder of boys.

THEORIES OF PEDOPHILIA

Psychoanalytic theories emphasize that pedophiles choose children as partners because they elicit less castration anxiety than do adults (Fenichel, 1945). Others have hypothesized an aversion to adult females and an association with homosexuality. The research evidence, however, does not support these theoretical views (Langevin, 1983; Langevin, Hucker, Ben-Aron, et al., 1985). The behavioral or social learning theories stress the importance of early conditioning, direct reinforcement, or modeling experiences, such as the presence of sexual abuse in the offender's past or an early sexual experience with a younger child. The single most popular theory of pedophilia is the "abused-abuser hypothesis," which proposes that individuals who were sexually abused in childhood are predisposed to developing pedophilia. As Garland and Dougher (1990) commented, despite the popularity of this view there is surprisingly little empirical support. There are at least three problems with this hypothesis: (1) although most victims of child sexual abuse are females, the vast majority of pedophiles are males; (2) only half of all child molesters have a personal history of sexual victimization by an adult in childhood (Weeks & Widom, 1998); and (3) some pedophiles allege having been sexually abused in childhood as a ploy to reduce their perceived responsibility for their sexual offenses (Freund, Watson, & Dickey, 1990). Thus, most individuals who were sexually molested as children do *not* develop pedophilia (Hanson & Slater, 1988; Salter et al., 2003).

Araji and Finkelhor (1985) have advanced a four-factor model of pedophilia. According to them, pedophilia may be understood in terms of (a) *emotional congruence*, or the emotional need to relate to children (e.g., faulty emotional development, feelings of inadequacy); (b) *blockage*, or the inability to attain alternative sources of gratification (e.g., social skills deficits, fear of adult partners); (c) *disinhibition*, referring to any influence that lowers the person's self-control (e.g., alcoholism, impulsivity); and (d) *sexual arousal* to prepubertal partners. Araji and Finkelhor (1985) noted that most existing theories of pedophilia include one or more of these factors. This proposed model is promising, as it stresses that no single factor will be found in every case of pedophilia. This model takes into account several factors that are common among pedophiles, but it does not fully explain why they occur. Many pedophiles, for example, feel inadequate with adult partners and are sexually attracted to children, but the model does not explain where these problems originate.

One of the influential theories of sexual offending was proposed by Marshall (1989) and Marshall, Hudson, and Hodkinson (1993). According to the model, secure parent-child attachment is essential for achieving intimate and mutually rewarding adult relationships. Inadequate attachment bonds can result from (1) poor parenting (e.g., inconsistency, lack of warmth, unresponsiveness, insensitivity, rejection, etc.), (2) discontinuities in parenting (e.g., loss of a parent, placement in foster care, etc.), or (3) serious family dysfunction (e.g., chaotic family, severe parental conflict, criminality in a parent, etc.). Lacking a secure attachment to a parent figure, children are left feeling insecure, anxious, and frustrated, often leading to behavior problems, such as delinquency, substance abuse, and aggression (Smallbone & Dadds, 2001). Afraid of others and mistrustful, these youths are especially unprepared for normal relationships with opposite-sex peers. These problems persist into adulthood, as these individuals feel isolated, lonely, and incapable of forming intimate relationships with peers (Smallbone & Dadds, 1998). They fear rejection, in the way they were rejected or neglected by their own parents. "Poor attachments in childhood, then, lead to an incapacity for intimacy, which produces painful feelings of emotional loneliness, and may ultimately lead to aggressive behavior" (Marshall et al., 1993, p. 174). Unable to form normal intimate relationships as adults, some of these individuals may resort to force and sexual coercion (as do rapists and exhibitionists) or seek out potential partners who are less emotionally threatening (as do pedophiles). According to this model, a man who lacks social skills and who feels inadequate and undesirable may be attracted to children because they are less rejecting and less critical than adults, thereby allowing an illusion of power, self-worth, and sexual desirability to the pedophile (Garlick, Marshall, & Thornton, 1996; Seidman, Marshall, Hudson, & Robertson, 1994).

The feelings of loneliness and problems with intimacy may be particularly difficult and painful for adults who were raised in cultures that promote sexual intimacy and traditional gender role stereotypes. In such cultures, those vulnerable may be especially prone to accepting mixed messages about sex and gender. Therefore, these men may be more likely to internalize distorted views of women (i.e., objectification of women) and of sex (e.g., sex as a conquest and a measure of a man's worth). This theory of sexual offending is promising because it incorporates the developmental sequence and various factors that could shape deviant urges and fantasies. It is also supported by a wealth of research that demonstrates that inadequate parent-child attachment bonds are linked to a host of behavioral and emotional problems later in life (see Goldberg, 1997). Sex offenders consistently report insecure attachment as predicted by the theory (Lyn & Burton, 2005).

CONCLUSIONS

Pedophilia is a serious problem in society. Many men and women report being victims of sexual abuse during childhood. According to one national survey (Laumann, Gagnon, Michael, & Michaels, 1994), nearly 12 percent of men and 17 percent of women reported that they had been sexually touched as children by an older adolescent or an adult. In most cases, it occurred between the ages of 7 and 10, and it progressed to oral sex and intercourse in 10–30 percent of the cases. For many victims, the abuse causes short-term and long-term problems in life (see Chapters 5 and 6 in this volume).

Pedophiles are usually men who have some degree of sexual preoccupation with immature children. For some, it is an exclusive sexual preference, but others have also had adult partners. Men with an exclusive sexual preference for children tend to have a larger number of victims and it is often a focus of their emotional, social, and sexual lives. As a group, pedophiles often lack social skills and feel inadequate in their relationships. This is not, however, universal. In some cases, child molestation is only part of a lengthy pattern of problematic behaviors at home and at school; these offenders tend to be antisocial, impulsive, and emotionally immature. Some pedophiles have a marked preference for a type of victim and specific sexual activities; others seem more indiscriminate. Many if not most pedophiles report troubled childhoods involving emotional, physical, or sexual abuse. Inadequate parent-child attachment and related problems are commonly reported by pedophiles and other sex offenders. These experiences are likely important factors in the developmental pathway to pedophilia.

REFERENCES

Abel, G. G., Becker, J. V., Mittelman, M., Cunningham-Rathner, J., Rouleau, J. L., & Murphy, W. D. (1987). Self-reported sex crimes of nonincarcerated paraphiliacs. *Journal of Interpersonal Violence, 2*, 3–25.

American Psychiatric Association. (1952). *Diagnostic and statistical manual of mental disorders*. Washington, DC: Author.

American Psychiatric Association. (1994). *The diagnostic and statistical manual of mental disorders* (4th ed.). Washington, DC: Author.

American Psychiatric Association. (2000). *The diagnostic and statistical manual of mental disorders* (4th ed., Text rev.). Washington, DC: Author.

Araji, S., & Finkelhor, D. (1985). Explanation of pedophilia: Review of empirical research. *Bulletin of the American Academy of Psychiatry and Law, 13*, 17–37.

Avery-Clark, C. A., & Laws, D. R. (1984). Differential erection response patterns of sexual child abusers to stimuli describing activities with children. *Behavior Therapy, 15*, 71–83.

Barbaree, H. E., & Marshall, W. L. (1989). Erectile responses among heterosexual child molesters, father-daughter incest offenders and matched non-offenders: Five distinct age preference profiles. *Canadian Journal of Behavioral Science, 21*, 70–82.

Barbaree, H. E., & Seto, M. C. (1997). Pedophilia: Assessment and treatment. In D. R. Laws & W. O'Donohue (Eds.), *Sexual deviance: Theory, assessment, and treatment* (pp. 175–193). New York: Guilford.

Bard, L. A., Carter, D. L., Cerce, D. D., Knight, R. A., Rosenberg, R., & Schneider, B. (1987). A descriptive study of rapists and child molesters: Developmental, clinical, and criminal characteristics. *Behavioral Sciences and the Law, 5*, 203–220.

Cohen, M. L., Seghorn, T., & Calmas, W. (1969). Sociometric study of the sex offender. *Journal of Abnormal Psychology, 74*, 249–255.

Dorr, D. (1998). Psychopathy in the pedophile. In T. Millon, E. Simonsen, M. Birket-Smith, & R. D. Davis (Eds.), *Psychopathy: Antisocial, criminal, and violent behavior* (pp. 304–320). New York: Guilford.

Emmers-Sommer, T. M., Allen, M., Bourhis, J., Sahlstein, E., Laskowski, K., Falato, W., et al. (2004). A meta-analysis of the relationship between social skills and sexual offenders. *Communication Reports, 17*, 1–10.

Erickson, W. D., Walbek, N. H., & Seely, R. K. (1988). Behavior patterns of child molesters. *Archives of Sexual Behavior, 17*, 77–86.

Fenichel, O. (1945). *The psychoanalytic theory of neurosis.* New York: Norton.

Freund, K., McKnight, C. K., Langevin, R., & Cibiri, S. (1972). The female child as a surrogate object. *Archives of Sexual Behavior, 2*, 119–133.

Freund, K., Watson, R., & Dickey, R. (1990). Does sexual abuse in childhood cause pedophilia: An exploratory study. *Archives of Sexual Behavior, 19*, 557–568.

Garland, R. J., & Dougher, M. J. (1990). The abused/abuser hypothesis of child sexual abuse: A critical review of theory and research. In J. R. Feierman (Ed.), *Pedophilia: Biosocial dimensions* (pp. 488–509). New York: Springer-Verlag.

Garlick, Y., Marshall, W. L., & Thornton, D. (1996). Intimacy deficits and attribution of blame among sexual offenders. *Legal and Criminological Psychology, 1*, 251–288.

Goldberg, S. (1997). Attachment and childhood behavior problems in normal, at-risk, and clinical samples. In L. Atkinson & K. J. Zucker (Eds.), *Attachment and psychopathology* (pp. 171–195). New York: Guilford.

Green, R. (2002). Is pedophilia a mental disorder? *Archives of Sexual Behavior, 31*, 467–471.

Groth, N. A., & Birnbaum, H. J. (1978). Adult sexual orientation and attraction to underage persons. *Archives of Sexual Behavior, 7*, 175–181.

Hanson, R. K., Gizzarelli, R., & Scott, H. (1994). The attitudes of incest offenders: Sexual entitlement and the acceptance of sex with children. *Criminal Justice and Behavior, 21*, 187–202.

Hanson, R. K., & Slater, S. (1988). Sexual victimization in the history of sexual abusers: A review. *Annals of Sex Research, 1*, 485–499.

Langevin, R. (1983). *Sexual strands: Understanding and treating sexual anomalies in men.* Hillsdale, NJ: Lawrence Erlbaum.

Langevin, R., Hucker, S. J., Ben-Aron, M. H., Purins, J. E., & Hook, H. J. (1985). Why are pedophiles attracted to children? Further studies of erotic preference in heterosexual pedophilia. In R. Langevin (Ed.), *Erotic preference, gender identity, and aggression in men: New research studies* (pp. 181–210). Hillsdale, NJ: Lawrence Erlbaum.

Langevin, R., Hucker, S. J., Handy, L., Purins, J., Russon, A. E., & Hook, H. J. (1985). Erotic preference and aggression in pedophilia: A comparison of heterosexual, homosexual, and bisexual types. In R. Langevin (Ed.), *Erotic preference, gender identity, and aggression in men: New research studies* (pp. 137–160). Hillsdale, NJ: Lawrence Erlbaum.

Lanyon, R. I. (1986). Theory and treatment in child molestation. *Journal of Consulting and Clinical Psychology, 54*, 176–182.

Laumann, E. O., Gagnon, J. H., Michael, R. T., & Michaels, S. (1994). *The social organization of sexuality: Sexual practices in the United States.* Chicago: The University of Chicago Press.

Laws, D. R., & O'Donohue, W. (1997). Introduction: Fundamental issues in sexual deviance. In D. R. Laws & W. O'Donohue (Eds.), *Sexual deviance: Theory, assessment, and treatment* (pp. 1–21). New York: Guilford.

Lee, J. K. P., Jackson, H. J., Pattison, P., & Ward, T. (2002). Developmental risk factors for sexual offending. *Child Abuse and Neglect, 26*, 73–92.

Levin, S. M., & Stava, L. (1987). Personality characteristics of sex offenders: A review. *Archives of Sexual Behavior, 16*, 57–79.

Lyn, T. S., & Burton, D. L. (2005). Attachment, anger, and anxiety of male sexual offenders. *Journal of Sexual Aggression, 11*, 127–137.

Marshall, W. L. (1989). Intimacy, loneliness, and sexual offenders. *Behaviour Research and Therapy, 27*, 491–503.

Marshall, W. L. (1997). Pedophilia: Psychopathology and theory. In D. R. Laws & W. O'Donohue (Eds.), *Sexual deviance: Theory, assessment, and treatment* (pp. 152–174). New York: Guilford.

Marshall, W. L., Barbaree, H. E., & Christophe, D. (1986). Sexual offenders against female children: Sexual preferences for age of victims and type of behaviour. *Canadian Journal of Behavioral Science, 18*, 424–439.

Marshall, W. L., Hudson, S. M., & Hodkinson, S. (1993). The importance of attachment bonds in the development of juvenile sex offending. In H. E. Barbaree, W. L. Marshall, & S. M. Hudson (Eds.), *The juvenile sex offender* (pp. 164–181). New York: Guilford.

Marshall, W. L., & McKnight, R. D. (1975). An integrated treatment program for sexual offenders. *Canadian Psychiatric Association Journal, 20*, 133–138.

McAnulty, R. D., Adams, H. E., & Dillon, J. (2001). Sexual deviation: The paraphilias. In H. E. Adams & P. B. Sutker (Eds.), *Comprehensive handbook of psychopathology* (3rd ed.). New York: Plenum.

Okami, P., & Goldberg, A. (1992). Personality correlates of pedophilia: Are they reliable indicators? *Journal of Sex Research, 29,* 297–328.

Overholser, J. C., & Beck, S. (1986). Multimethod assessment of rapists, child molesters, and three control groups on behavioral and psychological measures. *Journal of Consulting and Clinical Psychology, 54,* 682–687.

Prentky, R. A., Knight, R. A., & Lee, A. F. S. (1997). *Child sexual molestation: Research issues.* National Institute of Justice Research Report. Washington, DC: U. S. Department of Justice.

Quinsey, V. L., Chaplin, T. C., & Carrigan, W. F. (1979). Sexual preferences among incestuous and nonincestuous child molesters. *Behavior Therapy, 10,* 562–565.

Quinsey, V. L., Harris, G. T., & Rice, M. E. (1995). Actuarial prediction of sexual recidivism. *Journal of Interpersonal Violence, 10,* 85–105.

Salter, D., McMillan, D., Richards, M., Talbot, T., Hodges, J., Bentovim, A., et al. (2003). Development of sexually abusive behaviour in sexually victimized males: A longitudinal study. *Lancet, 361,* 471–476.

Segal, Z. V., & Marshall, W. L. (1985). Heterosexual social skills in a population of rapists and child molesters. *Journal of Consulting and Clinical Psychology, 53,* 55–63.

Seidman, B. T., Marshall, W. L., Hudson, S. M., & Robertson, P. J. (1994). An examination of intimacy and loneliness in sex offenders. *Journal of Interpersonal Violence, 9,* 518–534.

Serin, R. C., Malcolm, P. B., Khanna, A., & Barbaree, H. E. (1994). Psychopathy and deviant sexual arousal in incarcerated sexual offenders. *Journal of Interpersonal Violence, 9,* 3–11.

Seto, M. C. (2004). Pedophilia and sexual offenses against children. *Annual Review of Sex Research, 15,* 321–361.

Simon, L. (2000). An examination of the assumptions of specialization, mental disorder, and dangerousness in sex offenders. *Behavioral Sciences and the Law, 18,* 275–308.

Smallbone, S. W., & Dadds, M. R. (1998). Childhood attachment and adult attachment in incarcerated adult male sex offenders. *Journal of Interpersonal Violence, 13,* 555–573.

Smallbone, S. W., & Dadds, M. R. (2001). Further evidence for a relationship between attachment insecurity and coercive sexual behavior in non-offenders. *Journal of Interpersonal Violence, 16,* 22–35.

Smallbone, S. W., & Wortley, R. K. (2004). Criminal diversity and paraphilic interests among adult males convicted of sexual offenses against children. *International Journal of Offender Therapy and Comparative Criminology, 48,* 175–188.

Stermac, L. E., & Segal, Z. V. (1989). Adult sexual contact with children: An examination of cognitive factors. *Behavior Therapy, 20,* 573–584.

Wakefield, J. C. (1992). The concept of mental disorder: On the boundary between biological facts and social values. *American Psychologist, 47*, 373–388.

Ward, R., Hudson, S. M., Johnston, L., & W. L. Marshall (1997). Cognitive distortions in sex offenders: An integrative review. *Clinical Psychology Review, 17*, 479–507.

Weeks, R., & Widom, C. S. (1998). Self-reports of early childhood victimization among incarcerated adult male felons. *Journal of Interpersonal Violence, 13*, 346–361.

5

Sexual Assault

Karen S. Calhoun, Jenna McCauley, and Megan E. Crawford

Sexual assault is an enormous problem in the United States as well as internationally. Not only does it impact the lives of millions of individuals, but it also has huge costs to society in the form of economic loss, health burdens, and social problems. The emotional aftermath, short- and long-term disruption in functioning, psychological and physical health problems, increase in suicide risk, and increased vulnerability to additional forms of sexual and physical violence are but a few of the consequences. Survivors are affected most directly, but others in their lives (family, partners, friends, etc.) suffer serious consequences as well.

In this chapter, we will review definitions, impact, risk factors, prevention and intervention, and support services available to victims. The focus will be on adult victims of sexual assault, since child sexual abuse has somewhat different rates, definitions, and related issues.

DEFINING SEXUAL ASSAULT

While the occurrence of rape is a concern of growing importance, incidence estimates often suffer from flawed measurement methods and general underreporting, especially of rapes perpetrated by acquaintances (Koss, 1992). According to some estimates, as few as one in ten rapes are reported. Additionally, the definitions of rape, attempted rape, and sexual assault may be discrepant between researchers and legal/epidemiological sources. These two issues will be briefly discussed below. While these discrepancies affect any review of prevalence data, the important point is this: rape is a far too common occurrence and has a broad range of potential consequences and risk factors.

In defining various degrees of sexual violence, two main approaches are followed. The first set of definitions is found within the legal realm and is used for the periodic reporting of incidence rates. *Forcible rape* is a crime punishable by law, and thus it is legally defined by the FBI Uniform Crime Report as "the carnal knowledge of a female forcibly and against her will" (Rantala, 2000). This definition includes both attempted and completed rapes, but only includes female victims. The National Incidence Based Reporting System broadens the definition to include both female and male victims, defining *rape* as "the carnal knowledge of a person forcibly, and/or against that person's will; or not forcibly or against that person's will where that person is incapable of giving consent because of his/her temporary or permanent mental or physical incapacity." Additional legal terms which may apply to sexual assault experiences include *aggravated assault*, an unlawful attack by one person upon another for the purpose of inflicting severe or aggravated bodily injury; this type of assault is usually accompanied by the use of a weapon or another force likely to produce death or great bodily harm, and *simple assault*, aggravated assault without the display of a weapon. It is worth noting that legal definitions vary by state.

While important for purposes of filing legal charges and calculating annual incidence rates, the definitions are not as commonly used in research on sexual assault as are those germane to the public health sector. Within this perspective, *sexual violence* is defined as "any sexual act, attempt to obtain a sexual act, unwanted sexual comments or advances, or acts to traffic, or otherwise directed, against a person's sexuality using coercion, by any person regardless of their relationship to the victim, in any setting, including but not limited to home and work" (Jewkes, Sen, & Garcia-Moreno, 2002). As you can see, this definition is quite broad, leaving room for a variety of victim experiences. More specifically, *rape* may be defined as "physically forced or otherwise coerced penetration of the vulva or anus using a penis, other body parts, or an object." *Attempted rape* is a noncompleted rape. Within the context of these definitions, *coercion* applies to physical force, psychological intimidation, blackmail or other threats, or taking advantage of an individual who is incapable of giving consent. (For a review of the discrepancies of legal and public health sector definitions, see Kilpatrick, 2004.)

In an effort to resolve the disparate and often overlapping terminology, the Centers for Disease Control (Basile & Saltzman, 2002) published a compendium of uniform definitions and recommended data elements. Sexual violence was divided into five categories: a completed sex act without victim consent or involving a victim unable to consent or refuse, an attempted sex act without victim consent or involving a victim unable to consent or refuse, abusive sexual contact, noncontact sexual abuse (such as exhibitionism), and sexual violence unspecified. "Sex act" is uniformly defined as "contact between the penis and vulva or the penis and anus, involving penetration, however slight; contact between the mouth and penis, vulva, or anus; or penetration of the anal or genital opening of another person by hand, finger, or other object." The inability to consent may be due to age, illness, disability, being asleep, or the influence of alcohol or other drugs. Inability to refuse may be due to the use of weapons, physical violence, threats of physical violence, real or perceived coercion, intimidation or pressure, or the misuse of authority.

Within the realm of violence researchers, the most commonly agreed upon definition of *rape* has been defined by Koss (1992) as "nonconsensual vaginal, anal, or oral penetration, obtained by force, by threat of injury or bodily harm, or when the victim is incapable of giving consent (i.e., due to impairment by drugs or other intoxicants)." Although this definition is widely used in the literature on sexual assault, it has several limitations. In addition to the exclusion of attempted rape and other forms of sexual assault, the current definition includes stranger, acquaintance, date, and marital rape and does not necessarily lend itself to distinction among these victim-offender relationships, further clouding the intricacies of the impact that these factors may have in terms of postrape adjustment and potential risk factors. The term "sexual coercion" is frequently used to describe methods of aggression that do not involve force or violence, but occur more frequently in assault where the victim has some prior relationship with the offender (Koss, Dinero, Seibel, & Cox, 1988).

A range of sexual violence is subsumed by the term *sexual assault*. This term commonly includes sex acts such as unwanted fondling or sex play in addition to more severe forms of assault such as attempted or completed rape. While less severe forms of assault may result in physical and psychological consequences for the victim, a general finding is that more severe assaults are differentiated by their more significant impact on the lives of the victims.

Researchers are currently working toward a common lexicon. In the meantime, there is some commonality among the definitions to be highlighted. One such commonality is that whether legally defined or defined by researchers, *rape* may occur either by force or coercion and involves some form of penetration. *Attempted rape* is usually considered to be the lack of completion of these activities. *Sexual assault* may include a wide range of unwanted sexual activity that may range from an unwanted kiss, to unwanted sex play, to rape.

PREVALENCE ESTIMATES

Even considering underreporting and the lack of uniform definitions, the prevalence rates for rape are notably high. Prevalence of rape within a community sample has been estimated at 14 percent (Kilpatrick, Edmunds, & Seymour, 1992). According to the National Violence Against Women Survey (NVAWS), one in six women have experienced an attempted or completed

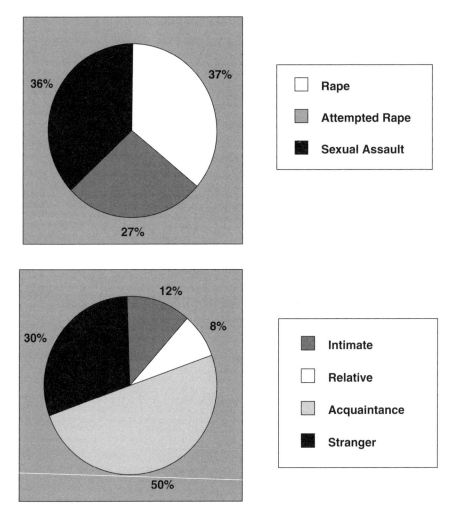

Figure 5.1. Estimates from National Crime Victim Survey results, 2003.

Source: Bureau of Justice Statistics.

rape (Tjaden & Thoennes, 2000). Among college women, estimates are even higher than those within the general population (Sorenson, Stein, Siegel, Golding, & Burnham, 1987). In a college sample of women, Gidycz et al. (1997) found that approximately 17 percent had experienced a rape, while an additional 33 percent had experienced some other form of sexual assault. Greene and Navarro (1998) found 27 percent of first-year college women were sexually assaulted over the course of a twelve-week semester. The combined effects of these estimates indicate that sexual assault is a frequent occurrence, impacting thousands of women each year. Although adolescent and young adult women are the most common targets of sexual assault, women of all ages, ethnicities, and backgrounds are victims.

Figure 5.1 gives an estimate of the relative incidence of rape, attempted rape, and sexual assault, according to the most recent National Crime Victim Survey results. It also indicates the incidence broken down by perpetrator type. Half of all perpetrators are acquaintances, including dates, neighbors, friends of friends, classmates, etc. Just under one third are strangers, 12 percent are spouses or intimate partners, and the rest are relatives.

CONSEQUENCES

Rape is a trauma that is often a devastating experience for its survivors. It results in both acute and chronic symptoms that may range from temporary emotional and physical reactions like fear and bruising, to more long-term psychological and health conditions such as major depression or fibromyalgia. Early research on the recovery of rape victims reported that almost 40 percent of women stated that recovery took "several years," while over 25 percent reported that they did not feel they had yet fully recovered at four to six years postrape. It is important to keep in mind that each person is different and may present with a wide array of immediate symptoms as a result of sexual assault, which may or may not progress to the development of chronic conditions. The subsequent material summarizes some of the potential immediate and long-term consequences with which rape survivors may be faced. It is by no means exhaustive, but represents a guide to the more common and prevalent reactions of women following the experience of rape.

Immediate Consequences of Sexual Assault

Victims of sexual assault may experience a range of reactions immediately following the trauma, including disorientation, numbness, feelings of vulnerability, shame, guilt and fear, and somatic symptoms. In 1974, Burgess and Holmstrom were the first researchers to collect self-report data from community samples of rape victims on the immediate and long-term effects of rape. To date, their research on the "rape trauma syndrome," as they coined it, remains a keystone in the discussion of immediate reactions to rape.

Burgess and Holmstrom (1979) divided the immediate reactions of rape victims into two basic types: the expressed style and the controlled style. Women who expressed their emotion tended to report feelings of fear and anxiety and exhibited behaviors such as crying, smiling, tenseness, and restlessness. The controlled style consisted of a masking of emotion and generally subdued affect. A fairly equal number of women expressed each style. It is worthwhile to remember that women who have experienced a sexual assault may present with a broad spectrum of emotional and physical conditions that are as varied as the circumstances of their victimization.

Acute reactions that appear within the first few weeks following the assault included a range of somatic and emotional conditions. For women experiencing physically forced sex, physical trauma may be common, including bruising and irritation. Other somatic reactions include tension headaches, fatigue, sleep disturbances, appetite reduction, nausea, hypersensitivity, and gynecological symptoms such as vaginal discharge, bleeding, itching, burning sensation, and generalized pain.

In terms of emotional reactions, fear is a primary feeling described by rape survivors. Women may report being afraid to be alone or fear of places that resemble the site of their attack. Women may also experience heightened anxiety throughout the course of their normal day and during their participation in routine activities. Other reactions common to victims of rape include humiliation, embarrassment, anger, revenge, and self-blame.

Long-Term Impact of Sexual Assault

For some women, short-term symptoms persist and may develop into long-term consequences. It is important to stress that not all victims of sexual assault will experience any or all of the symptoms and consequences discussed. However, it is also important to become aware of several of the more common long-term consequences that research has linked with the experience of sexual assault. As with the immediate impact, these consequences touch upon the realms of physical/somatic health, relationships, risky sexual behavior, and psychological sequelae. A very general introduction to these topics is provided below.

Physical and Somatic Health Consequences

Physical and somatic conditions associated with sexual assault encompass a broad range of chronic illness and reproductive health problems. Chronic conditions more likely to be diagnosed within a population of rape victims include, but are not limited to, arthritis, gastrointestinal disorders, headaches, chronic pain disorders (e.g., fibromyalgia), premenstrual symptoms, chronic pelvic pain, and psychogenic seizures.

Women with a history of sexual assault have approximately 1.6 times the odds of experiencing poor health as people without a history of assault (Golding, Cooper, & George, 1997). Assaults by strangers in particular are associated with an increased risk of poor health outcomes. These poor health outcomes lead to increased utilization of healthcare as well as a significant financial burden in medical costs. Women with a history of assault are more likely to rate themselves as unhealthy, visit their physician almost twice as often, and have medical costs 2.5 times higher than those of women without a history of sexual assault. The more frequent and severe the assault experience, the more adverse the health outcomes.

Another potential health consequence of rape is contraction of an array of sexually transmitted infections (STIs) and AIDS. Koss and Heslet (1992) found that up to 30 percent of rape victims tested positive for some form of sexually transmitted infection. As an additional risk, recent research has pointed to a link between previous victimization and risky sexual behaviors that may increase one's risk for STIs. Some women with a history of sexual assault have been found to have a significantly higher number of sex partners, engage in high-risk sexual practices, and be less likely to use condoms during sexual activity than nonvictims.

Social and Relational Impact

A far greater percentage of rape victims (71 percent) report a decrease in sexual activity. And, among the potential long-term consequences of rape are sexual dysfunction and disruption of preexisting heterosexual relationships. Women often report a significant level of impairment of functioning at work or school, as well as an increase in problems with family relationships. Whether women choose to disclose their experience to their friends and families or not, the experience of rape may have a long-term impact on how they interact within their interpersonal relationships.

Psychological Sequelae

Rape often leaves its mark via psychological conditions such as fear, anxiety, low self-esteem, social adjustment issues, depression, dysthymia, and posttraumatic stress disorder (PTSD). One study, which surveyed over 3,000 households and compared women with a history of sexual assault to those without such history, found that sexual assault predicted the later onset of major depressive episodes, substance use disorders, and anxiety disorders such as phobia, panic disorder, and obsessive-compulsive disorder. Depression and PTSD are the two most commonly experienced long-term psychological consequences of rape.

Depression is characterized by depressed mood most of the day every day, diminished interest and pleasure in once pleasurable activities, significant weight loss or gain, sleep disturbances, diminished ability to concentrate, and recurrent thoughts of death. In addition to acute symptoms of depression following a rape, women may also experience long-term depression (for reviews, see Koss, Bailey, & Yuan, 2003; Crowell & Burgess, 1996). Approximately 50 percent of rape survivors report depressive symptoms one month following the attack. Of these, over 40 percent meet the diagnostic criteria for depression. For comparison, the normal rate of depression for women in the United States is approximately 20 percent (Atkeson, Calhoun, Resick, & Ellis, 1982). Results from epidemiological research have indicated that those with a history of childhood or adult sexual assault are 2.4 times more likely to be diagnosed with major depression than controls. Other research has shown that over 20 percent of a sample of assault victims had a lifetime diagnosis of dysthymia (low-grade, chronic depression), almost 40 percent met the criteria for major depression, and over 40 percent were diagnosed with some form of depressive disorder. Rates of lifetime diagnosis with depression are higher for women victimized in childhood than for those first victimized in adulthood. However, both groups of women are significantly more likely to have a lifetime diagnosis of depression than nonvictimized women.

PTSD was first noted and studied within populations of war veterans following their return from combat. It was noted that a certain portion of these men experienced more difficulty in their readjustment to civilian life, expressed through a cluster of symptomatology. Soon, these similar symptoms began to be noted in populations other than those with combat experience. Among civilians, sexual assault is one of the largest contributors to the subsequent development of PTSD. The diagnosis of PTSD includes a myriad of symptoms that must persist more than one month following a trauma. It is noteworthy that several of these symptoms are common, acute experiences (i.e., less than one month postassault) for women who have been raped, and should enough of these symptoms be present, may garner the diagnosis of acute stress disorder. These symptoms are clustered into three main groups: reexperiencing (i.e., intrusive recollections, distressing dreams, acting or feeling as if the event is happening again, reactivity or distress upon being exposed to related external or internal cues), numbing (i.e., avoidance of thoughts, feelings, and memories related to the trauma), and increased arousal or hypervigilance. The PTSD diagnosis is only applicable should the symptoms continue to plague the survivor for more than one month. Estimates of the lifetime prevalence rates for PTSD among victims of completed rape are 60 to 65 percent. Kilpatrick et al. (1992) found that women with a history of sexual assault were over six times more likely to suffer from PTSD when compared to women without such history. In sum, PTSD is an all too common part of the postrape sequelae, with effects that may cause significant interference with daily life.

In addition to PTSD, survivors of sexual assault may experience a general increase in fear and anxiety. Calhoun, Atkeson, and Resick (1982) compared victims to nonvictims of sexual assault on longitudinal measures of various domains of fear. Overall, victims were significantly more fearful than nonvictims. While the amount of fear expressed among the victim group declined over the twelve-month follow-up period, these women remained significantly more anxious than those in the nonvictim control group. This fear may take many forms, from overall "edginess" or "jumpiness" to agoraphobia, and may express itself in fears such as fear of the dark, of being alone, or of being in large groups of people.

SEXUAL ASSAULT AND SUBSTANCE USE

In addition to the psychological sequelae of sexual assault trauma, another noteworthy relationship is between sexual assault experiences and lifetime prevalence rates of substance abuse or dependence. One study found that the odds for developing alcohol or drug use disorders more than doubled for women with a history of sexual assault (Burnam, Stein, & Golding, 1988). Clinicians and researchers report that women seeking treatment for substance use disorders (SUDs) have much higher rates of physical and sexual assault when compared with women in the general population. This relationship appears to be evident among women with a history of childhood sexual abuse.

Although the link between sexual assault and SUDs has been well documented, it is difficult to disentangle the direction and time sequencing of this relationship. Citing research designs reliant upon retrospective report of data, insufficient methodology, psychological symptomology, substance use, and often complex interactions of abuse, researchers have yet to fully determine which comes first—sexual assault or increased use of substances. However, attempts are being made to more clearly delineate the order of onset of these conditions. For example, White and Humphrey (1997) collected longitudinal data over the course of three years of over 700 college women. They found that women who experienced a sexual assault in one given year of the study had nearly doubled their odds of reporting heavy drinking in the following year. Currently, support is strongest for the existence of a bidirectional, at times even cyclical, relationship between sexual assault and substance use.

Supporting Theory

While the temporal directionality of the relationship between sexual assault and alcohol abuse appears to be bidirectional, researchers have formed and tested a hypothetical explanation for the occurrence of alcohol abuse subsequent to sexual assault. This theory has been coined the "self-medication hypothesis." Although this theory has been applied to a broad spectrum of substances, a majority of the research involving women who have experienced sexual assault focuses upon alcohol specifically. According to this theory, women who have experienced a traumatic event (such as sexual assault) are left to deal with the aftermath, which may include many of the symptoms previously discussed, like depressed mood, general anxiety, and PTSD. Alcohol use serves as a coping mechanism in that it may temporarily numb symptoms of anxiety, depression, or PTSD. Some researchers have termed the use of alcohol for the reduction of unpleasant emotions as "chemical avoidance." Because chemical avoidance is often effective on a short-term basis (e.g., it reduces anxiety), the drinking behavior is reinforced by the reduction in distress. This increases the likelihood of that same drinking behavior upon subsequent experience of unpleasant emotions. Over time, when used repeatedly and often exclusively, drinking becomes a maladaptive mechanism for coping. Laboratory research has supported this model. Results of studies, such as one by Levenson, Oyama, and Meek (1987) demonstrating that alcohol was effective in decreasing both physiological and subjective measures of stress following the administration of a small electric shock (physiological stressor) and a self-disclosing speech (psychological stressor), help to clarify how alcohol use may be negatively reinforced among victims of sexual assault.

Miranda et al. (2002) found that college women with a history of sexual assault experienced increased levels of psychological distress, which, consequently, was related to an increased use of alcohol. An additional consideration when examining this model is the role that alcohol expectancies (e.g., the belief that drinking alcohol will make one more relaxed and more sociable, and may help ease anxiety) may play in social situations. Many women may consume alcohol to help them cope with social anxiety or heightened sensitivity to intimate situations.

Consequences of Heavy Drinking

Alcohol use is one of the most common consequences of sexual assault experiences and is not without its own medical, psychological, and practical ramifications. Its impact may range from temporary impairment to no longer being able to fulfill work or familial responsibilities, interaction with other medications, social and legal problems, and alcohol-related birth defects. If left untreated for long periods of time, alcohol abuse may also lead to long-term health problems such as alcohol-related liver disease, heart disease, pancreatitis, and certain forms of cancer.

Increased Risk for Use of Other Substances

Although we have focused mainly on the development of alcohol-related problems following an assault, it is also worth noting that a strong relationship between previous victimization and the use of illegal substances has also been documented. A history of sexual assault more than doubles the odds of drug abuse or dependence. The self-medication hypothesis can be used to explain this relationship. However, the relationship between sexual assault and drug abuse is cyclical in nature, perhaps even more so than with alcohol abuse. That is, women who have been assaulted are more likely to use illicit drugs, and use of illicit drugs places women at greater risk for future victimization.

SEXUAL ASSAULT AND SUICIDE

Perhaps one of the most troubling consequences related to sexual assault involves an increase in suicidal ideation and suicide attempts among its victims. Studies of adult women indicate the existence of a link between sexual assault and suicidal behaviors. Rates of suicide are four times greater among sexually victimized women (Kilpatrick et al., 1992). Women who experience sexual assault at multiple phases of their lives (i.e., victims of childhood sexual abuse who are then revictimized as adults) show the greatest odds of exhibiting lifetime suicide attempts. The relationship between victimization and suicidal behavior is often mediated by the occurrence of other stressful life events, depression, PTSD, and alcohol dependence symptoms. Other suggested mediators of the sexual assault–suicide relationship that have not yet received as much empirical support include attributions of blame, hopelessness, and searching for meaning in one's victimization.

REVICTIMIZATION

In addition to the many physical and psychological consequences common in the aftermath of a sexual assault, women with a history of victimization also appear to be at increased risk for future sexual assaults. Although many variables have been recognized as potential risk factors for victimization, research consistently identifies a previous history of sexual abuse as one of the strongest predictors of future sexual victimization (Himelein, 1995; Koss & Dinero, 1989). Although prevalence rates vary, they suggest that up to 72 percent of women with a child or adolescent sexual abuse history will experience additional sexual assaults, with similar rates being documented across a variety of samples including college students, clinical populations, and community samples (Messman & Long, 1996). While most of this research has relied on retrospective reporting of victimization experiences, studies that follow women over time have identified a trend for revictimization as well. Gidycz, Hanson, and Layman (1995) followed female college students over a nine-month period, and found that sexual assault survivors were approximately twice as likely to experience victimization during their first three months of participation, and at subsequent six- and nine-month follow-up periods, this risk increased significantly. Specifically, women who were victimized during the initial three months of participation were three times more likely than nonvictims to experience victimization during the subsequent three-month follow-up period, and at nine months, participants were twenty times more likely than nonvictims to experience additional sexual victimization if they had been assaulted during the earlier time period.

These high prevalence rates are particularly alarming when one considers the impact of multiple assault experiences on a woman's functioning and well-being. All of the negative consequences experienced by rape survivors become exponentially worse for revictimized women, including higher rates of depression, anxiety, posttraumatic stress symptoms, hostility, somatic complaints, and suicide attempts (Ellis, Atkeson, & Calhoun, 1982; Messman-Moore, Long, & Siegfried, 2000). In addition, revictimized women experience more interpersonal dysfunction than single-assault victims, with fewer and less fulfilling social relationships, and problems with assertiveness, sociability, submissiveness, intimacy, responsibility, and control (Classen, Field, Koopman, Nevill-Manning, & Spiegel, 2001; Cloitre, Scarvalone, & Difede, 1997; Ellis et al.,

1982). While the majority of research on revictimization has focused on repeated sexual victimization, the adjustment of sexual assault survivors is further complicated by an increased risk for other forms of trauma. For example, Messman-Moore and Long (2000) found that women with a child sexual abuse history were also at increased risk for adult physical abuse and psychological maltreatment. Increased recognition of the problems associated with the phenomenon of revictimization has led to much research in recent years in an attempt to understand the so-called vicious cycle or link between the assault experiences (Mandoki & Burkhart, 1989). In spite of this significant growth in the literature, however, there is still insufficient evidence to support any of the suggested theories or explanations behind why victimization experiences are not evenly distributed throughout the population.

Although the exact mechanisms involved in risk for revictimization are still uncertain, several variables may increase a woman's vulnerability for multiple victimization experiences. The list of suggested mediators has been extensive, including such widely divergent variables as stable personality characteristics of the survivor, disturbed interpersonal relationships, and greater self-blame following the initial sexual assault experience (for reviews, see Arata, 2002; Breitenbecher, 2001). Research focused on risk perception seems to have received the most consistent empirical support. It suggests that revictimized women have more difficulty identifying threatening cues in dating situations (Breitenbecher, 2001). This impaired ability to detect risk may decrease the likelihood of a woman successfully resisting unwanted sexual advances from a potential perpetrator, putting her at higher risk for victimization. Several experimental studies using an audiotaped vignette of a date rape have documented that revictimized women took significantly longer than single-assault or nonvictims in identifying when the man in the situation had "gone too far," which suggests that revictimized women may have poorer risk recognition (Marx, Calhoun, Wilson, & Meyerson, 2001; Wilson, Calhoun, & Bernat, 1999). However, not all studies on threat perception have supported the same conclusions, suggesting that even with adequate risk recognition, "accurate perception of risk must translate into effective action" (Cue, George, & Norris, 1996, p. 502). A recent study suggested that revictimization was predicted by a woman's behavioral response to risky situations rather than her ability to identify threatening cues, which emphasizes the need to examine variables that may be preventing some women from engaging in self-protective behaviors (Messman-Moore & Brown, in press). Other factors that may reduce risk perception or influence a woman's ability to effectively resist unwanted sexual advances include alcohol and drug use, level of assertiveness, and psychological distress, all of which have received partial support as underlying explanations for revictimization (Greene & Navarro, 1998; Gidycz, Coble, Latham, & Layman, 1993). While these variables point to the importance of a woman's behavior in increasing risk for revictimization, one must also separately consider the role of a woman's beliefs and perceived self-efficacy in increasing her vulnerability for multiple sexual victimization experiences. According to Bandura (1977), a person's self-efficacy determines "whether coping behavior will be initiated, how much effort will be expended, and how long it will be sustained in the face of obstacles and aversive experiences." Thus, a woman with low self-efficacy regarding her ability to resist unwanted sexual advances may be less likely to engage in protective behaviors with potential perpetrators. Self-efficacy was found to be a protective factor in studies designed to evaluate a program aimed at reducing revictimization risk (Calhoun et al., 2002; Marx et al., 2001). Together, these results highlight the role of a woman's thoughts and beliefs as a possible factor in revictimization. Despite increased attention to this phenomenon, the inconsistency of findings on the subject of revictimization limits the ability of researchers and community health providers to intervene with this population of women and reduce their risk for future assaults. However, while the need continues for research on the mechanisms responsible for putting some women at greater risk, evidence continues to build for the role of previous victimization as one of the strongest risk factors for sexual assault.

RISK FACTORS FOR SEXUAL ASSAULT

Despite limited understanding of revictimization and its underlying causes, general risk factors for sexual assault have been more extensively researched. Theories on sexual assault and associated risk factors have evolved considerably over the past two decades. Several variables have consistently been shown to increase a woman's vulnerability for sexual assault. Using a nationally representative sample of college women, Koss and Dinero (1989) simultaneously examined variables associated with three models or hypotheses, including vulnerability-creating traumatic experiences, social-psychological vulnerability, and vulnerability-enhancing situations. As discussed above, previous traumatic experiences seem to be well established as risk factors for repeat victimization. Observations of victims of sexual abuse have influenced the development of a concept known as traumatic sexualization. Described by Finkelhor and Browne (1985), traumatic sexualization "refers to a process in which a child's sexuality (including both sexual feelings and sexual attitudes) is shaped in a developmentally inappropriate and interpersonally dysfunctional fashion as a result of sexual abuse" (p. 531). These influential early experiences may lead to more liberal sexual attitudes and higher levels of consensual sexual activity at younger ages, which in turn have been identified as risk factors for adult sexual assault (Himelein, 1995; Koss, 1985). Another possible explanation for the relationship between early traumatic experiences and sexual assault risk is the intermediate role of psychological distress and behaviors used to reduce negative affect. A recent study suggested that levels of depression, anxiety, and hostility resulting from child sexual abuse was significantly related to the use of sexual activity as a strategy for reducing this dysphoria, which in turn significantly increased their vulnerability for adult sexual assault experiences (Orcutt, Cooper, & Garcia, in press). Therefore, the distress caused by exposure to early traumatic experiences may lead to maladaptive coping strategies that increase a woman's risk for sexual assault, such as contact with multiple sexual partners and impaired sexual decision making (Orcutt et al., in press).

Social-psychological characteristics have been commonly suggested as potential sources of risk for sexual victimization. Although there is some evidence supporting the role of assertiveness and social poise in protecting a woman from experiencing victimization, research has failed thus far in identifying any consistent personality profile that distinguishes rape survivors from nonvictims. Some characteristics that are frequently suggested as possible risk variables are a woman's attitudes and beliefs about violence, traditional views of femininity, and acceptance of rape myths. The social control theory posits that some women are socialized to be more accepting of violence, to submit to traditional passive female roles, and to believe in common rape myths, all of which increase their likelihood of being targeted by potential perpetrators (Koss & Dinero, 1989). Research thus far has failed to support this theory, however, with the majority of findings suggesting that there are no differences between nonvictims and sexual assault survivors on measures of sex-role stereotyping, acceptance of interpersonal violence, and adversarial sexual beliefs (Amick & Calhoun, 1987; Koss, 1985).

The third model, suggested by Koss and Dinero (1989), consists of various situational characteristics surrounding the assault itself and the possible role that these variables play in increasing a woman's risk for sexual assault. Studies aimed at understanding these risk factors have emphasized the possible influence of alcohol or substance use by both the survivor and perpetrator, location of the assault, dating behaviors, and frequency of sexual activity. Being in an isolated location with a potential acquaintance rapist has been considered a risk factor. As many as 75 percent of sexual assaults occur within private residences, with these experiences being approximately twice as likely to occur in the man's apartment (Miller & Marshall, 1987; Muehlenhard & Linton, 1987). The seclusion of these environments may reduce a woman's opportunity to escape the situation and successfully resist any unwanted sexual advances. The location may also influence the perceived justifiability of sexual aggression, as research suggests that both men and women believe that rape is more justified if a couple goes to the man's apartment (Muehlenhard, 1988). Other context-specific variables that influence people's perceptions of rape justifiability include the woman initiating the date and allowing the man to pay for all the dating expenses (Muehlenhard, 1988). These research findings imply that risk for victimization may increase in these dating contexts. However, it is important to note that while for some participants the perceived justifiability of rape increased in these dating situations, the vast majority of students (77.5 percent) surveyed indicated that rape was never justifiable under any circumstance.

Therefore, while women may benefit from increased awareness of how these dating behaviors may be misinterpreted by potential assailants, they do not represent negligent actions or behaviors that justify the sexual assault.

In an attempt to integrate the risk factors suggested by these three theoretical models, Koss and Dinero (1989) examined the combined influence of these variables on risk for sexual victimization in order to identify the best set of predictors or risk factors. Looking at fourteen variables hypothesized to increase a woman's vulnerability, findings suggested that taken together, only four of these variables were responsible for predicting a woman's odds of being raped at a rate greater than chance: a previous history of sexual abuse, sexual attitudes, alcohol use, and sexual activity. Thus, the strongest predictors seem to be related to sexual history and alcohol use.

Alcohol Use as a Risk Factor

Among all of these situational variables, alcohol and drug use seems to be the most well-supported and frequently documented risk factor for sexual victimization experiences. In a retrospective examination of risk factors for sexual assault, Muehlenhard and Linton (1987) found that mere use of alcohol or drugs was not related to sexual assault experiences; however, heavy usage was identified as a risk factor. Retrospective data support the finding that when women are intoxicated, men are most likely drinking as well. However, in assaults in which the victim was not drinking, the perpetrator had been drinking in only about half of the incidents. This finding is only a very basic illustration of the complexities inherent in the relationship between alcohol and sexual assault, and an in-depth delineation of the detailed research findings is beyond the scope of this chapter. However, several broad categories of knowledge concerning alcohol as a risk factor for sexual assault are worth attention. Due to the complexity intimated by previous research findings, a review by Abbey et al. (2002) suggested that alcohol use be examined as a risk factor falling into three categories of assault context: those in which the perpetrator was intoxicated, those in which both parties were intoxicated, and those in which neither was intoxicated.

Assaults in which both parties were using intoxicants (primarily alcohol, while some assaults involved alcohol with the use of additional substances) were more likely to find their genesis outside the home of either the perpetrator or the victim, and were less likely to involve a perpetrator who was an intimate partner than incidents in which only the man or neither party was drinking. Conversely, sexual assaults involving alcohol use were more likely to involve a perpetrator who was an acquaintance or casual date, and more likely to involve some time spent at a party or a bar. These incidents were also more likely to culminate in rape as opposed to sexual coercion.

Research detailing the association of "perpetrator-only" alcohol use with factors such as severity of assault and physical injury to the victim has found a strong correlation between amount of alcohol consumed by the perpetrator and the severity of assault. More recent findings suggest that this relationship is curvilinear. Perpetrators who have not consumed alcohol and those who have consumed heavy amounts of alcohol are less likely to complete a rape. Men who have not consumed alcohol may be more willing to comprehend and respond to a woman's resistance. Men who have been drinking heavily may not physiologically be able to complete the rape or overcome resistance. Interestingly though, research is consistent in finding a linear relationship between the quantity of alcohol the perpetrator consumed prior to the event and the amount of physical aggression used during the assault. The more men drink, the more violent the assault becomes. Victims of assaults involving only perpetrator use of alcohol are more likely to be low in sexual assertiveness and have higher rates of childhood sexual abuse. Additionally, they tend to experience higher rates of partner physical violence (than mutual use victims and nonvictims) and lower income levels.

An interesting twist to the alcohol-sexual assault link is the consideration of the bar environment itself. Is there something about being in a bar that makes women more vulnerable to assault? Researchers are beginning to think so. By interviewing and collecting data from women who frequent bars, researchers began to detect alarmingly high rates of experienced aggression. Approximately one-third of the women interviewed in one such study were victims of either attempted or completed rape. A follow-up study (Parks & Zetes-Zanatta, 1999) indicated that victimization was predicted by more frequent exposure to the bar environment but not by the actual amount of alcohol consumed by the woman or whether the consumption led to intoxication. This study suggests that context alone (including exposure to men who are drinking), independent of alcohol use at the time of assault, is related to an increased risk for sexual assault.

In addition to alcohol risk that is event related, research has linked lifetime (also referred to as global) use of alcohol with increased risk of sexual assault. For example, Testa, Livingston, Vanzile-Tamsen, and Frone (2003) found that adolescent history of alcohol and drug use predicted the subsequent occurrence of incapacitated rape. Although somewhat disparate in their findings, studies with populations of college women tend to find that higher levels of global alcohol use are associated with sexual victimization experiences. Within community samples of women, having been diagnosed with a substance use disorder is correlated with victimization.

Although the relationship between lifetime misuse of alcohol (and other substances) and sexual assault has been suggested, it is still unclear exactly how they are linked. Potential explanations may lie in the third variable. For example, global substance use and sexual victimization share similar historical risk factors (i.e., previous trauma, younger age, single relationship status). Additionally, high levels of substance use are associated with other high-risk behaviors and tendencies toward sensation seeking that make women more vulnerable to sexual assault (e.g., engaging in unprotected sex, high number of sexual partners). Finally, high levels of global use of alcohol increase women's risk for assault by increasing their likelihood of being in high-risk environments (e.g., bars) and their likelihood of using intoxicants at the time of the assault. Abbey, Ross, McDuffie, and McAuslan (1996) found that alcohol consumption during consensual sex was related to alcohol consumption at the time of sexual assault. In a study involving over 25,000 college-aged women, Mohler-Kuo, Dowdall, Koss, and Wechsler (2004) found that the ones who were involved in the use of illicit drugs, heavy drinking in high school, and attending colleges with high rates of episodic heavy drinking (binge drinking) were at a higher risk for being raped while intoxicated.

Why is alcohol a risk factor for sexual assault? What is it about intoxication that places women at greater risk for being assaulted? Several suggestions include cognitive and motor impairment, perceptions of drinking women, as well as the context in which drinking often places women.

Cognitive and motor impairment is sometimes discussed within the context of the alcohol myopia theory (Steele & Josephs, 1990). According to the alcohol myopia theory, intoxicated individuals are more likely to focus on situational cues that are the most salient in their environment to the exclusion of other potentially important cues. For example, when a woman is intoxicated within a social setting, the focus of her attention, according to the myopia theory, would be on various aspects of the social setting and socialization. Her attention would not likely be given to potential danger or assault cues, which would be inconsistent with the dominant focus of attention. Potential consequences of this myopic focus may include a decreased ability to register the meaning of facial expressions (particularly anger).

Because assaults involving an intoxicated woman often begin within social contexts, cognitive impairments, such as attention deficits, may also make it more difficult for women to enact an appropriate resistance strategy. Norris, Nurius, and Dimeff (1996) found that blood alcohol levels among college-aged women were inversely related to resistance strategies, both physical and verbal. Additionally, researchers have found that alcohol decreases response to displeasing stimuli (Stritzke, Patrick, & Lang, 1995), meaning that women who are intoxicated may be more likely to experience a blunted reaction to assault strategies.

This impairment in a woman's ability to resist sexual assault is often paired with others' perceptions of drinking women. Although, in general, research shows that men find women who drink heavily less attractive and are less likely to want to enter a relationship with a heavy drinker, men are also more likely to perceive these women as being more aroused, more sexual, and more likely to initiate intercourse. In a laboratory study (Abbey et al., 2002), trained observers rated intoxicated women as being more sexy, outgoing, sociable, friendly, expressive, talkative, relaxed, and humorous than low-dose participants. More applied research within a college population of males found that 75 percent of the sample admitted to getting a woman drunk or high as a means of increasing their chances of having sex with the woman (Mosher & Anderson, 1986).

It has become clear that heavy alcohol consumption and frequenting bars/clubs place women at an increased risk for assault. If drinking is such a risky activity for women to participate in, the question remains then, why do women drink? Several very basic explanations have been posited, including, but not limited to, alcohol expectancies, self-medication, and context/social pressure or support of behavior.

No one drinks expecting to be assaulted. As a matter of fact, it is quite the opposite. In addition to the amount of alcohol consumed, researchers often investigate the motivations behind the consumption of alcohol. One motivation is alcohol expectancy. Alcohol expectancies are, very basically, what one believes will happen to them following their consumption of alcohol. There is support for a relationship between a history of sexual victimization and a higher level of positive alcohol expectancies. For example, Corbin, Bernat, Calhoun, McNair, and Seals (2001) found that when compared with nonvictimized controls, women with a history of attempted or completed rape reported a greater degree of positive outcome expectancies that included a reduction in tension, sexual enhancement, and global positive changes. As such, women may not be expecting drinking to result in assault, but rather to produce these various positive outcomes.

The self-medication theory discussed previously is worth inclusion as a potential reason for continued and increased use of alcohol, despite its consistent identification as a risk factor. Again, according to this theory, women may consume alcohol as a means of coping with or numbing/avoiding unpleasant emotional affect.

Finally, context is an important factor to consider in a discussion of why women at greater risk for sexual assault may continue to drink. Specifically, drinking is a common occurrence in college populations of both men and women, both with and without a history of assaulting or being assaulted. Within this setting, parties and frequenting bars are fairly typical occurrences. Additionally, these environments contain several other positive reinforcements, such as socialization, relaxation, and the potential for meeting others with whom one may be interested in pursuing a relationship.

To conclude, several thoughts are important to keep in mind. Drinking and increased risk of sexual assault have been consistently linked with one another by researchers. Above and beyond the amount of alcohol consumed by the victim, several other important factors include drinking by the male perpetrator as well as exposure to the riskier environment of bars and parties. Although intoxication produces a range of effects that make it more difficult for women to detect and react to threat cues, there are a number of factors maintaining women's pattern of drinking despite their increased risk for assault. However, it is important to also note that this relationship between sexual assault and alcohol consumption does not mean that if women abstained from drinking, their risk for assault would disappear. There are potentially confounding factors that may better account for the occurrence of assault than consumption of alcohol. Future research hopes to more closely elucidate additional mechanisms for this relationship, both direct and indirect, as well as search for intervening factors that may moderate this relationship, reducing the risk of sexual assault for those women who drink.

Identification of risk factors has been an important step in research on sexual assault as it increases our understanding of how to take preventative action and educate women on how they can reduce their risk. However, it is important to emphasize that even the most conscientious efforts made by a woman to avoid engaging in any of these risky behaviors, such as alcohol use or increased sexual activity, cannot by itself guarantee that she will not experience a sexual assault in her lifetime. The ultimate responsibility for any victimization experience lies with the perpetrator, and although knowledge of risk factors can reduce prevalence rates, every sexual assault occurs under different circumstances and is precipitated by different events or behaviors, making all risk factors equally worthy of attention and consideration.

INTERVENTION AND PREVENTION

Primary Prevention

Although research on sexual victimization and our understanding of associated risk factors have steadily increased in recent years, rates of victimization continue to be distressingly high. Given the well-established and extensive range of negative consequences suffered by women in the aftermath of assault, the importance of directing attention toward prevention and risk-reduction efforts cannot be overemphasized. In order to eliminate or at least reduce the occurrence of sexual victimization, the most logical place to make an impact is with prevention programs aimed at potential perpetrators, as their actions ultimately determine whether an assault takes place. Programs aimed at male audiences typically involve components related to reducing rape-myth acceptance and increasing empathy for victims, and some recent programs have shown success at changing participants' attitudes toward rape (Foubert, 2000; O'Donohue, Yeater, & Fanetti, 2003). Although these attitudes are related to sexual aggression, there is still a lack of evidence for the success of these programs in changing actual behavior and reducing rates of sexual assault (Yeater & O'Donohue, 1999).

While the effectiveness of prevention programs targeting males remains in question, however, there is a more pressing need to educate women on rape statistics and potential risk factors so that they may begin to take steps on their own to reduce their vulnerability. Although sexual assault prevention programs have been widely implemented on college campuses, the effectiveness of these programs at producing lasting change and reducing prevalence has not been studied adequately. Most of these programs have emphasized attitudinal change through education and awareness of prevalence, rape myths, societal factors involved in promoting the occurrence of rape, and common risk factors and consequences of sexual victimization, and very few investigated whether program participation actually influenced subsequent victimization rates (Yeater & O'Donohue, 1999). In one of the first studies to evaluate the success of a prevention program in producing both an increase in protective dating behaviors and a decrease in rates of victimization, Hanson and Gidycz (1993) implemented a program for female college students that focused on awareness of rape myths, risk factors, and available strategies and precautionary behaviors associated with rape resistance. The program was successful not only in increasing knowledge about sexual assault and reducing risky dating behaviors, but also in reducing rates of sexual victimization for program participants in comparison to the control group. However, while these results appear promising, the success of this program was not universal, as the reduction in victimization experiences was only true for women without a previous history of victimization. For those women who had already experienced a sexual assault, this particular prevention failed to decrease their risk for future victimization. Subsequent modifications of this program have produced inconsistent findings regarding its effectiveness at reducing the incidence of sexual assault (Breitenbecher & Gidycz, 1998; Breitenbecher & Scarce, 1999). Evaluations of programs targeting mixed-gender audiences have also documented positive changes in attitudes toward rape, but the magnitude of this change was small and was unrelated to a reduction in victimization experiences (Gidycz et al., 2001; Pinzone-Glover, Gidycz, & Jacobs, 1998). More research is needed not only to identify the critical elements of these programs that contributed to their relative success, but also to identify ways to generalize their findings to women with a previous history of victimization and women in community and clinical populations. However, the original findings produced in the Hanson and Gidycz (1993) study are encouraging because they highlight the potential that women have to successfully reduce their risk for sexual assault. Because sexual victimization has such devastating costs to both women and society in general, prevention on this level is ideal, and although initial findings from these studies are limited, they suggest that with further research, this may be an attainable goal.

Prevention of Sexual Revictimization

Given the significant role of previous victimization as a risk factor for sexual assault, many researchers have emphasized the importance of targeting previous victims when designing prevention programs. Efforts to do this have been limited by the current inconsistencies in the literature on revictimization and the underlying mechanisms responsible for increasing a woman's risk for multiple assaults. Without an established theoretical basis or explanation for why this phenomenon occurs, the creation of successful prevention programs for revictimization remains a considerable challenge. Simply modifying empirically supported prevention programs so that they include information relevant for revictimization has failed to make an impact on prevalence rates, and in fact failed to reduce risk for nonvictims as well, contrary to previous findings (Breitenbecher & Gidycz, 1998; Breitenbecher & Scarce, 1999). More recent research, however, on a risk reduction program specifically designed to address the issue of revictimization, has resulted in reductions in prevalence rates following participation. This program consisted of two 2-hour sessions involving a presentation and discussion of sexual assault definitions, statistics, offender characteristics, risk factors, and common postassault reactions. In addition, the topics of how to recognize risk in dangerous situations, problem-solving skills, assertiveness, and communication skills were presented to program participants. Results of a pilot study with a brief follow-up (Marx et al., 2001) indicated that the women who completed the program demonstrated significantly lower rates of rape revictimization than the control group, and also indicated greater increases in self-efficacy. A large multisite study of this program replicated the original findings and extended them in a two-year follow-up (Calhoun et al., 2002). Thus, the program investigated by these two studies shows a great deal of potential for reducing rates of sexual assault among previously victimized women. Because of this population's increased risk for subsequent sexual assault experiences, the success of this program at reducing rates is a promising step toward understanding and preventing the phenomenon of revictimization.

Support Services

Although some of these recently developed early interventions for rape victims show potential for reducing the immediate and long-term distress experienced by women in the aftermath of an assault, the value of both formal and informal support in helping women cope with victimization cannot be overemphasized. For many years now, increased awareness and activism on behalf of rape survivors has led to the creation of more widely available support services in a variety of contexts that women may utilize as part of their healing process. Some of these formal community resources include the legal or criminal justice system, medical services, mental health professionals, and rape crisis centers, all of which offer varying types of support, information, and advocacy for victimized women. While every survivor must decide for herself which of these services to make use of during her recovery process, each of these resources can provide valuable support in helping women cope with a sexual assault experience.

The emergence of rape crisis centers nationwide has created a particularly important resource for sexually victimized women. In 2001, there were approximately 1,200 active organizations in the United States offering services such as a twenty-four-hour information and crisis hotline, counseling, and legal and medical advocacy for victims (Campbell & Martin, 2001). Rape crisis centers also play an important role in providing services to the entire community in the form of outreach programs designed to educate the public and increase awareness about the prevalence and consequences of sexual victimization (O'Sullivan & Carlton, 2001). The vast majority of women who seek support from rape crisis centers characterize their experience with these organizations as healing, and evaluations of center services indicate that they are effective at providing survivors with support, information, and assistance in making decisions (Campbell, Wasco, Ahrens, Sefl, & Barnes, 2001; Wasco et al., 2004). Despite the valuable programs offered by rape crisis centers, research suggests that their services are underutilized. Campbell et al. (2001) surveyed a community sample of adult rape survivors and found that only 21 percent had sought support services from a rape crisis center, and even more troubling, 91 percent of these women were Caucasian, indicating that ethnic minority women in particular are not taking advantage of the assistance offered by rape crisis centers. However, a recent study suggested that although few victims used rape crisis centers, for those who did, 94.2 percent rated them as being helpful, an approval rate that was higher than for any other source of support (Golding, Siegel, Sorenson, Burnam, & Stein, 1989). Thus, while rape crisis centers offer a number of important and effective services to survivors of sexual assault, women may not be adequately informed of the resources and advocacy they can provide.

Another support service available to sexual assault victims is the criminal justice system. If a survivor decides to report a sexual assault to the police, law enforcement agents may investigate the crime and identify the perpetrator after which a prosecutor may decide whether to press charges and potentially convict the perpetrator for his crime (Campbell, 1998). In addition, the criminal justice system is involved in victim compensation programs that vary by state and are designed to reimburse victims for costs incurred as a direct result of the crime, such as lost wages, medical expenses, and counseling (for information about these programs by state, contact the Office for Victims of Crime, www.ojp.usdoj.gov/ovc). Although seeking justice against sex offenders is undoubtedly a worthwhile endeavor, very few women report their rape to the police, and of those reported, only 12 percent result in a successful conviction (Frazier & Haney, 1996). While some women do have positive experiences working with the criminal justice system, the majority of survivors characterize their contact with the legal system as hurtful with outcomes that contradicted their wishes, particularly for victims who were raped by acquaintances without the presence of a weapon and who sustained few physical injuries (Campbell et al., 2001; Campbell, 1998). Thus, every survivor must decide for herself whether the legal process and associated complexities is something she would like to pursue as part of her healing process.

Finally, another important service provided to rape victims in the aftermath of an assault is medical care, usually provided through hospital emergency rooms. In addition to collection of forensic evidence, women who seek medical care are examined and treated for any physical injuries, tested for sexually transmitted diseases, and provided with information regarding risk for pregnancy and emergency contraception (Campbell, 1998). Vaginal and perianal trauma is indicated in approximately half of rape victims who seek medical care, and up to 30 percent of these women contract sexually transmitted diseases from their assault experience (Goodman, Koss, & Russo, 1993). Thus, even without severe physical injury, survivors should be encouraged to seek medical care in order to detect the presence of any health risks. Also, the medical exam conducted to collect forensic evidence can confirm a woman's report of nonconsensual activity if performed within seventy-two hours of an assault (Dunlap, Brazeau, Stermac, & Addison, 2004). Therefore, medical professionals have the opportunity to provide many valuable services to sexually assaulted women. As with the criminal justice system, very few women seek out medical care following a sexual assault (Golding et al., 1989; Campbell et al., 2001). However, the rates of reporting to medical professionals increased 60 percent between 1974 and 1991, particularly by women who were raped by acquaintances (Magid et al., 2004). Suggested reasons for this increase include changing attitudes toward acquaintance rape, increased media awareness, and improved community education about the nature and significant prevalence of acquaintance rape (Magid et al., 2004). While this increase in victims seeking medical care is encouraging, it appears that there are still barriers preventing some women from seeking medical care. Research suggests that women are most likely to seek support from medical professionals if they were raped by a stranger, and if they experienced severe injuries (Ullman & Filipas, 2001). In addition, for those victims who did seek out medical assistance, approximately one-third classified their experience as hurtful, with less than half of the victims receiving information on risk for pregnancy (49 percent), emergency contraception (43 percent), and information on sexually transmitted diseases (39 percent) or HIV risk (32 percent) (Campbell et al., 2001). Therefore, while there are many valuable and necessary services provided to victims by medical professionals, many women are not seeking out this type of care at all, and for those who do, many of their needs are still neglected in the process.

Because the physical and psychological consequences of a sexual assault can be so extensive, use of these formal support services and available resources may help considerably with the recovery process, but the trend across rape crisis centers, criminal justice workers, and medical professionals suggests that a large proportion of survivors are not taking advantage of the individual contributions these services can offer. In order to understand the barriers to women seeking support services, focus groups have been employed to interview sexually assaulted women about their reasons for not utilizing these available organizations (Logan, Evans, Stevenson, & Jordan, 2005). Across rural and urban communities, women identified such barriers as limited or costly services, lack of awareness about what services are available, encounters with service providers who lack education on sexual assault issues, shame and fear of blame from others, insensitive healthcare providers, community pressure to keep quiet about their victimization experience, and lack of control over legal and court processes (Logan et al., 2005). Whether these barriers are misperceptions or not, it is clear that education for women, service providers, and the general community is greatly needed to reduce the likelihood of these fears being realized by survivors who seek support services.

However, while it would appear that formal support services are not fully utilized by rape victims, it is clear that informal support seeking is much more prevalent among sexually assaulted women. Among self-identified sexual assault survivors, rates of support seeking from friends and relatives were as high as 94.2 percent, and using an epidemiological survey approach, rates of disclosure to friends and relatives were 59.3 percent (Golding et al., 1989; Ullman & Filipas, 2001). Therefore, while some women may not be fully benefiting from available community resources, they do seem to be more likely to seek support from friends and family members. In addition, women reporting to these informal support services seem to be receiving less negative social reactions, which are predictive of better adjustment (Ullman, 1996). A recent study suggested that on average, when women disclose sexual assault experiences to a friend, these friends do not blame the survivor and the disclosure can have a positive impact on their friendship (Ahrens & Campbell, 2000). However, when friends have strong feelings of ineffectiveness and emotional distress, this can actually have a negative impact on the relationship, and men in particular tend to be more likely to blame the survivor and have more feelings of confusion and ineffectiveness following a woman's disclosure of sexual assault (Ahrens & Campbell, 2000). Despite this potentially greater difficulty for male significant others to cope with the rape of a loved one, a recent study suggested that the most uniquely helpful response experienced by sexual assault survivors was emotional support from their romantic partner, indicating that male significant others can play an important role in helping a loved one through her recovery (Filipas & Ullman, 2001). Other reactions and forms of support endorsed by victims as being particularly helpful included emotional support from friends, tangible aid, having other survivors share their experience with them, having romantic partners and friends listen to them, experiencing validation and belief from others, and not being discouraged from talking about their assault (Filipas & Ullman, 2001). Because women are much more likely to disclose their sexual assault to friends, family members, and romantic partners, their reaction and involvement in helping the survivor cope is an essential ingredient throughout a woman's healing process (Koss & Harvey, 1991). Significant others should be encouraged to seek information and resources from formal support services such as rape crisis centers and mental health professionals, as well as publications and books that are available to educate loved ones on rape and how to best support the survivor (see McEvoy & Brookings, 1991).

Early Interventions for Rape Victims

Although reducing the incidence of sexual assault is the primary goal of prevention efforts, there is still a need for effective interventions for women who have already experienced a sexual assault. As previously described, the physical and psychological consequences experienced by rape victims are extensive and often debilitating, and initial levels of distress have been shown to be directly related to later outcome (Resick, 1993; Rothbaum, Foa, Riggs, Murdock, & Walsh, 1992). However, the individual reactions to sexual assault can be widely different, indicating that there may be protective factors involved in preventing some of the negative aftereffects of a victimization experience. With this in mind, research has begun to examine more closely the experiences of rape victims after their assault occurs in order to understand factors that may contribute to their symptomatology and find ways to reduce the impact of those variables. Foa, Hearst-Ikeda, and Perry (1995) created a brief intervention for rape victims involving four weekly sessions in the weeks immediately following an assault. These sessions incorporated cognitive-behavioral treatment approaches and were effective at reducing posttraumatic stress symptoms immediately following the intervention. Although participants in the intervention group displayed a more rapid reduction in distress than participants who did not receive the intervention, there were no differences between the groups at five and a half months postassault. Despite this short-lived advantage over participants who did not receive the intervention, however, this study indicates that women can significantly reduce their suffering in the immediate aftermath of an assault experience through these relatively brief intervention methods.

One experience thought to contribute to the trauma and distress of sexually victimized women is the forensic rape exam performed at hospitals following an assault. Although many hospitals have rape crisis counselors available to meet with victims, this experience is by nature an invasive procedure that can significantly increase anxiety and distress. A recent study on acute rape responses has introduced a video to be watched by survivors immediately preceding their forensic exam that discusses not only the process of what will happen during the exam, but also common reactions to sexual assault and strategies survivors may implement to reduce their anxiety and fear-related responses as they recover from their victimization experience (Resnick, Acierno, Holmes, Kilpatrick, & Jager, 1999). These preliminary findings are promising in that the video successfully created a reduction in distress during the exam, which was later connected with fewer PTSD symptoms at a six-week follow-up. Given the cost-efficiency and ease of implementation of such a video, the success of such an intervention is commendable. However, while interventions such as these may successfully reduce a woman's distress following a sexual assault, the degree of trauma experienced by rape victims in many cases requires more extensive and involved clinical treatment.

Treatment for Long-Term Posttraumatic Symptoms

Although a majority of women who experience sexual assault demonstrate an amazing level of resilience, an interpersonal trauma as severe as rape may lead to the development of posttraumatic symptoms that require long-term, intensive psychotherapy. As previously discussed, posttraumatic stress disorder (PTSD) is a clinical diagnosis that describes a cluster of symptoms one may continue to experience more than one month postassault. These symptom clusters include avoidance (particularly of reminders of the event or related cues and emotional numbing), reexperiencing (including flashbacks, nightmares, and reexperiencing of emotions of the event), and hypervigilance (which includes difficulty falling or staying asleep, outbursts of anger, difficulty concentrating). Should these symptoms persist, they can greatly interfere with a survivor's functioning and enjoyment of daily life.

Fortunately, treatments are available that are specifically tailored to address the symptoms that characterize posttraumatic reactions. A very brief overview of several of the available treatments for PTSD is presented here. While a broad spectrum of treatment approaches exists, this brief overview will focus on the treatments that have garnered empirical support through studies of treatment outcomes.

Most models of treatment with demonstrated efficacy consist of some combination of three main treatment modes. These modes are sometimes referred to as *exposure, anxiety management training*, and *cognitive therapy*. Various treatment packages may involve a unique combination of some or all of these components, with or without additional components. Some treatments may combine these typical "PTSD components" with treatment addressing potential comorbid conditions such as substance use or depression. It is important that the treatment plan match the needs of the individual and thus while common elements of effective treatments have been identified, treatment for PTSD may remain somewhat ideographic to meet the needs of each client (for a review of empirically supported treatments for PTSD, see Keane & Barlow, 2002).

Exposure therapy aims to reduce anxiety through exposure to the traumatic memory that is typically either *in vivo*, a reenactment of the actual event, or *imaginal*, using imagery to recall the traumatic event in detail. In addition to these more traditional methods, virtual reality technology is being applied to exposure treatment. Regardless of mode, the purpose of exposure is to reduce symptoms of avoidance while at the same time increasing a survivor's sense of mastery over a given experience and its memory. Exposures are most often conducted in a gradual manner. That is, the client progresses through her particular set of exposure situations in a way that allows her to progressively face more difficult (anxiety-producing) situations.

Anxiety management training aims to teach survivors an assortment of skills that will help them cope with and manage (as the name suggests) their anxiety and its symptoms. This form of treatment may include things such as anger management skills, relaxation training, trauma education, interpersonal skill training, job skills training, etc. While, in general, research has shown that this form of treatment alone is not as effective in the long term as exposure treatment, it has shown effectiveness and may be an especially beneficial addition to a treatment package that includes exposure.

Resick and Schnicke (1993) have developed a treatment for PTSD specifically geared toward survivors of rape. The treatment, called *cognitive processing therapy*, combines the third element, cognitive restructuring, with a form of exposure that involves writing about the traumatic event in graded levels of detail. The cognitive restructuring component provides a means of addressing potential distortions in thoughts about or resulting from the assault.

An additional avenue of assistance for survivors of assault suffering from PTSD is psychopharmacological intervention. While pharmacological treatments for PTSD are in somewhat earlier stages of development, treatment outcome studies have lent support to the use of selective serotonin reuptake inhibitors such as sertraline (Brady, Pearlstein, Asnis, Baker, Rothbaum, Sikes, et al., 2000). In most cases, these should be combined with psychotherapy.

Whatever the treatment option a survivor may choose to pursue, the most important point is that there are options. In order to become more informed of the options that may exist in any particular area, there are several worthwhile resources that are a good start for seeking out treatment. Some of these resources include state psychological associations, which will typically be able to provide a list of therapists and some brief description of the populations they serve. An additional potential resource for those seeking a treatment similar to the ones described above is the Association for Behavioral and Cognitive Therapies (www.aabt.org). This site has listings of member psychologists and other professionals around the country, many of whom specialize in the treatment of PTSD and other related problems, and may be a helpful starting point for those seeking treatment. Finally, for those living near a large research university, doctoral programs often operate training clinics, which may serve as a resource for further information and treatment.

Regardless of the services and resources a sexual assault survivor uses to best cope with her experience, it is clear that the reactions and quality of services provided by formal and informal support systems can impact the overall adjustment and well-being of survivors in the aftermath of an assault. As suggested by Koss and Harvey (1991), "together these reactions will define the victim's position relative to the larger society and will contribute to or detract from her sense of personal and social power. As these intersecting communities act or fail to act on her behalf, the woman raped literally will rebuild her sense of self" (p. 96).

REFERENCES

Abbey, A., Ross, L. T., McDuffie, D., & McAuslan, P. (1996). Alcohol and dating risk factors for sexual assault among college women. *Psychology of Women Quarterly, 20*(1), 147–169.

Abbey, A., Zawacki, T., Buck, P. O., Testa, M., Parks, K., Norris, J., et al. (2002). How does alcohol contribute to sexual assault? Explanations from laboratory and survey data. *Alcoholism: Clinical and Experimental Research, 26*(4), 575–581.

Ahrens, C. E., & Campbell, R. (2000). Assisting rape victims as they recover from rape: The impact on friends. *Journal of Interpersonal Violence, 15*(9), 959–986.

Amick, A. E., & Calhoun, K. S. (1987). Resistance to sexual aggression: Personality, attitudinal, and situational factors. *Archives of Sexual Behavior, 16*, 153–163.

Arata, C. M. (2002). Child sexual abuse and sexual revictimization. *Clinical Psychology: Science & Practice, 9*(2), 135–164.

Atkeson, B. M., Calhoun, K. S., Resick, P. A., & Ellis, E. M. (1982). Victims of rape: Repeated assessment of depressive symptoms. *Journal of Consulting and Clinical Psychology, 50*(1), 96–102.

Bandura, A. (1977). Self-efficacy: Toward a unifying theory of behavioral change. *Psychological Review, 84*, 191–215.

Basile, K. C., & Saltzman, L. E. (2002). *Sexual violence surveillance: Uniform definitions and recommended data elements.* Atlanta, GA: Centers for Disease Control and Prevention.

Brady, K., Pearlstein, T., Asnis, G. M., Baker, D., Rothbaum, B., Sikes, C. R., et al. (2000). Efficacy and safety of sertraline treatment of posttraumatic stress disorder: A randomized controlled trial. *Journal of the American Medical Association, 283*(14), 1837–1844.

Breitenbecher, K. H. (2001). Sexual revictimization among women: A review of the literature focusing on empirical investigations. *Aggression and Violent Behavior, 6*, 415–432.

Breitenbecher, K. H., & Gidycz, C. A. (1998). An empirical evaluation of a program designed to reduce the risk of multiple sexual victimization. *Journal of Interpersonal Violence, 13*, 472–488.

Breitenbecher, K. H., & Scarce, M. (1999). A longitudinal evaluation of the effectiveness of a sexual assault education program. *Journal of Interpersonal Violence, 14*, 459–478.

Burgess, A.W., & Holmstrom, L. L. (1974). Rape trauma syndrome. *American Journal of Psychiatry, 131*(9), 981–986.

Burgess, A. W., & Holmstrom, L. L. (1979). Rape: Sexual disruption and recovery. *American Journal of Orthopsychiatry, 49*(4), 648–657.

Burnam, M. A., Stein, J. A., & Golding, J. M. (1988). Sexual assault and mental disorders in a community population. *Journal of Consulting and Clinical Psychology, 56*(6), 843–850.

Calhoun, K. S., Atkeson, B. M., & Resick, P. A. (1982). A longitudinal examination of fear reactions in victims of rape. *Journal of Counseling Psychology, 29*(6), 655–661.

Calhoun, K. S., Gidycz, C. A., Wilson, A. E., Van Wynsberghe, A., Outman, R., Marioni, N., et al. (2002, November). *Long-term evaluation of a group risk reduction program for sexual revictimization.* Poster presented at the 36th Annual Meeting of the Association for Advancement of Behavior Therapy, Reno, NV.

Campbell, R. (1998). The community response to rape: Victims' experiences with the legal, medical, and mental health systems. *American Journal of Community Psychology, 26*, 355–379.

Campbell, R., & Martin, P. Y. (2001). Services for sexual assault survivors: The role of rape crisis centers. In C. M. Renzetti, J. L. Edleson, & R. K. Bergen (Eds.), *Sourcebook on violence against women* (pp. 227–241). Thousand Oaks, CA: Sage.

Campbell, R., Wasco, S. M., Ahrens, C. E., Sefl, T., & Barnes, H. E. (2001). Preventing the "second rape": Rape survivors' experiences with community service providers. *Journal of Interpersonal Violence, 16*, 1239–1259.

Classen, C., Field, N. P., Koopman, C., Nevill-Manning, K., & Spiegel, D. (2001). Interpersonal problems and their relationship to sexual revictimization among women sexually abused in childhood. *Journal of Interpersonal Violence, 16*, 495–509.

Cloitre, M., Scarvalone, P., & Difede, J. (1997). Posttraumatic stress disorder, self and interpersonal dysfunction among sexually retraumatized women. *Journal of Traumatic Stress Disorder, 10*, 437–452.

Corbin, W. R., Bernat, J. A., Calhoun, K. S., McNair, L. D., & Seals, K. L. (2001). The role of alcohol expectancies and alcohol consumption among sexually victimized and nonvictimized college women. *Journal of Interpersonal Violence, 16*(4), 297–311.

Crowell, N. A., & Burgess, A. W. (Ed.). (1996). *Understanding violence against women.* National Research Council, Commission on Behavioral & Social Sciences & Education. Washington, DC: National Academy Press.

Cue, K. L., George, W. H., & Norris, J. (1996). Women's appraisals of sexual-assault risk in dating situations. *Psychology of Women Quarterly, 20*, 487–504.

Dunlap, H., Brazeau, P., Stermac, L., & Addison, M. (2004). Acute forensic medical procedures used following a sexual assault among treatment-seeking women. *Women and Health, 40*, 53–65.

Ellis, E. M., Atkeson, B. M., & Calhoun, K. S. (1982). An examination of differences between multiple- and single-incident victims of sexual assault. *Journal of Abnormal Psychology, 91*, 221–224.

Filipas, H. H., & Ullman, S. E. (2001). Social reactions to sexual assault victims from various support sources. *Violence and Victims, 16*, 673–692.

Finkelhor, D., & Browne, A. (1985). The traumatic impact of child sexual abuse: A conceptualization. *American Journal of Orthopsychiatry, 55*, 530–541.

Foa, E. B., Hearst-Ikeda, D., & Perry, K. J. (1995). Evaluation of a brief cognitive-behavioral program for the prevention of chronic PTSD in recent assault victims. *Journal of Consulting and Clinical Psychology, 63*, 948–955.

Foubert, J. D. (2000). The longitudinal effects of a rape-prevention program on fraternity men's attitudes, behavioral intent, and behavior. *Journal of American College Health, 48*, 158–163.

Frazier, P. A., & Haney, B. (1996). Sexual assault cases in the legal system: Police, prosecutor, and victim perspectives. *Law and Human Behavior, 20*(6), 607–628.

Gidycz, C. A., Coble, C. N., Latham, L., & Layman, M. J. (1993). Sexual assault experience in adulthood and prior victimization experiences: A prospective analysis. *Psychology of Women Quarterly, 17*, 151–168.

Gidycz, C. A., Hanson, K., & Layman, M. J. (1995). A prospective analysis of the relationships among sexual assault experiences. *Psychology of Women Quarterly, 19*, 5–29.

Gidycz, C. A., Layman, M. J., Crothers, M., Gylys, J., Matorin, A., & Dowdall, C. (1997, May). *An evaluation of an acquaintance rape prevention program: Impact on attitudes and behavior.* Paper presented at the meeting of the Midwestern Psychological Association, Chicago, IL.

Gidycz, C. A., Layman, M. J., Rich, C. L., Crothers, M., Gylys, J., Matorin, A., et al. (2001). An evaluation of an acquaintance rape prevention program: Impact on attitudes, sexual aggression, and sexual victimization. *Journal of Interpersonal Violence, 16*, 1120–1138.

Golding, J. M., Cooper, M. L., & George, L. K. (1997). Sexual assault and health perceptions: Seven general population studies. *Health Psychology, 16*(5), 417–425.

Golding, J. M., Siegel, J. M., Sorenson, S. B., Burnam, M. A., & Stein, J. A. (1989). Social support sources following sexual assault. *Journal of Community Psychology, 17*, 92–107.

Goodman, L. A., Koss, M. P., & Russo, N. F. (1993). Violence against women: Mental health effects: Part II. Conceptualizations of posttraumatic stress. *Applied and Preventive Psychology, 2*(3), 123–130.

Greene, D. M., & Navarro, R. L. (1998). Situation-specific assertiveness in the epidemiology of sexual victimization among university women: A prospective path analysis. *Psychology of Women Quarterly, 22*, 589–604.

Hanson, K. A., & Gidycz, C. A. (1993). Evaluation of a sexual assault prevention program. *Journal of Consulting and Clinical Psychology, 61*, 1046–1052.

Himelein, M. J. (1995). Risk factors for sexual victimization in dating: A longitudinal study of college women. *Psychology of Women Quarterly, 19*, 31–48.

Jewkes, R., Sen, P., & Garcia-Moreno, C. (2002). Sexual violence. In E. G. Krug, L. L. Dahlberg, J. A. Mercy, A. B. Zwi, & R. Lozano (Eds.), *World report on violence and health* (pp. 149–181). Geneva, Switzerland: World Health Organization.

Keane, T. M., & Barlow, D. H. (2002). Posttraumatic stress disorder. In D. H. Barlow (Ed.), *Anxiety and its disorders: The nature and treatment of anxiety and panic* (2nd ed., pp. 418–453). New York: Guilford Press.

Kilpatrick, D. G. (2004). What is violence against women? Defining and measuring the problem. *Journal of Interpersonal Violence, 19*(11), 1209–1234.

Kilpatrick, D. G., Edmunds, C., & Seymour, A. (1992). *Rape in America: A report to the nation*. Charleston: Medical University of South Carolina, National Victims Center & the Crime Victims Research and Treatment Center.

Koss, M. P. (1985). The hidden rape victim: Personality, attitudinal, and situational characteristics. *Psychology of Women Quarterly, 9*, 193–212.

Koss, M. P. (1992). The underdetection of rape: Methodological choices influence incidence estimates. *Journal of Social Issues, 48*, 61–75.

Koss, M. P., Bailey, J. A., & Yuan, N. P. (2003). Depression and PTSD in survivors of male violence: Research and training initiatives to facilitate recovery. *Psychology of Women Quarterly, 27*(2), 130–142.

Koss, M. P., & Dinero, T. E. (1989). Discriminant analysis of risk factors for sexual victimization among a national sample of college women. *Journal of Consulting and Clinical Psychology, 57*, 242–250.

Koss, M. P., Dinero, T. E., Seibel, C. A., & Cox, S. L. (1988). Stranger and acquaintance rape: Are there differences in the victim's experience? *Psychology of Women Quarterly, 12*(1), 1–24.

Koss, M. P., & Harvey, M. R. (1991). *The rape victim: Clinical and community interventions*. Newbury Park, CA: Sage.

Koss, M. P., & Heslet, L. (1992). Somatic consequences of violence against women. *Archives of Family Medicine, 1*, 53–59.

Levenson, R. W., Oyama, O. N., & Meek, P. S. (1987). Greater reinforcement from alcohol for those at risk: Parental risk, personality risk, and sex. *Journal of Abnormal Psychology, 96*, 242–253.

Logan, T. K., Evans, L., Stevenson, E., Jordan, C. E. (2005). Barriers to services for rural and urban survivors of rape. *Journal of Interpersonal Violence, 20*, 591–616.

Magid, D. J., Houry, D., Koepsell, T. D., Ziller, A., Soules, M. R., Jenny, C. (2004). The epidemiology of female rape victims who seek immediate medical care: Temporal trends in the incidence of sexual assault and acquaintance rape. *Journal of Interpersonal Violence, 19*, 3–12.

Mandoki, C. A., & Burkhart, B. R. (1989). Sexual victimization: Is there a vicious cycle? *Violence and Victims, 4*, 179–190.

Marx, B. P., Calhoun, K. S., Wilson, A. E., & Meyerson, L. A. (2001). Sexual revictimization prevention: An outcome evaluation. *Journal of Consulting and Clinical Psychology, 69*, 25–32.

McEvoy, A. W., & Brookings, J. B. (1991). *If she is raped: A guidebook for husbands, fathers, and male friends* (2nd ed.). Holmes Beach, FL: Learning.

Messman, T. L., & Long, P. J. (1996). Child sexual abuse and its relationship to revictimization in adult women: A review. *Clinical Psychology Review, 16*, 397–420.

Messman-Moore, T. L., & Brown, A. L. (in press). Risk perception, rape and sexual revictimization: A prospective study of college women. *Psychology of Women Quarterly*.

Messman-Moore, T. L., & Long, P. J. (2000). Child sexual abuse and revictimization in the form of adult sexual abuse, adult physical abuse, and adult psychological maltreatment. *Journal of Interpersonal Violence, 15*(5), 489–502.

Messman-Moore, T. L., Long, P. J., & Siegfried, N. J. (2000). The revictimization of child sexual abuse survivors: An examination of the adjustment of college women with child sexual abuse, adult sexual abuse, and adult physical abuse. *Child Maltreatment, 5*, 18–27.

Miller, B., & Marshall, J. C. (1987). Coercive sex on the university campus. *Journal of College Student Personnel, 28*, 38–47.

Miranda, R., Mironda, R., Meyerson, L. A., Long, P. J., Marx, B. P., & Simpson, S. M. (2002). Sexual assault and alcohol use: Exploring the self-medication hypothesis. *Violence and Victims, 17*(2), 205–217.

Mohler-Kuo, M., Dowdall, G. W., Koss, M. P., & Wechsler, H. (2004). Correlates of rape while intoxicated in a national sample of college women. *Journal of Studies on Alcohol, 65*(1), 37–45.

Mosher, D. L., & Anderson, R. D. (1986). Macho personality, sexual aggression, and reactions to guided imagery of realistic rape. *Journal of Research in Personality, 20*(1), 77–94.

Muehlenhard, C. L. (1988). Misinterpreted dating behaviors and the risk of date rape. *Journal of Social and Clinical Psychology, 6*, 20–37.

Muehlenhard, C. L., & Linton, M. A. (1987). Date rape and sexual aggression in dating situations: Incidence and risk factors. *Journal of Counseling Psychology, 34*(2), 186–196.

Norris, J., Nurius, P., & Dimeff, L. (1996). Through her eyes: Factors affecting women's perception of and resistance to acquaintance sexual aggression threat. *Psychology of Women Quarterly, 20*, 123–145.

O'Donohue, W., Yeater, E. A., & Fanetti, M. (2003). Rape prevention with college males: The roles of rape myth acceptance, victim empathy, and outcome expectancies. *Journal of Interpersonal Violence, 18*, 513–531.

Orcutt, H. K., Cooper, M. L., & Garcia, M. (in press). Use of sexual intercourse to reduce negative affect as a prospective mediator of sexual revictimization. *Journal of Traumatic Stress*.

O'Sullivan, E., & Carlton, A. (2001). Victim services, community outreach, and contemporary rape crisis centers: A comparison of independent and multiservice centers. *Journal of Interpersonal Violence, 16*, 343–360.

Parks, K. A., & Zetes-Zanatta, L. M. (1999). Women's bar-related victimization: Refining and testing a conceptual model. *Aggressive Behavior, 25*(5), 349–364.

Pinzone-Glover, H. A., Gidycz, C. A., & Jacobs, C. D. (1998). An acquaintance rape prevention program: Effects on attitudes toward women, rape-related attitudes, and perceptions of rape scenarios. *Psychology of Women Quarterly, 22*, 605–621.

Rantala, R. (2000). *Effects of NIBRS on crime statistics* (Special Report, NCJ 178890). Washington, DC: U.S. Department of Justice, Office of Justice Programs, Bureau of Justice Statistics.

Resick, P. A. (1993). The psychological impact of rape. *Journal of Interpersonal Violence, 8*, 223–255.

Resick, P. A., & Schnicke, M. K. (1993). *Cognitive processing therapy for rape victims: A treatment manual.* Thousand Oaks, CA: Sage.

Resnick, H., Acierno, R., Holmes, M., Kilpatrick, D. G., & Jager, N. (1999). Prevention of post-rape psychopathology: Preliminary finding of a controlled acute rape treatment study. *Journal of Anxiety Disorders, 13*(4), 359–370.

Rothbaum, B. O., Foa, E. B., Riggs, D. S., Murdock, T., & Walsh, W. (1992). A prospective examination of post-traumatic stress disorder in rape victims. *Journal of Traumatic Stress, 5*, 455–475.

Sorenson, S. B., Stein, J. A., Siegel, J. M., Golding, J. M., & Burnham, M. A. (1987). The prevalence of adult sexual assault: The Los Angeles Epidemiologic Catchment Area Project. *American Journal of Epidemiology, 126*, 1154–1164.

Steele, C. M., & Josephs, R. A. (1990). Alcohol myopia: Its prized and dangerous effects. *American Psychologist, 45*(8), 921–933.

Stritzke, W. G. K., Patrick, C. J., & Lang, A. R. (1995). Alcohol and human emotion: A multidimensional analysis incorporating startle-probe methodology. *Journal of Abnormal Psychology, 104*(1), 114–122.

Testa, M., Livingston, J. A., Vanzile-Tamsen, C., & Frone, M. R. (2003). The role of women's substance use in vulnerability to forcible and incapacitated rape. *Journal of Studies on Alcohol, 64*(6), 756–764.

Tjaden, P., & Thoennes, N. (2000). Prevalence and consequences of male-to-female and female-to-male intimate partner violence as measured by the National Violence Against Women Survey. *Violence Against Women, 6*(2), 142–161.

Ullman, S. E. (1996). Correlates and consequences of adult sexual assault disclosure. *Journal of Interpersonal Violence, 11*, 554–571.

Ullman, S. E., & Filipas, H. H. (2001). Correlates of formal and informal support seeking in sexual assault victims. *Journal of Interpersonal Violence, 16*, 1028–1047.

Wasco, S. M., Campbell, R., Howard, A., Mason, G. E., Staggs, S. L., Schewe, P. A., et al. (2004). A statewide evaluation of services provided to rape survivors. *Journal of Interpersonal Violence, 19*, 252–263.

White, J. W., & Humphrey, J. A. (1997). A longitudinal approach to the study of sexual assault: Theoretical and methodological considerations. In M. Schwartz (Ed.), *Researching sexual violence against women: Methodological and personal perspectives* (pp. 22–42). Thousand Oaks, CA: Sage.

Wilson, A. E., Calhoun, K. S., & Bernat, J. A. (1999). Risk recognition and trauma–related symptoms among sexually revictimized women. *Journal of Consulting and Clinical Psychology, 67*, 705–710.

Yeater, E. A., & O'Donohue, W. (1999). Sexual assault prevention programs: Current issues, future directions, and the potential efficacy of interventions with women. *Clinical Psychology Review, 19*, 739–771.

6

Incest Victims and Offenders

Rita Kenyon-Jump ◆

Incest, the sexual exploitation of a child by a family member, is socially ab-horred, yet occurs far too frequently and is clearly linked to psychopathology and social dysfunction in children, adolescents, and adults. What follows is a review of the research on incest, including the most widely accepted defini-tion, prevalence data, (the number of cases found in a population at a given time), descriptions of the characteristics of both survivor and offender, the psychological effects (problems or disorders) that result from experiencing childhood sexual abuse by a family member, and effective treatments to assist survivors of childhood sexual trauma in reclaiming their lives. I have attempted to cover the effects of incest on male and female survivors at various devel-opmental stages, such as during childhood, adolescence, and adulthood as well as in different victim–perpetrator relationships, such as mother–son incest, father–daughter incest, and with extended family members. I have also pro-vided current thinking into male and female juvenile and adult incest of-fenders.

Much of the research on childhood sexual abuse combines intrafamilial (immediate and extended family members) and extrafamilial (acquaintances and strangers) child sexual abuse victims into one sexually abused group, and typically they are compared with a group of persons who have not experienced sexual abuse. Studies will report the percentage of incest and nonfamilial sexually abused participants in the sexual abuse group but use the combined group for the statistical comparisons. This makes it more difficult to determine the differences and similarities between people who have experienced incest and those who have experienced sexual abuse by nonfamily members. When possible, I have delineated the effects of childhood sexual abuse specifically attributed to intrafamilial abuse.

DEFINITION AND PREVALENCE

Three types of populations are typically studied in research on childhood sexual abuse: community samples, clinical samples, and college student samples, and the bulk of the research is retrospective, meaning that the participants in the research are being asked to remember details from their past; thus, the data are not always as accurate as they might be if it was gathered at the time of the abuse. Information regarding incidence of reported childhood sexual assault is also gleaned from law enforcement data banks, such as the National Incident-Based Reporting System (NIBRS) operated through the U.S. Department of Justice, Bureau of Justice Statistics. Although it is widely accepted that cases of child sexual abuse reported to law enforcement agencies represent only a small fraction of the total number of childhood sexual abuse victims, such information can still be valuable. Recent data from NIBRS reveal that almost half (49 percent) of all child sexual assault victims under the age of 6 were assaulted by family members—51 percent of female victims and 42 percent of male victims (U.S. Department of Justice, 2000). The percentage of those experiencing incest among reported child victims of sexual assault decreases somewhat for both males and females as the children age, with 44 percent of female victims and 38 percent of male victims in the age range of 6–11 years and 24 percent of both male and female victims aged 12–17 being victims of incest (U.S. Department of Justice, 2000).

Diana Russell (1986) conducted the seminal prevalence study of incest with a probability sample of 930 women in the San Francisco area. She defined incest as any kind of exploitive sexual contact or attempted contact that occurred between relatives, no matter how distant the relationship, whether they were blood relatives or not, before the victim turned 18 years old. The relative with whom the respondent had sexual or attempted sexual contact had to be five years or more older than the respondent or, if the offending relative was less than five years older, the experience was considered abusive if there was evidence that it was unwanted, if the relative initiated the contact, and if it caused the respondent some degree of distress or some long-term effects. The other most cited research on child sexual abuse was Finkelhor's (1979) study of 530 female college students. His research addressed both intrafamilial and extrafamilial childhood sexual abuse, and his definition of incest was not limited to sexual contact but also included sexual propositions and exhibition.

Finkelhor (1979) reported that 10 percent of the women in his sample were sexually abused by a relative and when no age limit was applied the prevalence increased to 20 percent. Russell (1986) reported that 16 percent of her sample identified at least one experience of incestuous abuse, and 12 percent of these women had been sexually abused by a relative before reaching the age of 14.

A more recent retrospective survey involving over 8,000 non-institutionalized civilian men and women between the ages of 15 and 54 years from all forty-eight contiguous states indicated that the prevalence for child-hood sexual abuse (defined as rape and molestation), combining both in-trafamilial (relatives and steprelatives) and extrafamilial (acquaintances and strangers) abuse, was 13.5 percent for females and 2.5 percent for males. For intrafamilial rape or molestation the prevalence for females was 7.6 percent and for males 0.8 percent (Molnar, Buka, & Kessler, 2001). Briere and Elliott (2003) found that 32.3 percent of the female and 14.2 percent of the male participants in a national, geographically stratified, random sample of adults reported having experienced childhood sexual abuse and, of that sample, 46.8 percent had been sexually abused within their immediate or extended family. All of these statistics reveal a consistent and significant number of victims of childhood sexual abuse over a period of many years.

FAMILY ENVIRONMENT

There have been conflicting reports of the independent effects of family environment and childhood sexual abuse in predicting long-term negative outcomes for males and females who were sexually abused in childhood. Some report that the childhood family environment rather than the abuse is re-sponsible for the psychological difficulty that survivors of childhood trauma exhibit (Beitchman et al., 1992; Flemming, Mullen, Sibthorpe, & Bammer, 1999; Merrill, Thomsen, Sinclair, Gold, & Milner, 2001; Peters, 1988, cited in Fassler, Amodeo, Griffin, Clay, & Ellis, 2005), while others assert that child-hood sexual abuse has been linked to multiple short- and long-term psycho-logical problems both in child and adult survivors of childhood sexual abuse and has been associated with psychiatric disorders whether or not the abuse is part of a larger collection of family adversities (Dinwiddie et al., 2000; Fassler et al., 2005; Kendler et al., 2000; Molnar, Buka, & Kessler, 2001; Mullen, Martin, Anderson, Romans, & Herbison, 1996; Nelson et al., 2002; Peleikis, Mykletun, & Dahl, 2004; Stevenson, 1999; Weiss, Longhurst, & Mazure, 1999). Rind, Tromovitch, and Bauserman (1998) indicated in their meta-analysis of child sexual abuse studies using college samples that the family background risk factors predicted more risk for adult psychological distress than did child sexual abuse in the college student population. They also suggested that in clinical samples with a higher proportion of persons with intrafamilial childhood sexual abuse, the experience of childhood sexual abuse may be more of a predictor than the family background. Thus, it may be in the case of incest that sexual abuse is the significant risk factor.

PSYCHOLOGICAL EFFECTS OF INCESTUOUS ABUSE

Sexual abuse by a family member is associated with more psychological distress and social adjustment symptoms than extrafamilial childhood abuse (Browne & Finkelhor, 1986; Finkelhor, 1979; Herman, Russell, & Trocki, 1986; Jackson, Calhoun, Amick, Maddever, & Habif, 1990; Kelly, Wood, Gonzalez, MacDonald, & Waterman, 2002; Ketring & Feinauer, 1999; Molnar, Buka, & Kessler, 2001; Russell, 1986; Tsai, Feldman-Summers, & Edgar, 1979; Wind & Silvern, 1992). When comparing female victims of childhood sexual abuse, father–daughter incest is the most psychologically damaging sexually abusive relationship (Finkelhor,1979; Russell, 1986) and when both male and female intrafamilial sexual abuse victims are studied, those abused by their fathers also scored significantly higher on symptoms related to dissociation, anxiety, depression, postsexual abuse trauma, and sleep disturbance than males and females abused by acquaintances, strangers, and other family members (Ketring & Feinauer, 1999). Perpetration by a father/father figure produced significantly higher mean trauma scores even when controlling for the severity of the sexual trauma. In addition, abuse by other family members resulted in significantly more negative symptoms than that experienced by persons who were sexually abused by strangers (Ketring & Feinauer, 1999).

Younger children are more likely to be abused by family members (Fischer & McDonald, 1998) and sexual abuse at a young age, before 7–8 years of age, has been associated with more psychological disturbance (Nash, Zivney, & Hulsey, 1993) and more physical injury (Fischer & McDonald, 1998). Intrafamilial sexual trauma is typically repetitive and of a longer duration than abuse by nonfamily members (Cole & Putnam, 1992; Fischer & McDonald, 1998; Ruggiero, McLeer, & Dixon, 2000). Duration of the abuse has been found to be associated with poorer adjustment in adulthood (Bennett, Hughes, & Luke, 2000; Rodriguez, Vande Kemp, & Foy, 1998). Internalization of the abuse (i.e., attributing self-blame) is correlated with duration of abuse and has been found to explain more of the adulthood maladjustment of childhood sexual abuse survivors than duration of the abuse, relationship to the offender, or age of onset of the abuse (Steel, Sanna, Hammond, Whipple, & Cross, 2004).

There is a longer delay in disclosure of abuse in incest, with more coercion to keep the abuse a secret and greater fear of what will happen to the family if the sexual abuse is revealed (Fischer & McDonald, 1998; Kogan, 2004; Lawson, 1993; Russell, 1986; Sheinberg & Fraenkel, 2001). The more closely related the sexually victimized child is to the perpetrator, the less likely that the child will disclose the abuse (Wyatt & Newcomb, 1990). The younger the child is when disclosing incest, the more likely she will receive a negative reaction whether she discloses to a parent or friend (Roesler & Wind, 1994) and the less likely that the sexual assault will result in an arrest (U.S. Department of Justice, 2000). In fact, over half of a sample of female incest survivors reported that their parent either ignored the disclosure, responded with anger, or blamed the victim (Roesler & Wind, 1994). Mothers with a history of childhood sexual trauma display more distress than mothers who have not been sexually abused when their children disclose sexual abuse (Deblinger, Stauffer, & Landsberg, 1994). Mothers have been found to be most supportive of their children upon disclosure of incest when the perpetrator is an ex-spouse (Everson, Hunter, Runyon, Edelsohn, & Coulter, 1989), biological father, uncle, cousin, or grandfather (Sirles & Franke, 1989) and least supportive when a current, unmarried partner (Everson et al., 1989; Sirles & Franke, 1989) or stepfather (Sirles & Franke, 1989) is the offender. Telling of the abuse will not ensure that the abuse will stop. In a retrospective survey of 228 female survivors of incest, the abuse continued for at least a year for over half of the respondents who had disclosed their abuse prior to age 18, and in over a fourth of the cases, the abuse did not stop for over a year following the disclosure (Roesler & Wind, 1994).

Intrusiveness (i.e., anal, vaginal, oral penetration) of the sexual abuse does not differ between groups of children abused by family members or nonfamily members; both groups of children experience force and penetration (Hall, Mathews, & Pearce, 2002).

Child and Adolescent Survivors of Incest

Children who have experienced incest engage in more sexualized behavior, such as touching sex parts in public, asking others to engage in sexual behavior, and touching another child's private parts. They also exhibit more self-stimulating behaviors than children molested by nonfamily members, with male victims of sexual abuse displaying significantly more sexualized behavior than females (Estes & Tidwell, 2002). Younger children are more likely to engage in self-stimulating behaviors than are older children, and younger males are more likely to do so than younger females (Estes & Tidwell, 2002). Sexualized behavior and posttraumatic stress are the two most common problematic consequences of sexual abuse during childhood (Kendall-Tackett, Williams, & Finkelhor, 1993).

Male and female preschool children who have been sexually abused are likely to experience emotional distress, sexualized behavior, sleep problems, bedwetting, sadness, and regression to an earlier developmental level (Fontella, Harrington, & Zuravin, 2000).

A lower level of functioning is associated with an older age of onset of abuse, greater frequency and longer duration of sexual abuse, and disclosure first to someone other than the victim's mother (Ruggiero et al., 2000). Ruggiero et al. (2000) indicated that the children in the study who were abused by stepfathers and fathers had higher global functioning and fewer symptoms of avoidant behavior. Their finding was opposite of those who report that abuse by fathers and stepfathers is the most damaging (Finkelhor, 1979; Ketring & Feinauer, 1999; Russell, 1986). A possible explanation of this could be that they included adult relatives other than fathers and stepfathers in their extrafamilial group and did not define if the perpetrator children in the extrafamilial group were related to the offended children. Including family members may have lowered the functioning of the extrafamilial group.

Adolescents are at particular risk for developing psychological problems as a result of sexual abuse (Feiring, Taska, & Lewis, 1999). Peer interaction is crucial for normal adolescent development, and the secrecy of sexual abuse, especially incestuous abuse, can isolate an adolescent from his/her peer group (Marvasti & Dripchak, 2004a; O'Brien, 1987; Schultz, 1990). Adolescence is also a time for developing one's identity, including a sexual identity. It is confusing for young girls to view themselves as their own age when they have been forced to engage in activities intended for adults (Sheinberg & Fraenkel, 2001). Girls, more so than boys, experience increased personal vulnerability and perceive the world as a dangerous place (Feiring et al., 1999). Male and female adolescents with histories of sexual abuse report more distress than adolescents who have not experienced sexual abuse, with sexually abused female adolescents more likely to experience depression than sexually abused male adolescents (Meyerson, Long, Miranda, & Marx, 2002). Both male and female sexually abused adolescents report more symptoms of depression and hopelessness than similar adolescents without histories of sexual trauma (Martin, Bergen, Richardson, Roeger, & Allison, 2004). Sexually abused girls with severe family conflict experience higher levels of depression (Meyerson et al., 2002). Incest prior to the age of 14 significantly increases the risk of a lifetime incidence of major depression (Pribor & Dinwiddie, 1992).

Adolescent male and female sexual abuse victims are more likely to think about suicide, make suicidal threats or attempts, or deliberately self-injure than their nonabused counterparts. However, boys who experienced sexual abuse respond more negatively than girls (Martin et al., 2004; Molnar, Berkman, & Buka, 2001; Ystgaard, Hestetun, Loeb, & Mehlum, 2004). They have a tenfold increased risk of making suicidal plans and threats and a fifteenfold increased risk of attempting suicide compared to nonabused males, even after controlling for symptoms of depression, hopelessness, and family functioning. In abused girls, depression, hopelessness, and poorer family functioning make it more likely that they will become suicidal (Martin et al., 2004). High levels of distress related to the sexual trauma are strongly associated with suicidal ideas and plans in both male and female adolescents (Martin et al., 2004). Males with low levels of distress are also likely to make suicidal threats while those with high levels of distress will deliberately harm themselves in addition to making threats (Martin et al., 2004).

Sexually and physically abused adolescent boys and girls are more likely to use alcohol and other drugs at a young age, including a greater variety of substances, and engage in more frequent attempts to "self-medicate painful emotions" than are nonabused adolescents (Harrison, Fulkerson, & Beebe, 1997, p. 536). In a sample of 122,824 public school sixth, ninth, and twelfth grade students in Minnesota, 25.6 percent of the female students and 6.8 percent of the male students endorsed having experienced sexual abuse either by an older family member or an older nonfamily member; of this group of sexually abused adolescents, 64 percent of the males and 46 percent of the females who reported intrafamilial sexual abuse also reported extrafamilial sexual abuse (Harrison et al., 1997). Substance use and abuse is especially problematic for adolescents, as it interferes with the development of appropriate coping skills and negatively impacts social and academic functioning (Harrison et al., 1997).

Childhood sexual abuse during adolescence increases the risk for later sexual victimization (Ryan, Kilmer, Cauce, Wantanabe, & Hoyt, 2000) and is strongly associated with attempted suicide in homeless adolescents (Feitel, Margetson, Chamas, & Lipman, 1992; Ryan et al., 2000) and with high levels of depression and anxiety in adolescents (Meyerson et al., 2002; Ryan et al., 2000). Adolescent male victims of sexual abuse have a higher risk of suicidal ideation, sexual risk-taking, substance abuse, delinquency, and eating disorders than adolescent males without a history of sexual abuse (Chandy, Blum, & Resnick, 1999). Male and female high school students with a history of childhood sexual victimization engage in high-risk sexual behaviors, such as having consensual intercourse before age 15, having two or more sexual partners in the previous three months, and sex resulting in pregnancy. The risk of multiple partners, substance use at last intercourse, and sex resulting in pregnancy is four to five times greater for high school boys who experienced sexual abuse compared with boys with no such history (Raj, Silverman, & Amaro, 2000). High school-aged girls who experienced childhood sexual abuse are twice as likely to have early intercourse, three or more sex partners ever, and to become pregnant than are girls who have not experienced sexual abuse during their childhood (Raj et al., 2000).

Adolescents who have a history of childhood sexual abuse are at an increased risk of eating disorders as well (Chandy et al., 1997; Neumark-Sztainer, Story, Hannan, Beauhring, & Resnick, 2000). Those who experienced incest are significantly more likely than adolescents who have not been sexually abused to engage in bingeing and purging with their eating, to express dissatisfaction with their bodies, and to report a loss of control with regard to their eating habits (Wonderlich et al., 2001).

Adult Female Survivors of Childhood Incest

Mood disorders, anxiety disorders, especially posttraumatic stress disorder (PTSD), substance use disorders, eating disorders, and personality disorders have been linked to the experience of childhood sexual abuse in adult women (Cole & Putnam, 1992; Gladstone, Parker, Mitchell, Malhi, Wilhelm, & Austin, 2004; Hofmann, Levitt, Hofman, Greene, Litz, & Barlow, 2001; Molnar, Buka, & Kessler, 2001; Owens & Chard, 2003; van Gerko, Hughes, Hamill, & Waller, 2005; Weiss et al., 1999).

Female inpatients who have been diagnosed with major depressive disorder and who have experienced childhood sexual trauma are four times less likely to recover from their depression within twelve months than those depressed female inpatients with no history of child sexual abuse and, at a five-year follow-up, chronic depression is significantly more prevalent in those with histories of childhood sexual abuse (Zlotnick, Ryan, Miller, & Keitner, 1995). Childhood sexual abuse has also been linked to longer episodes of depression in female outpatients (Zlotnick, Mattia, & Zimmerman, 2001) and in females with comorbid anxiety and major depressive disorders (Zlotnick, Warshaw, Shea, & Keller, 1997). Outpatients with histories of childhood sexual abuse are significantly more likely to be diagnosed with PTSD, multiple psychological disorders (e.g., major depression combined with an anxiety disorder), and borderline personality disorder (Zlotnick et al., 2001) than patients with no histories of childhood sexual abuse. Although this study of 235 depressed outpatients combined those who experienced incest with those who experienced extrafamilial abuse in their sample of sexually abused subjects, 25 percent of the sample endorsed having experienced childhood sexual abuse and 52 percent of those experienced incest (Zlotnick et al., 2001). The odds of PTSD are higher for sexually abused females who have experienced rape by steprelatives and acquaintances than by strangers (Molnar, Buka, & Kessler, 2001). Others have concluded that childhood sexual abuse is a substantial risk factor for chronic, recurrent major depressive episodes (Browne & Finkelhor, 1986; Pribor & Dinwiddie, 1992; Saunders, Villeponteaux, Lipovsky, Kilpatrick, & Veronen, 1992). In fact, a history of childhood sexual abuse in females was associated with fourteen of seventeen lifetime mood, anxiety, and substance abuse disorders (Molnar, Buka, & Kessler, 2001). In a study of 301 women in New Zealand who met lifetime criteria for an eating disorder, affective disorder, and/or substance abuse, women with a lifetime diagnosis of depression were twice as likely to report a history of incest than women who had no history of depression (Bushnell, Wells, & Oakley-Brown, 1992, cited in Weiss et al., 1999).

Substance abuse is strongly linked with childhood sexual abuse, more so than any other psychiatric disorder (Kendler et al., 2000; Teusch, 2001) and, in particular, with victims of incest (Wonderlich et al., 2001). Female victims of incest who do not receive treatment for their trauma have more difficulty in the early stages of alcohol sobriety than women without a history of incest or childhood sexual trauma and are also more likely to relapse (i.e., use alcohol again) (Kovach, 1986). Incest is also associated with lifetime difficulty with crack cocaine (Freeman, Collier, & Parillo, 2002).

Survivors of incest frequently engage in promiscuity and oversexualization of relationships (Gordy, 1993). Children molested by a parent have difficulty distinguishing between affection and sex because of the confusing blurring between parental love and incest (Marvasti & Dripchak, 2004a). As adults, they often are revictimized because of a lack of social judgment in determining which situations are safe and which are risky, an overall belief that one does not have the right to object or resist sexual advances, and a lack of confidence and assertiveness that can be paralyzing in the face of unwanted sexual advances (Marvasti & Dripchak, 2004a). Women with histories of incest typically have difficulty with trust, intimacy in their marriage and dating relationships, and managing their sexuality (Cole & Putnam, 1992).

Female adult victims of childhood sexual abuse, especially those who experienced incest, self-mutilate (including cutting and burning themselves) and self-injure (including hitting themselves, placing ice on parts of their bodies, scratching to the point of bleeding, and adding salt to the site of the cutting) (Gladstone et al., 2004; Marvasti & Dripchak, 2004b; Molnar, Berkman, & Buka, 2001; Ystgaard et al., 2004). Self-injurious behavior allows incest victims to "demonstrate control and ownership of their bodies" (p. 39) and also is a safer expression of anger and rage (Marvasti & Dripchak, 2004b). Hospitalized females who self-mutilate and repeatedly attempt suicide are more likely to have histories of sexual trauma and physical abuse than women who have not made repeated suicide attempts and who do not self-mutilate (Ystgaard et al., 2004). Suicidal behavior is more prevalent among persons who have reported childhood sexual abuse than persons who have not, with the odds of suicide attempts two to four times higher for female victims of childhood sexual abuse. In fact, 12 percent of all females raped as children will attempt suicide even if they do not have a psychiatric disorder or any other experiences of childhood trauma, and 7 percent of all females who were molested will attempt suicide (Molnar et al., 2001).

As noted with adolescents, adult women with a history of childhood sexual abuse are also more likely to be raped and develop PTSD in adulthood than are nonvictims (Gladstone et al., 2004; Kessler & Bieschke, 1999; Peleikis et al., 2004). The risk of sexual revictimization of incest victims in adulthood is also higher than that for childhood victims of nonfamilial abuse. The odds of sexual coercion of incest victims as compared to women abused by nonfamily members were 5.13 times higher and the odds for rape were 4.58 times higher (Kessler & Bieschke, 1999).

In a recent study of 299 women with a diagnosed eating disorder, those who reported childhood sexual abuse had higher levels of bingeing, vomiting, use of laxatives, and use of diuretics; in addition, they differed significantly from those without a history of sexual abuse in body image disturbance (defined as distorted), a negative evaluation of self based upon body shape (van Gerko et al., 2005). Although the researchers asked the participants if their abuse was intrafamilial, they unfortunately did not report this data in the study and explained that they had "not recorded in a sufficiently systematic way" to allow this information to be used in the analysis (p. 377). Other studies have found similar links to eating disorders and body image disturbance (Kendler et al., 2000; Waller, 1992; Waller, Hamilton, Rose, Sumra, & Baldwin, 1993).

Adult Male Survivors of Childhood Incest

There is relatively little research specifically on male victims of incest as compared to the study of females. In her review and critique of the literature on mother-son sexual abuse, Lawson (1993) highlighted that such abuse is rarely reported to child protective authorities or police, is most likely to be disclosed in long-term psychotherapy, and, when the abuse is subtle, is often not thought of as abuse. She reported that "in cases of mother-son sexual abuse, the taboo against disclosure is far stronger than the taboo against the behavior itself" (p. 264). In the research that has been conducted with male victims of childhood sexual abuse, distinctions often have not been made between those abused by family members and nonfamilial offenders. In recent years, more attention has been paid to mother-son sexual abuse, but research on father-son sexual abuse remains lacking.

Even with the paucity of research on male survivors of childhood sexual abuse, it is clear that such abuse has a negative impact on the lives of these boys and men. Male incest survivors have reported severe, long-term, negative effects on social, sexual, family, and physical areas of their lives (Ray, 1996), and men who experienced either incest or extrafamilial abuse have reported difficulty forming and maintaining sexual relationships, avoidance of intimacy, and problems initiating and sustaining their careers (Gill & Tutty, 1999).

Mother-son incest is associated with more self-reported difficulties than all other victim-perpetrator relationships, including that of father and son (Kelly et al., 2002). Specifically, males abused by their mothers report more sexual problems, dissociation, aggression, and interpersonal problems than males not abused by their mothers and, even controlling for those abused by their fathers, mother-son incest is still associated with significant problems in sexual functioning, dissociation, and interpersonal problems. In addition, these males report more symptoms of PTSD than men who have had no experiences of any parental abuse (Kelly et al., 2002).

Father-son incest is associated with more PTSD symptoms compared with males not abused by their fathers, even with no differences in the intrusiveness (i.e., penetration) of the sexual acts (Kelly et al., 2002). Mother-son incest is somewhat less intrusive than that of the other groups of perpetrators; however, there are men in the mother-son group who experience intercourse. Males abused by their mothers, or females in general, are more likely to report a heterosexual orientation while there is no significant relationship between sexual abuse by a father and sexual orientation as an adult. Mother-son incest survivors who initially perceive the sexual abuse positively or with a mixed reaction experience the most severe, long-term adjustment difficulties, especially problems with anger, trust, and aggression in intimate relationships (Kelly et al., 2002).

Suicidal behavior is more prevalent among men who have reported childhood sexual abuse than men who have not, with the odds of suicide attempts four to eleven times higher for male victims (Molnar et al., 2001). Even male victims of child rape who have no other childhood adversities or psychiatric disorders are far more likely to make a serious suicide attempt than are nonvictims. However, males victims with a psychiatric disorder are likely to attempt suicide at a younger age than male victims who do not also have a psychiatric disorder (Molnar, Berkman, & Buka, 2001).

Younger boys (i.e., age 7 and under) as compared to older boys (i.e., age 10 and older) are more likely to be sexually abused by a family member, especially a parent (Fischer & MacDonald, 1998; Kelly et al., 2002), while older boys are more likely to be abused by nonrelatives but persons familiar to them. Sexual abuse by a family member also places a male child at risk for extrafamilial sexual abuse. Approximately two-thirds of the males who experience sexual abuse by a family member also report sexual abuse by a nonrelative outside of the immediate family (Harrison et al., 1997).

Males who experience incest are less likely than females who have been abused by family members to be removed from the home (Spiegel, 2003), which places them at risk for continued abuse. Male incest victims are also less likely than female incest victims to report the abuse at the time of its occurrence or in their lifetime (Gill & Tutty, 1999; Spiegel, 2003).

COPING

Negative attributional style has been defined as the tendency for people to ascribe the "cause of a negative event to themselves (internal), across situations (global), and over time (stable)" and has been associated with psychological distress following childhood sexual abuse (Steel et al., 2004, p. 787). Attributions of shame and self-blame are associated with depression and lower self-esteem in children as early as two months after disclosure of the abuse (Feiring et al., 1999). Accepting responsibility for the abuse, internalization of the abuse, resistance, and confrontive coping all contribute to serious psychological problems in adulthood (Steel et al., 2004). Failing to use social support as a coping strategy also leads to more psychological distress in adulthood (Steel et al., 2004).

Duration of the abuse is correlated with internalization of abuse, which in turn is related to a poorer adjustment in adulthood. For example, the longer the abuse takes place, the more likely the victim will blame him-/herself. Others (Bennett et al., 2000; Rodriguez et al., 1998) also found a positive relationship between duration of abuse and significant psychological distress but did not look at the coping styles. The older the child at the time of abuse, the poorer the adjustment in adulthood, as the older the victim, the more likely he/she will accept responsibility for the abuse (Steel et al., 2004). Older victims may experience increased negative symptomatology because they have awareness that the sexual experiences are unacceptable and harmful (Ruggiero et al., 2000).

In general, victims appear to have poorer outcomes if they deny the abuse, distance themselves from the abuse, or otherwise minimize the abuse. Furthermore, the long-term impact of childhood sexual abuse may be lessened if the victim tells another person about the abuse and problem-solves possible strategies to end the abuse (Guelzow, Cornett, & Dougherty, 2002). Endler and Parker (as cited in Guelzow et al., 2002) proposed three coping strategies used by persons when placed in stressful situations. They identified emotion-focused coping (i.e., self-blame for being too emotional, preoccupation with worry) and avoidance-focused coping (i.e., engaging in activities to ignore the abuse) as maladaptive, while task-focused coping (i.e., outlining priorities and developing and following through on a course of action) is viewed as adaptive. Family support is likely to reduce extreme long-term consequences from childhood sexual abuse and decrease the impact of childhood sexual abuse (Guelzow et al., 2002). A mother's support is an important mediating variable when the perpetrator of the abuse is familial, while lack of a father's support increases the likelihood of emotion-focused coping (Guelzow et al., 2002).

In their study of over 100 female survivors of incest, Brand and Alexander (2003) found that avoidance-focused coping and emotion-focused coping were the most used styles of coping and were associated with poorer adult functioning. Use of avoidance seems to be dysfunctional in the long run as it prevents the development of effective coping strategies. They found little use of task-focused coping and explained how this highlights the extreme powerlessness of children who are being sexually abused. They suggested that sexually victimized children's main method of protecting themselves is to attempt to manage their emotional reactions. Contrary to the finding of others, seeking social support was associated with more distress. Victims of incest typically report significantly less family support than victims of extrafamilial sexual abuse (Stroud, 1999) and for this reason telling of the abuse is not always effective in ending the abuse (Roesler & Wind, 1994). Brand and Alexander (2003) also suggest that when "abuse is frequent, chronic, and/or perpetrated by a family member, distancing from the current abuse may be beneficial" (p. 291). They also hypothesized that children who are able to distance themselves may function better as adults because the distancing strategy could make them more resilient. Thus, it is not clear-cut when seeking support will be helpful or harmful. Perhaps if the mother believes her child and takes action to protect the child, then the social support may prevent adulthood distress.

Developmental factors affect a child's capacity to handle stress and sexually abused children react to incest differently depending upon age and developmental level (Cole & Putnam, 1992). Preschool victims use the coping style of denial and dissociation and are unable to use instrumental coping strategies of refusal and avoidance because they cannot tell others of the abuse and cannot get away from their family member perpetrator. Sexual abuse during the elementary school years interferes with development of social self-competence because children who experience severe guilt, shame, and confusion regarding their sexual abuse are unlikely to feel secure enough to make friends or create any type of social support away from home. Adolescence is a significant period of social and sexual identity development. Incest during adolescence may interrupt learning to use reasoning, reflection, and planning, which leaves incest survivors relying on denial, dissociation, and other immature coping strategies and places them at greater risk for severe psychological problems (Cole & Putnam, 1992).

NONOFFENDING MOTHERS

Early work in the area of incest tended to blame mothers and promoted a belief that mothers were aware of the incest prior to the disclosure and colluded with the perpetrator on a conscious or unconscious level. However, the vast majority of mothers believe their children when they disclose the sexual abuse and make an effort to protect them (Joyce, 1997).

Crawford (1999) concluded in her review of literature on the role of nonoffending mothers in intrafamilial sexual abuse of daughters that these mothers are a mixed group with each needing individual assessment by professionals to determine if that mother is capable of supporting, protecting, and assisting in her daughter's healing. Lastly, Bolen (2003) also focused on the literature pertaining to nonoffending mothers of sexually abused children with an emphasis on intrafamilial abuse and suggested that there has been a sociohistorical context in which nonoffending mothers are held accountable for the abuse of their children in the eyes of child protection professionals, whereas there appears to be no similar level of responsibility for the nonoffending father.

There is conflicting information regarding a mother's history of childhood sexual abuse being a risk factor for sexual abuse of her own children. Some studies have shown that a mother's history of childhood sexual abuse, especially incest, is a risk factor for her own children to be sexually abused, especially by a father or stepfather (Faller, 1989; Joyce, 1997; McCloskey & Bailey, 2000; Russell, 1986), while others found no difference in the mother's history of sexual abuse with regard to sexual abuse of her children, including incest (Estes & Tidwell, 2002). Mothers who abuse alcohol and drugs place their children at greater risk for sexual abuse than mothers who do not (McCloskey & Bailey, 2000).

Daughters whose mothers experienced incest have reported a negative impact upon them as children that transcended into their adulthood. Research suggests that mothers who have been victims of incest themselves suffer long-term negative effects, including parenting difficulties as a result of problems related to their own sense of organization, control, and confidence (Cole & Putnam, 1992). A negative attitude toward one's own body and sexuality, viewing all women as victims, difficulty integrating sex and intimacy, impaired judgment of the trustworthiness of others, hypervigilance, lack of assertiveness, lack of parenting skills, difficulty recognizing and expressing anger, eating disorders, and external locus of control were found in both the mothers who experienced incest and their daughters. In addition, the daughters attributed many of their own psychological problems to their mother's parenting and history of incest, including sexually acting out, sexualized relationships with males, feeling defective, fear of all men, impaired functioning in their occupations, and substance abuse (Voth & Tutty, 1999).

OFFENDERS

Characteristics of Adult Male Incest Offenders

Men who abused children known to them but unrelated have been found to have more years of education than those who molest children in their extended or immediate families and those who molest children unknown to them (Greenberg et al., 2000). Sex offenders with low levels of education are more likely to offend again than are those with more education (Hanson & Bussiere, 1998).

Men who abuse their daughters or stepdaughters are thought to be less antisocial and have lower levels of psychopathology than child molesters who offend strangers, extended family members, or acquaintances (Greenberg et al., 2000; Rice & Harris, 2002), with those who abuse biological daughters not only showing the lowest level of psychopathology among groups of child molesters but also not scoring above the cutoff to indicate psychopathology (Rice & Harris, 2002).

No significant differences have been found between sexually offending biological fathers and stepfathers with regard to the number of victims, the age of the victim, use of threats or force, penetration, and the influence of alcohol and drugs. There are few victims for each group and little use of force or threats. Half of the biological offenders and half of the stepfather offenders engage in oral, vaginal, or anal penetration, and a quarter of both groups report using drugs or alcohol at the time of the offense (Greenberg, Firestone, Nunes, Bradford, & Curry, 2005). There are no differences between incestuous biological fathers and stepfathers with regard to their own histories of childhood sexual abuse and physical abuse; however, over 50 percent of these men had been sexually and/or physically abused. While there are also no differences between these incestuous offenders with regard to recidivism, criminal charges, or being placed outside of the home prior to age 16, over a third had a criminal record and had been placed outside of their homes prior to age 16 (Greenberg et al., 2005).

Childhood sexual victimization of incest offenders presents a complex picture. Male sex offenders who were abused by family members as children are more likely to have female victims and less likely to bribe their victims than are male offenders who were abused by strangers or acquaintances (Craissati, McClurg, & Browne, 2002). Those males abused by strangers are more likely to abuse males or a combination of both males and females (Craissati et al., 2002).

Familial offenders more so than nonfamilial offenders minimize their behavior (Webster & Beech, 2001) and view their victims as adults (Wilson, 1999). Some studies have shown that nonfamilial offenders are more likely to blame their victims and are less likely to admit their responsibility (Miner & Dwyer, 1997; Webster & Beech, 2001), while others found the contrary (Parton & Day, 2002).

Arousal Patterns of Incest Offenders

Exclusively incestuous male offenders who abuse female children generally have more deviant arousal and deviant sexual preferences than males who are not sex offenders, but are less deviant than males who abuse children outside of their families (Freund, Watson, & Dickey, 1991; Greenberg et al., 2005; Rice & Harris, 2002; Seto, Lalumiere, & Kuban, 1999). Exclusively intrafamilial father-daughter child molesters are not as predatory as and are less antisocial than extrafamilial child abusers (Rice & Harris, 2002). There is conflicting information regarding deviant arousal using phallometric measures with biological fathers and stepfathers. Greenberg et al. (2005) reported that biological fathers are significantly less aroused by children than are stepfathers; however, others (Rice & Harris, 2002; Seto et al., 1999) found that biological fathers do not differ from stepfathers with regard to arousal to child stimuli. Incestuous biological fathers respond less than extended family molesters and child molesters who abused females both within and outside of the family (Seto et al., 1999). Yet, when comparisons are made between intrafamilial male offenders and extrafamilial offenders with a single victim, the two groups have identical mean phallometric deviance differentials indicating sexual attraction to children (Rice & Harris, 2002).

Recidivism

While researchers have consistently demonstrated lower sexual and violent recidivism (i.e., offending again) rates for those molesting their biological daughters and stepdaughters as compared to child molesters who molest acquaintances, strangers, and extended family members (Firestone et al., 1999; Greenberg et al., 2000; Hanson & Bussière, 1998), it is difficult to know true rates of recidivism with incest offenders, as incestuous abuse is often not reported or detected (Greenberg et al., 2000) and pleas to lesser offenses are frequently made to save the child victims from the trauma of testifying in court. Of importance, however, is the realization that in absolute terms, the recidivism of incestuous biological and stepfathers is not low (Rice & Harris, 2002).

Characteristics of Female Incest Offenders

It has long been believed that females, especially mothers, do not abuse children. This belief so permeates our Western culture that even knowledgeable professionals, such as police officers, social workers, child protection workers, psychologists, and psychiatrists, have minimized and dismissed the possibility. In a study of such professionals' responses to female offenders of children, female sex offenders were less likely than male child sexual abusers to be investigated by the police or involved in social service agencies, and female child molesters were allowed to voluntarily discontinue involvement with child protection agencies (Hetherton & Beardsall, 1998). Another study of eighty-three confirmed cases of child sexual abuse by females revealed that only one of the females was criminally prosecuted, even when there was also significant physical abuse, such as "burning, beating, biting or pinching the breasts or genitals of the children or tying them up during acts of sexual assault" (Ramsay-Klawsnik, 1990, cited in Denov, 2003, p. 49). It is also a common belief that when women do sexually abuse children, especially their own, they do so in conjunction with a male (Mathews, Mathews, & Speltz, 1990, cited in Kelly et al., 2002).

Adult female sex offenders present complicated interactions between victim and offender characteristics as well as patterns of offending. Convicted adult female incest offenders are most likely to abuse children ranging in age from 12 to 17 years and are next likely to abuse children ranging in age from 6 to 11 years; while female incest offenders do not neatly fit into any one of the six types of female sex offenders, they are most likely to fall into the category of Young Adult Child Exploiters who molest both male and female children under the age of 7 (Vandiver & Kercher, 2004).

One study showed that the vast majority of female adult and juvenile sex offenders have experienced intrafamilial sexual abuse, and the tendency for incest continues in their offending histories with 46 percent of the adult female sex offenders sexually molesting their daughters, 39 percent molesting their sons, and 92 percent with a "mother or maternal figure tie with their victims (daughter, son, nephew, niece)" (Tardif, Auclair, Jacob, & Carpentier, 2005, p. 162). And over half of the sample of female juvenile perpetrators also molested family members (brothers, half-brothers, stepsisters) (Tardif et al., 2005). Extreme conflict in the mother–child relationship in both the adult and juvenile female sexual perpetrators plays a crucial role in these women and girls becoming perpetrators. Having had a sexually and physically abusive father is also a risk factor in the adult offenders whereas an absent or uninvolved father is implicated for the juvenile offenders (Tardif et al., 2005).

Typically, clinicians and researchers have believed that children who are sexually abused by other children are less distressed than children abused by adults; however, recent research has indicated that this is not the case. Children abused by both adult offenders (over age 18) and offenders under age 17 display clinically relevant levels of behavioral and emotional problems, with one-fourth of each of the groups experiencing suicidal ideation (Shaw et al., 2000). Both groups of victims experience excessive sexual problems, sexual concerns, sexual preoccupation, sexual fears, and unwanted sexual feelings. Furthermore, those abused by juveniles experienced even more of these problems. Children abused by children are more likely to be abused by siblings and more likely to display more sexual problems (Shaw et al., 2000). Thus, sexual acts between children, even with a minimum of three years' difference in age, result in similar levels of emotional and behavioral distress found in children abused by adults (Shaw et al., 2000).

TREATMENT

Group treatments are particularly effective for victims of incest because being in a group decreases isolation and provides an awareness that others have also experienced incest. Groups typically last ten weeks with follow-up six months later. Group treatments for women victims of childhood incest effectively reduce symptoms of anxiety, avoidance, dissociation, and depression, increase self-esteem and the ability to protect oneself, and decrease feelings of guilt, shame, and self-blame (Alexander, Neimeyer, Follette, Moore, & Harter, 1989; Carver, Stalker, Stewart, & Abraham, 1989; Hazzard, Rogers, & Angert, 1993; Herman & Schaatzow, 1984; Morgan & Cummings, 1999; Roberts & Lie, 1989; Zlotnick, Shea, et al., 1997).

Several studies showed conflicting results regarding the impact of individual therapy in addition to the group experience. Some research shows that prior individual therapy contributes to more successful outcomes from the group treatment (Hazzard et al., 1993; Westbury & Tutty, 1999), while other research found no additional benefit from concurrent individual therapy (Morgan & Cummings, 1999).

A treatment model that focuses on shame-based behaviors may significantly decrease a woman's risk for sexual revictimization, increase her ability to express emotions, such as rage and humiliation, and decrease self-blame (Kessler & Bieschke, 1999). Shame is also a significant emotion that results in negative consequences for male victims of incest and is important to target in treatments for men and boys. Psychiatric disorders most prevalent with survivors of childhood incest reflect impairments in self- and social functioning and suggest use of a developmental model for treatment (Cole & Putnam,

1992). Interventions that target ruminative behaviors, affect modulation, and active problem-solving are indicated for adolescent females while adolescent boys need assistance in tolerating emotions without acting out sexually and learning to ask for help and support (Feiring et al., 1999).

While group therapy has been studied more than individual therapy and has been thought to be the most effective with adult survivors of childhood sexual trauma, two general approaches to group therapy have emerged. Trauma-focused group therapy focuses on a survivor's symptoms and past environment while present-focused group therapy emphasizes the current environment and symptoms (Speigel, Classen, Thurston, & Butler, 2004). Trauma-focused therapy involves telling the story of one's trauma and has the benefit of exposure and desensitization in reducing symptoms related to trauma (Foa & Meadows, 1997). Present-focused therapy alleviates symptoms by focusing on current problem behaviors without discussing specifics of the trauma (Spiegel et al., 2004; Classen, Koopman, Nevill-Manning, & Spiegel, 2001). Both approaches have particular strengths; the present-focused group decreases the risk of vicarious traumatization while the trauma-focused group allows the survivor's story and voice to be heard and acknowledged. To date, there has been only one randomized clinical pilot study, with a larger study underway, that has attempted to ascertain which approach is most effective (Spiegel et al., 2004). Interestingly, neither group reduced trauma symptoms. However, the trauma-focused group was effective in decreasing interpersonal problems while the present-focused group showed promise in reducing sexual revictimization (Spiegel et al., 2004).

Outcome studies of group treatment for males who have experienced incest are almost nonexistent. Clinicians and researchers who work with males who have experienced both intrafamilial and extrafamilial sexual abuse insist that to apply the constructs, paradigms, and treatment strategies designed for female survivors of childhood trauma to male survivors would be ineffective at best and a disservice at worst (Spiegel, 2003). Two published studies with males who experienced childhood sexual abuse did not differentiate between those males who were molested by family members and those who were not but showed promise for treatment (Sharpe, Selley, Low, & Hall, 2001; Morrison & Treliving, 2002). One approach for working with male victims of sexual abuse is called the SAM (Sexual Abuse of Males) Model and is based upon research, therapy, and practice specific to men and boys (Spiegel, 2003).

Trauma-focused cognitive behavior therapy and cognitive behavior therapy with children who have experienced sexual abuse have been shown to be effective in reducing PTSD, depression, behavior problems, sexualized behavior, abuse-related attributions, shame, and anxiety while also increasing social competence and improving parenting (Cohen, Mannarino, & Knudsen, 2005; Cohen & Mannarino, 1996, 1997, 1998; Cohen, Deblinger, Mannarino, & Steer, 2004; Deblinger, Lippman, & Steer, 1996; Deblinger, Steer, & Lippman, 1999; King et al., 2000).

CONCLUSIONS

Incest is a serious ongoing problem in our society that continues to be unreported and underreported and has significant negative, long-term consequences for its victims, both male and female. Untreated childhood sexual abuse creates problems that last a lifetime. We must do a better job of detecting incest by specifically inquiring of this experience in our clinical populations. The unexplored nature of incest with males needs to be studied along all developmental levels in order to design effective treatments. In the outcome-based world of psychological treatment, we need to provide treatment that has proven to be effective and efficacious. Discovering and treating sexual abuse during childhood and adolescence could prevent significant impairment, re-victimization, and disruption in the lives of adult survivors of childhood incest as well as reduce the transgenerational risk of incest.

REFERENCES

Alexander, P. C., Neimeyer, R. A., Follette, V. M., Moore, M. K., & Harter, S. (1989). A comparison of group treatment of women sexually abused as children. *Journal of Consulting and Clinical Psychology, 57*, 479–483.

Beitchman, J. H., Zucker, K. J., Hood, J. E., DaCosta, G. A., Akman, D., & Cassavia, E. (1992). A review of the long-term effects of child sexual abuse. *Child Abuse & Neglect, 16*, 101–118.

Bennett, S. E., Hughes, H. M., & Luke, D. A. (2000). Heterogeneity in patterns of child sexual abuse family functioning and long-term adjustment. *Journal of Interpersonal Violence, 15*(2), 134–137.

Bolen, R. M. (2003). Nonoffending mothers of sexually abused children: A case of institutionalized sexism? *Violence Against Women, 9*(11), 1336–1366.

Brand, B. L., & Alexander, P. C. (2003). Coping with incest: The relationship between recollections of childhood coping and adult functioning in female survivors of incest. *Journal of Traumatic Stress, 16*(3), 285–293.

Briere, J., & Elliott, D. M. (2003). Prevalence and psychological sequelae of self-reported childhood physical and sexual abuse in a general population sample of men and women. *Child Abuse & Neglect, 27*, 1205–1222.

Browne, M. W., & Finkelhor, D. (1986). Impact of child sexual abuse: A review of the research. *Psychological Bulletin, 99*, 66–77.

Carver, C. M., Stalker, C., Stewart, E., & Abraham, B. (1989). The impact of group therapy for adult survivors of childhood sexual abuse. *Canadian Journal of Psychiatry, 34*, 753–758.

Chandy, J. M., Blum, R. W., & Resnick, M. D. (1996). Gender-specific outcomes for sexually abused adolescents. *Child Abuse & Neglect, 20*(12), 1219–1231.

Classen, C., Koopman, C., Nevill-Manning, K., & Spiegel, D. (2001). A preliminary report comparing trauma-focused and present-focused group therapy against a wait-listed condition among childhood sexual abuse survivors with PTSD. *Journal of Aggression, Maltreatment and Trauma, 4,* 265–288.

Cohen, J. A., Deblinger, E., Mannarino, A. P., & Steer, R. A. (2004). A multisite, randomized controlled trial for sexually abused children with PTSD symptoms. *Journal of the American Academy of Child and Adolescent Psychiatry, 43,* 393–402.

Cohen, J. A., & Mannarino, A. P. (1996). A treatment outcome study for sexually abused preschool children: Initial findings. *Journal of the American Academy of Child and Adolescent Psychiatry, 35,* 42–50.

Cohen, J. A., & Mannarino, A. P. (1997). A treatment study of sexually abused preschool children: Outcome during a one-year follow-up. *Journal of the American Academy of Child and Adolescent Psychiatry, 36,* 1228–1235.

Cohen, J. A., & Mannarino, A. P. (1998). Interventions for sexually abused children: Initial treatment findings. *Child Maltreatment, 3,* 17–26.

Cohen, J. A., Mannarino, A. P., & Knudsen, K. (2005). Treating sexually abused children: A 1 year follow-up of a randomized controlled trial. *Child Abuse & Neglect, 29,* 135–145.

Cole, P. M., & Putnam, F. W. (1992). Effect of incest on self and social functioning: A developmental psychopathology perspective. *Journal of Consulting and Clinical Psychology, 60*(2), 174–184.

Craissati, J., McClurg, G., & Browne, K. (2002). Characteristics of perpetrators of child sexual abuse who have been sexually victimized as children. *Sexual Abuse: Journal of Research and Treatment, 14*(3), 225–239.

Crawford, S. L. (1999). Intrafamilial sexual abuse: What we think we know about mothers, and implications for intervention. *Journal of Child Sexual Abuse, 7*(3), 55–72.

Deblinger, E., Lippman, J., & Steer, R. (1996). Sexually abused children suffering posttraumatic stress symptoms: Initial treatment outcome findings. *Child Maltreatment, 1,* 310–321.

Deblinger, E., Stauffer, L., & Landsberg, C. (1994). The impact of a history of child sexual abuse on maternal response to allegations of sexual abuse concerning her child. *Journal of Child Sexual Abuse, 3*(3), 67–74.

Deblinger, E., Steer, R., & Lippman, J. (1999). Two-year follow-up study of cognitive-behavioral therapy for sexually abused children suffering posttraumatic stress symptoms. *Child Abuse & Neglect, 23,* 1371–1378.

Denov, M. S. (2003). To a safer place? Victims of sexual abuse by females and their disclosures to professionals. *Child Abuse & Neglect, 27,* 47–61.

Dinwiddie, S., Heath, A. C., Dunne, M. P., Bucholz, K. K., Madden, P. A., Slutske, W. S., et al. (2000). Early sexual abuse and lifetime psychopathology: A co-twin control study. *Psychological Medicine, 30,* 41–52.

Estes, L. S., & Tidwell, R. (2002). Sexually abused children's behaviours: Impact of gender and mother's experience of intra- and extra-familial sexual abuse. *Family Practice, 19*(1), 36–44.

Everson, M., Hunter, W., Runyon, D., Edelsohn, G., & Coulter, M. (1989). Maternal support following disclosure of incest. *American Journal of Orthopsychiatry, 59,* 197–207.

Faller, K. C. (1989). Why sexual abuse? An exploration of the intergenerational hypothesis. *Child Abuse & Neglect, 13,* 543–548.

Fassler, I. R., Amodeo, M., Griffin, M. L., Clay, C. M., & Ellis, M. E. (2005). Predicting long-term outcomes for women sexually abused in childhood: Contribution of abuse severity versus family environment. *Child Abuse & Neglect, 29,* 269–284.

Feiring, C., Taska, L., & Lewis, M. (1999). Social support and children's and adolescents' adaptation to sexual abuse. *Journal of Interpersonal Violence, 13*(2), 240–260.

Feitel, B., Margetson, N., Chamas, J., & Lipman, C. (1992). Psychosocial background and behavioral and emotional disorders of homeless and runaway youth. *Hospital & Community Psychiatry, 43,* 155–159.

Finkelhor, D. (1979). *Sexually victimized children.* New York: Free Press.

Firestone, P., Bradford, J. M., McCoy, M., Greenberg, D. M., Curry, S., & Larose, M. R. (1999). Predictions of recidivism in incest offenders. *Journal of Interpersonal Violence, 14,* 511–531.

Fischer, D. G., & McDonald, W. L. (1998). Characteristics of intrafamilial and extrafamilial child sexual abuse. *Child Abuse & Neglect, 22*(9), 915–929.

Flemming, J., Mullen, P. E., Sibthorpe, B., & Bammer, G. (1999). The long-term impact of childhood sexual abuse in Australian women. *Child Abuse & Neglect, 23*(2), 145–159.

Foa, E. B., & Meadows, E. A. (1997). Psychosocial treatments for posttraumatic stress disorder: A critical review. *Annual Review of Psychology, 48,* 449–480.

Fontella, C., Harrington, D., & Zuravin, S. J. (2000). Gender differences in the characteristics and outcomes of sexually abused preschoolers. *Journal of Child Sexual Abuse, 9*(2), 21–40.

Freeman, R. C., Collier, K., & Parillo, K. M. (2002). Early life sexual abuse as a risk for crack cocaine use. *American Journal of Alcohol Abuse, 28*(1), 109–131.

Freund, K., Watson, R., & Dickey, R. (1991). Sex offenses against female children perpetrated by men who are not pedophiles. *Journal of Sex Research, 28,* 409–423.

Gill, M., & Tutty, L. M. (1999). Male survivors of childhood sexual abuse: A qualitative study and issues for clinical consideration. *Journal of Child Sexual Abuse, 7*(3), 19–33.

Gladstone, G. L., Parker, G. B., Mitchell, P. B., Malhi, G. S., Wilhelm, K., & Austin, M. (2004). Implications of childhood trauma for depressed women: An analysis of pathways from childhood sexual abuse to deliberate self-harm and revictimization. *American Journal of Psychiatry, 161*(8), 1417–1425.

Gordy, P. L. (1993). Group work that supports adult victims of childhood incest. *Social Casework, 64,* 300–307.

Greenberg, D., Bradford, J., Firestone, P., & Curry, S. (2000). Recidivism of child molesters: A study of victim relationship with the perpetrator. *Child Abuse & Neglect, 24*(11), 1485–1494.

Greenberg, D. M., Firestone, P., Nunes, K. L., Bradford, J. M., & Curry, S. (2005). Biological fathers and stepfathers who molest their daughters: Psychological, phallometric, and criminal features. *Sexual Abuse: A Journal of Research and Treatment, 17*(1), 39–46.

Guelzow, J. W., Cornett, P. F., & Dougherty, T. M. (2002). Child sexual abuse victims' perception of paternal support as a significant predictor of coping style and global self-worth. *Journal of Child Sexual Abuse, 11*(4), 53–72.

Hall, D. K., Mathews, F., & Pearce, J. (2002). Sexual behavior problems in sexually abused children: A preliminary typology. *Child Abuse & Neglect, 26*, 289–312.

Hanson, R. K., & Bussière, M. T. (1998). Predicting relapse: A meta-analysis of sexual offender recidivism studies. *Journal of Consulting and Clinical Psychology, 66*, 348–362.

Harrison, P. A., Fulkerson, J. A., & Beebe, T. J. (1997). Multiple substance abuse among adolescent physical and sexual abuse victims. *Child Abuse & Neglect, 21*(6), 529–539.

Hazzard, A., Rogers, J. H., & Angert, L. (1993). Factors affecting group therapy outcomes for adult sexual abuse survivors. *International Journal of Group Psychotherapy, 43*, 453–468.

Herman, J., Russell, D., & Trocki, K. (1986). Long-term effects of incestuous abuse in childhood. *American Journal of Psychiatry, 143*, 1293–1296.

Herman, J., & Schaatzow, E. (1984). Time-limited group therapy for women with a history of incest. *International Journal of Group Psychotherapy, 34*, 605–616.

Hetherton, J., & Beardsall, L. (1998). Decisions and attitudes concerning child sexual abuse: Does the gender of the perpetrator make a difference to child protection professionals? *Child Abuse & Neglect, 22*(12), 1265–1283.

Hofmann, S. G., Levitt, J. T., Hofman, E. C., Greene, K., Litz, B. T., & Barlow, D. H. (2001). Potentially traumatizing events in panic disorder and other anxiety disorders. *Depression and Anxiety, 13*, 101–102.

Jackson, J. L., Calhoun, K. S., Amick, A. E., Maddever, H. M., & Habif, V. L. (1990). Young adult women who report intrafamilial sexual abuse: Subsequent adjustment. *Archives of Sexual Behavior, 19*(3), 211–221.

Joyce, P. A. (1997). Mothers of sexually abused children and the concept of collusion: A literature review. *Journal of Child Sexual Abuse, 6*(2), 75–92.

Kelly, R. J., Wood, J. J., Gonzalez, L. S., MacDonald, V., & Waterman, J. (2002). Effects of mother-son incest and positive perceptions of sexual abuse experiences on the psychosocial adjustment of clinic-referred men. *Child Abuse & Neglect, 26*, 425–441.

Kendall-Tackett, K. A., Williams, L. M., & Finkelhor, D. (1993). The effects of sexual abuse on children: A review and synthesis of recent empirical findings. *Psychological Bulletin, 113*, 164–181.

Kendler, K., Bulik, C. M., Silberg, J., Hettema, J. M., Myers, J., & Prescott, C. A. (2000). Childhood sexual abuse and adult psychiatric and substance use disorders in women: An epidemiological and cotwin control analysis. *Archives of General Psychiatry, 57*(10), 953–959.

Kessler, B. L., & Bieschke, K. J. (1999). A retrospective analysis of shame, dissociation, and adult victimization in survivors of childhood sexual abuse. *Journal of Counseling Psychology, 46*(3), 335–341.

Ketring, S. A., & Feinauer, L. L. (1999). Perpetrator-victim relationship: Long-term effects of sexual abuse for men and women. *American Journal of Family Therapy, 27*, 109–120.

King, N. J., Tongue, B. J., Mullen, P., Myerson, N., Heyne, D., Rollings, et al. (2000). Treating sexually abused children with posttraumatic stress symptoms: A randomized clinical trial. *Journal of the American Academy of Child and Adolescent Psychiatry, 39*, 1347–1355.

Kogan, S. M. (2004). Disclosing unwanted sexual experiences: Results from a national sample of adolescent women. *Child Abuse & Neglect, 28*, 147–165.

Kovach, J. (1986). Incest as a treatment issue for alcoholic women. *Alcoholism Treatment Quarterly, 3*, 1–15.

Lawson, C. (1993). Mother-son sexual abuse: Rare or underreported? A critique of the research. *Child Abuse & Neglect, 17*, 261–269.

Martin, G., Bergen, H. A., Richardson, A. S., Roeger, L., & Allison, S. (2004). Sexual abuse and suicidality: Gender differences in a large community sample of adolescents. *Child Abuse & Neglect, 28*, 491–503.

Marvasti, J. A., & Dripchak, V. L. (2004a). Psychiatric co-morbidities in female survivors of sexual trauma: Trauma related syndrome and revictimization. In J. A. Marvasti (Ed.), *Psychiatric treatment of victims and survivors of sexual trauma: A neurobiological approach* (pp. 19–35). Springfield, IL: Charles C. Thomas.

Marvasti, J. A., & Dripchak, V. L. (2004b). Psychopathology in survivors of incestuous abuse: Self-mutilation, trichotillomania, restless leg syndrome, & anorexia nervosa. In J. A. Marvasti (Ed.), *Psychiatric treatment of victims and survivors of sexual trauma: A neurobiological approach* (pp. 37–50). Springfield, IL: Charles C. Thomas.

McCloskey, L. A., & Bailey, J. A. (2000). The intergenerational transmission of risk for child sexual abuse. *Journal of Interpersonal Violence, 15*(10), 1019–1035.

Merrill, L. L., Thomsen, C. J., Sinclair, B. B., Gold, S. R., & Milner, J. S. (2001). Predicting the impact of child sexual abuse on women: The role of abuse severity, parental support, and coping strategies. *Journal of Consulting and Clinical Psychology, 69*(6), 992–1006.

Meyerson, L. A., Long, P. J., Miranda, R., Jr., & Marx, B. P. (2002). The influence of childhood sexual abuse, physical abuse, family environment, and gender on the psychological adjustment of adolescents. *Child Abuse & Neglect, 26*, 387–405.

Miner, M. H., & Dwyer, S. M. (1997). The psychosocial development of sex offenders: Differences between exhibitionists, child molesters, and incest offenders. *International Journal of Offender Therapy and Comparative Criminology, 41*(1), 36–44.

Molnar, B. E., Berkman, L. F., & Buka, S. L. (2001). Psychopathology, childhood sexual abuse and other childhood adversities: Relative links to subsequent suicidal behaviour in the US. *Psychological Medicine, 31*, 965–977.

Molnar, B. E., Buka, S. L. & Kessler, R. C. (2001). Child sexual abuse and subsequent psychopathology: Results from the national comorbidity survey. *American Journal of Public Health, 91*(5), 753–760.

Morgan, T., & Cummings, A. L. (1999). Change experienced during group therapy for female survivors of childhood sexual abuse. *Journal of Consulting and Clinical Psychology, 67*, 28–36.

Morrison, A., & Treliving, L. (2002). Evaluation of outcome in a dynamically oriented group for adult males who have been sexually abused in childhood. *British Journal of Psychotherapy, 19*, 59–76.

Mullen, P. E., Martin, J. L., Anderson, J. C., Romans, S. E., & Herbison, G. P. (1996). The long-term impact of the physical, emotional, and sexual abuse of children: A community study. *Child Abuse & Neglect, 20*, 7–21.

Nash, M. R., Zivney, O., & Hulsey, T. (1993). Characteristics of sexual abuse associated with greater psychological impairment among children. *Child Abuse & Neglect, 17*, 401–408.

Nelson, E. C., Heath, A. C., Madden, P. A., Cooper, M. L., Dinwiddie, S. H., Bucholz, K. K., et al. (2002). Association between self-reported childhood sexual abuse and adverse psychosocial outcomes: Results from a twin study. *Archives of General Psychiatry, 59*, 139–145.

Neumark-Sztainer, D., Story, M., Hannan, P. J., Beauhring, T., & Resnick, M. D. (2000). Disorder eating among adolescents: Associations with sexual physical abuse and other familial psychosocial factors. *International Journal of Eating Disorders, 28*, 249–258.

O'Brien, J. D. (1987). The effects of incest on female adolescent development. *Journal of American Academy of Psychoanalysis, 15*, 83–92.

Owens, G. P., & Chard, K. M. (2003). Comorbidity and psychiatric diagnoses among women reporting child sexual abuse. *Child Abuse & Neglect, 27*, 1075–1082.

Parton, F., & Day, A. (2002). Empathy, intimacy, loneliness and locus of control in child sex offenders: A comparison between familial and nonfamilial child sexual offenders. *Journal of Child Sexual Abuse, 11*(2), 41–57.

Peleikis, D. E., Mykletun, A., & Dahl, A. A. (2004). The relative influence of childhood sexual abuse and other family background risk factors on adult adversities in female outpatients treated for anxiety disorders and depression. *Child Abuse & Neglect, 28*, 61–76.

Pribor, E. F., & Dinwiddie, S. H. (1992). Psychiatric correlates of incest in childhood. *American Journal of Psychiatry, 149*, 52–56.

Raj, A., Silverman, J. G., & Amaro, H. (2000). The relationship between sexual abuse and sexual risk among high school students: Findings from the 1997 Massachusetts Youth Risk Behavior Survey. *Maternal and Child Health Journal, 4*(2), 125–134.

Ray, S. L. (1996). Adult male survivors of incest: An exploratory study. *Journal of Child Sexual Abuse, 5,* 103–114.

Rice, M. E., & Harris, G. T. (2002). Men who molest their sexually immature daughters: Is a special explanation required? *Journal of Abnormal Psychology, 111*(2), 329–339.

Rind, B., Tromovitch, P., & Bauserman, R. (1998). A meta-analytic examination of assumed properties of child sexual abuse using college samples. *Psychological Bulletin, 124,* 22–53.

Roberts, L., & Lie, G. (1989). A group therapy approach to treatment of incest. *Social Work with Groups, 12,* 77–90.

Rodriguez, N., Vande Kemp, H., & Foy, D. W. (1998). Posttraumatic stress disorder in survivors of childhood sexual and physical abuse: A critical review of the empirical research. *Journal of Child Sexual Abuse, 7*(2), 17–45.

Roesler, T. A., & Wind, T. W. (1994). Telling the secret: Adult women describe their disclosures of incest. *Journal of Interpersonal Violence, 9*(3), 327–338.

Ruggiero, K. J., McLeer, S. V., & Dixon, J. F. (2000). Sexual abuse characteristics associated with survivor psychopathology. *Child Abuse & Neglect, 24*(7), 951–964.

Russell, D. E. H. (1986). *The secret trauma: Incest in the lives of girls and women.* New York: Basic Books.

Ryan, K. D., Kilmer, R. P., Cauce, A. M., Wantanabe, H., & Hoyt, D. R. (2000). Psychological consequences of child maltreatment in homeless adolescents: Untangling the unique effects of maltreatment and family environment. *Child Abuse & Neglect, 24*(3), 333–352.

Saunders, B. E., Villeponteaux, L. A., Lipovsky, J. A., Kilpatrick, D. G., & Veronen, L. J. (1992). Child sexual assault as a risk factor for mental disorders among women. *Journal of Interpersonal Violence, 7,* 189–204.

Schultz, R. (1990). Secrets of adolescence: Incest and developmental fixations. In R. P. Kluft (Ed.), *Incest-related syndromes of adult psychopathology* (pp. 133–159). Washington, DC: American Psychiatric Press.

Seto, M. C., Lalumiere, M. L., & Kuban, M. (1999). The sexual preferences of incest offenders. *Journal of Abnormal Psychology, 108*(2), 267–272.

Sharpe, J., Selley, C., Low, L., & Hall, Z. (2001). Group analytic therapy for male survivors of childhood sexual abuse. *Group Analysis, 34,* 195–209.

Shaw, J. A., Lewis, J. E., Loeb, A., Rosado, J., & Rodriguez, R. A. (2000). Child on child sexual abuse: Psychological perspectives. *Child Abuse & Neglect, 24*(12), 1591–1600.

Sheinberg, M., & Fraenkel, P. (2001). *The Relational Trauma of Incest: A family-based approach to treatment.* New York: Guilford.

Sirles, E., & Franke, R. (1989). Factors influencing mothers' reactions to intrafamily sexual abuse. *Child Abuse & Neglect, 13,* 131–139.

Spiegel, D., Classen, C., Thurston, E., & Butler, L. (2004). Trauma-focused versus present-focused models of group treatment for women sexually abused in childhood. In L. Koenig, L. S. Doll, A. O'Leary, and W. Pequegnat (Eds.) *From child sexual abuse to adult sexual risk: Trauma, revictimization, and intervention* (pp. 251–268). Washington, DC: American Psychological Association.

Spiegel, J. (2003). *Sexual abuse of males: The SAM model of theory and practice.* New York: Brunner-Routledge.

Steel, J., Sanna, L., Hammond, B., Whipple, J., & Cross, H. (2004). Psychological sequelae of childhood sexual abuse: Abuse-related characteristics, coping strategies, and attributional style. *Child Abuse & Neglect, 28,* 785–801.

Stevenson, J. (1999). The treatment of long-term sequelae of child abuse. *Journal of Child Psychology and Psychiatry, 40,* 89–111.

Stroud, D. D. (1999). Familial support as perceived by adult victims of childhood sexual abuse. *Sexual Abuse, 11,* 159–175.

Tardif, M., Auclair, N., Jacob, M., & Carpentier, J. (2005). Sexual abuse perpetrated by adult and juvenile females: An ultimate attempt to resolve a conflict associated with maternal identity. *Child Abuse & Neglect, 29,* 153–167.

Teusch, R. (2001). Substance abuse as a symptom of childhood sexual abuse. *Psychiatric Service, 52,* 1530–1532.

Tsai, M., Feldman-Summers, S., & Edgar, M. (1979). Childhood molestation: Variables related to differential impact on psychosexual functioning in adult women. *Journal of Abnormal Psychology, 88,* 407–417.

U.S. Department of Justice. (2000). *Sexual assault of young children as reported to law enforcement: Victim, incident, and offender characteristics.* (NCJ 182990). Washington, DC: Department of Justice, Bureau of Justice Statistics.

Vandiver, D. M., & Kercher, G. (2004). Offender and victim characteristics of registered female sex offenders in Texas: A proposed typology of female sexual offenders. *Sexual Abuse: A Journal of Research and Treatment, 16*(2), 121–137.

van Gerko, K., Hughes, M. L., Hamill, M., & Waller, G. (2005). Reported childhood sexual abuse and eating-disordered cognitions and behaviors. *Child Abuse & Neglect, 29,* 375–382.

Voth, P. F., & Tutty, L. M. (1999). Daughter's perceptions of being mothered by an incest survivor: A phenomenological study. *Journal of Child Sexual Abuse, 8*(3), 25–43.

Waller, G. (1992). Sexual abuse and the severity of bulimic symptomology. *British Journal of Psychiatry, 161,* 90–93.

Waller, G., Hamilton, K., Rose, N., Sumra, J., & Baldwin, G. (1993). Sexual abuse and body-image distortion in the eating disorders. *British Journal of Clinical Psychology, 32,* 350–352.

Webster, S. D., & Beech, A. R. (2001). The nature of sexual offenders' affective empathy: A grounded theory analysis. *Sexual Abuse: A Journal of Research and Treatment, 12,* 249–261.

Weiss, E. L., Longhurst, J. G., & Mazure, C. M. (1999). Childhood sexual abuse as a risk factor for depression in women: Psychosocial and neurobiological correlates. *American Journal of Psychiatry, 156*(6), 816–828.

Westbury, E., & Tutty, L. M. (1999). The efficacy of group treatment for survivors of childhood abuse. *Child Abuse & Neglect, 23,* 31–44.

Wilson, R. J. (1999). Emotional congruence in sexual offenders against children. *Sexual Abuse: A Journal of Research and Treatment, 11,* 33–48.

Wind, T. W., & Silvern, L. (1992). Type and extent of child abuse as predictors of adult functioning. *Journal of Family Violence, 7,* 261–281.

Wonderlich, S. A., Crosby, R. D., Mitchell, J. E., Thompson, K. M., Redlin, J., Demuth, G., et al. (2001). *Eating disturbance and sexual trauma in childhood and adulthood.* New York: Wiley.

Wyatt, G. E., & Newcomb, M. (1990). Internal and external mediators of women's sexual abuse in childhood. *Journal of Consulting and Clinical Psychology, 58,* 758–767.

Ystgaard, M., Hestetun, I., Loeb, M., & Mehlum, L. (2004). Is there a specific relationship between childhood sexual and physical abuse and repeated suicidal behavior? *Child Abuse & Neglect, 28,* 863–875.

Zlotnick, C., Mattia, J., & Zimmerman, M. (2001). Clinical features of survivors of sexual abuse with major depression. *Child Abuse & Neglect, 25,* 357–367.

Zlotnick, C., Ryan, C. E., Miller, I. W., & Keitner, G. I. (1995). Childhood abuse and recovery from major depression. *Child Abuse & Neglect, 19,* 1513–1516.

Zlotnick, C., Shea, T. M., Rosen, K., Simpson, E., Mulrenin, K., Begin, A., et al. (1997). An affect-management group for women with posttraumatic stress disorder and histories of childhood sexual abuse. *Journal of Traumatic Stress, 10,* 425–436.

Zlotnick, C., Warshaw, M., Shea, M. T., & Keller, M. B. (1997). Trauma and chronic depression among patients with anxiety disorders. *Journal of Consulting and Clinical Psychology, 65,* 333–336.

7

Treatment of Sex Offenders

Lester W. Wright, Jr., and Angela P. Hatcher ◆

INTRODUCTION

The term "sex offender" can be defined as any individual who, because of the nature of his or her sexual behavior, has come into contact with the legal system. The sexual behavior for which the individual has gotten into trouble might have been coercive in nature, as in the case of rape, or it might have been for what is known in psychology as paraphilic behavior. Paraphilias, formerly known as sexual deviations, represent a group of heterogeneous disorders. The common theme in this group is that they involve sexual urges, fantasies, and behaviors that are viewed as atypical and often socially unacceptable (American Psychiatric Association, 2000). The essential features of a paraphilia in the *Diagnostic and Statistical Manual of Mental Disorders* (*DSM-IV-TR*, a diagnostic guide used by mental health professionals) are recurrent, intense sexually arousing fantasies, sexual urges, or behaviors generally involving (1) nonhuman objects, (2) the suffering or humiliation of oneself or one's partner, or (3) children or other nonconsenting persons. For some clients, the atypical fantasies are essential for sexual arousal and, therefore, they are always incorporated into sexual behavior, even if just in fantasy. For others, the atypical urges and fantasies are occasional, and they may still engage in normative sexual practices.

The *DSM-IV-TR* states that paraphilias, regardless of their prevalence, are typically persistent; however, they do sometimes diminish with age. Because perpetrators of sexual offenses are most commonly men, we will limit our discussion to the treatment of male sex offenders.

It is important to remember that not all atypical sexual behaviors fall into the sex offense category. Likewise, what is considered deviant behavior can change and vary across cultures. As a result, treatment is generally limited to those individuals whose sexual behavior involves nonconsenting partners, including pedophilia, exhibitionism, voyeurism, and frotteurism, or to those individuals whose atypical sexual arousal is personally problematic. It has been found that men whose sexual fantasies center on fetishes, including cross-dressing or masochism, rarely request treatment; they seek a consenting partner who either shares or tolerates their atypical sexual interests (McAnulty & Burnette, 2004).

THEORETICAL FOUNDATIONS

In order to effectively treat sex offenders, it is important to have a thorough understanding of how atypical sexual arousal is developed and maintained. Behavioral modification is the main component of most contemporary treatment programs for paraphilias and other types of sex offenses (Abel et al., 1984; Barnard, Fuller, Robbins, & Shaw, 1989). Behavioral treatments are based on the assumption that atypical sexual interest is primarily learned behavior. Conditioning, the process whereby learning occurs, can either be operant or classical in nature. In the case of atypical sexual arousal, it is thought that a combination of both types of conditioning is responsible for the learning process. Operant conditioning generally occurs when a reinforcing consequence immediately follows a response and increases the future frequency of that response, or when an aversive consequence immediately follows a response and decreases the future frequency of that response. Classical conditioning occurs when a neutral stimulus acquires the eliciting properties of an unconditioned stimulus through pairing the unconditioned stimulus with a neutral stimulus.

As for the role of conditioning of atypical sexual interest, with regard to classical conditioning, a neutral, or in this case previously nonsexually arousing, stimulus becomes sexually arousing by repeatedly being paired with a stimulus that is sexually arousing. The sexually arousing stimulus that the neutral stimulus is paired with may be an unconditioned, or unlearned stimulus, or it might be a conditioned, or learned stimulus. Operant conditioning, in this situation, would be important in the reinforcement of behavior as sexually arousing. Specifically, masturbation to atypical fantasies will increase their strength to sexually arouse and also function as mental rehearsals in which future sexual offenses are planned (Marshall & Barbaree, 1990). Evidence for the relationship between atypical stimuli and orgasm is provided by a few early analogue laboratory studies. These studies (Rachman, 1966; Rachman & Hodgson, 1968) paired pictures of boots to nude pictures of adult women and led to increased responding (i.e., sexual arousal) to the fetishistic stimuli (i.e., the boots). Abel and Blanchard (1974), Evans (1968), Laws and Marshall (1991), and McGuire, Carlisle, & Young (1965) provide support for the use of masturbation to alter sexual interests; however, Herman, Barlow, and Agras (1974) and Marshall (1974) found it difficult to produce such arousal. It is important to remember that while atypical sexual arousal can be conditioned in a laboratory, this does not provide proof that atypical sexual interests develop along similar lines (Laws & O'Donohue, 1997). Regardless of how it developed, inappropriate or atypical sexual arousal is thought to be a significant factor in the cause and maintenance of sexual offending (Ward, Hudson, & Keenan, 2000), and, as such, learning to have a sexual preference for, and arousal to, consenting adult partners is viewed as necessary for changing one's sexual practices (Ward & Stewart, 2003).

There is good evidence that atypical sexual behavior, at least in the short term, is amenable to behavioral modification techniques (Feierman & Feierman, 2000), which are based on the above theoretical assumptions. The goal is to decrease the strength of the atypical arousal and to increase normative sexual arousal. Support for these principles comes from several lines of research. Stava, Levin, and Schwanz (1993), for example, demonstrated that it was the aversive component of covert sensitization trials, rather than merely distraction or habituation, that was responsible for reductions in sexual arousal to pedophilic stimuli in a 30-year-old pedophile.

Broadly speaking, treatment for sex offenders includes strategies to decrease atypical arousal and increase appropriate arousal. However, because men who commit sex offenses often have multiple deficits, including social skills deficits, poor impulse control, and low victim empathy, most treatment programs employ multiple modalities to address these problems. Likewise, treatment for sex offenders may also include skills training, sex education, and cognitive restructuring. Finally, relapse prevention is included in most sex offender treatment programs as a means of preventing the offender from committing another sex offense.

DECREASING ATYPICAL AROUSAL

Early behavioral interventions for atypical sexual arousal focused primarily on decreasing atypical arousal through aversive conditioning procedures. Using these procedures, atypical sexual arousal is decreased by repeatedly pairing atypical fantasies and urges with aversive stimuli so that rather than eliciting sexual arousal, the atypical fantasies eventually acquire aversive properties and are no longer sexually arousing. Three aversive conditioning procedures are described below: aversion therapy using either electrical or olfactory aversion, covert sensitization, and masturbatory satiation. In addition to these procedures, medication is sometimes used to decrease sexual arousal.

Aversion Therapy

The goal of aversion therapy is to decrease the sexually arousing properties of atypical fantasies and images; this is accomplished by pairing the atypical fantasies and images with an aversive stimulus. McAnulty and Adams (1992) noted that while there does appear to be evidence in the literature for the effectiveness of aversive conditioning in treating paraphilic disorders, the use of aversion therapy is sometimes challenged on ethical and moral grounds.

There are two types of aversion therapy, differentiated primarily by the type of aversive stimulus that is used. Electrical aversion involves the use of a mild but painful shock (McAnulty & Adams, 1992). Olfactory aversion involves the use of a noxious odor, such as ammonia. For each type of aversion therapy, the aversive stimuli are immediately presented when the individual engages in atypical imagery or fantasy.

Covert Sensitization

Another form of aversive conditioning, covert sensitization, was introduced by Cautela (1967). Just as with other forms of aversive conditioning, the purpose of this procedure is to decrease the level of an undesired behavior. While covert sensitization is a form of aversive conditioning, it does not involve the actual presentation of an aversive stimulus. Cautela claimed that this procedure is covert in that the aversive stimuli are presented in the imagination only.

In this procedure the individual is asked to fantasize using his atypical fantasy; however, before the fantasy reaches the point of actually engaging in the atypical behavior, the individual is instructed to imagine an aversive image (e.g., getting caught by the police, spending time in jail, etc.) as a way to reduce the sexually arousing properties of the atypical fantasy (Cautela, 1967). In order for this procedure to be most effective, it is typically recommended that the aversive image that is used be one that the client would find most aversive. Likewise, images that are realistic are likely to be most effective.

With regard to effectiveness, in a review of the literature, Little and Curran (1978) noted that there have been several controlled, within-subject studies that provide empirical support for the use of covert sensitization in the treatment of sexual deviance. Likewise, Brownell, Hayes, and Barlow (1977) effectively used covert sensitization in the treatment of two exhibitionists, a sadist, a transvestite, and a child molester. Using a combination of orgasmic reconditioning, described below, and covert sensitization, Lande (1980) successfully treated an individual with a history of fire setting accompanied by masturbation.

Masturbatory Satiation

The technique of masturbatory satiation is intended to decrease an individual's arousal to atypical fantasies by pairing the atypical fantasies with boredom. When using the procedure, the individual is instructed to masturbate to orgasm while fantasizing about something that is normal or appropriate. Once the individual has reached orgasm, he is instructed to continue masturbating for forty-five minutes to one hour during which time the preferred atypical fantasy is used (Witt & Sager, 1988). Continuing to masturbate to an atypical fantasy after orgasm is punishing to the person, rather than rewarding and makes the atypical fantasy less exciting and, therefore, less likely to be used in the future. Using this technique the person learns that the normal fantasies help him have an orgasm and that the atypical fantasies produce boredom and may cause him pain or embarrassment.

Medication Management

The use of medications to treat sex offenders is controversial. Grubin (2000) pointed out that some cognitive-behavioral therapists perceive the use of medications as "cheating" and that the use of medications might suggest to the offender that his ability to control his offending is limited because his sexual drives are not completely under his power. The most commonly used classes of medications are antiandrogens and selective serotonin reuptake inhibitors (SSRIs).

Hyde and DeLamater (2006) stated that sexual arousability is dependent on maintaining the level of androgen in the bloodstream above a certain level. Therefore, antiandrogen drugs are sometimes used either to reduce the production of androgen or to block the effects of androgen. The two most commonly used antiandrogen medications are cyproterone acetate and medroxyprogesterone acetate (Depo-Provera). By either blocking the production of androgens or blocking their effects, these medications reduce sexual drive as well as the individual's ability to respond physically (i.e., get an erection) to sexual stimuli (Grubin, 2000).

The SSRIs, frequently prescribed for depression and anxiety, are also sometimes used in the treatment of sex offenders. In their review of the literature, Greenberg and Bradford (1997) reported that SSRIs have been useful in reducing fantasies, sexual urges, masturbation, and paraphilic behavior in exhibitionists, fetishists, voyeurs, and child molesters. Grubin (2000) suggested that SSRIs may be most beneficial for those individuals whose sexual offending has an obsessive-compulsive quality to it.

Hyde and DeLamater (2006) suggested that antiandrogen and SSRIs in the treatment of sex offenders should only be used as one element of a more comprehensive treatment program. Likewise, Grubin (2000) stated that most men want to quit taking the medication at some point as a test, because of side effects, or because they are unhappy with being asexual. Regardless of the reason, it is important that individuals who have committed sex offenses have other skills at their disposal to prevent committing another offense. It should also be mentioned that the use of these medications, just as with any other medication, does not guarantee the desired effect.

INCREASING APPROPRIATE AROUSAL

Early attempts to change atypical behavior were not especially successful since clinicians focused exclusively on eliminating atypical arousal without attending to normative arousal (Barlow, 1973). Many individuals whose atypical sexual arousal has been lifelong and exclusive do not have sexual fantasies or urges that contain "normal" stimuli, such as consenting adult sexual interactions. Because eliminating the individual's atypical urges does not guarantee the emergence of normal urges to replace them, conditioning procedures to enhance sexual arousal to appropriate stimuli (i.e., consenting adult sexual partners) were developed.

Orgasmic Reconditioning

Orgasmic reconditioning is one of the techniques designed to enhance arousal to appropriate stimuli (e.g., adult heterosexual and/or homosexual partners) by pairing appropriate stimuli with orgasm. It is also sometimes referred to as directed masturbation, masturbation training, or masturbatory reconditioning; however, some of these terms have specific meanings. According to McAnulty and Adams (1992), "The rationale for orgasmic reconditioning is based on the assumption that stimuli acquire sexually arousing properties through their pairing with pleasurable sensations, namely sexual arousal and orgasm" (p. 188). There are currently four distinct forms of masturbatory reconditioning: (a) thematic shift (Marquis, 1970; Thorpe, Schmidt, & Castell, 1964); (b) fantasy alternation (Abel, Blanchard, Barlow & Flanagan, 1975; Van-Deventer & Laws, 1978); (c) directed masturbation (Kremsdorf, Holmen, & Laws, 1980; Maletzky, 1985); and (d) satiation (Marshall & Lippens, 1977). The most frequently used type of orgasmic reconditioning, and the one that we will discuss, is thematic shift.

Thematic shift orgasmic reconditioning, as originally used by Marquis (1970), required the client to masturbate using atypical stimuli until the point of ejaculatory inevitability, at which time the client was to switch to an appropriate fantasy. The aim is to increase the attractiveness of the conventional fantasy by such association (Hawton, 1983). As therapy progresses, the client is instructed to begin using an appropriate fantasy earlier and earlier in his masturbatory sessions until he can ultimately use appropriate fantasies from the beginning of masturbation to orgasm (McAnulty & Adams, 1992). Initially, the client may lose his arousal and erection when he switches to the appropriate fantasy. If this happens, the client is instructed to switch to his preferred fantasy to achieve a high level of arousal and then return to the appropriate fantasy. Bancroft (1974) found that gradual reshaping of atypical fantasies is more effective than trying to masturbate without using the atypical/nonnormative fantasy at all.

Quinsey and Earls (1990) concluded that evidence for the effectiveness of orgasmic reconditioning is limited in depth and significance. Laws and Marshall (1991), while optimistic, stated that there are insufficient data to conclude that orgasmic reconditioning is a clearly effective treatment for sexual deviations of any kind over the long term. Several studies (Davison, 1968; Marquis, 1970) reported success in using orgasmic reconditioning with clients, but treatment did not rely on orgasmic reconditioning exclusively. Marshall and Eccles (1991) consider orgasmic reconditioning to be one component of a comprehensive program to modify one's sexual behavior.

SKILLS TRAINING

Social Skills Training

Deficient social skills are an important factor in understanding sexual deviations (Quinsey, 1977). The rationale for social skills training is quite simple. If an individual does not feel competent to interact with someone in an age-appropriate manner then he or she is more apt to interact with someone younger and/or with someone in an inappropriate manner. The aim of social skills training is to teach an individual how to develop social relationships that could eventually lead to a consensual intimate relationship with an appropriate partner. Some of the early work in skills training, called heterosocial skills training, was conducted with men and women to teach them how to interact with adult partners of the opposite sex (Bellack & Morrison, 1982; Curran, 1977; Curran & Monti, 1982). Some of the skills taught in social skills training include how to initiate a conversation, appropriate eye contact, how to respect another's personal space, how to take turns in a conversation without interrupting, how to end a conversation, as well as how and when it is appropriate to touch another person. Other programs have been designed to assist individuals who engage in a range of atypical sexual behaviors (Abel et al., 1984; Marshall & Barbaree, 1988; McFall, 1990; Rooth, 1980). The skills training component is often incorporated into a comprehensive treatment program that is designed to fit the individual's needs. When working with someone who does not appear to be socially skilled, a distinction must be made between a person with skills deficits and a person whose performance in social situations is inhibited (Arkowitz, 1981; Bellack & Morrison, 1982). If the individual has skills deficits then skills acquisition is in order. If the individual has the requisite skills but does not use them, then the individual will require some type of treatment to enable the use of these skills. Usually social skills are inhibited by anxiety/irrational fears. The individual may require some anxiety reduction technique, such as desensitization, that is, helping the person to relax in the presence of something that makes him anxious or scared; or perhaps some cognitive restructuring, which is explained below, to challenge rationalizations, or the thoughts people have that make it okay for them to engage in atypical behavior, and change distorted thinking (McMullin, 1986; Murphy, 1990).

Assertiveness Training

Stermac and Quinsey (1986) found that a significant number of rapists lack social competence skills, particularly assertiveness skills. Likewise, it is often the case that sex offenders need to be taught the difference between assertive, aggressive, passive, and passive-aggressive behaviors. An individual who possesses assertive skills is able to respond to problematic situations by making requests when something is wanted and by refusing inappropriate requests (Schroeder & Black, 1985). When acting in an assertive manner, one protects his rights as well as the rights of others (Lange & Jakubowski, 1976). When acting aggressively, one is protecting one's rights but trampling on the rights of others. An aggressive person may overact in some situations, become angry, and be abusive toward others; these types of people usually want things done their way and do not take turns or negotiate fairly (Dow, 1994). A person who is passive is allowing his rights to be neglected while protecting the rights of others. A passive person may not express opinions, does not refuse unreasonable requests, and allows others to have their way most of the time. A person who is passive-aggressive acts as if he is subjugating his rights and protecting the rights of others but will trample on the rights of others behind their backs. Individuals who are constantly passive may lash out in an aggressive manner when they get tired of having their rights violated. The goal of assertiveness training is to teach individuals that everybody has rights and how to protect their rights without violating the rights of others. Cognitive restructuring may be necessary to help the offender realize that he has rights and that it is alright to say no to certain requests or that it is alright to make appropriate requests of others. Individuals with low self-esteem and negative core beliefs, such as "I am stupid" or "I am worthless," often place the rights of others ahead of their own rights. When this happens the person often feels angry and taken advantage of and may act out sexually in an atypical way to get even or to feel better. Several models of assertiveness training can be used, depending upon the situation. Basic assertion involves a simple expression of standing up for one's rights, beliefs, feelings, or opinions and can also be used to express affection (Lange & Jakubowski, 1976). Empathic assertion allows you to convey sensitivity to another and is useful in situations in which you have a relationship with an individual (Lange & Jakubowski, 1976). Escalating assertion (Rimm & Masters,

1974) involves starting with a response that can accomplish the speaker's goal with a minimum of effort and negative emotion and has a small possibility of negative consequences (Lange & Jakubowski, 1976). If, however, the other person fails to respond to a request and continues to violate one's rights, the speaker escalates the assertion and becomes increasingly firm. The broken record model of assertiveness (Smith, 1975) is probably best used in situations in which one does not have a relationship with the individual and does not plan to start such a relationship. When using the broken record model, the individual basically sounds like a record that is stuck repeating the same phrase over and over.

Anger Management

For some offenders, sex and aggression are inextricably linked. Individuals develop scripts for interpersonal relationships through their observations and interactions with others. Negative events from their past, such as poor parenting, parental rejection, inconsistent and harsh discipline, violence between parents, physical and sexual abuse, being exposed to inappropriate models, as well as many others can lead to distorted internal dialogue and a faulty belief system about one's environment (Fagen & Wexler, 1988; Marshall & Barbaree, 1990). These aggressive cognitive scripts that develop throughout one's childhood and adolescence could become blueprints for aggression depending on whether the behaviors exhibited are punished or rewarded (Huesmann, 1988). The aim of anger management is to reduce the intensity of the anger that is experienced and to control the way the individual behaves when anger is elicited.

Turkat (1990) proposed treating aggression problems using graduated exposure to stimuli that elicit anger. He suggested constructing a hierarchy of anger-eliciting stimuli and training the individual to engage in a competing response, such as distracting oneself with another thought or activity or using a relaxation technique to get rid of the anger. The idea is that one cannot be angry and relaxed at the same time. Cognitive restructuring, or changing how one thinks about something, can be used with offenders who hold adversarial attitudes toward their partners and for those who use interpersonal violence to attain desired goals. Skills training—for example, assertiveness and social skills training—may be necessary to supplement the offender's armament of tools to use in interpersonal relationships. Teaching the client to take a time-out is also a good technique to allow him to compose his thoughts and calm down before he responds when he is angry. Stress management and communication skills training may be implemented if necessary.

Victim Empathy Training

Empathy is the awareness and understanding of another's thoughts and feelings. It is widely accepted by clinicians within the field that a lack of empathy plays a major role in the etiology and maintenance of sex offending. The data from studies assessing empathy in sex offenders, however, have provided mixed results (Geer, Estupinan, & Manguno-Mire, 2000). Researchers examining empathy in sex offenders have recently begun to investigate the nature of empathic responding to determine if this is a general deficit or if it is circumscribed to a class of victims. Fernandez, Marshall, Lightbody, and O'Sullivan (1999) assessed the level of empathy in child molesters and a control group of nonoffenders for three types of victims: an accident victim, a general sexual abuse victim, and their own victim. They found that child molesters displayed the same amount of empathy as nonoffenders toward the victim of an accident. However, relative to the accident victim, the child molesters demonstrated a deficit in empathy toward a general sexual abuse victim, that is, not their own victim. Similarly, the child molesters displayed significantly less empathy toward their own victim than toward the general sexual abuse victim. This finding is important as it calls into question a long-held assumption that sex offenders lack empathy/lack the ability to experience empathy. Despite the lack of clear-cut evidence for the role of empathy, most treatment programs for sex offenders include a component designed to increase an offender's capacity for victim empathy to reduce recidivism.

SEX EDUCATION

Barbaree and Seto (1997) suggested that sex education be included in a comprehensive treatment program for sex offenders. Given that myths and misinformation about sexuality abound, it is likely that an offender lacks information and/or has incorrect information. The aim of sex education is to make the individual more comfortable with sexual information and to improve one's sexual skills by providing comprehensive knowledge of the sexual anatomy, sexual response, sexual technique, and communication skills. Kolvin (1967) suggested that sexual education, counseling, and reassurance alone could generate behavior change. Sex education can be provided in a group format, and/or self-help books can be given to the client to read on his own time.

SEX THERAPY

Clients who have a sexual dysfunction may require sex therapy to correct the problem. Conditions such as erectile disorder, premature ejaculation, or delayed ejaculation may cause the client to be embarrassed or to get angry and act out with his partner. The end result is that the person could seek out nonconsenting or underage partners and become abusive if provoked. The goal of sex therapy is to restore normal functioning so that he will be comfortable with his sexual performance and will hopefully seek out appropriate partners, or be comfortable with his dysfunction and learn other ways to please his partner. There are empirically validated techniques for treating sexual dysfunctions and these can be administered in individual therapy. Leiblum and Rosen (2000) and Wincze and Carey (2001) offer treatment recommendations for sexual dysfunctions.

COGNITIVE RESTRUCTURING

Our thoughts, appraisals, and expectancies can elicit or modulate our mood and physiological processes, influence the environment, and serve as stimuli for behavior (Turk, Rudy, & Sorkin, 1992). Conversely, mood, physiology, environmental factors, and behavior can influence thought processes (Turk et al., 1992). The goals of cognitive therapy are to help the client identify and correct maladaptive thoughts, to retrain the client to think more logically and realistically, and to modify any irrational core beliefs (Abel et al., 1984; Turk et al., 1992). Murphy (1990) found that sexual aggressors reported such cognitive distortions as claims that the victim enjoyed the assault, blaming the victim, and a general belief in rape myths. This self-deceptive and distorted thinking, which is based on false assumptions, misperceptions, and self-serving interpretations, helps the sex offender justify his behavior (Feierman & Feierman, 2000). The application of cognitive-behavioral therapy to sexual disorders evolved from the research on anxiety disorders and depression.

Cognitive restructuring involves teaching the client to challenge irrational attitudes and beliefs, not only about sexuality, but also about how he views the world and life in general. The client is taught to self-monitor his thoughts, to recognize maladaptive thought patterns, and to log his irrational thoughts on tracking sheets that are used in therapy to monitor progress (Beck, Rush, Shaw, & Emery, 1979). The client is instructed to dispute the irrational thoughts and state evidence as to why the thoughts are irrational. The client is then encouraged to state a rational response and provide evidence for the validity of this response. Clients usually have difficulty recognizing their distorted thoughts and may argue that their distorted thoughts are accurate since they have evidence as to the veracity of their thoughts and beliefs. However, the evidence provided by the client can usually be identified as another type of cognitive distortion. As the client becomes better at identifying his irrational thoughts and beliefs, he reduces the amount of time spent thinking irrationally and is able to make better decisions that lead to more desirable outcomes. Once the client starts to change his attitude and thought patterns and begins to see events and situations more realistically, the therapist can begin to work on the client's core beliefs to help the client see himself in a more positive manner. Negative core beliefs such as "I'm stupid" or "I'm powerless" can be tackled and replaced by more accurate beliefs once the client no longer engages in distorted thinking. By experiencing these negative core beliefs about oneself—for example, "I'm stupid"—the person feels inadequate around people his own age. He then spends time with individuals younger than himself, perhaps children, so that he feels smarter than them, which can lead to sexual abuse. If a man has a negative core belief that he is powerless, he might rape a woman or a child to prove that he has power over that person. By helping the offender to realize that the negative core belief is incorrect, he can then develop an accurate core belief that does not lead to distorted thinking and/or inappropriate behavior.

An alternative to using cognitive restructuring to help clients change their thinking in order to change their negative feelings or problem behavior is to use acceptance-based therapy to help people accept their negative thoughts and feelings rather than change them (Hayes, Stossahl, & Wilson, 1999; Hayes & Wilson, 1994). Acceptance, in this paradigm, refers to the willingness to experience a full range of thoughts, emotions, memories, bodily states, and behavioral predispositions, including those that are problematic, without necessarily having to change them, escape from them, act on them, or avoid them (Paul, Marx, & Orsillo, 1999). According to LoPiccolo (1994), using acceptance-based therapies allows the client to relinquish the struggle to gain control over his thoughts, which then allows him to develop and engage in more adaptive, alternative behaviors.

RELAPSE PREVENTION

Relapse prevention is a self-control program designed to teach individuals who are trying to change their behavior how to anticipate and cope with the problem of relapse (Laws, 1989, p. 2). The aim of relapse prevention is to prevent the recurrence of a problematic behavior (Hanson, 2000; Ward & Hudson, 1998), which is frequently accomplished by helping the individual identify and control or avoid triggers of the behavior (Hyde & DeLamater, 2006). Relapse prevention is frequently used as an adjunct to cognitive-behavioral therapy but has also been used as a stand-alone program. The program has a psychoeducational thrust that combines behavioral skills training, cognitive therapy, and lifestyle change (Larimer & Marlatt, 1994; Laws, 1989). This method of treatment teaches coping strategies to avoid lapses, which are viewed as opportunities to learn which stimuli control behavior, and relapses, which are viewed as failures (Maletzky, 1997). The model, as described by Pithers (1990), is based on the work of Marlatt and Gordon (1985), who developed this procedure for treating addictive behaviors.

Behavior chains and cycles are central concepts to relapse prevention (Maletzky, 1997). A sex offense is viewed as a sequence or chain of behaviors that ultimately leads to the offending behavior. A number of antecedents and assumptions precede the final act. With relapse prevention, the client is taught to analyze the chain of behaviors and assumptions that lead to the offending behavior. Clients are taught the value of breaking the chain of behaviors as early in the chain as possible to avert another offense. In the early stages of treatment the client is instructed to keep records of his lapses and triggers to create self-awareness and self-scrutiny (Maletzky, 1997). By helping the client anticipate events that predispose a lapse—that is, making a mistake, such as a child molester wanting to engage in sexual fantasies about children (as opposed to actually masturbating to fantasies about children, which would be a relapse)—and by having escape strategies to exit high-risk situations, lapses can often be circumvented. Additionally, stimulus control procedures are put in place to make the client accountable and to decrease offending opportunities. If a client has a relapse, the event is used as an opportunity to learn from his mistakes, and he is encouraged to begin using his treatment plan immediately. In summary, the essential components of relapse prevention include:

1. Identifying situations in which the individual is at high risk of relapse (feeling sad, lonely, etc.) and teaching the client to identify these high-risk situations and to avoid them.

2. Identifying lapses as behaviors that do not constitute full-fledged relapses, but which may be precursors to full-blown relapse (fantasizing about a child, walking near a playground, etc.), and teaching the client to identify lapses.

3. Teaching the client coping strategies to use both in high-risk situations and after lapses to prevent relapse.

While internal self-management strategies are important to stop the offending behavior (Pithers, 1990), it is also useful to include measures of external control, such as involving the client's family and coworkers (Maletzky, 1997). Therapy sessions often involve reviewing the situations the client found difficult and helping him engage in problem-solving to alleviate the problem. Maletzky (1997) warns that this process must be engaged in repeatedly so that it becomes a behavioral habit rather than an intellectual process. Relapse prevention can be conducted in either group or individual format.

IS TREATMENT OF SEX OFFENDERS EFFECTIVE?

Sex offenders have historically been viewed as difficult to treat, if not hopeless. This skepticism is based in part on the denial that is common among sex offenders and the prevailing belief that sexual preferences cannot be altered. There is also a common assumption that a person who has committed one sexual offense will invariably commit others. A number of studies give us reason to reconsider these notions. Overall recidivism rates do increase with the length of follow-up, but they are not 100 percent; in fact, one review concluded that 55 percent of sex offenders recidivate. Hanson and Bussière (1998), in their analysis of sexual offender recidivism studies, found that on average, the sexual offense recidivism rate is low (13.4 percent), with rapists having a higher average rate of recidivism than child molesters. Treatment does seem to help some offenders. Hall (1995) concluded that treatment produces a 30 percent reduction in recidivism. Treatment outcome rates, on a short-term basis, are significantly better than no treatment at all and often rival the outcome rates for many other *DSM-IV-TR* psychiatric disorders (Feierman & Feierman, 2000).

Treatment plans should be tailored to the individual offender based on his need and risk level in order to increase his chances of overcoming his problems. Anyone working with sexual offenders should be prepared to be patient and flexible because many offenders do not wish to change but are forced to do so as a result of external pressure, usually a family member or the legal system. Laws (2003) stated that resistance should be viewed as a phase of treatment rather than an obstacle. Therapists must help clients work through the resistance, or precontemplation, phase before contemplating actual change (Laws, 2003).

In most cases, any treatment technique in isolation will be ineffective and a combination of procedures is likely to be needed (Hawton, 1983). The client's unique behavioral excesses and deficits should guide the therapist in choosing which techniques to use. Assessment should include the presence of disinhibiting factors such as alcohol or drugs, stress or emotional states, the use of pornography, and the role of atypical fantasies in the commission of a sexual offense (Finkelhor, 1984). Treatment for sex offenders should generally cover a variety of issues such as distorted cognitions, sexual issues, victim empathy, social skills training, problem-solving, life skills, stress management, and relapse prevention training (Hudson, Marshall, Ward, Johnston, & Jones, 1995). We concur with Grossman, Martis, and Fichtner (1999), who concluded, "What emerges from the literature is a strong suggestion that a comprehensive cognitive-behavioral program should involve components that reduce atypical arousal while increasing appropriate arousal and should include cognitive restructuring, social skills training, victim empathy awareness, and relapse prevention" (p. 360). The research assessing the treatment of sex offenders demonstrates that treatment does seem to reduce recidivism among sexual offenders.

REFERENCES

Abel, G. G., Becker, J. B., Cunningham-Rathner, J., Rouleau, J. L., Kaplan, M., & Reich, J. (1984). *Treatment manual: The treatment of child molesters.* (Available from G. G. Abel, Behavioral Medicine Institute of Atlanta, 1401 Peachtree street, Northeast Atlanta, GA 30309).

Abel, G. G., & Blanchard, E. B. (1974). The role of fantasy in the treatment of sexual deviation. *Archives of General Psychiatry, 30,* 467–475.

Abel, G. G., Blanchard, E. B., Barlow, D. H., & Flanagan, B. (1975, December). *A case report of the behavioral treatment of a sadistic rapist.* Paper presented at the 9th Annual Convention of the Association for the Advancement of Behavior Therapy, San Francisco, CA.

American Psychiatric Association. (2000). *Diagnostic and statistical manual of mental disorders* (4th ed., text revision). Washington, DC: Author.

Arkowitz, H. (1981). Assessment of social skills. In M. Hersen & S. Bellack (Eds.), *Behavioral assessment: A practical handbook* (2nd ed., pp. 296–327). New York: Pergamon.

Bancroft, J. (1974). *Deviant sexual behaviour: Modification and assessment.* Oxford: Clarendon.

Barbaree, H. E., & Seto, M. C. (1997). Pedophilia: Assessment and treatment. In D. R. Laws & W. O'Donohue (Eds.), *Sexual deviance: Theory, assessment, and treatment* (p. 184). New York: Guilford.

Barlow, D. H. (1973). Increasing heterosexual responsiveness in the treatment of sexual deviation: A review of the clinical and experimental evidence. *Behavior Therapy, 4,* 655–671.

Barnard, G. W., Fuller, A. K., Robbins, L., & Shaw, T. (1989). *The child molester: An integrated approach to evaluation and treatment.* Philadelphia: Brunner/Mazel.

Beck, A. T., Rush, A. J., Shaw, B. F., & Emery, G. (1979). *Cognitive therapy of depression: A treatment manual.* New York: Guilford.

Bellack, A. S., & Morrison, R. L. (1982). Interpersonal dysfunction. In A. S. Bellack, M. Hersen, & A. E. Kazdin (Eds.), *International handbook of behavior modification and therapy* (pp. 717–747). New York: Plenum Press.

Brownell, K. D., Hayes, S. C., & Barlow, D. H. (1977). Patterns of appropriate and deviant sexual arousal: The behavioral treatment of multiple sexual deviations. *Journal of Consulting and Clinical Psychology, 45,* 1144–1155.

Cautela, J. R. (1967). Covert sensitization. *Psychological Reports, 20,* 459–468.

Curran, J. P. (1977). Skills training as an approach to the treatment of heterosexual-social anxiety: A review. *Psychological Bulletin, 84,* 140–157.

Curran, J. P., & Monti, P. M. (1982). *Social skills training: A practical handbook for assessment and treatment.* New York: Guilford.

Davison, G. C. (1968). Elimination of a sadistic fantasy by a client-controlled counterconditioning technique. *Journal of Abnormal Psychology, 73,* 84–90.

Dow, M. G. (1994). Social inadequacy and social skill. In L. W. Craighead, W. E. Craighead, A. E. Kazdin, & M. J. Mahoney (Eds.), *Cognitive and behavioral interventions: An empirical approach to mental health problems* (pp. 123–140). Boston: Allyn & Bacon.

Evans, D. R. (1968). Masturbatory fantasy and sexual deviation. *Behaviour Research and Therapy, 6,* 17–19.

Fagen, J., & Wexler, S. (1988). Explanations of sexual assault among violent delinquents. *Journal of Adolescent Research, 3,* 363–385.

Feierman, J. R., & Feierman, L. A. (2000). Paraphilias. In L. T. Szuchman & F. Muscarella (Eds.), *Psychological perspectives on human sexuality* (pp. 480–518). New York: Wiley.

Fernandez, Y. M., Marshall, W. L., Lightbody, S., & O'Sullivan, C. (1999). The Child Molester Empathy Measure: Description and examination of its reliability and validity. *Sexual Abuse: A Journal of Research and Treatment, 11,* 17–31.

Finkelhor, D. (1984). *Child sexual abuse: New theory and research.* New York: Free Press.

Geer, J. H., Estupinan, L. A., & Manguno-Mire, G. M. (2000). Empathy, social skills, and other relevant cognitive processes in child molesters. *Aggression and Violent Behavior, 5,* 99–126.

Greenberg, D., & Bradford, J. M. W. (1997). Treatment of the paraphilic disorders: A review of the selective serotonin reuptake inhibitors. *Sexual Abuse: A Journal of Research and Treatment, 9,* 349–360.

Grossman, L. S., Martis, B., & Fichtner, C. G. (1999). Are sex offenders treatable? A research overview. *Psychiatric Services, 50,* 349–361.

Grubin, D. (2000). Complementing relapse prevention with medical intervention. In D. R. Laws, S. M. Hudson, & T. Ward (Eds.), *Remaking relapse prevention with sex offenders: A sourcebook* (pp. 201–212). Thousand Oaks, CA: Sage.

Hall, G. C. N. (1995). Sexual offender recidivism revisited: A meta-analysis of recent treatment studies. *Journal of Consulting and Clinical Psychology, 63,* 802–809.

Hanson, R. K. (2000). What is so special about relapse prevention? In D. R. Laws, S. M. Hudson, & T. Ward (Eds.), *Remaking relapse prevention with sex offenders: A sourcebook* (pp. 3–26). Thousand Oaks, CA: Sage.

Hanson, R. K., & Bussière, M. T. (1998). Predicting relapse: A meta-analysis of sexual offender recidivism studies. *Journal of Consulting and Clinical Psychology, 66,* 348–362.

Hawton, K. (1983). Behavioural approaches to the management of sexual deviations. *British Journal of Psychiatry, 143,* 248–255.

Hayes, S. C., Stossahl, K. D., & Wilson, K. G. (1999). *Acceptance and commitment therapy: An experiential approach to behavior change.* New York: Guilford.

Hayes, S. C., & Wilson, K. G. (1994). Acceptance and commitment therapy: Altering the verbal support for experiential avoidance. *Behavior Analyst, 17,* 289–304.

Herman, S. H., Barlow, D. H., & Agras, W. S. (1974). An experimental analysis of exposure to "elicit" heterosexual stimuli as an effective variable in changing arousal patterns in homosexuals. *Behaviour Research and Therapy, 12,* 315–345.

Hudson, S. M., Marshall, W. L., Ward, T., Johnston, P. W., & Jones, R. L. (1995). Kia Marama: A cognitive-behavioural program for incarcerated child molesters. *Behaviour Change, 12,* 69–80.

Huesmann, L. R. (1988). An information-processing model for the development of aggression. *Aggressive Behavior, 14,* 13–24.

Hyde, J. S., & DeLamater, J. D. (2006). *Understanding human sexuality* (9th ed.). Boston: McGraw-Hill.

Kolvin, I. (1967). Aversion imagery treatment in an adolescent. *Behaviour Research and Therapy, 5,* 245–248.

Kremsdorf, R. B., Holmen, M. L., & Laws, D. R. (1980). Orgasmic reconditioning without deviant imagery: A case report with a pedophile. *Behaviour Research and Therapy, 18,* 203–207.

Lande, S. D. (1980). A combination of orgasmic reconditioning and covert sensitization in the treatment of a fire fetish. *Journal of Behavior Therapy and
Experimental Psychiatry, 11,* 291–296.

Lange, A. J., & Jakubowski, P. (1976). *Responsible assertive behavior: Cognitive/
behavioral procedures for trainers.* Champaign, IL: Research Press.

Larimer, M. E., & Marlatt, G. A. (1994). Addictive behaviors. In L. W. Craighead, W. E. Craighead, A. E. Kazdin, & M. J. Mahoney (Eds.), *Cognitive
and behavioral interventions: An empirical approach to mental health problems*
(pp. 157–168). Boston: Allyn & Bacon.

Laws, D. R. (2003). Harm reduction and sexual offending: Is an intraparadigmatic
shift possible? In T. Ward, D. R. Laws, & S. M. Hudson (Eds.), *Sexual
deviance: Issues and controversies* (pp. 280–296). Thousand Oaks, CA: Sage.

Laws, D. R. (Ed.). (1989). *Relapse prevention with sex offenders.* New York: Guilford.

Laws, D. R., & Marshall, W. L. (1991). Masturbatory reconditioning with sexual
deviates: An evaluative review. *Advances in Behaviour Research and Therapy,
13,* 13–25.

Laws, D. R., & O'Donohue, W. (Eds.). (1997). *Sexual deviance: Theory, assessment,
and treatment.* New York: Guilford.

Leiblum, S. R., & Rosen, R. C. (Eds.). (2000). *Principles and practice of sex therapy.*
(3rd ed.). New York: Guilford.

Little, L. M., & Curran, J. P. (1978). Covert sensitization: A clinical procedure in
need of some explanations. *Psychological Bulletin, 85,* 513–531.

LoPiccolo, J. (1994). Acceptance and change: Content and context in psychotherapy. In S. C. Haynes, N. S. Jacobson, V. M. Follete, & M. J. Dougher
(Eds.), *Acceptance and change: Content and context in psychotherapy* (pp. 149–
170). Reno, NV: Context Press.

Maletzky, B. M. (1985). Orgasmic reconditioning. In A. S. Bellack & M. Hersen
(Eds.), *Dictionary of behavior therapy techniques* (pp. 157–158). New York:
Pergamon.

Maletzky, B. M. (1997). Exhibitionism: Assessment and treatment. In D. R. Laws &
W. O'Donohue (Eds.), *Sexual deviance: Theory, assessment, and treatment*
(pp. 40–74). New York: Guilford.

Marlatt, G. A., & Gordon, J. R. (Eds.). (1985). *Relapse prevention: Maintenance
strategies in the treatment of addictive behaviors.* New York: Guilford.

Marquis, J. N. (1970). Orgasmic reconditioning: Changing sexual object choice
through controlling masturbation fantasies. *Journal of Behavior Therapy &
Experimental Psychiatry, 1,* 263–271.

Marshall, W. L. (1974). The classical conditioning of sexual attractiveness: A
report of four therapeutic failures. *Behavior Therapy, 5,* 298–299.

Marshall, W. L., & Barbaree, H. E. (1988). The long-term evaluation of a behavioral treatment program for child molesters. *Behaviour Research and
Therapy, 26,* 499–511.

Marshall, W. L., & Barbaree, H. E. (1990). An integrated theory of the etiology of
sexual offending. In W. L. Marshall, D. R. Laws, & H. E. Barbaree (Eds.),

Handbook of sexual assault: Issues, theories, and treatment of the offender (pp. 257–275). New York: Plenum Press.

Marshall, W. L., & Eccles, A. (1991). Issues in clinical practice with sex offenders. *Journal of Interpersonal Violence, 6*, 68–93.

Marshall, W. L., & Lippens, K. (1977). The clinical value of boredom: A procedure for reducing inappropriate sexual interests. *Journal of Nervous and Mental Disease, 165*, 283–287.

McAnulty, R. D., & Adams, H. E. (1992). Behavior therapy with paraphilic disorders. In S. M. Turner, K. S. Calhoun, & H. E. Adams (Eds.), *Handbook of clinical behavioral therapy* (2nd ed., pp. 175–201). New York: Wiley.

McAnulty, R. D., & Burnette, M. M. (2004). *Exploring human sexuality: Making healthy decisions* (2nd ed.). Boston: Allyn & Bacon.

McFall, R. M. (1990). The enhancement of social skills: An information-processing analysis. In W. L. Marshall, D. R. Laws, & H. B. Barbaree (Eds.), *Handbook of sexual assault: Issues, theories, and treatment of the offender* (pp. 311–330). New York: Plenum Press.

McGuire, R. J., Carlisle, J. M., & Young, B. G. (1965). Sexual deviations as conditioned behaviour: A hypothesis. *Behaviour Research and Therapy, 2*, 185–190.

McMullin, R. E. (1986). *Handbook of cognitive therapy techniques.* New York: W. W. Norton.

Murphy, W. D. (1990). Assessment and modification of cognitive distortions in sex offenders. In W. L. Marshall, D. R. Laws, & H. E. Barbaree (Eds.), *Handbook of sexual assault: Issues, theories, and treatment of the offender* (pp. 331–342). New York: Plenum Press.

Paul, R. H., Marx, B. P., & Orsillo, S. M. (1999). Acceptance-based psychotherapy in the treatment of an adjudicated exhibitionist: A case example. *Behavior Therapy, 30*, 149–162.

Pithers, W. D. (1990). Relapse prevention with sexual aggressors. In W. L. Marshall, D. R. Laws, & H. E. Barbaree (Eds.), *Handbook of sexual assault: Issues, theories, and treatment of the offender* (pp. 343–361). New York: Plenum Press.

Quinsey, V. L. (1977). The assessment and treatment of child molesters: A review. *Canadian Psychological Review, 18*, 204–220.

Quinsey, V. L., & Earls, C. M. (1990). The modification of sexual preference. In W. L. Marshall, D. R. Laws, & H. E. Barbaree (Eds.), *Handbook of sexual assault: Issues, theories, and treatment of the offender* (pp. 343–361). New York: Plenum Press.

Rachman, S. (1966). Sexual fetishism: An experimental analogue. *Psychological Record, 16*, 293–296.

Rachman, S. J., & Hodgson, R. J. (1968). Experimentally induced sexual fetishism: Replication and development. *Psychological Record, 18*, 25–27.

Rimm, D. C., & Masters, J. C. (1974). *Behavior therapy: Techniques and empirical findings.* New York: Academic Press.

Rooth, G. (1980). Exhibitionism: An eclectic approach to management. *British Journal of Hospital Medicine, 23*, 366–370.

Schroeder, H. E., & Black, M. J. (1985). Unassertiveness. In M. Hersen & A. S. Bellack (Eds.), *Handbook of clinical behavior therapy with adults* (pp. 509–530). New York: Plenum Press.

Smith, M. J. (1975). *When I say no I feel guilty.* New York: Dial Press.

Stava, L., Levin, S. M., & Schwanz, C. (1993). The role of aversion in covert sensitization in the treatment of pedophilia: A case report. *Journal of Child Sexual Abuse, 2,* 1–13.

Stermac, L. E., & Quinsey, V. L. (1986). Social competence among rapists. *Behavioral Assessment, 8,* 171–185.

Thorpe, J. G., Schmidt, E., & Castell, D. (1964). A comparison of positive and negative (aversive) conditioning in the treatment of homosexuality. *Behaviour Research and Therapy, 1,* 357–362.

Turk, D. C., Rudy, T. E., & Sorkin, B. A. (1992). Chronic pain: Behavioral conceptualizations and interventions. In S. M. Turner, K. S. Calhoun, and H. E. Adams (Eds.), *Handbook of clinical behavioral therapy* (2nd ed., pp. 373–396). New York: Wiley.

Turkat, I. D. (1990*). The personality disorders: A psychological approach to clinical management.* New York: Pergamon.

VanDeventer, A. D., & Laws, D. R. (1978). Orgasmic reconditioning to redirect sexual arousal in pedophiles. *Behavior Therapy, 9,* 748–765.

Ward, T., & Hudson, S. M. (1998). A model of the relapse process in sex offenders. *Journal of Interpersonal Violence, 13,* 700–725.

Ward, T., Hudson, S. M., & Keenan, T. (2000). The assessment and treatment of sexual offenders against children. In C. R. Hollins (Ed.), *Handbook of offender assessment and treatment* (pp. 358–361). London: Wiley.

Ward, T., & Stewart, C. A. (2003). Criminogenic needs or human needs: A theoretical model. *Psychology, Crime, & Law, 9,* 125–143.

Wincze, J. P., & Carey, M. P. (2001). *Sexual dysfunction: A guide for assessment and treatment* (2nd ed.). New York: Guilford.

Witt, P., & Sager, W. (1988). Procedures for treating deviant sexual arousal patterns. In P. A. Keller and S. R. Heyman (Eds.), *Innovations in clinical practice: A source book* (volume 7, pp. 89–98). Sarasota, FL: Professional Resource Exchange.

SUGGESTED READINGS

Laws, D. R., & O'Donohue, W. (Eds.). (1997). *Sexual deviance: Theory, assessment, and treatment.* New York: Guilford.

Ward, T., Laws, D. R., & Hudson, S. M. (Eds.). (2003). *Sexual deviance: Issues and controversies.* Thousand Oaks, CA: Sage.

Wincze, J. P., & Carey, M. P. (2001). *Sexual dysfunction: A guide for assessment and treatment* (2nd ed.). New York: Guilford.

8

The Management of Sex Offenders: Introducing a Good Lives Approach

Rachael M. Collie, Tony Ward, and Theresa A. Gannon

Sexual offending is a socially significant and complex problem that has become the focus of intensive research and treatment efforts over the last thirty years. The public's anxiety and concern about the release of sex offenders to the community is understandable; sexual offending affects some of the most vulnerable members of our community, and is inherently difficult to understand. What would make an adult sexually interested in a child, or lead one adult to force another to have sex against his/her will? Ideas that those who commit sexual crimes are "sick" or "evil" and "untreatable" are reinforced by media portrayals of sensational albeit rare cases of sexual murder. No matter how explanations for sexual offending are cast, the resulting fear and disgust heightens public pressure to defer the release of offenders, or to guarantee that release is conditional on "curing" the underlying pathology.

These concerns have deterred corrective efforts away from considering offenders' welfare, and have ensured that public safety drives treatment efforts with sex offenders in much of the Western world (i.e., Canada, UK, Australia, New Zealand). Thus, the goal of treatment is simply to reduce sex offender risk and minimize the harm caused by offenders. This perspective toward sex offender treatment is called the *risk management* approach or *Risk-Need Model* (RNM). Within this approach, the main aim of treatment is to identify deficits or problems with the offenders' psychological and behavioral functioning that are commonly associated with sexual offending (e.g., offense-supportive beliefs or deviant sexual arousal) and to eliminate, reduce, or contain the extent of these problems to control and reduce reoffending. In summary, the primary aim of treatment is to make society a safer place by reducing the occurrence of future sexual offenses in those sex offenders who are returning to the community.

Efforts over the last two to three decades have shown that sexual offender programs can be successfully implemented within the prison and community, and that the predominant risk management approach to sexual offender treatment does appreciably reduce future sexual offending (Hollin, 1999; Marshall & McGuire, 2003). For example, a recent review of treatment outcome studies found that treatments with a risk management approach (i.e., cognitive-behavior and relapse prevention programs) reduced sexual reoffending from 17.4 percent to 9.9 percent in treated sexual offenders (Hanson et al., 2002). The same review found that treatment also reduced the nonsexual reoffending rate from 51 percent to 32 percent (Hanson et al., 2002). The magnitude of these reductions in reoffending are at the more effective end of the spectrum compared to treatment programs for nonsexual (general) offenders, are roughly similar to the overall effects of psychotherapy (when all forms are combined together), and are larger than many of the effects found for established medical treatments, such as bypass surgery and the use of aspirin to reduce myocardial infarction (Marshall & McGuire, 2003). Hence, in many regards, current treatment approaches for sex offenders represent a significant achievement and can be considered a success.

Despite the effectiveness of the risk management approach to sex offender treatment, we believe this approach has a number of flaws that mean it may not be the most effective means we have of managing sexual offenders in the community. The main criticism is that risk management exclusively focuses on risk, or offending, and gives insufficient attention to the factors associated with a healthy law-abiding life. In short, we think the effectiveness of sex offender treatment can be improved by incorporating an explicit focus on offender well-being in treatment. Thus, in this chapter, we advocate for a dual focus on risk management and offender well-being, where offenders learn to manage their risk of reoffending within the broader goal of learning to lead a better kind of life. A better kind of life is one in which an individual meets his needs in socially acceptable and personally satisfying ways. It is our contention that embedding the task of achieving and maintaining behavior change within a model of personal well-being, identity, and lifestyle makes treatment more meaningful for offenders, optimizing their motivation to "buy in" to, and benefit from, the treatment opportunities offered. Thus, by enhancing treatment in these ways we believe that the effectiveness of sex offender treatment can be further improved. Ultimately, improving the effectiveness of treatment leads to fewer sexual crimes and increased public safety.

In this chapter, we first describe the fundamental tenets of the risk management approach to sex offender treatment, how treatment works when based purely on a risk management model, and some of the issues we think are problematic for effective sex offender management using this approach. Second, we describe the relatively new approach to sex offender management called the Good Lives Model (GLM) and describe how the GLM incorporates the risk management principles while also adopting a much more holistic approach to sex offender management. Finally, we outline how treatment could be implemented using the GLM and draw main conclusions about this approach and its strengths. We note from the outset that we use male pronouns when referring to offenders. Although there is increasing recognition of women as perpetrators, by far the vast majority of sexual offenses are committed by men, and almost all research has been conducted with male offenders.

RISK MANAGEMENT AND THE RISK-NEED MODEL

The risk management approach to sex offender treatment has been the dominant perspective for many years now and represents a substantial and impressive achievement (see Andrews & Bonta, 2003; Gendreau, 1996; McGuire, 2002). The risk management approach relies on the following basic ideas: Criminal behavior or offending is associated with a number of risk factors. A risk factor is anything that, when measured at time one (e.g., during imprisonment), predicts the occurrence of offending at time two (e.g., five years after release from prison). Thus, reducing or eliminating risk factors linked to offending will lead to reductions in future offending.

Of course, many of the factors known to predict future offending are related to past offending. For example, the age that offending began, the number of past offenses, and age at first imprisonment all reliably predict involvement in future offending, including sexual offending (e.g., Gendreau, Little, & Goggin, 1996; Hanson & Bussière, 1998). Such historical or *static risks* are largely unchangeable and so their value is in helping predict offending over time. In contrast, other factors known to predict offending are related to situational and psychological factors. For example, holding values or beliefs that crime is justified and causes little harm is a *psychological* risk factor correlated with future offending, while having easy access to criminal opportunities such as unsupervised access to victims is a *situational* risk factor (Andrews & Bonta, 2003; Hanson & Harris, 2000). Unlike unchangeable static risk factors, psychological and situational risk factors can change over time. Hence they are called *dynamic risk factors*. According to the risk management approach, reducing or eliminating dynamic risk factors will lead to reductions in future offending. The value of dynamic risk factors therefore is that they become the clinical problems that should be explicitly targeted in treatment to reduce likelihood of future reoffending.

Extensive effort has gone into identifying the factors that can reliably predict future sexual recidivism. Until recently, much of this research has focused on static risk factors resulting in greater agreement about the static

Static Risk Factors

Demographic Factors

- Younger age
- Marital status (single)

General Criminality

- Total number of prior offenses (any/nonsexual)

Sexual Criminal History

- Number of prior sexual offenses
- Stranger victims (versus acquaintance)
- Extrafamilial victims (versus related victims)
- Early age of onset of sexual offending
- Male child victim
- Diverse sexual crimes

Adverse childhood environment

- Separation from biological parents

Dynamic/Psychological Risk Factors

Sexual Deviancy

- Any deviant sexual interest
- Sexual interest in children
- Paraphilic interests (e.g., exhibitionism, voyeurism, cross-dressing)
- Sexual preoccupations (high rates of sexual interests & activities, paraphilic or nonparaphilic)
- High (feminine) scores on MMPI Masculinity-Femininity Scale

Antisocial Orientation

- Antisocial/psychopathic personality disorder
- Antisocial traits, such as general self-regulation problems, impulsivity, poor problem-solving, employment instability, any substance abuse, intoxicated during offense, procriminal attitudes, hostility
- History of rule violation, including noncompliance with supervision & violation of conditional release

Intimacy Deficits

- Emotional identification with children
- Lack of intimate relationship
- Conflicts in intimate relationships

Sexual Attitudes

- Attitudes tolerant of sexual crime

Figure 8.1. Risk factors for sexual offense recidivism.

Sources: Hanson & Bussière (1998) and Hanson & Morton-Bourgon (2004).

(historical) risk factors for sexual recidivism than the dynamic (psychological) risk factors. Figure 8.1 summarizes the static and dynamic risk factors identified in the two most recent and complementary meta-analyses on sexual recidivism (see Hanson & Bussière, 1998; Hanson & Morton-Bourgon, 2004). Of note, the risk factors presented are those that were consistently associated with sexual recidivism across several studies (each risk factor is aggregated across three to thirty-one studies). Also, the risk predictors vary in their predictive strength; some are more strongly associated with future sexual recidivism than others. For example, sexual deviancy and antisocial/psychopathic personality were found to be stronger predictors of sexual recidivism than intimacy deficits or adverse childhood environment.

Research has only more recently begun to address the situational or acute risk factors for sexual recidivism. Results from the most comprehensive study of acute risk factors are presented in Figure 8.2 (see Hanson & Harris, 2000). Situational or acute risk factors are usually not predictive of sexual recidivism over the longer term, but instead they indicate when a particular offender is more likely to reoffend. For example, personal distress variables, such as negative mood, show no or only a very weak association with future sexual recidivism in studies of large groups of sexual offenders (Hanson & Bussière, 1998; Hanson & Morton-Bourgon, 2004), but in those offenders who do recidivate, sexually negative mood is often reported in the relapse process. One way of understanding this fact is that negative mood *per se* does not predict future sexual recidivism across offenders but the way that negative mood is managed by offenders (e.g., regulating mood using deviant sexual fantasy and/ or masturbation), particularly by those at higher risk for reoffending, is linked to sexual recidivism (Hanson & Morton-Bourgon, 2004).

Risk management has become synonymous with the Risk-Need approach. According to the Risk-Need Model (RNM), effective treatment depends upon classifying offenders according to three main principles: Risk, Need, and Responsivity (Andrews & Bonta, 2003). First, the *risk principle* states that offenders' risk of reoffending should be assessed and that the intensity of treatment delivered to the offender should match this assessed level of risk. Thus, according to the risk principle, offenders with highest risk should receive the most intense treatment (i.e., the largest "dose"), whereas offenders with lowest risk should receive minimal or no treatment. In practice, risk assessment instruments combine a number of risk factors to produce an estimate of risk. Thus, the more risk factors present for an offender, the higher the level of assessed risk and in turn the greater the intensity of recommended treatment.

Second, the *need principle* specifies that treatment should primarily target dynamic risk factors (i.e., those factors potentially amenable to change) associated with risk of future offending. In the RNM, psychological and situational dynamic risk factors are relabeled as *criminogenic needs*.[1] Examples of sexual offending criminogenic needs are deviant sexual arousal, intimacy

---

Self-management

- Victim access
- Sees self as no risk to recidivate

Attitudes

- Low remorse/victim blaming

Psychological Symptoms

- Anger
- Negative mood
- Psychiatric symptoms
- General hygiene problems

Drug Use

- Substance abuse
- Started anti-androgens (sex drive reduction medication) the month before recidivating

Social Adjustment

- General social problems

Cooperation with Supervision

- Overall cooperation with supervision (low)
- Disengaged from supervision
- Manipulative
- No-show/late for appointments

Figure 8.2. Acute (situational) risk factors for sexual offense recidivism.

Source: Hanson & Harris (2000).

deficits and loneliness, and problems with emotional regulation (Hanson & Harris, 2000). In contrast, other clinical problems with weak or nonexistent statistical relationships to reoffending are labeled *noncriminogenic needs*. Examples of noncriminogenic needs are low self-esteem, anxiety, and personal distress (Andrews & Bonta, 2003). Noncriminogenic needs are deemed largely irrelevant as primary treatment targets because changing them is not linked to reductions in reoffending (Ward & Stewart, 2003).

In practice, the RNM is often accompanied by a *relapse prevention* treatment framework or component. Relapse prevention teaches offenders to recognize the situational and psychological dynamic risk factors associated with past offending, such as being alone with children or feeling very down. Offenders are then taught how best to avoid or respond to these risk situations and psychological states so as to minimize their chances of reoffending (Ward & Hudson, 2000).

Third, the *responsivity principle* is concerned with a program's ability to reach and make sense to the offenders for whom it was designed. In other words, program delivery should be matched to offenders' characteristics to maximize their absorption of the program material so they then can make the desired changes to stop offending. Potential treatment responsivity barriers arise from offenders' characteristics or program characteristics (either individually or in combination). For example, an offender may not think his offending is wrong or may perceive little benefit from participating in a program (i.e., the offender has low treatment motivation). Alternatively, an offender may be keen for treatment but struggle to understand and apply the program material because the program pitches the material too high for his individual ability (i.e., the offender has a low IQ and/or the program emphasizes cognitive and verbal skills), or is delivered by therapists who have little understanding of the offender's cultural background (i.e., the program is culturally mismatched with the offender's ethnicity and culture).

In practice, the responsivity principle is implemented using treatment programs that favor a cognitive-behavioral, skill-oriented delivery style (Andrews & Bonta, 2003). Such programs are highly structured, directive, and combine a psycho-educational approach with a skills development one. In addition, some programs address offenders' unique responsivity issues, such as social anxiety, depression, and so on, by providing prior or adjunct individual therapy and/or by modifying the standardized program to take into account such issues. Some responsivity barriers are also noncriminogenic needs (i.e., clinical problems experienced by the offender that have a weak or nonexistent statistical relationship with reoffending). Thus, if noncriminogenic needs moderate the effectiveness of treatment then they can be targeted to the extent necessary to assist the offender to engage in and benefit from treatment.

In addition to the basic Risk-Need-Responsivity principles described above, the role of *assessment integrity* and *professional discretion* are highlighted by Andrews and Bonta (2003). *Assessment integrity* requires that both the assessment approaches underpinning the classification decisions and the principles informing the classification decisions are carried out as they are prescribed. In contrast, *professional discretion* requires that treatment providers be flexible and use their clinical judgment to override the three principles (i.e., Risk, Need, and Responsivity) if warranted under certain circumstances. Clearly, agencies and clinicians need to arrive at a balance between implementing the RNM rigidly as designed and exercising flexibility for individual circumstances and differences.

In summary, the RNM makes a number of basic claims about how to maximize the effectiveness of treatment. First, risk assessment should drive treatment dosage. The more risk factors present for any offender, generally the greater that offender's risk of reoffending and, in turn, the greater the intensity of recommended treatment. Second, matching risk and treatment dosage results in better outcomes, that is, lower recidivism. The implications are that best outcomes are achieved by channeling treatment resources into higher-risk offenders (i.e., those with the most risk factors). Conversely, giving low-risk offenders high levels of treatment is wasteful and may actually *increase* their chances of reoffending (Andrews & Bonta, 2003). Third, treatment that directly targets criminogenic needs or dynamic risk factors rather than other clinical problems (i.e., noncriminogenic needs) will result in better outcomes. Fourth, offenders' other clinical problems or characteristics that affect their responsiveness to treatment should be addressed to the extent necessary for the offender to engage and learn in the program.

RNM Sexual Offender Treatment

As we alluded to earlier, the RNM of sex offender treatment is dominated by relapse prevention treatment approaches. Relapse prevention was first developed by Marlatt and Gordon (1985) to describe the process of relapse in individuals suffering from serious alcohol problems. The approach assisted recovering alcohol abusers to recognize the factors that trigger abstinence failure and promoted the use of cognitive-behavioral methods for responding adaptively to those triggers. Five years later, the relapse prevention model was adapted to describe the sexual offense relapse process (Pithers, 1990) and has remained the dominant approach to sexual offender treatment ever since (Laws, 2000; Ward & Hudson, 2000).

Relapse prevention with sex offenders has two main goals. The first is to teach individuals to recognize the situational and psychological risk factors associated with their offending (Ward & Hudson, 2000). Offenders are typically taught to identify their *offense cycle or process*; that is, the sequence of psychological and situational risk factors or decision points that predisposed and immediately precipitated their offending. The offense cycle is broken into various phases to enable the easy identification of risk factors. Typical phases include: background problems and lifestyle issues (i.e., offense precursors), offense planning, entering high-risk situations, offending, and postoffense evaluations. In this way, the offender is taught how problems and decisions at one point in time or in one aspect of his life contribute to offending occurring at a later point. To illustrate, an offender might identify how his loneliness and social isolation was a background problem (i.e., *offense precursor*) that created an incentive for seeking out the company of children (i.e., *offense planning*). Socializing with children would be labeled a *high-risk situation* because sense of self-control over deviant sexual thoughts and feelings may become compromised in children's company. All aspects of the offender's sexually abusive behavior, whether officially prosecuted or not, would be included in the *offending phase* (e.g., inappropriate touching or fondling a fully clothed child). Finally, *post-offense evaluations* that either exacerbated background problems (e.g., feeling guilty and further isolating himself) or diminished offending responsibility (e.g., rationalizing that the offense was accidental) are highlighted as perpetuating the cycle of offending.

The second major goal of relapse prevention is to teach offenders coping skills to more adaptively respond to their risk factors and therefore to lessen the chances of reoffending. Treatment techniques typically include psycho-education and cognitive-behavioral methods organized into treatment modules. Each treatment module is usually linked to different aspects of the offenders' offense cycle; thus the offense cycle acts as a continuous thread, through which treatment components are planned and integrated.

A useful illustration of a state-of-the-art RNM sexual offender program is the Kia Marama child sexual offender treatment program that operates in New Zealand (Ward, 2003). Although delivered only to child sexual offenders, this type of program is commonly delivered to both child and adult sexual offenders in other countries. In brief, the Kia Marama program is thirty-three weeks long and provided to groups of eight to ten men on three days per week for up to three hours per day. Where individual therapy is provided, the primary purpose is to enable a participant to engage in the group program. The program comprises discrete modules that are sequenced accordingly: norm building; understanding offending (i.e., the offense cycle); arousal reconditioning; victim impact and empathy; mood management; relationship skills; and relapse prevention. A brief description of each component follows.

Norm Building

The main aims are to establish the social rules for the group, encourage motivation to engage in the program, and encourage accepting personal responsibility for offending and offense-related risk factors. The treatment philosophy is explained; the men are told that the program does not aim to cure them but rather to teach them to control their behavior through understanding their offending and learning ways to break the offense pattern. Each group generates group rules that will assist them to function effectively to achieve the program aim. Rules typically cover confidentiality (prohibiting the discussion of issues raised in the group with people outside the group), communication procedures (e.g., using "I" statements, turn-taking), the importance of accepting responsibility for one's own issues, and challenging other group members constructively and assertively (rather than aggressively or colluding).

Understanding Offending

The main aims are for each man to fully understand his offense cycle and the role of his various risk factors, and to understand how distorted thinking has facilitated his cycle. Men are encouraged to develop an understanding of how background factors (e.g., low mood, lifestyle imbalances,[2] sexual difficulties, intimacy problems) set the scene for their own offending. The men are then encouraged to be honest about the steps taken to set up an opportunity for offending, whether involving explicit planning or unintentional choices, and to be honest about the nature of their offending. Men are assisted to see how their own particular postoffense reactions added to background difficulties and perpetuated reoffending risk.

Arousal Reconditioning

This module focuses on the role of deviant arousal in offending and teaches techniques to reduce deviant sexual interest. Inappropriate or deviant sexual arousal to children is hypothesized to be an important factor causing and maintaining sexual offending (Marshall & Barbaree, 1990). In essence, the pairing of orgasm to imagined or real sexual contact with children is thought to condition offenders' sexual responsiveness to children. Thus, the arousal reconditioning module aims to teach each man techniques to *unpair* or recondition deviant sexual arousal patterns. Men are taught imaginal (or covert) sensitization, a technique that involves pairing deviant sexual arousal (and other early aspects of the offense cycle) with the negative consequences of apprehension in the offenders' imagination and with an alternate escape script. Directed masturbation is another technique used that attempts to strengthen sexual arousal to appropriate images and thoughts, while satiation procedures attempt to reduce arousal to deviant sexual fantasies.

Victim Impact and Empathy

A lack of empathic concern for victims and an inability or refusal to seriously consider the traumatic effects of sexual abuse is a common feature of many sex offenders. This pattern of empathy deficit is thought to reflect the dysfunctional and distorted thinking patterns of the offenders, rather than a general deficiency in capacity to be empathic (although for some offenders this can be the case) (Ward, Keenan, & Hudson, 2000). This module aims to enhance each man's understanding of the negative impact of his offending and promote normal empathy so he is less willing to inflict that harm again. A range of psycho-education tasks are used to teach men about the negative effects of sexual abuse in general, and each man is required to recognize and acknowledge the effects for his own victims in a written task and role-plays.

Mood Management

The mood management module aims to teach knowledge and skills to enhance emotion regulation. Men are taught to identify and distinguish a range of feelings that are commonly linked with offending, such as sadness, fear, and anger, and to focus on those feelings associated with their risk of reoffending. A range of cognitive-behavior techniques used in mainstream mood or emotion management are taught in the module, the main aim being to help men avoid making emotion-focused snap decisions.

Relationships

In this module, men consider the importance of intimate relationships and the ways that they can enhance appropriate intimate relationships through a variety of psycho-educational tasks. Communication and problem-solving techniques are taught. Education about healthy sexuality and sexual dysfunction is also included.

Relapse Prevention

The final module is an extension of the relapse prevention focus that has run throughout the program. By this stage, men should have learned to self-monitor their risk factors and to use a range of cognitive and behavioral techniques to respond more effectively when risk factors emerge or are operating. Particular emphasis is placed on "breaking the cycle" as early as possible to ensure that the risk of reoffending is always minimized. The men present a revised understanding of their offense cycle in the form of a personal statement. Men are encouraged to understand that risk management incorporates both an internal risk management component (i.e., internal self-monitoring and coping skills) and an external risk management component that involves external monitoring and support from prosocial family and friends who are prepared to help him achieve his goal of avoiding reoffending. Thus, in his personal statement, each man is required to link each of his risk factors to the internal and external risk management strategies that are designed to reduce risk.

Reintegration Component

A reintegration component runs alongside the group program that focuses on each man's release planning and strengthens his proposed support network in the community. Prosocial support people (e.g., professionals, family, and friends) are identified by program staff together with the man, and these support people are informed about the man's participation and progress in treatment. In the latter stages of the program, reintegration meetings are typically held that involve the man and his support network. In these meetings the man presents and discusses his offense pattern, relapse prevention, and release plan with his support network, who in turn evaluate and strengthen his understanding, relapse, and release plan. A key purpose of these reintegration meetings is to equip the man's support network to be able to externally monitor the man's progress in the community and to act to reduce or disclose high-risk situations when they emerge.

Although the various sexual offender programs differ in their organizing structure, a number of common features characterize the RNM of sexual offender treatment. First, the treatment emphasizes a formulation of the offense-related *risk* factors. Second, treatment is problem-focused. Third, treatment mostly teaches skills to *avoid* or *reduce* risk factors/problems. More specifically, treatment teaches some eliminative skills and strategies (i.e., techniques to suppress the problem) and some constructional or prosocial skills and strategies (i.e., techniques that build new repertoires of behavior) (McGuire, 2002). However, the constructional or prosocial skills are often only broadly tied to adaptive or healthy outcomes rather than tied to individualized formulations of prosocial personal, interpersonal, or lifestyle goals. Fourth, all participants complete all modules and receive the same dose of each module irrespective of individual offense-related risk factors. For example, all men at Kia Marama complete the sexual arousal reconditioning module although not all child sexual offenders exhibit deviant sexual interest to children (Marshall, 1997). Fifth, treatment is predominantly, if not exclusively, group-based.

Problems with the RNM

The RNM is clearly effective, and has resulted in lower recidivism rates for sex offenders (Andrews & Bonta, 2003; Hanson et al., 2002). However, we believe the RNM and attendant relapse prevention approach have weaknesses that limit the ability to provide *meaningful* treatment, thus reducing the potential *effectiveness* of this treatment. An appropriate metaphor that captures our primary concern about the RNM is that of a pincushion. The RNM views sex offenders as compilations of disconnected risk factors or criminogenic needs (i.e., pins) that are all embedded within offenders' personalities, lifestyles, and cultural and social environments (i.e., the pincushion). The main aim of treatment is to remove as many of these risk factors or pins as possible so that overall level of risk is reduced. Unfortunately, the danger is that by primarily focusing treatment on the pins, rather than the pincushion (or whole person), individuals are viewed as disembodied bearers of risk rather than integrated agents or individuals.

Viewing risk factors independently, and in isolation from individuals' overall psychological and social functioning, fails to make clear how various risk factors relate to each other, why various risk factors exist and how they produce offending (i.e., the underlying causal mechanisms of the risk factor), or what psychological or social needs are being met by offending. Contemporary theory about the causes of sexual offending strongly suggests that there are various interrelationships between individual risk factors that operate to produce sexual offending (Beech & Ward, 2004). Simply viewing risk factors as independent entities conceals the more complex causal mechanisms that exist. Just like removing pins from a pincushion leaves gaps or holes where the pins once existed, removing risk factors from offenders' lives also runs the risk of leaving holes or gaps in the ways psychological and social needs were previously met. When offenders are treated *strictly* according to the RNM, the intermediate indicators of treatment success are significant reductions in the offenders' dynamic risk factors. For example, the offender shows less sexual interest in children, endorses fewer distorted beliefs about sex with children, and shows knowledge of the situations he should avoid (i.e., relapse prevention). What may not be addressed or considered is whether the offender has other socially acceptable and personally satisfying ways of meeting the psychological and social needs once met by offending.

Like all humans, sex offenders have inherent human needs that require fulfillment (Deci & Ryan, 2000). In contrast to the pincushion model, we argue that the primary purpose of treatment should be to help offenders learn new ways of living that are both *socially acceptable* and *personally satisfying*. In essence, we believe that "good lives" and risk management are like two sides of the same coin. Focusing on a *good life* and offender well-being helps offenders learn what to do to have a satisfying life where offending is unnecessary. In turn, this approach results in the automatic reduction of risk factors that once flagged a good life problem.

A number of related concerns about the basic RNM stem from or have contributed to the development of the GLM that we present in the following section. First, many of the core treatment techniques using the RNM and attendant relapse prevention approach are framed in negative terms. For example, treatment focuses on *extinguishing* deviant sexual arousal, *eliminating* problematic attitudes, *reducing* cognitive distortions (i.e., biased thinking), and *avoiding* high-risk situations (e.g., avoiding use of substances or babysitting young children for friends). We think an important focus of treatment is on what kind of life to lead, not simply what problems or situations to avoid or reduce. Stopping offending involves replacing the old patterns associated with offending with new ways of living life. Broadly discussing or speculating about *alternative prosocial options* is insufficient. The best way to learn something new is to develop specific goals and focus attention on achieving those goals. We suggest that treatment should focus on building strengths or capabilities to enable offenders to meet their needs in acceptable ways, rather than promoting narrow skills purely for managing risk factors.

Second, human beings have a range of basic or inherent human needs that motivate us to pursue certain experiences and outcomes (Deci & Ryan, 2000). The categorization of needs into criminogenic and noncriminogenic does not reflect this kind of understanding of human need (Ward & Stewart, 2003). In the RNM "needs" are defined entirely by their statistical relationship to subsequent offending. No attempt is made to link an understanding of criminogenic needs to broader psychological models of human need and functioning. Although knowing the correlates or predictors of offending is relevant information, what is more important for treatment is why an offender sexually offended (i.e., knowing the cause, not just the symptoms).

In the GLM, criminogenic needs/dynamic risk factors are reframed as the internal or external obstacles that interfere with offenders' meeting their basic human needs in personally rewarding and socially acceptable ways. For example, offenders' antisocial attitudes are viewed as an internal obstacle to meeting the basic human need of intimacy in relationships. A common theme to antisocial thinking is that other people are hostile and malevolent individuals who will hurt or take advantage if given the opportunity. Thus antisocial thinking creates suspicion, hostility, and mistrust that distorts the perception of interpersonal encounters and interferes with establishing the trusting and secure relationships that provide intimacy.

Fourth, the RNM gives no attention to the role of personal identity and personal agency in the change process. Although both are intuitively relevant, little research exists on the role of personal identity or personal agency in the process of desisting from offending. A notable exception is Maruna's (2001) study on the self-narratives of offenders who either desisted from crime or persisted with crime. The results revealed that desisters and persisters differed little in their personality traits, but substantially in their personal identities. *Persistent offenders* tended to live according to a *condemnation script* that emphasized little possibility for change and an impoverished sense of personal agency or self-efficacy. In contrast, *desisters* tended to live according to a *redemption script* where they viewed themselves as inherently good people whose pattern of crime resulted from negative external events and misdirected attempts to assert some form of power or control. For desisters, change involved giving new meaning to past events and gaining a sense of power and control over their destiny.

Fifth, the principle and issue of treatment responsivity is not sufficiently developed, a fact that is acknowledged also by advocates of the RNM (Andrews & Bonta, 2003; Ogloff & Davis, 2004). Treatment responsivity barriers can be both criminogenic needs (e.g., impulsivity and antisocial thinking) and noncriminogenic needs (e.g., low self-esteem, anxiety, and psychological distress). Although the responsivity principle affords a valid reason for addressing noncriminogenic needs, the primary focus of treatment always emphasizes criminogenic needs. Instead, we believe treatment engagement and effectiveness can be maximized if issues of emotional safety, self-esteem, and emotional well-being are explicitly considered and attended to throughout the treatment process.

Sixth, the RNM is silent on the crucial role of context or ecological variables in the process of rehabilitation. Offenders do not commit offenses in a vacuum and equally cannot be expected to make changes in a vacuum. Instead, each offender is embedded in a local social, cultural, personal, and environmental context. Offenders' contexts should be considered so that treatment focuses on the specific skills and resources necessary to function adaptively in those specific contexts. For example, an offender who returns to live in a rural area will face somewhat different barriers to social integration than an offender who returns to live in an urban area. Equally, the skills and resources relevant to individuals from various ethnic or socioeconomic groups are likely to be different in important ways. Tailoring the development of internal (e.g., skills, attitudes) and external resources (e.g., social supports, work opportunities) to each offender's distinct social contexts is likely to improve treatment relevance and effectiveness.

In summary, we acknowledge that the RNM and the attendant relapse prevention approach to sex offender treatment has a number of merits. Most notable is the RNM's strong empirical base and simplicity; programs consistent with the RNM are typically shown to reduce the rates of sexual reoffending. However, the RNM fails to conceptualize offending within broader psychological models of human needs, motivation, and functioning. Insufficient attention is focused on how to live a better kind of life in which inherent human needs are being met in personally satisfying and socially acceptable ways. Treatment needs are compartmentalized into those that lead to reductions in offending (i.e., criminogenic needs) and those that do not (i.e., responsivity barriers), whereas in practice, issues of motivation, personal agency, and personal identity are always present and influencing the change process. Explicitly recognizing the role of these influences and utilizing them in treatment affords an opportunity to make treatment not only more meaningful for offenders, but also more effective.

A POSITIVE APPROACH TO SEX OFFENDER MANAGEMENT: A GOOD LIVES MODEL

The Good Lives Model (GLM) is a capabilities- or strength-based treatment approach (Rapp, 1998). By being strength-based, we mean that the aim of treatment emphasizes equipping individuals with the necessary psychological and social conditions to achieve well-being in socially acceptable and personally satisfying ways. The aim of strength-based approaches is to enhance individuals' capacity to live meaningful, constructive, and ultimately happy lives so that they can desist from further offending (Ward, Polaschek, & Beech, 2005).

The GLM is underpinned by three related core ideas. First, humans are viewed as active, goal-seeking beings who constantly attempt to construct a sense of meaning and purpose in their lives. Second, all human actions reflect attempts to meet inherent human needs or *primary human goods* (Emmons, 1999; Ward, 2002). Primary human goods are actions, states of affairs, or experiences that are inherently beneficial to humans and are naturally sought out for their own intrinsic properties rather than as a means to some other end (Arnhart, 1998; Deci & Ryan, 2000; Emmons, 1999; Schmuck & Sheldon, 2001). Examples of primary human goods are autonomy, competence, and relatedness (Deci & Ryan, 2000). Third, instrumental or secondary goods provide the concrete means or strategies for achieving primary human goods. For example, being in a relationship provides an opportunity to obtain the primary human good of intimacy (a subclass of relatedness); intimacy is the experience of familiarity, closeness, and understanding necessary for optimum psychological functioning and well-being.

The pursuit and achievement of primary human goods is integral to individuals' sense of meaning and purpose in their life, and in turn their well-being. In other words, when individuals are able to secure the full range of primary human goods (i.e., meet their inherent human needs), their well-being flourishes. For such individuals their good lives plan is working well. However, when individuals are unable to secure a number of primary human goods, constructing meaningful and purposeful lives is frustrated and well-being is compromised; the good lives plan is dysfunctional. According to the GLM, the presence of dynamic risk factors simply alerts clinicians to problems in the way offenders are seeking to achieve primary human goods and construct meaningful and purposeful lives. Different categories of risk factors point to problems in the pursuit of different types of primary human goods. For example, social isolation indicates difficulties in the ways the goods of intimacy and community are sought and may indicate social skills deficits and/or lack of social opportunities and resources.

Research findings from a number of disciplines (i.e., anthropology, evolutionary theory, philosophy, practical ethics, psychology, social policy, and social science) appear to converge on nine types of primary goods (see Arnhart, 1998; Aspinwall & Staudinger, 2003; Cummins, 1996; Emmons, 1999; Linley & Joseph, 2004; Murphy, 2001; Nussbaum, 2000; Rescher, 1990). No one of these goods is "better" to attain than others; rather, all in some form or another are necessary for a fulfilling life. The main categories of primary human goods sought are *life* (i.e., healthy living, optimal physical functioning, sexual satisfaction), *knowledge* (i.e., wisdom and information), *excellence in work and play* (i.e., mastery experiences), *excellence in agency* (i.e., autonomy, self-directedness), *inner peace* (i.e., freedom from emotional turmoil and stress), *relatedness* (i.e., intimate, family, romantic, and community relationships), *spirituality* (i.e., finding meaning and purpose in life), *happiness*, and *creativity*. As a comprehensive list, these nine primary human goods are, of course, multifaceted and may be broken down into related subclusters of goods. For example, the primary good of relatedness may be further subdivided into the goods of intimacy, friendship, support, caring, reliability, honesty, and so on. Table 8.1 summarizes these primary human goods and outlines potential secondary (instrumental) human goods that individuals may use to secure their primary human goods.

Individuals are unique in the priorities or weight they give to different types of goods due to cultural context, personal preferences, strengths, and opportunities. For example, an individual from a culture that places greater social value on *relatedness* than *excellence in agency* per se may internalize that value and prioritize pursuit of group mastery over individual mastery (i.e., greater well-being is achieved when the group does well rather than when the individual does well). Thus, all individuals have their own unique *good lives plan* that reflects the priority given to the various primary human goods and the secondary goods or strategies chosen to achieve the primary goods. In essence, an individual's good lives plan reflects an individual's *personal identity*; it is like an internalized metascript that guides the kind of life a person seeks and the type of person he tries to be.

A good life is attainable when an individual possesses both the *internal* skills and capabilities and *external* opportunities and supports to achieve primary

Table 8.1. Primary Human Goods and Potential Secondary Goods

Primary Goods	Secondary Goods (examples)
Life • Healthy living • Optimal physical functioning • Sexual satisfaction	• Leisure & sporting involvement • Attention to diet • Maintain intimate relationship
Knowledge • Wisdom • Information	• Work, career • Education • Reading
Excellence in work & play • Mastery experiences	• Involvement in work, career, sport, hobbies, interests • Engage in training, mentoring program
Excellence in agency • Autonomy • Self-directedness	• Achieve financial independence • Seek employment that matches desire for autonomy/direction
Inner peace • Freedom from emotional turmoil and stress	• Achieve lifestyle balance • Maintain positive relationships • Learn emotional regulation skills • Physical exercise
Relatedness • Intimate • Family • Romantic • Community	• Work on building intimacy within relationships • Invest in establishing & maintaining a romantic relationship • Have children, be an active parent • Involvement in community groups & activities
Spirituality • Meaning & purpose in life	• Practice religious beliefs • Live life according to values • Engage in cherished life projects
Happiness	• Engage in relationships & activities that bring joy & pleasure
Creativity	• Work, parenting, music, art, gardening

human goods in a socially acceptable manner. For a fulfilling and balanced life, it is important that the full range of primary goods is attained within an individual's lifestyle. In the case of individuals who offend, problems reside in four major types of difficulties: (1) problems in the *means* used to secure goods (e.g., seeking intimacy through child sexual abuse); (2) a lack of *scope* or variety in the goods being sought (e.g., devaluing relatedness or intimacy resulting in a lack of socially acceptable means to achieve sexual satisfaction); (3) the presence of *conflict* among the goods sought (e.g., wanting both autonomy of sexual freedom and intimacy within the same relationship); and (4) a lack of skills or capacity to adapt the good sought or means chosen to changes in circumstances (e.g., impulsive decision making). To illustrate, an offender might achieve a sense of intimacy and mastery in a sexual relationship with a child. Clearly, sexual abuse is an inappropriate way of seeking intimacy and mastery and is unlikely to result in higher levels of well-being. However, although the activity is harmful, the drive for a sense of intimacy and mastery is a common human pursuit.

In summary, the GLM proposes that humans pursue primary human goods because such goods are inherently beneficial and linked to our sense of meaning, purpose, and well-being. Individuals each have a unique *good lives plan* that reflects their personal identity and is influenced by individual preferences, strengths, cultural context, and opportunities. No one good lives plan is supreme (Den Uyl, 1991; Rasmussen, 1999), so primary human goods should not be combined in exactly the same way for all individuals, although all should be present. Put another way, humans all need the essential nutrients for a healthy diet and optimal functioning, yet each individual obtains these through different dietary preferences. When a person sexually offends, the GLM proposes that there is a problem in his good lives plan. That is, there are problems in the way he is pursuing his primary human goods and seeking to meet inherent human needs (e.g., the plan may lack sufficient scope, include inappropriate means, lack coherence, or the offender may have planning deficits). Within the GLM, dynamic risk factors simply inform the therapist that problems exist and steer the therapist toward an understanding of the nature of these problems.

IMPLEMENTING THE GLM

We propose the GLM and Risk-Need approaches should be combined to provide a more sophisticated treatment for sexual offenders with a dual focus on attending to optimal human functioning and individual risk factors. Here, risk factors are used as markers of specific problems in an offender's good lives plan, providing a rehabilitation framework that deals more systematically with motivation, the functions of offending, and treatment responsivity. According to the GLM, treatment should proceed on the assumption that effective rehabilitation requires acquisition of the competencies and external supports necessary to achieve a better good lives plan. Thus, the goal of treatment should be to enhance human well-being (i.e., good lives) as this will reduce risk.

A treatment plan should be explicitly constructed in the form of a good lives formulation. The good lives formulation should take into account offenders' preferences, strengths, primary goods, and relevant environments when specifying the internal conditions (e.g., competencies, beliefs) and external conditions (e.g., opportunities, social environment) required to achieve his primary goods. Tinkering with standard treatment plans is insufficient: the good lives formulation should be explicit, specific, individualized, and centered around an offender's personal identity, primary goods, and lifestyle (see Ward, Mann, & Gannon, 2005 for a detailed discussion).

Conceptualizing criminogenic needs (i.e., dynamic risk factors) as internal or external obstacles that frustrate or block the achievement of primary human goods integrates the GLM and the RNM. In other words, criminogenic needs indicate some form of impairment in the good lives plan; either a healthy good lives plan was never present or a healthy good lives plan was present but was compromised in some way. There is likely to be common relationships between different types of risk factors and distinct primary human goods. For example, deviant sexual interests indicate that some of the necessary internal and external conditions for healthy sexuality and relationships are distorted or missing in some way. Internal obstacles may include deviant sexual scripts, inappropriate sexual knowledge, or fears concerning intimacy. External obstacles may include social isolation or physical characteristics/disability that compromise relationship opportunities.

Risk factors and appropriate self-management are not ignored; instead, they are explicitly contextualized as part of achieving the individual's good lives plan. For example, most child molesters will still need to avoid working with children or adhere to very strict conditions placed around such work. Although this type of risk management may be necessary for reduced re-offending it is not sufficient for long-term desistence. Instead, long-term desistance from offending appears to result from the process of an individual constructing and achieving a healthy good lives plan that is reflected in his or her personal identity and lifestyle. In the following sections, we sketch out the main foundations of the GLM of sexual offender assessment and treatment. The interested reader, however, can find more detailed information on GLM treatment in Ward, Mann, and Gannon, 2005 or Ward and Mann, 2004.

GLM Assessment

The GLM approach to assessment has distinctive content and style dimensions. As described earlier, the traditional RNM focuses assessment on eliciting offenders' personal history relevant to offending, offenders' understanding of their offending, and measuring a range of potential risk factors with psychological tests. In addition to these traditional foci, the GLM assessment model places equal importance on discovering the offenders' own goals, life priorities, strengths, achievements, and aims for their intervention. The purpose is to understand how clients conceptualize their own lives, and how they prioritize and operationalize their range of primary human goods. The result is a balance between assessment of risk and vulnerability, and assessment of client strengths and personal identity.

The GLM requires a particular, collaborative style. If the primary purpose of assessment is to establish the client's risk for reoffending on society's behalf, it is likely the client has little reason to engage openly. Instead, the contingencies favor trying to impress the assessor as being low risk by concealing or minimizing offending and the related risk areas. However, if the interests of the client are given explicit recognition and value, there is a greater likelihood that the client can see personal benefits to engaging more fully in the assessment process. The latter approach reflects the aims of the GLM assessment model. A collaborative approach to assessment can be facilitated by presenting evidence to the client as a collaborative investigation. Results of assessment procedures, such as phallometric testing (i.e., physiological testing of sexual response patterns) and psychological testing, can be fed back to the client and the client can be asked to help draw conclusions from them.

Perhaps most important to the collaborative assessment approach advocated by the GLM is that strengths and life achievements are considered to be as important as offense-related needs in determining treatment plans and prognosis. Mann and Shingler (2001) recently produced a set of guidelines for collaborative risk assessment to help reconcile the goals of the assessor with the goals of the client. The early indicators are that using collaborative risk assessment strategies greatly improves the relationship between therapy staff and clients. More impressively, there is a subsequent positive effect on motivation and treatment retention.

Taking direct interest in clients' conceptualization of their lives, priorities, and desires for the future in a respectful and collaborative way sets the scene for developing treatment plans where potential benefits are more apparent. For example, undertaking extensive treatment to learn what went wrong and how to avoid or cope better in risky situations so as to reduce reoffending may seem necessary but not particularly appealing. In fact, it may seem an extension of the punishment given for the crime. In contrast, undertaking extensive treatment to realize goals, promote well-being, and live a satisfying life free from further offending is a more attractive option and less likely to conflict with the individual's goals. The assessment process is therefore a potential motivational intervention in its own right, the outcome of which is an individual beginning treatment with a clear sense of how the treatment is relevant and why it is worthwhile.

GLM Treatment

A GLM approach to sex offender treatment is informed by an explicit and particular understanding of sex offenders and the therapeutic task. First, the GLM acknowledges that a large proportion of sex offenders have developmental histories marked by a diversity of adversarial experiences. These adversarial experiences may involve negative developmental experiences (e.g., physical or sexual abuse, instability in the family or caregiver arrangements, and so on) and/or may involve experiences that were missing in development (e.g., there was emotional neglect, insecure relationships, lack of positive personal and interpersonal modeling, and so on). Hence, sex offenders are seen as individuals who have lacked the opportunity and resources necessary to develop an adequate good lives plan. Second, sexual offending represents an attempt to achieve human goods that are desired and normative, but where the skills or capabilities necessary to achieve them are lacking. Third, the absence or problems in achieving some primary human goods appear to be more strongly related to sexual offending than others. These goods are agency (i.e., autonomy and self-directedness), inner peace (i.e., freedom from emotional turmoil and stress), and relatedness (i.e., including intimate, romantic, family, and community) (Ward & Mann, 2004). Fourth, reducing the risk of sexual reoffending is achieved by assisting sexual offenders to develop the skills and capabilities necessary to achieve the full range of primary human goods, with particular emphasis on agency, inner peace, and relatedness. Fifth, treatment is seen as an activity that adds to a sexual offender's repertoire of personal functioning, rather than being an activity that removes or manages a problem. Restricting activities that are highly related to sexual offending or offense-related problems may be necessary but should not be the primary focus of treatment. Instead, the goal should be to assist clients to live as normal a life as possible, where restrictions are only used when necessary.

The aims of GLM treatment are always specified as approach goals (Emmons, 1999; Mann, 2000; Mann, Webster, Schofield, & Marshall, 2004). Approach goals involve defining what individuals will achieve and gain, in contrast to avoidance goals that specify what will be avoided or ceased. Specifying the aims of treatment as approach goals has several advantages. For example, goals that are life-enhancing rather than problem-avoiding are more likely to create intrinsic motivation for change rather than the motivation for change being extrinsically driven (i.e., to avoid trouble with the law). Goals that focus on what the offender wants to obtain in life are more in line with what offenders want to achieve. The reality is that most offenders are much more focused on their own problems and quality of life than the harm they have caused their victims. Hence, incorporating offenders' goals as well as society's goals into treatment is more likely to tap into offenders' intrinsic motivation for change.

Research shows some advantages to using approach goal programs. Cox, Klinger, and Blount (1991) found that alcohol abusers who participated in an approach-goal focused program were less likely to lapse than individuals working toward avoidance goals. Mann et al. (2004) found teaching traditional relapse prevention ideas and skills to sex offenders with an approach-goal focus rather than the traditional avoidance and risk reduction focus resulted in greater engagement in treatment (i.e., greater homework compliance and disclosure of problems). Instead of teaching offenders what risk factors to notice and avoid, offenders were taught personal and interpersonal qualities to notice and work toward for a more adaptive personal identity. At program completion, offenders in the approach-goal group were equally able to articulate their personal risk factors but were rated as more genuinely motivated for living a nonoffending lifestyle than offenders in the avoidance-goal group.

Treatment using the GLM involves two broad steps: First, the offender must learn to think of himself as someone who can secure all the important primary human goods in socially acceptable and personally satisfying ways. In other words, the offender has to learn to believe that change is possible and that change is worthwhile. Second, the treatment program should aim to help offenders develop the scope, strategies, coherence, and capacities necessary for living a healthy personal good lives plan. To achieve this, individuals' offending should be understood in the context of the problematic or unhealthy good lives plan operating when the offending occurred, or until now. Also, the treatment goals should be understood as the steps necessary to help the individual construct and achieve the healthy personal good lives plan.

Many of the specific activities of traditional RNM programs can be utilized in a GLM program. However, the goal of each intervention will be explicitly linked to the GLM theory and offered in a style consistent with the GLM principles. Ward and colleagues (Ward & Mann, 2004; Ward, Mann, & Gannon, 2005) recently reviewed the traditional targets of sex offender treatment and reinterpreted these in light of the GLM. For example, a common target of sex offender treatment is offenders' sexual preferences for children. According to the GLM, sexual preferences for children point to the following potential problems and treatment approaches: (i), the offender uses inappropriate means to achieve sexual satisfaction and sexual intimacy (through which the primary human goods of *life* and *relatedness* that we outlined earlier are achieved, respectively). Treatment should focus on helping the offender develop a wider range of strategies for achieving sexual satisfaction and sexual intimacy (i.e., provide appropriate means to achieve these goods); (ii), the offender lacks scope in his good lives plan and places too much emphasis on achieving sexual satisfaction or sexual intimacy at any cost. The offender should be helped to learn to value and invest in a broader range of primary human goods (i.e., improve the scope of the good lives plan); and (iii), the offender uses inappropriate means to achieve agency or mastery and attempts to achieve these through sexual domination of a minor. Treatment should help the offender develop a wider range of strategies for achieving agency and mastery in both appropriate sexual relationships and in nonsexual situations (i.e., provide appropriate means for achieving these goods). The extent that any one of these formulations is accurate for an individual offender would be ascertained through the assessment process. It is also entirely feasible that a different link to a primary human good may exist. The GLM is not intended to be a rigidly prescriptive approach; rather, what is important is that the problem area is understood in terms of the individual's good lives plan and treatment aims to achieve a healthy good lives plan (in which offending is not necessary or compatible).

Adopting a combined GLM and RNM treatment approach requires re-thinking some of the ways that sex offender treatment programs are packaged and operationalized. As discussed earlier, RNM sex offender treatment programs tend to be highly structured psycho-educational programs where a series of skills are taught in sequential modules. Although a one-size-fits-all program structure has advantages in terms of the simplicity of streaming individuals for treatment, the rigidity of such an approach is inconsistent with the emphasis on making treatment explicitly relevant and tailored to the individual offender. An alternative approach is to develop individualized formulation-based GLM treatment programs that tie intervention modules or areas specifically to the offenders' good lives formulations and plans. Offering formulation-based interventions is not the same as offering unstructured treatment. Unstructured treatments have been shown to have no impact on recidivism rates (Gendreau, 1996; Andrews & Bonta, 2003), so they obviously are not sufficient. Formulation-based treatment derives clear structure from the formulation, treatment methods, and treatment processes used, and is capable of providing a transparent program model that is auditable.

Few formulation-based treatment programs for sex offenders currently exist on which to base a GLM treatment approach. One exception is a program run by William Marshall et al. in Canada (Marshall, Anderson, & Fernandez, 1999), where group members work through a series of assignments at their own pace. Assignments include both offense-related topics and topics related to achieving human goods, such as intimacy, attachment, and emotional well-being. While one way to deliver an assignment or topic-based program is for each participant to complete each assignment at his or her own pace, another option is for participants to only complete treatment components or modules derived from their formulation. Although a departure from the current practice, it would be possible to manualize the major clinical areas addressed in a modularized program. Each program participant would have a selection of the modules based on his or her individualized formulation. In practice, some modules could be designed as core modules that are relevant to all program participants so participants can continue to meet as a group and obtain the benefits of a group process. Others could be selected based on individual need. For example, a core module focused on *building and maintaining progress toward a good lives plan* could include psycho-education about good lives plans, basic self-management skills, problem-solving and motivation enhancement skills. Other modules could focus on sexual health, interpersonal competence, self-esteem, anxiety management, and so on, and be completed on an *as needed* basis either in other groups or individually, depending on the resources and operational constraints of the agency. An example of a highly individualized program that uses manualized treatment components, much like choosing the best tools from a tool kit, is Multi-Systemic Therapy (MST;

Henggeler, Melton, Smith, Schoenwald, & Hanley, 1993; Henggeler, Schoenwald, Borduin, Rowland, & Cunningham, 1998). Designed for youth with serious mental health and offending problems, MST has proven to be an innovative and very successful program that is supported by rigorous treatment integrity processes and evaluation research.

Whatever decisions are made about the best method to organize and deliver the program, it would be important to have a carefully controlled system of recording what treatment had been offered so evaluations of treatment efficacy can be undertaken. Clear guidelines for determining which treatment components were and were not included in the treatment plan would also be required to ensure consistency in decision making. We strongly advocate that adoption of the GLM also include adoption of a rigorous empirical approach to program evaluation and continuous improvement.

CONCLUSIONS

In this chapter we have presented a new theory of sex offender rehabilitation. The GLM is a strength-based approach to working with offenders that has the major aim of equipping offenders with the necessary internal and external resources to live better lives. In the GLM, criminogenic needs or dynamic risk factors are conceptualized as distortions in the internal and external resources necessary to live healthy lives. Although criminogenic needs are important for understanding the occurrence of sexual offending, they should not be the sole focus of treatment. Instead, we advocate embedding the RNM within the GLM to create a twin focus on establishing good lives and avoiding inflicting harm. Such an approach grounds individuals' offending within a broad understanding of their functioning, personal identity, lifestyle, and social context and provides a rich and comprehensive guide for clinicians who undertake the difficult task of treating sex offenders.

By making treatment more meaningful for offenders and optimizing offenders' intrinsic motivational and change processes, we believe we can increase the effectiveness of treatment and, in turn, increase public safety. In particular, the GLM provides us an opportunity to explore a better means of reaching unmotivated or treatment-resistant offenders and enhancing the maintenance of positive changes following treatment completion in the community. The combined approach also provides the potential to be more efficient with those offenders who are already motivated and well on the road to change.

We believe that the GLM and principles will continue to grow and exert influence in clinical practice with sex offenders. Of course, full integration of such principles is dependent upon the outcome data from programs that have begun to pilot the model. It is our hope that researchers' and practitioners' interest in the GLM will flourish and produce a sizable evidence base upon which the GLM can be more fully evaluated. However, adopting the GLM approach will require researchers, practitioners, and the public to be open to new innovations in sex offender rehabilitation and to be willing for treatment to explicitly work toward offenders' well-being.

NOTES

1. Strictly speaking, some dynamic risk factors may not be criminogenic needs. For example, some risk assessment instruments look at the recency of criminal behavior, such as the number of assaults committed over the last twelve months. Although such dynamic risk factors may change over time (e.g., there are more or fewer assaults committed over the last twelve months), they still do not represent the psychological or situational clinical problems that are targeted in treatment.

2. Lifestyle imbalance is created when life is dominated by activities perceived as hassles or demands (shoulds) compared with activities perceived as pleasures or self-fulfilling (wants). Lifestyle imbalance is often associated with a perception of self-deprivation that can trigger a desire for indulgence in an avoided or abstained behavior (Marlatt, 1985).

REFERENCES

Andrews, D. A., & Bonta, J. (2003). *The psychology of criminal conduct* (3rd ed.). Cincinnati, OH: Anderson.

Arnhart, L. (1998). *Darwinian natural right: The biological ethics of human nature.* Albany: State University of New York Press.

Aspinwall, L. G., & Staudinger, U. M. (Eds.). (2003). *A psychology of human strengths: Fundamental questions and future directions for a positive psychology.* Washington, DC: American Psychological Association.

Beech, A. R., & Ward, T. (2004). The integration of etiology and risk in sexual offenders: A theoretical framework. *Aggression & Violent Behavior, 10,* 31–63.

Cox, M., Klinger, E., & Blount, J. P. (1991). Alcohol use and goal hierarchies: Systematic motivational counseling for alcoholics. In W. R. Miller & S. Rollnick (Eds.), *Motivational interviewing: Preparing people to change addictive behavior* (pp. 260–271). New York: Guilford.

Cummins, R. A. (1996). The domains of life satisfaction: An attempt to order chaos. *Social Indicators Research, 38,* 303–328.

Deci, E. L., & Ryan, R. M. (2000). The "what" and "why" of goal pursuits: Human needs and the self-determination of behavior. *Psychological Inquiry, 11,* 227–268.

Den Uyl, D. (1991). *The virtue of prudence.* New York: Peter Lang.

Emmons, R. A. (1999). *The psychology of ultimate concerns.* New York: Guilford.

Gendreau, P. (1996). Offender rehabilitation: What we know and what needs to be done. *Criminal Justice and Behavior, 23,* 144–161.

Gendreau, P., Little, T., & Goggin, C. (1996). A meta-analysis of the predictors of adult offender recidivism: What works! *Criminology, 34,* 575–607.

Hanson, R. K., & Bussière, M. T. (1998). Predicting relapse: A meta-analysis of sexual offender recidivism studies. *Journal of Consulting & Clinical Psychology, 66*, 348–362.

Hanson, R. K., Gordon, A., Harris, A. J. R., Marques, J. K., Murphy, W., Quinsey, V. L., et al. (2002). First report of the collaborative outcome data project on the effectiveness of psychological treatment for sex offenders. *Sexual Abuse: A Journal of Research and Treatment, 14*, 169–194.

Hanson, R. K., & Harris, A. J. R. (2000). Where should we intervene? Dynamic predictors of sex offense recidivism. *Criminal Justice and Behavior, 27*, 6–35.

Hanson, R. K., & Morton-Bourgon, K. (2004). Predictors of sexual recidivism: An updated meta-analysis 2004–02. Public Works & Government Services Canada. Retrieved July 1, 2005, from www.psepc-sppcc.gc.ca/publica tions/corrections/pdf/200402_e.pdf

Henggeler, S. W., Melton, G. B., Smith, L. A., Schoenwald, S. K., & Hanley, J. (1993). Family preservation using multisystemic therapy: Long-term follow-up to a clinical trial with serious juvenile offenders. *Journal of Child and Family Studies, 2*, 283–293.

Henggeler, S. W., Schoenwald, S. K., Borduin, C. M., Rowland, M. D., & Cunningham, P. B. (1998). *Multisystemic treatment for antisocial behavior in children and adolescents.* New York: Guilford.

Hollin, C. R. (1999). Treatment programs for offenders: Meta-analysis, "what works" and beyond. *International Journal of Law and Psychiatry, 22*, 361–372.

Laws, D. R. (2000). Relapse prevention: Reconceptualization and revision. In C. R. Hollin (Ed.), *Handbook of offender assessment and treatment* (pp. 297–307). Chichester, UK: Wiley.

Linley, P. A., & Joseph, S. (Eds.). (2004). *Positive psychology in practice.* New York: Wiley.

Mann, R. E. (2000). Managing resistance and rebellion in relapse prevention. In D. R. Laws, S. M. Hudson, & T. Ward (Eds.), *Remaking relapse prevention with sex offenders* (pp. 187–200). Thousand Oaks, CA: Sage.

Mann, R. E., & Shingler, J. (2001, September). *Collaborative risk assessment with sexual offenders.* Paper presented at the National Organization for the Treatment of Abusers, Cardiff, Wales.

Mann, R. E., Webster, S. D., Schofield, C., & Marshall, W. L. (2004). Approach versus avoidance goals in relapse prevention with sexual offenders. *Sexual Abuse: A Journal of Research and Treatment, 16*, 65–75.

Marlatt, G. A. (1985). Relapse prevention: Theoretical rationale and overview of the model. In G. A. Marlatt & J. R. Gordon (Eds.), *Relapse prevention: Maintenance strategies in the treatment of addictive behaviors* (pp. 3–70). New York: Guilford.

Marlatt, G. A., & Gordon, J. R. (Eds.). (1985). *Relapse prevention: Maintenance strategies in the treatment of addictive behaviors.* New York: Guilford.

Marshall, P. (1997). *The prevalence of convictions for sexual offending.* No. 55. London: Home Office Research Statistics Directorate.

Marshall, W. L., Anderson, D., & Fernandez, Y. (1999). *Cognitive-behavioural treatments of sex offenders.* Chichester, UK: Wiley.

Marshall, W. L., & Barbaree, H. E. (1990). An integrated theory of the etiology of sexual offending. In W. L. Marshall, D. R. Laws, & Barbaree, H. E. (Eds.), *Handbook of sexual assault: Issues, theories, and treatment of the offender* (pp. 257–275). New York: Plenum.

Marshall, W. L., & McGuire, J. (2003). Effect sizes in the treatment of sexual offenders. *International Journal of Offender Therapy and Comparative Criminology, 47,* 653–663.

Maruna, S. (2001). *Making good: How ex-convicts reform and rebuild their lives.* Washington, DC: American Psychological Association.

McGuire, J. (2002). Integrating findings from research reviews. In J. McGuire (Ed.), *Offender rehabilitation and treatment: Effective programmes and policies for reducing reoffending* (pp. 3–38). Chichester, UK: Wiley.

Murphy, M. C. (2001). *Natural law and practical rationality.* New York: Cambridge University Press.

Nussbaum, M. C. (2000). *Women and human development: The capabilities approach.* New York: Cambridge University Press.

Ogloff, J., & Davis, M. R. (2004). Advances in offender assessment and rehabilitation: Contributions of the Risk-Needs-Responsivity approach. *Psychology, Crime, & Law, 10,* 229–242.

Pithers, W. D. (1990). Relapse prevention with sexual aggression: A method for maintaining therapeutic gain and enhancing external supervision. In W. L. Marshall, D. R. Laws, & H. E. Barbaree (Eds.), *Handbook of sexual assault: Issues, theories, and treatment of the offender* (pp. 343–361). New York: Plenum.

Rapp, C. A. (1998). *The strengths model: Case management with people suffering from severe and persistent mental illness.* New York: Oxford University Press.

Rasmussen, D. B. (1999). Human flourishing and the appeal to human nature. In E. F. Paul, F. D. Miller, & J. Paul (Eds.), *Human flourishing* (pp. 1–43). New York: Cambridge University Press.

Rescher, N. (1990). *Human interests: Reflections on philosophical anthropology.* Stanford, CA: Stanford University Press.

Schmuck, P., & Sheldon, K. M. (Eds.). (2001). *Life goals and well-being.* Toronto, Ontario: Hogrefe & Huber.

Ward, T. (2002). Good lives and the rehabilitation of offenders: Promises and problems. *Aggression and Violent Behavior, 7,* 513–528.

Ward, T. (2003). The explanation, assessment, and treatment of child sexual abuse. *International Journal of Forensic Psychology, 1,* 10–25.

Ward, T., & Hudson, S. M. (2000). A self-regulation model of relapse prevention. In D. R. Laws, S. M. Hudson, & T. Ward (Eds.), *Remaking relapse prevention with sex offenders: A sourcebook* (pp. 79–101). Thousand Oaks, CA: Sage.

Ward, T., Keenan, T., & Hudson, S. M. (2000). Understanding cognitive, affective, and intimacy deficits in sexual offenders: A developmental perspective. *Aggression & Violent Behavior, 5,* 41–62.

Ward, T., & Mann, R. (2004). Good lives and the rehabilitation of offenders: A positive approach to sex offender treatment. In P. A. Linley & S. Joseph (Eds.), *Positive psychology in practice* (pp. 598–616). New York: Wiley.

Ward, T., Mann, R., & Gannon, T. (2005). *The comprehensive model of good lives treatment for sex offenders: Clinical implications.* Manuscript submitted for publication.

Ward, T., Polaschek, D. L., & Beech, A. R. (2005). *Theories of sexual offending.* Chichester, UK: Wiley.

Ward, T., & Stewart, C. A. (2003). Criminogenic needs or human needs: A theoretical critique. *Psychology, Crime, & Law, 9*, 125–143.

9

Offender Profiling

Laurence J. Alison and Jonathan S. Ogan ◆

> Anecdotes are one thing . . . hard evidence is a totally different thing.
> The "Amazing Randi," Master Magician and Skeptic

This chapter seeks to challenge the several assumptions on which many "traditional" offender profiling methods are based and to illustrate the pitfalls of too heavy a reliance on methods that have been widely presented in the media and in fictional portrayals. We also give a brief overview of the relatively less-well-discussed (or least media-friendly) developments within psychology and behavioral science that are now successfully assisting the police with sexual assault, rape, and murder enquiries. We begin by defining what we mean by "traditional," explore the assumptions on which it is based, and challenge them. We then continue with a discussion of the more varied and diverse means by which psychologists can contribute to major investigations, including a consideration of decision making and suspect prioritization. Our principal argument is that senior officers engaged in major enquiries deserve the best advice possible and that the most suitable method for enhancing the professional standing of profiling and other behavioral contributions is to ensure that they are built on a logical and systematic scientific foundation and not speculation, whim, intuition, or anecdote.

"A MORON IN A HURRY COULD SEE IT WOULD NOT STAND UP IN COURT"[1]

In the United Kingdom, a severe blow was delivered to offender profiling in the Rachel Nickell murder case.[2] A clinical psychologist developed a profile based on the supposed fantasies on the apparently sexually related murder of a young woman in one of London's public parks. The resultant advice supplied by the profiler was used to direct a police undercover operation, in which the enquiry team hoped the suspect (Colin Stagg) would reveal some guilty knowledge of the offense (i.e., that only the actual offender would know about). This guilty knowledge or a confession was never forthcoming and there was no compelling evidence against Stagg. Indeed, there is some recent plausible speculation that a variety of other suspects who were not focused on with the same verve are far more compelling. However, at the earliest stages of the trial, even before the evidence was heard before the jury, the case was thrown out. The judge, Justice Ognall, severely criticized the use of "profiling" and behavioral advice in this particular investigation—in part because of its lack of scientific foundations and the apparent unquestioned intuition on which it was based (Britton, 1997). He argued that the enquiry was run with an "excess of zeal" and classified the case as an example of "misconduct of the grossest kind."

This case doubtless had a negative impact on profiling in the United Kingdom. However, the hiatus provided academics and practitioners with the time to review the subject and how to move profiling forward to standardize advisory output. Moreover, there was a clear remit to ensure that advice should offer practical results and be based on a firmly scientific foundation. Prior to this painful introspection, profiling in the United Kingdom had been a phenomenon that was trying to run before it could even crawl, let alone walk. The approach taken by Britton was largely based on his experience and the format generally involved the provision of inferences about the "type" of offender responsible and the "types" of characteristics associated with this "type" of offense behavior. Alison and West (2005) referred to this approach, which is still used by many advisors in the United States and a number of European countries, as "traditional" profiling.

By traditional offender profiling, we broadly mean the range of advice given in major criminal investigations in which an "expert" draws up a list of demographic details of an offender based upon inferences about the type of person whom she or he thinks has committed the crime (see Alison & West, 2005 for a detailed review). We need to distinguish this from more contemporary approaches, which are less well considered, but will be covered in the latter half of this chapter. Traditional profiling is now less well used than it was ten years ago and is best exemplified in the accounts of ex-FBI officers in the United States (for example, Ressler & Shactman's *Whoever Fights Monsters*, 1992) and by one or two clinical psychologists in the United Kingdom (e.g., see Britton's 1997 *The Jigsaw Man*). It is the most frequently represented portrayal of what offender profilers do in crime fiction (TV, films, and books) although its weaknesses have gradually led to a decline in how often it is used by police investigators. In traditional methods, "types" of offenders are inferred from characteristics of the crime scene (i.e., whether the offender used a garrotte or a gun, whether he bound the victim or spent time speaking with him or her). The idea of an expert with special insight into the minds of killers and who can, through an examination of the crime scene, draw conclusions about the type of person who committed it is an enticing prospect and perhaps is the reason why this approach is the one most frequently reflected in the media. The archetype of visionary crime fighter, succeeding where the rest of the enquiry team has failed, seems to have a very firm grip on the public's imagination. However, we will show that such portrayals, as well as some of the now actual but outdated approaches that these were based on, represent a very incomplete and naïve view of theories of personality as well as what is possible in profiling. Doubtless, such archetypes will continue to entertain us in TV shows, films, and books, but it is important that we understand that this glorification of the expert as mystical crime fighter should be appreciated as based on anecdote and fiction and not on fact.

In contrast, in this chapter, we will show that what is far more important for us to gain a psychological "purchase on" is the central figure of any investigation, namely the senior investigating officer (SIO), *not* the "expert" pulled in to assist the enquiry. Indeed, psychologists wishing to contribute to major investigations would do well to consider their expertise in relation to understanding how the SIO will make decisions, lead his or her team, and network with the local community, the family of the victim(s), and, potentially, even state or federal government. We illustrate that the skills required to be a successful detective are far from just being a good sleuth and, although the detective's role can be enhanced by working with psychologists, a good investigating officer cautiously approaches external advice and is fully aware of how to critically evaluate it and incorporate it wisely into the investigation. However, before we consider the range of contributions to investigation beyond the simpleminded view of profiling types of offenders, we outline the justifications for our very skeptical view of traditional profiling.

BASIC ASSUMPTIONS

According to *Sexual Homicide: Patterns and Motives*, an often-cited "handbook" on offender profiling, it is possible to establish what sort of person has committed a crime based on the offender's behavior at a crime scene (Ressler, Burgess, & Douglas, 1988). So, with this assumption in mind, a profiler could, for example, in examining the injuries of the victim, the level of ransacking, and the method of entry to the property, predict the type of person "whodunnit." This process would involve reading the fine details of the crime scene and coming up with the kind of person responsible. This might include the offender's age, personality, social competencies, and even the type of car the offender drives. Perhaps the most popular example of this style of profiling is the supposed distinction between organized and disorganized killers. This model of offender behavior assumes that each type will have a distinct and consistent method of committing crimes. The details of this model are summarized in the following tables. Burgess, Douglas, and Ressler (1985) derived the system in interviews with thirty-six offenders who volunteered to speak to FBI officers.

Burgess et al. argue that these two "styles of offending" match up with two equally distinct offender types, organized and disorganized (see Table 9.1). For example, an individual engaging in the organized behaviors is the sort of person who would be married, have a good work record, and generally be more social than his dysfunctional, socially inept, disorganized counterpart. The style of offending is also thought to reflect the poor personal hygiene habits associated with disorganized offenders (see Tables 9.2 and 9.3).

Although this system holds great appeal (once one had learned what was present in an organized killing and a disorganized killing, one would simply learn by rote memory the list of characteristics associated with one or the other), criminal behavior is, sadly, much more complex than this simple twofold system. Let us consider an analogy: If we think about the behavior of people we know, we might be able to say whether they keep a reasonably tidy house or not ("organized" or "disorganized" house owners). We might even find that there are some very basic differences in the way these people think. Thus, we might want to measure the extent to which individuals who keep their house in pristine condition are more particular in the organization of their office space. We might also measure the extent to which their level of organization relates to other behaviors such as punctuality. The former

Table 9.1. Crime Scene Characteristics

Organized Crime Scene	Disorganized Crime Scene
Planned offense	Spontaneous offense
Victim is a stranger	Victim is a stranger
Controlled conversation	Minimal conversation
Scene reflects control	Scene is random/sloppy
Demands submissive victim	Sudden violence to victim
Restraints used	Minimal use of restraints
Aggressive prior to death	Sex after death
Body hidden	Body left in view
Weapon/evidence absent	Weapon/evidence present
Transports victim	Body left at scene

Source: Burgess et al. (1985).

Table 9.2. Organized Perpetrator Characteristics

Perpetrator Characteristics	Postoffense Behavior
High intelligence	Returns to crime scene
Socially adequate	Volunteers information
Sexually competent	Police groupie
Lives with father	Anticipates questioning
High birth order	May move body
Harsh discipline	May dispose of body
Controlled mood	to advertise crime
Masculine image	
Charming	**Best Interview Strategies**
Situational cause	Direct strategy
Geographically mobile	Be certain of details
Occupationally mobile	Only admit what he has to
Follows media	
Model prisoner	

Source: Burgess et al. (1985).

measure would tell us how consistently tidy they are in different environments and the latter measure would be one indication of how the organization of their house measures up (or not) with other behaviors that we might hypothesize are organized behaviors. Both of these are plausible hypotheses (although similar efforts have not been tested or examined in relation to

Table 9.3. Disorganized Perpetrator Characteristics

Perpetrator Characteristics	Postoffense Behavior
Below average intelligence	Returns to crime scene
Socially inadequate	May attend funeral/burial
Unskilled occupation	Memorial in media
Low birth order status	May turn to religion
Father's work unstable	May keep diary/newspaper
Harsh/inconsistent discipline as a child	clippings
Anxious mood during crime	May change residence
Minimal use of alcohol during crime	May change job
Lives alone	May have personality change
Lives/works near crime scene	
Minimal interest in media	**Best Interview Strategies**
Significant behavior change	Empathize with him
Nocturnal habits	Indirectly introduce evidence
Poor personal hygiene	Counselor approach
Secret hiding places	Nighttime interview
Usually does not date	
High-school dropout	

Source: Burgess et al. (1985).

offense behavior).[3] However, it is a far more ambitious psychologist who would argue that all of the people we know who keep their house very tidy are of a narrowly defined age range, of exactly the same social competence, and drive exactly the same type of car. Although there might be some loose associations (with younger individuals tending toward the less tidy end of the spectrum) it is probable that there is considerable variation among individuals and that this variation does not neatly match up with sociodemographic features (age, gender, ethnicity, etc.).

Moreover, there is probably a range of levels of tidiness rather than a system in which an individual was either tidy or untidy. Might we be able to say, for example, that incredibly tidy Dave is tidier than Jan, and that Jan is in turn tidier than our filthy friend Mick? Might it also be the case that most of the people we know could not be classified as at extreme ends of the spectrum? Thus, although we might know one or two people like Mick and Dave, most of the people we know would be more like Jan—that is, reasonably tidy. Therefore, for an offender classification system with only two types to prove successful would mean that very few offenders were hybrids or in the mid-range. Instead, the overwhelming majority would have to be at one end of the spectrum or the other.

Finally, if only we have a snapshot (say an hour) to look around an individual's house at some random point in his or her life (e.g., on the morning after Dave has had a dinner party for fifteen people and when Mick is preparing to sell his house and has tidied up for prospective buyers), we might get a very different view of the person. Similarly, in the offenses we examine, we have to be sure that the situation does not have too powerful an effect on the offender's behavior.

Therefore, for all sorts of complex reasons, including the fact that behaviors are usually on a continuum, the fact that psychological processes do not normally map neatly onto demographics such as age, and the fact that situations often have a powerful influence on behavior, this simple twofold system is unlikely to prove very useful.

Alison and Canter (1999) argued that organization might more fruitfully be considered a continuum rather than an either/or system. They claimed that the behaviors may represent various levels of planning, rather than discrete types, and that this might be reflected in crime scenes actually having a mixture of organized and disorganized behaviors. While Burgess et al.'s original system concedes that hybrids exist (i.e., contain both organized and disorganized elements), we have found that a majority of examples contain "both elements" (i.e., most are "Jans" and not "Micks" or "Daves") and, as such, the utility of the two discrete types to profile the likely background characteristics of offenders loses its power as a method for discriminating among individuals (Canter, Alison, Alison, & Wentink, 2004). Indeed, there is some suggestion in our study of such offenders that most of them are relatively organized, but it is the nature of their "type" of disorganization that varies.

Second, the belief that profilers can predict an offender's background characteristics relies on two major assumptions: consistency and homology.

Consistency and Homology

For profiling to work, perpetrators have to remain consistent across a number of crimes (in the same way that Dave must always be tidy and Mick always filthy). If during the first crime an offender gags and binds the victim, the second they kiss and compliment the victim, and the third they punch and stab the victim, then clearly it would be impossible to claim that certain clusters of behaviors are closely associated with certain clusters of offender backgrounds. Happily though, there is a fair amount of research that suggests that offenders are somewhat consistent. This has been demonstrated in rape, burglary, and, more recently, serial murder (see Salfati & Taylor, forthcoming).

The second assumption (homology), however, is more controversial (Mokros & Alison, 2002). Homology assumes that where two different offenders have the same personality they will commit a crime in the same way. Similarly, if two crime scenes are similar then they will have both been committed by the same type of person. This would mean that if Mick, whose house is untidy, is 24 years old, lives with his mother, and collects *Playboy* magazine, then all people with a similar level of untidiness in their house would also have to be about 24 years old, live with their mother, and collect pornography. In the crime example we would have a system where rapists who gag and bind victims would be more likely to be between 25 and 30. Conversely, those who kiss and compliment the victim are likely to be between 30 and 35. While there is some evidence that certain crime scene behaviors are associated with certain background characteristics, there is no compelling evidence that "clusters" of behaviors can be closely matched with particular clusters of background characteristics.

There is a subtle but very important distinction between the claim that clusters of behaviors are related to clusters of background characteristics "compared" to the claim that single behaviors are related to single characteristics. To further elucidate, let's take two examples:

1. The offender did not leave any fingerprints at the rape crime scene. It is therefore my assertion that this offender is likely to be a prolific burglar. Research by Professor X (1987) indicates that 76 percent of offenders who do not leave fingerprints have more than seven previous convictions for burglary.

2. This offense demonstrates that the offender is a "planner" rapist—there are no fingerprints, the crime scene is tidy, there is no ransacking, and he has only stolen electrical goods and children's clothes (both of which can be easily sold for gain). "Planner" rapists are between the ages of 25 and 30, feel no remorse, are likely to be in a semiskilled job, and are likely to be married.

The first is called a "one to one relationship" and typifies the sorts of claims made by profilers who may refer to themselves as crime analysts or behavioral advisors (these individuals might be considered the "new generation" of contemporary profilers). The second example reflects the more traditional method of profiling and is in line with the previous work of some FBI agents (most of whom are now retired) who advised in the early days of profiling in the 1970s, as well as an increasingly dwindling selection of individuals from a variety of backgrounds who appear to be happy to put themselves forward as expert profilers.

Traditional profiling methods (as in point 2) make far more ambitious claims than those offered by the behavioral advisor approach. Indeed, what is so enticing is the seeming promise of a rich and detailed character assessment or "pen portrait" of the offender. However, this approach assumes that offenders' behaviors are a product of stable personality traits (consistency) and that all offenders who share a particular personality (a "planner type") will behave in the same way (homology). Thus, the traditional view makes a number of inferential leaps (see Figure 9.1) in which one derives a type from a cluster of behaviors and a cluster of background characteristics from those different types.

However, research has indicated that this model fails to hold water. Several studies have now tested this process and consistently failed to find these sorts of relationships (see Davies, Wittebrood, & Jackson, 1998; House, 1997; Mokros & Alison, 2002).

Many developments have emerged since, and the FBI and their associated academic colleagues have begun to produce many more academically rigorous studies (particularly in relation to the study of child abduction—see, for example, Boudreaux, Lord, & Dutra, 1999; Boudreaux, Lord, & Jarvis, 2001; Prentky, Knight, & Lee, 1997), but prior to these more recent studies, and even though there was little to no empirical support for the theories upon which traditional methods relied. Witkin (1996) demonstrated that the demand for

---

1. Crime scene: Perpetrator takes a weapon to the crime scene, gags victim, leaves no fingerprints

---

2. Inference #1 = Therefore we have a "planner rapist"

---

3. Inference #2 = "Planner rapists" all share the same group of background characteristics—i.e., all the same age, same marital circumstances, same professions, etc.

Figure 9.1. Traditional model of offender profiling, revealing the number of inferential leaps based on an evaluation of the crime scene.

profiles was high, with the FBI having a number of full-time profilers who, collectively, were involved in around 1,000 cases per year. Unfortunately, it has taken some time for science to catch up with and question the methods that had previously been relied upon. Furthermore, science is only just beginning to develop more reliable bases upon which to advise crime investigations (issues that we shall consider shortly). However, despite its more labored journey, the scientific method is gradually weeding out the bogus approaches and providing more fruitful, reliable, tested, and transparent evidence-based methods for assisting the police. Part of the contribution lies in a change of tact, from the exclusive focus on the killer and his likely "psychological profile," to contributions that consider the way the police collect information, make decisions, and direct and lead a team that they must motivate during times of stress, often with difficult challenges that require them to deal effectively and sensitively with the community they serve and often rely upon. Thus, behavioral advisors and profiles are now realizing that their contribution may lie more productively in a greater appreciation of the myriad issues that are involved in investigating crime.

BEYOND THE CRIME SCENE

This is an important juncture at which to point out the small part that, to date, profiling has played in apprehending killers. Copson's (1995) study indicated that in less than 10 percent of cases did a profile lead to the identification of the offender. Thus, it is worth keeping the utility of the method in perspective. Doubtless, profiling has been utilized wisely and judiciously and has proved operationally useful. Indeed, recent promising scientific developments are beginning to emerge that have adopted a more systematic and critical approach. However, it is worth considering other methods by which psychologists might assist the police in the apprehension of offenders and the successful resolution of major enquiries. Keppel (1989) notes that very little has been written with regard to how serial killers are caught, other than the investigative techniques undertaken at the original crime scene. He points to several solvability factors in homicide investigation that go beyond the crime scene. These include the quality of police interviews of eyewitnesses, the circumstances that led to the initial stop and arrest of the murderer, the circumstances that established probable cause to search and seize physical evidence from person/property of suspect, the quality of the investigation at the crime scene, and the quality of the scientific analysis of the physical evidence seized from the suspect and its comparison to physical evidence recovered from victims and murder scenes. These are all issues that can be assisted through contact with and advice from psychologists. Recent work has indicated that the way in which this information is collected and collated can be improved with guidance from a psychological perspective. Apart from Keppel's work, the bulk of discussions regarding solvability have been critical of the police's role in the investigation and have frequently concluded that the police force has had little to do with solving crime (Greenwood, 1970; Greenwood, Chaiken, & Petersilia, 1977). Even certain FBI officers (Ressler, Burgess, D'Agostino, & Douglas, 1984) have admitted that many of the United States's most notorious serial murderers have been caught either through happenstance or during some unrelated routine police procedure. Keppel (1989), though, is dismissive of the role of chance. Instead, he views this as an opportunity eagerly grasped by a smart cop: "what usually occurs is that some patrol officer on routine duty comes across the killer, it then takes alert and intelligent investigators to turn the opportunity into a final resolution of the case" (p. 68). We have argued that bringing to bear a psychological and systematic approach to several aspects of policing (leadership, information collection, decision making, and so on) can make these "chances" more probable.

Alison and Whyte (2005) identified a number of factors involved in apprehension. Their descriptive study considered 101 single-offender American serial murder cases. The average age for these offenders was approximately 30 years old, with the youngest at 17 years old and the eldest 52 years old. Many previous studies have indicated that serial killers are in their late twenties or early thirties (Hickey, 1991). In our sample these offenders killed a total of 617 victims ranging from three to twenty-three people killed as a series.

Figure 9.2 outlines the frequency distribution for the methods by which the present sample of serial murderers were apprehended (the apprehension variables). In many cases there were several apprehension variables that contributed to an individual's capture. However, the most frequent contributions were from eyewitness testimony, the fact that the offender had previously been institutionalized, that he had committed another crime in a similar way (and so the crimes were linked) and, most frequently of all, because the offender committed another (often less serious) crime that led to the offender's capture.

The overlapping nature of these apprehension variables is captured in Figure 9.3. We have classified these as belonging to five central issues: the way in which the offender's own behavior assists in his own apprehension, the role of an informant, the role of the direct work of a detective, the role of the victim, or, at the core of the overwhelming majority of cases, the role that the offender's previous crimes have in apprehension.

OLD SINS CAST LONG SHADOWS

As we noted, it is unusual for one factor to be solely responsible for catching killers. Instead, factors tend to co-occur in varying degrees within thematically prescribed "clusters." That is to say, in a case where there is forensic evidence, it is often also supported by eyewitness information (variables within the *detective* cluster); whereas, in cases where there is a confession, it is more likely that the offender knows the victim (variables within the *offender* cluster). Alison and Whyte (2005) termed these as "roles" that relate

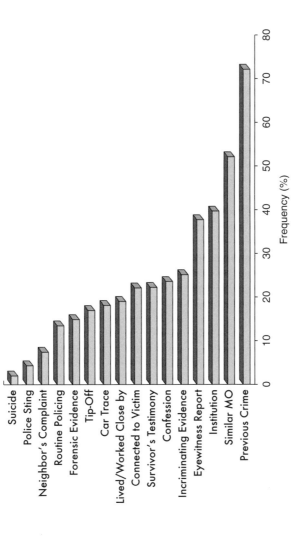

Figure 9.2. Frequency distribution for methods of apprehension in a sample of eighty-seven serial murderers.

OFFENDER

Lives/works near victim, knows victim, confesses

INFORMANT

Police sting, tip-off, complaints from neighbor

CORE VARIABLES

Prior institutionalization, similar MO, prior crimes

DETECTIVE

Forensic evidence, eyewitness, car trace, routine policing

VICTIM

Survivor testimony, victim's belongings found at suspect's home

Figure 9.3. Schematic representation of co-occurrences.

to different emphases on the part of different "participants" in the overall picture of serial murderer apprehension. We have labeled these roles: *detective, offender, victim,* and *informant,* with the central box consisting of aspects that relate to the offenders' *previous history of offending.* This central region is common to most apprehension cases and overlaps with all four of the other regions. Thus, in many cases, solid and robust recording and tracking of an offender's previous history is the quality that most frequently assists in apprehension. The offender's past literally catches up with him!

Statistics reveal that detective work is directly relevant in 79 percent of cases, followed by offender = 67 percent, victim = 48 percent, and finally, informant = 23 percent. This demonstrates that apprehension (in serial killer cases) depends very significantly on good detective work and the ability to capitalize on the information gained, followed by "errors" on the offenders' part, followed by the impact of the victim, and finally, the use of informants.

As one may expect, the *detective* region contains variables that encompass police procedures: forensic and eyewitness reports, the crime scene, the "mugshot," car (either tire marks or a vehicle left nearby, or one seen by a witness), and a chance encounter during routine policing. This lends some support to the "smart cop theory"—putting two and two together and effecting an arrest.

However, the most pertinent factor throughout the investigative process is the impact of the offenders' past criminal activities—a factor that relies on accurate, robust, and reliable recording systems. Aside from the direct investigative implications of recording offenders' previous convictions accurately, all profiling decision support systems must rely on accurate archives (House, 1997; Egger, 1998; Keppel & Weis, 1993).

However, as Ogan and Alison (2005) have argued, the process of dealing with such decision support systems and taking advice from those who operate them is one small component of detective work. The job of the detective will seldom be restricted to "sleuthing" and, instead, involves a multilayered set of aims and objectives. This is perhaps best summed up by the management pyramid of Figure 9.4.

Indeed, far from being a macho "supercop," successful SIOs will possess a myriad of interpersonal and diplomatic, managerial, media-handling, and administrative and logistical skills—a far cry from the stereotypical TV portrayal of the "rogue cop" who bends the rules but gets results! The structure of the pyramid implies that if the broader foundations are rocked or managed ineffectively, the integrity of the management of the incident will be compromised. For example, insensitivity to the local community can damage community relations that can last for many years and suppress intelligence and information. This has been the sad inheritance of the Stephen Lawrence enquiry in England.[4] The case involved the murder of a young black male in London. The subsequent public inquiry flagged institutional racism as endemic within the Metropolitan Police, an allegation given more credence by the perceived lack of police success with the case. This subsequently led to a fractious relationship between the police and the local black community, severely damaging relationships for many years. The police have had to work very hard to regain the trust of the community, and a variety of initiatives in recent years have been largely successful in this process of repair. Efforts included changes in how the police liaise, recruit from, and work alongside ethnic groups. It is therefore important to have some understanding of the wider context within which policing and investigation emerge and to recognize that behavioral advice is one component in a very large and sophisticated system. Profiling is simply one element within the wider remit of behavioral advice and, as such, really is at the very tip of the narrowest point of the management pyramid.

Incident
(the enquiry itself)

Enquiry team
(those who are working on the incident, team skills, team atmosphere)

Family and local community
(race and diversity, family liaison)

Organizational climate of the police environment
(current attitudes that impact on the police generally)

Political and local/national government issues
(federal and state government-driven agendas and current practice)

Figure 9.4. Management pyramid in critical incidents.

Source: Alison & West, 2005.

FROM "PROFILING" TO "PRIORITIZING"

Bearing in mind that a profile should yield operationally useful information to the police, there needs to be some way of describing how each piece of advice can be practically applied to an investigation. It is hard to argue why it might be useful to know whether an offender collects pornography. However, indicating a likely area in which he may reside may prove more operationally useful. Suspect prioritization is aimed at reducing the pool of suspects. In achieving this, each item in an investigative report would have to demonstrate on what basis a range of suspects could be narrowed down. Alison and Wilson (2005) have argued that this is most productively considered through a range of filters, rather than a list of likely characteristics of the offender. Thus, one would provide the following sort of filter:

"First consider all individuals within a 1 mile radius of the crime scene, who have any prior convictions for any kind of offense within the last year" (Geographic Filter).

"Then prioritize all those with any prior violent or sexual convictions" (Preconvictions Filter).

"Of this group, first consider all those matching the physical description provided by your victim" (Eyewitness Filter).

This system carries the assumption that the most reliable information is the geographic, followed by the preconvictions, followed by the eyewitness information, because if we are wrong about the first filter (and the offender lives farther than one mile away) all the other filters become redundant. However, if the eyewitness information is incorrect (research does indicate that it can be quite unreliable) and the geographic and preconviction filters are correct, our offender is still within the right search parameters. This system has proved effective in a variety of investigations, from rapes to kidnaps and child abductions (Alison, 2005). However, it is important to establish the right filters and their levels of reliability. This is important because it allows us (and the SIO) to know how much trust to put in any one filter. Thus, as well as moving toward a different approach in terms of the content of the advice, Alison, Goodwill, and Alison (2005) have argued that the structure of advisory reports is critical in ensuring that they are clearly interpreted and used judiciously.

NOT ALL CLAIMS ARE EQUAL

Alison, Smith, Eastman, and Rainbow (2003) reviewed Toulmin's (1958) philosophy of argument and how this can be used to generate advisory reports. They argued that "the strength of a 'Toulminian'" approach lies in its ability to deconstruct arguments into their constituent parts, thus allowing for close scrutiny of the strengths and weaknesses of various aspects of the argument" (Alison et al., 2005). So, if we have a hypothetical claim in a profile, for example: "The unknown offender lives within 5 km of the sexual assault site," a Toulminian approach would substantiate this assertion by demonstrating the grounds on which it is based, as well as the certainty of the claim (how confident we are in the claim), namely: "The offender is 75% likely (how certain we are) to live within 5 km of the rape (claim), since rapists tend not travel more than 5 km from home to offend (basis) as reported in a study by X & Y."

Compared to traditional offender profiling methods, this approach makes clear how reliable each claim is and, as such, enables the lead investigator to consider how much trust or emphasis she or he can put in any given claim. Thus, it provides room for speculation, intuition, and experience, as well as empirically based claims, but makes clear on which basis any given claim is made. Such clarity may well have saved the senior officers in the Nickell enquiry from too heavy a reliance on the profiler and saved the profiler from allegations of too heavy an involvement and influence over the enquiry team, since the bases for each of the claims should have been clearly articulated and recorded during the enquiry, as opposed to under cross examination by a tenacious attorney.[5]

AN INVESTIGATIVE CREDO

Although the temptation for psychologists to assist police with their enquiries can be great, and there is a laudable desire to "do good," inappropriate and unclear advice in high-profile cases can actually prove quite dangerous and drag an enquiry team in entirely the wrong direction. Sadly, there is little to assist psychologists in making decisions about whether to engage in an enquiry, or indeed, how to engage. The current British Psychological Society Codes of Conduct, as well as the American Psychological Association Ethical Guidelines, do provide a framework, but they are not designed specifically for contributing to crime investigations. However, Alison and West (2005) have put forward a number of questions that the profiler should contemplate during the initial contact, reviewing evidence, and writing-up stage. This Investigative Credo is as follows:

1. Will my report be provided on time?
2. Have I discussed fees and have these been agreed to?
3. Have I agreed to the objectives of the report?
4. Do I know who the central contact is in this enquiry if I need further details?
5. Do I have a realistic idea of how long this case will take me?
6. What features of the case are influencing current investigative priorities?
7. Has an exhaustive crime scene assessment been used to maximize the information that can be derived to determine the sequence of events and offender behavior?
8. Have I visited the crime scene and its environs so that I am aware of the geography of the case?

9. Is photographic evidence sufficient for me to appreciate the crime scene and its geographic significance?

10. Has an exhaustive assessment of the emerging statements been conducted to determine what information is convergent or corroborative; divergent or contradictory?

11. What information has been decided to be redundant for the investigation?

12. What features of the offense, alone or in combination, are influencing my interpretation?

13. What are my provisional hypotheses?

14. What are the investigative team's provisional hypotheses?

15. Am I influenced by 14?

16. Is my current interpretation congruent with any related theories?

17. Have any similar (historical) cases been identified as sources for further understanding?

18. Have any cases or incidents been identified as potential links?

19. Have I allowed myself to be subject to peer review?

20. What further enquiries have now been initiated?

21. Have my findings been influenced by external pressures, group dynamics, heuristics, or biases in a way that reduces their accuracy or usefulness?

22. Have I based my findings on a clearly defined evidence base, and used this evidence to support any recommendations made?

23. Which datasets have I accessed and are they relevant to the case under investigation?

24. Am I presenting my findings in a way that is unambiguous and will not lead to misunderstanding or misinterpretation?

25. Have I succeeded in meeting the objectives originally defined?

26. What has been the effectiveness of my advice?

27. Have I written up the facts of the case, the process of my decision making, my analysis, interpretation, and discussions with other experts?

THE TORTOISE AND THE HARE

Offender profiling has been inextricably linked to murder and, perhaps even more so, with serial killing. Thankfully, such cases are relatively rare events, and the rather skewed notion of probing the mind of killers does not fully capture the scope of work that is emerging in reference to what psychology can contribute. We need to remind ourselves though, that many of the assumptions that are promulgated in the media have not been scientifically scrutinized, so there needs to be some discretion exercised when evaluating profiling reports. On a more proactive note, developments are emerging as researchers test hypotheses and return to the tried and tested methods to scrutinize a variety of methods for assisting the police. With this has come the recognition that profiling is a small cog in a far larger machine, and for that machine to work effectively psychologists need to be more creative and expansive in their thinking. Gradually, work is emerging that has assisted us in our understanding of information collection, decision making, leadership, community relations, media, and prioritization. It is through this joint, multivariate endeavor that science will gradually catch up with and overtake the anecdotes and fictional portrayals and make a real contribution to crime investigation.

NOTES

1. A reference in *The Independent* (a UK newspaper) to the psychological evidence against Colin Stagg in the Nickell enquiry.

2. The first author was one of the several psychologists who provided a defense report in this case.

3. There are now several articles that have failed to find such relationships in offending behavior (see Alison, 2005 for a review).

4. "The Stephen Lawrence Inquiry," http://www.archive.official-documents .co.uk/document/cm42/4262/sli-00.htm

5. Jim Sturman, the legal representative for the defense, provides an interesting overview of this case in Sturman and Ormerod (2005).

REFERENCES

Alison, L. J. (2005). (Ed.). *The forensic psychologist's casebook: Psychological profiling and criminal investigation.* Cullumpton, Devon: Willan.

Alison, L. J., & Canter, D. V. (1999). Professional, legal, and ethical issues in offender profiling. In D. V. Canter & L. J. Alison (Eds.), *Profiling in policy and practice* (pp. 21–54). Aldershot, UK: Ashgate.

Alison, L. J., Goodwill, A., & Alison, E. (2005). Guidelines for profilers. In L. J. Alison (Ed.), *The forensic psychologist's casebook: Psychological profiling and criminal investigation* (pp. 277–297). Cullumpton, Devon: Willan.

Alison, L. J., Smith, M. D., Eastman, O., & Rainbow, L. (2003). Toulmin's philosophy of argument and its relevance to offender profiling. *Psychology, Crime and Law, 9*(2), 173–183.

Alison, L. J., & West, A. (2005). Conclusions: Personal reflections on the last decade. In L. J. Alison (Ed.), *The forensic psychologist's casebook: Psychological profiling and criminal investigation* (pp. 380–392). Cullumpton, Devon: Willan.

Alison, L. J., & Whyte, C. (2005). *Informant, offender, detective and victim roles in apprehension methods in serial murder* (Master's thesis, University of Liverpool, UK). Unpublished document.

Alison, L. J., & Wilson, G. (2005). Suspect prioritization in the investigation of sex offenders: From clinical classification and profiling to pragmatism. In L. J.

Alison (Ed.), *The forensic psychologist's casebook: Psychological profiling and criminal investigation* (pp. 68–89). Cullumpton, Devon: Willan.

Boudreaux, M., Lord, W., & Dutra, R. (1999). Child abduction: Age-based analyses of offender, victim and offense characteristics in 550 cases of alleged child disappearance. *Journal of Forensic Sciences, 44*(3), 539–553.

Boudreaux, M., Lord, W., & Jarvis, J. (2001). Behavioral perspectives on child homicide: The role of access, vulnerability and routine activities theory. *Trauma, Violence and Abuse, 2*(1), 56–78.

Britton, P. (1997). *The jigsaw man.* London: Bantam Press.

Burgess, J., Douglas, J., & Ressler, R. (1985). Classifying sexual homicide crime scenes. *FBI Law Enforcement Bulletin, 54,* 12–17.

Canter, D. V., Alison, A. J., Alison, E., & Wentink, N. (2004). The organized/disorganized typologies of serial murder: Myth or model? *Psychology, Public Policy, and Law, 10,* 7–36.

Copson, G. (1995). *Coals to Newcastle: Part 1. A study of offender profiling.* London: Police Research Group Special Interest Series, Home Office.

Davies, A., Wittebrood, K., & Jackson, J. L. (1998). *Predicting the criminal record of a stranger rapist* (Special interest series paper 12). London: Home Office, Policing and Reducing Crime Unit.

Egger, S. A. (1998). *The killers among us: An examination of serial murder and its investigation.* Englewood Cliffs, NJ: Prentice Hall.

Greenwood, P. W. (1970). *An analysis of the apprehension activities of the New York City Police Department.* Santa Monica, CA: RAND Corporation.

Greenwood, P. W., Chaiken, J. M., & Petersilia, J. (1977). *The criminal investigation process.* Lexington, MA: D. C. Heath.

Hickey, E. W. (1991). *Serial murderers and their victims.* Pacific Grove, CA: Brooks/Cole.

House, J. C. (1997). Towards a practical application of offender profiling: The RNC's criminal suspect prioritization system. In J. L. Jackson & D. A. Bekerian (Eds.), *Offender profiling: Theory, research and practice* (pp. 177–190). Chichester, UK: Wiley.

Keppel, R. D. (1989). *Serial murder: Future implications for police investigations.* Cincinnati, OH: Anderson.

Keppel, R. D., & Weis, J. G. (1993). *Improving the investigation of violent crime: The homicide investigation and tracking system.* Washington, DC: U.S. Department of Justice.

Mokros, A., & Alison, L. (2002). Is profiling possible? Testing the predicted homology of crime scene actions and background characteristics in a sample of rapists. *Legal and Criminological Psychology, 7,* 25–43.

Ogan, J., & Alison, L. J. (2005). Jack the Ripper and the Whitechapel murders: A very Victorian critical incident. In L. J. Alison (Ed.), *The forensic psychologist's casebook: Psychological profiling and criminal investigation* (pp. 23–46). Cullumpton, Devon: Willan.

Prentky, R., Knight, R., & Lee, A. (1997). Risk factors associated with recidivism among extrafamilial child molesters. *Journal of Consulting and Clinical Psychology, 65,* 141–149.

Ressler, R. K., Burgess, A. W., D'Agostino, R. B., & Douglas, J. E. (1984). *Serial murder: A new phenomenon of homicide.* Paper presented at the annual meeting of the International Association of Forensic Science, Oxford, England.

Ressler, R. K., Burgess, A. W., & Douglas, J. E. (1988). *Sexual homicide: Patterns and motives.* Lexington, MA: Lexington Books.

Ressler, R. K., & Shachtman, T. (1992). *Whoever fights monsters: My twenty years tracking serial killers for the FBI.* New York: St. Martin's Press.

Salfati, C. G., & Taylor, P. J. (forthcoming). Differentiating sexual violence: A comparison of sexual homicide and rape.

Toulmin, S. (1958). *The uses of argument.* Cambridge: Cambridge University Press.

Witkin, G. (1996). How the FBI paints portraits of the nation's most wanted. *U.S. News & World Report, 32.*

10

Severe Sexual Sadism: Its Features and Treatment

William L. Marshall and Stephen J. Hucker ◆

INTRODUCTION

The idea that some people are sexually stimulated by inflicting suffering (physical and psychological) on others has a long history in mental health literature. Krafft-Ebing (1886) was the first to clearly describe this clinical entity and his description of the features of sexual sadists has influenced diagnostic criteria ever since. However, instances of sexually sadistic acts appeared in the more popular literature far earlier than Krafft-Ebing's description. Baron Gilles de Rais was hanged in the fifteenth century for the rape, torture, and murder of several hundred children, and most people are aware of the behavior of the notorious Donation Alphonse François under his rather grandiose, self-adopted name of the Marquis de Sade. In the early part of the twentieth century, Stekel (1929) expanded on Krafft-Ebing's work distinguishing masochism (the sexualized experience of being subject to suffering) from sadism (the sexualized experience of inflicting suffering). It was Stekel's work, in particular, that led to the adoption of these terms in clinical work. In this chapter we will restrict our concerns to those people identified as sexual sadists and, more particularly, to those sexual offenders who meet criteria for sexual sadism.

Some sexual sadists, like Gilles de Rais, also murder their victims. However, some sexual offenders who are not sadists likewise kill their victims, sometimes to eliminate the only witness (other than themselves), sometimes as a result of rage, and sometimes for other reasons (see Grubin [1994] for a discussion of these reasons). Unfortunately, the literature on sexual sadism does not always clearly distinguish sadistic sexual murderers from other types of sexual murderers, and similarly, articles on serial sexual killers may fail to identify the subgroup of sexual sadists among their samples.

These problems make it difficult to review or summarize the existing literature. In addition, we (Marshall & Kennedy, 2003) found that although most authors indicated they had followed the criteria outlined in a relevant edition of the American Psychiatric Association's *Diagnostic and Statistical Manual of Mental Disorders* (*DSM*), the actual criteria used to identify their samples of sexual sadists was not a match for *DSM* criteria. Quite a number of researchers (Apsche, 1993; Brittain, 1970; Dietz, Hazelwood, & Warren, 1990; Egger, 1998; Fromm, 1973; Giannangelo, 1996; Gratzer & Bradford, 1995; Levin & Fox, 1985; Langevin, Ben-Aron, Wright, Marchese, & Handy, 1988; Myers, Scott, Burgess, & Burgess, 1995) claim that the crucial feature of sexual sadists is the exercise of power and control over the victim, while the other features (e.g., torture, humiliation, aggression) are seen as the means by which power and control is exercised. At other times, some of these same authors (e.g., Myers, Burgess, Burgess, & Douglass, 1999; Ressler, Burgess, & Douglas, 1988), as well as others (Seto & Kuban, 1996), describe the expression of violence or aggression as the key feature of sexual sadists. Whatever features are seen as diagnostic, all authors view sexual sadists as being sexually aroused by these features. *DSM-IV-TR* (American Psychiatric Association, 2000) describes sexual sadism as a paraphilia that involves "recurrent, intense sexually arousing fantasies, sexual urges, or behaviors involving acts (real, not simulated) in which the psychological or physical suffering (including humiliation) of the victim is sexually exciting to the person" (p. 574). Like all the features described in the literature (e.g., violence, torture, control, power, aggression, humiliation), the *DSM* requires that the psychological and physical suffering of the victim must be sexualized for the offender to meet criteria as a sexual sadist. The problem with this requirement is that the only person who can know with any degree of certainty that these acts generate (or are necessary for) sexual arousal, is the offender. Not surprisingly, few sexual offenders who commit violent or degrading acts willingly admit that such acts are sexually arousing to them. Indeed, very few sexual offenders of any type are readily forthcoming about what sexually excites them. Thus, the diagnostician must make an inference based on other information (e.g., details of the crime scene, reports by victims, the offender's life history and offense history) about the client's sexual motivation. The authors of *DSM-III* (American Psychiatric Association, 1980) recognized that the rather poor interdiagnostician reliability of earlier versions of *DSM* was the result of requiring diagnosticians to make inferences about their client's motivations or about other unobservable processes. As a result, from *DSM-III* onward, the subsequent editions of *DSM* have, for almost all diagnoses, attempted to specify observable criteria; the paraphilias, including sexual sadism, remain, unfortunately, an exception to this wise decision.

Despite this confusing state of diagnostic criteria (differing views of what is crucial, and a reliance on diagnostic inferences) some authors continue to try to integrate the findings on sexual sadists. Recently, for example, Proulx, Blais, and Beauregard (2005) have summarized what they believe the extant literature tells us about sexual sadists. They focused primarily on their own research studies and compared their findings with those generated by Dietz et al. (1990) and by Gratzer and Bradford (1995). Table 10.1 describes some of the data from each of these studies plus data that Marshall, Kennedy, and Yates (2002) extracted from files in Correctional Service of Canada (CSC) prisons where a diagnosis of sexual sadism had been applied by one or another psychiatric expert. As can be seen from the table, the percentage of each study group who enacted the listed behaviors was quite discrepant across these four reports. In some instances the differences are startling, particularly on the issue of the infliction of physical torture. It would appear that the CSC psychiatrists were using different diagnostic criteria than were the clinicians in the other studies, although even in Proulx et al.'s (2005) report the incidence of torture among sexual sadists seems very low given the *DSM* criteria on which the diagnosis was supposedly based. In examining the data in Table 10.1 on the incidence of humiliation, it is clear that the criteria employed by the FBI, ROH, and CSC diagnosticians, and to a significant extent by Proulx et al., could not have been a match for *DSM*. The diagnostic manual clearly specifies the psychological suffering (i.e., humiliation) of the victim to be critical to the diagnosis as is the physical suffering of the victim. Since none of the indices of physical suffering (i.e., torture, the use of aggression or violence) or of humiliation reveal that these were present in 100 percent of the cases (with the exception of torture for the FBI study), it seems safe to conclude that the diagnosis of sexual sadism in these studies did not follow *DSM* criteria rigorously at all. Thus we cannot

Table 10.1. Percentage Rates of Various Behaviors during Sexual Assault

	FBI[a]	ROH[b]	CSC[c]	Proulx et al.[d]
Abduction/confinement	76.7	64.3	22.0	18.6
Torture	100.0	78.6	9.8	30.2
Bondage	76.7	14.3	29.3	16.3
Aggression/violence	60.0	64.3	24.4	90.7
Suffocation	13.3	46.4	36.6	50.0*
Humiliation	23.3	0	12.2	53.7
Insertion of object	40.0	14.3	4.9	9.3

Sources: (a) adapted from Dietz et al. (1990); (b) adapted from Gratzer & Bradford (1995); (c) adapted from Marshall, Kennedy, & Yates (2002); (d) adapted from Proulx et al. (2005).

* Proulx et al. reported suffocation only for the sexual sadists who attacked children.

reliably conclude that the features described in these studies accurately convey what it is that sexual sadists do when they sexually offend, and we are on far more shaky ground when it comes to inferring sexual motivation in relation to any of these behaviors.

Proulx et al. also described personality features of their putative sexual sadists. The sadists, in comparison with a matched group of nonsadistic sexual offenders, displayed more schizoid, schizotypal, histrionic, and avoidant personality features. More interesting perhaps was Proulx et al.'s observations of the behaviors and experiences of the sadists in the forty-eight hours preceding their offense. They found that sadists were more likely than nonsadistic sexual offenders to have had a specific conflict with a woman during this preoffense period and to have had conflicts with women in general. They were also far more angry and sexually excited, and they reported fantasizing about deviant sexual acts prior to their offenses. In addition, the sadists in Proulx et al.'s study were far more likely to have planned their offense and to have deliberately selected the victim than were the nonsadistic offenders.

Although the differences in the percentage of subjects who displayed each feature across these three studies no doubt reflect both differing diagnostic practices and different samples of sexual sadists, there is some consistency in the features seen as crucial to this diagnosis. However, diagnostic inconsistency presents a real problem that, to date, has to some extent obfuscated the identification of the primary characteristics of sexual sadists. We now turn to a consideration of diagnostic issues.

DIAGNOSTIC ISSUES

In order to address the problems presented by sadistic sexual offenders, it is necessary to have a clear and agreed-upon definition of what constitutes sexual sadism. Research cannot proceed in a useful way unless all researchers are in agreement on the criteria necessary to identify sexual sadism. If researchers employ different definitions of the problem, then the data derived from research cannot be integrated in a way that would lead to an understanding of sexual sadism that could guide assessment and treatment. Since sadistic sexual offenders constitute a real threat to the community, it is essential that methodologically sound research be conducted that can appropriately inform treatment providers and decision-makers. Sexual sadists who commit offenses to satisfy their deviant desires may not always present as a high risk to reoffend based on actuarial measures, but their risk to harm if they do reoffend is always high. Thus, an agreed-upon set of criteria necessary to reliably diagnose sexual sadism is critical.

The *DSM* in its various incarnations has ostensibly been the agreed-upon guide for researchers attempting to study sexual sadism. We say "ostensibly" because in our review of the existing literature (Marshall & Kennedy, 2003) we found that although almost all authors claimed to adhere to *DSM* criteria, the actual criteria they specified were rarely a match for those specified in the *DSM*. Given these differences in the diagnostic criteria employed in various studies, it is no surprise that estimates of the incidence of sexual sadism range from 5 percent to 80 percent (Marshall & Kennedy, 2003). Of course, these different estimates may also result from the different samples examined in the various studies of sexual offenders.

Fortunately, there was a good deal of overlap in the studies we reviewed concerning the features that were considered indicative of sexual sadism. While our review revealed thirty-plus supposedly critical features, there was agreement among most researchers that the following are essential to the diagnosis of sexual sadism: torture or cruelty, victim suffering, humiliation of victim, use of force or violence, control over victim, sexual mutilation. Some authors (e.g., Brittain, 1970; Gratzer & Bradford, 1995; Myers et al., 1999) suggest that the motivation behind sexual sadism is the exercise of power and control over the victim, which has become sexualized in these men; that is, the exercise of power and control is sexually arousing to sexual sadists. These authors claim that all the other features (e.g., torture, cruelty, force and violence, humiliation) are enacted for the sole purpose of achieving and demonstrating this power and control.

Faced with the evident disagreement across studies revealed on the specifics of diagnostic criteria, Marshall and colleagues (2002) conducted two studies meant to evaluate the reliability of the diagnosis of sexual sadism. First, they extracted from the files held in three Canadian federal prisons psychiatric reports where the psychiatrists were asked to evaluate the dangerousness of various sexual offenders. All these assessments occurred over a ten-year period (1989–1999). All the evaluated offenders had previously been assessed as high risk to reoffend sexually using one or another actuarial risk assessment instrument. Combined with the actuarial instruments, the psychiatrists' evaluations were intended to reveal each offender's risk to reoffend and the associated likelihood of harm. Fifty-nine evaluations were located of which forty-one involved cases where the offender was diagnosed as a sexual sadist, while the remaining eighteen cases were given various other diagnoses. The fourteen evaluators were all experienced forensic psychiatrists who reported using *DSM-III-R* or *DSM-IV* criteria.

Marshall, Kennedy, and Yates (2002) compared the offenders who were given a diagnosis of sexual sadism with those who were not given such a diagnosis. The groups were compared on twenty offense features (extracted from extensive police and victim reports and from court records), ten sets of self-reported information, and seven data sets derived from phallometric assessments of sexual interests. All this information was available to the psychiatrists doing the evaluations. Contrary to expectations, those offenders who were not diagnosed as sexual sadists were significantly more likely to have beaten or tortured their victims than were those deemed to be sexual sadists. In addition, the nonsadists showed greater sexual arousal to nonsexual violence while the sadists displayed greater arousal to consenting sexual scenes. Marshall et al. calculated a composite sadistic score based on offense details, but again it was the nonsadists who scored the highest. It appears that the diagnosticians in the study did not systematically employ the information Marshall et al. used to compare the sadists and nonsadists. Perhaps they relied more on how the offender presented at interview. However, the only thing that predicted their diagnoses was what an earlier psychiatric report identified as the diagnosis. Apparently, once a diagnosis is made it tends to be perpetuated by subsequent diagnosticians even when the available information contradicts the diagnosis.

Since Marshall and Kennedy's (2002) literature review revealed that the authors of each study used idiosyncratic criteria to apply the diagnosis of sexual sadism, it may be that Marshall et al.'s (2002) first study simply revealed the idiosyncratic tendencies of each of the psychiatrists the prisons hired to evaluate the offenders. Marshall, Kennedy, Yates, and Serran (2002), therefore, decided to conduct a further study to examine the interdiagnostician reliability of sexual sadism. They carefully extracted information from the files of twelve of the offenders in their first study, six of whom had been identified as being sexual sadists while the other six were identified as having some other diagnosis (e.g., pedophilia, antisocial personality disorder). The information contained details of the life history of each offender, crime scene data and other details of his offense(s), the results of various psychological tests as well as the results of phallometric evaluations (which measure a person's sexual arousal to selected cues), and self-reported sexual interests and activities provided by the offenders. All this information on each of the twelve offenders was provided to fifteen internationally renowned forensic psychiatrists, each of whom had experience working specifically with sexually sadistic offenders. These experts were asked to complete several tasks, but the one of prime interest was the requirement that they decide whether each offender was or was not a sexual sadist. A resultant calculation revealed a percentage of agreement among the experts that was marginally above chance (75 percent agreement where chance agreement would be 53.3 percent). Generally, the statistic considered appropriate to determine inter-rater agreement is the *kappa* coefficient. For very important decisions it is generally agreed that a *kappa* coefficient of .9 is necessary, whereas for a decision having rather trivial consequences a *kappa* of .6 is acceptable (American Educational Research Foundation, 1999). Given that psychiatric diagnoses of sexual sadism (or not) markedly influence a variety of decisions (e.g., determining if an offender meets criteria for Dangerous Offender status, or is a Sexually Violent Predator, or a decision to release the offender to the community) that have very important implications for the safety of the community and for the offenders' freedom, it would seem necessary for interdiagnostician agreement to be high. Unfortunately, not only was the percent agreement among the experts quite low, but the *kappa* statistic revealed completely unsatisfactory interdiagnostician agreement (*kappa* = .14).

Clearly Marshall et al.'s two studies do not encourage confidence in the application of the diagnosis of sexual sadism.

Perhaps the best study yet of psychiatric diagnoses applied to sexual offenders was conducted by Levenson (2004). She examined diagnoses given to sexual offenders being considered by Florida courts for the application of a civil commitment as a Sexually Violent Predator (SVP). The successful application of this status means the offender is to be incarcerated indefinitely until it can be shown that he has so profited from treatment as to no longer be an unacceptable risk to the community. In these cases the courts require two acknowledged experts to independently evaluate the offender. For the SVP status to be applied, the offender must meet criteria for a paraphilia and be determined to be at high risk to reoffend. Levenson compared the diagnoses identified by each of the two independent assessors. The resultant *kappa* coefficient for sexual sadism was 0.3, which is far below acceptable standards. Evidently so-called experts in Florida do no better at diagnosing sexual sadism than did Marshall et al.'s samples of Canadian psychiatrists or international forensic psychiatrists.

Despite these disappointing data, we are not inclined to dismiss the relevance of sexually sadistic behaviors, but rather, we believe the present diagnostic practices are inadequate. We could urge forensic psychologists and psychiatrists to exercise greater care, or we could insist that they employ the same criteria. Perhaps, however, the problem resides in the insistence of the diagnostic manual that the sadist must be sexually aroused by the suffering and humiliation of the victim. Since no one but the offenders can know the answer to this question, and they are unlikely to reveal such interests, the diagnosis requires the clinician to infer sexual motivation in the infliction of cruelty, torture, or degradation. Such a reliance on inference is almost certain to limit the reliability of the diagnosis.

One way around this problem of inferring sexual motivation that has been adopted by some authors is to employ phallometric assessment (see Marshall & Fernandez [2003] for a review). Phallometric assessments involve the measurement of the client's erectile changes in response to the presentation of various sets of sexual stimuli. No one has yet developed a satisfactory stimulus set specifically for sadists, but several researchers have adapted current assessment stimuli designed for men who sexually assault adult females. Seto and Kuban (1996), for example, used arousal to a description of a brutal rape as an index of sexual sadism. Unfortunately, they found no differences between rapists they defined as sadists and rapists whom they determined were not sadists. Seto and Kuban's data match those found in similar studies (Barbaree, Seto, Serin, Amos, & Preston, 1994; Langevin et al., 1985; Rice, Chaplin, Harris, & Coutts, 1994). Proulx et al. (2005) modified their standard phallometric stimuli to include sets describing rapes that involved either extreme physical violence or had additional elements involving the humiliation of the victim. Proulx et al.'s stimulus sets are closer to the *DSM* criteria for sexual sadism than are any other available stimulus sets. In comparing rapists who were deemed to be sadists with rapists who did not meet the criteria, Proulx et al. found that the sadists showed significantly greater arousal to both the physically violent and humiliating scenes. These data suggest that specifically designed sadistic stimuli may reliably distinguish sadistic from nonsadistic sexual offenders. We have designed such stimuli but because of the extreme nature of the content we have not yet been able to get ethics approval for a study to examine the value of this phallometric procedure. In addition, such studies suffer from a seemingly inescapable conundrum; namely, that each group (i.e., sadists and nonsadists) must be distinguished prior to the phallometric evaluation and yet the phallometric test is being evaluated as a diagnostic tool in identifying sadism.

As an alternative to current diagnostic practices, we suggest that the actual behaviors of sexual sadists may provide a basis for more accurately and more reliably identifying these problematic offenders. In the study by Marshall, Kennedy, Yates, et al. (2002) where international experts were asked to identify sexual offenders as sadists or not, these experts were also required to rate the importance for diagnostic purposes of a variety of features of the offender's behavior. While the

Table 10.2. Experts' Ratings of Sadistic Features

Feature	Experts' Ratings of Importance
1. Offender exercises power/control/domination over victim	3.15
2. Offender humiliates/degrades victim	3.15
3. Offender tortures or is cruel to victim	3.14
4. Offender is sexually aroused by sadistic acts	3.14
5. Offender mutilates sexual parts of victim's body	2.72
6. Offender has history of choking consensual partners during sex	2.50
7. Offender engages in gratuitous violence toward or wounding of victim	2.35
8. Offender attempts to, or succeeds in, strangling, choking, or otherwise asphyxiating victim	2.21
9. Offender has history of nonsexual cruelty to other persons or animals	2.14
10. Offender keeps trophies of victim or keeps records of the offense	2.11
11. Offender carefully preplans offense	2.00
12. Offender engages in bondage with consensual partners during sex	2.00
13. Offender mutilates nonsexual parts of victim's body	1.85
14. Victim is abducted/confined	1.85
15. Evidence of ritualism in offense	1.85

Source: Adapted from Marshall, Kennedy, Yates, et al. (2002).

experts were not, as we have seen, able to agree on the diagnosis, they were in general agreement on what features are important in making a diagnosis. Table 10.2 describes the features identified by these experts as relevant and records the average ratings of the importance of each of these features. The rating scale ranged from 0 to 4 where 4 indicated that the feature was crucial to the diagnosis and 1 indicated it was somewhat relevant; 0 meant the feature was not relevant. In addition to the features described in Table 10.2, both cross-dressing and fire-setting have been suggested by some authors (Dietz et al., 1990; Gratzer & Bradford, 1995) as distinguishing features of sexual sadists, but experts in Marshall, Kennedy, Yates, et al.'s (2002) study rated both of these features as zero (i.e., not relevant).

We intend to develop a rating scale based on the features listed in Table 10.2 with ratings for each feature being weighted according to the values assigned by the experts in the Marshall, Kennedy, Yates, et al. (2002) study. The scale has been developed to the stage where we are now conducting inter-rater reliability studies in several locations worldwide. We will also examine the relationship between scores on the rating scale and various other features of the offense, offender, and actuarial risk measures. Whether such a dimensional approach, rather than a categorical diagnosis, will prove helpful remains to be seen, but there have been calls for the *DSM* to move to a more dimensional approach across all diagnoses (Widiger & Coker, 2003). In any event, it is clear that current diagnostic practices, as they apply to sexual sadism, are in need of serious repair.

TREATMENT

Given the present state of knowledge, we firmly believe that if a sexual offender clearly meets criteria for sexual sadism (or scores high on our Sadism Scale), then psychological treatment alone is insufficient. A combination of antiandrogens and psychological treatment (specifically, cognitive behavioral therapy) is, in our view, necessary to effectively minimize the risk of re-offending and thereby maximally protect the public. For sexual sadists the risk not only concerns the likelihood of a reoffense, but also includes the very high risk of considerable harm to the victim. For some sexual sadists (particularly those who have only one identified victim), scoring actuarial risk assessment instruments (see Doren [2002] for details) may indicate a low risk to reoffend, but this will not reveal anything about risk to harm. Antiandrogens may serve to reduce both the risk to reoffend and the risk to harm, but psychological interventions may also equip the offender with the skills, attitudes, and beliefs necessary to meet his needs in a prosocial manner.

Psychological Intervention

We have elsewhere described in detail the application of a cognitive behavioral treatment program designed specifically for sexual offenders and we have demonstrated its effectiveness (Marshall, Anderson, & Fernandez, 1999; Marshall, Marshall, Serran, & Fernandez, in press). We will not describe this program in detail here, but briefly outline its main features and how these might be adjusted for sexual sadists. The reader is referred to the original sources for greater details of this program. Table 10.3 describes the treatment targets. Those targets identified as "primary" are addressed with all sexual offenders although the procedures and degree of concentration are adjusted to meet the needs and capacities of each individual client (this represents what Andrews & Bonta [1998] call the "responsivity" principle). The additional targets listed in Table 10.3 simply identify the most common extra needs of sexual offenders and are not meant to exhaust all the possible array of additional problems any one client might have.

Acceptance of responsibility requires the client to give a full disclosure of the details of his offense, describe his history of prior offenses, indicate whatever planning he made to commit the offense, and reveal his persistent sexual fantasies. When having sexual sadists give a disclosure of their offense, it is best to avoid having the client provide the sexual, violent, and sadistic elements in any detail. They need to indicate what they have done but not in sufficient detail to allow them to become aroused. For example, the sadist may indicate that he sexually mutilated the victim but not provide specific details of the mutilation. He may say he deliberately humiliated the victim but should not describe this in graphic detail.

During the disclosure of their offense, as well as in discussing all other topics, sexual offenders display attitudes, beliefs, and perceptions that reveal their underlying inappropriate schemas. For sexual sadists the schemas of

Table 10.3. Treatment Targets for Psychological Intervention

Primary Targets	Additional Targets
Acceptance of responsibility	Anger/violence management
Self-esteem	Substance abuse
Autobiography	Reasoning and rehabilitation
Pathways to offending	
Victim empathy/harm	
Social skills	
Coping/mood management	
Sexual interests	
Self-management plans	
• Avoidance strategies	
• Good life plans	
• Release plans	
• Warning signs	
• Support groups	

particular relevance that guide their perceptions, expressed attitudes, and be-haviors, concern sex, violence, women and children, and their own sense of entitlement. Every surface expression of these schemas (e.g., their expressed attitudes, beliefs, and perceptions) needs to be challenged and alternative views need to be encouraged and reinforced.

Self-esteem is enhanced because doing so appears to enhance the offen-der's involvement and commitment to treatment, and enhancements of self-esteem are related to improvements in various other targets of treatment (see Marshall et al. [1999] for details). Having clients complete an autobiography helps them recognize the origins of their problems, assists the therapist in developing a broader understanding of the client, and facilitates, along with the offense disclosure, the beginning of the development of the offender's path-ways to offending. The offense pathway identifies the background factors that led to the creation of a frame of mind that allowed the offender to develop the specific steps required to offend. The background factors (e.g., problems with adult relations, anger at the world or women), the preparations to offend (e.g., planning, getting intoxicated), and the specific steps taken to be able to offend all need to be clearly elucidated. This is necessary so that eventually steps to circumvent these problems can be identified (i.e., self-management plans) and skills training (e.g., mood management, and the enhancement of coping skills and relationship skills) implemented to facilitate putting the client's self-management plans into action.

In discussions, numerous therapists have expressed concerns about having sexual sadists understand the harmful effects they have inflicted on their vic-tims, as is typically done to increase the empathy sexual offenders have toward their victims. Since sexual sadists are, by definition, excited by the prospect of harming their victims, it is suggested by these therapists that helping such offenders recognize the harm they have done will enhance their motivation to offend rather than reduce it. It is thought that sadists would enjoy, rather than be deterred by, the idea that their victim has suffered harm in the aftermath of the offense. This may, however, be a misplaced concern. Sadists clearly derive some pleasure (whether sexual or as a result of control, etc.) from their victim's suffering *during* the offense, but this does not mean that they are necessarily excited by postoffense suffering. Indeed, it seems to us unlikely that they are. To be aroused by suffering, the sadist has to be in the process of inflicting it on the victim. In his sexual fantasies the sadist imagines hurting and humiliating the victim, but he does not imagine this suffering to last after the imagined offense is over. There is no evidence suggesting that sexual sadists dwell on or are excited by the prospect of their victim continuing to suffer long-term. In our treatment of sadists, we find that most of them have either not thought about the postoffense suffering of their victim or they have expressed some degree of regret about the suffering. It appears they enjoy victim suffering during the offense but they are either indifferent to long-term consequences or they may actually prefer their offense not to have long-term consequences for the victim. In any event, sadists depersonalize their victims during the offense in order to inflict pain and degrade the victim. The process of identifying postoffense victim harm and its spillover effects on the victim's family serves to make the victim a real person with feelings, hopes, and all the other features that make someone human. Reducing the sadist's capacity to depersonalize other people should make it harder for him to offend in the future. Therefore, in alerting a sexual sadist to the long-term harm that his victim has experienced (or is likely to experience), the therapist must portray the victim as a real person with hopes and aspirations that have been disrupted by the offense. This, we believe, will cause the sadist to think of his victims (and all potential future victims) as fully formed people, thus reducing his capacity to depersonalize them in a way that allows him to treat them as objects for his peculiar pleasure.

Sadists are typically isolated individuals, or at least have serious problems in forming deep attachments to others. Teaching them the skills, attitudes, and self-confidence needed to effectively relate to others should allow them to feel not only more connected to others (and consequently less likely to depersonalize others) but also to feel less need to control others. The desperate need to have control over another person reflects the sadist's inability to feel any sense of control over various aspects of his own life, particularly in terms of his relationships with other people. Giving him the skills needed to meet his needs (including the need for control) should serve to reduce his attempts to control others by inappropriate means.

It appears that sadists exercise strong control over the expression of their emotions except when offending. They often present as cold and detached individuals, devoid of any real emotions. Attempts at suppressing emotions fail to give the person any experience at enjoying and modulating their emotions in an appropriate and satisfying way. Everybody experiences emotions, but some people attempt to suppress the expression of feelings, and this leads to all manner of problems (Kennedy-Moore & Watson, 1999). Also, poor emotional regulation (which in the case of sadists typically manifests as over-controlled emotional regulation) has numerous damaging consequences both for the individual and others (Baumeister & Vohs, 2004). Encouraging sadists to become more emotionally expressive may not only be beneficial; it should also provide the therapist with a window into the world of the client, which would not be available were the sadist to remain emotionally unexpressive. Problematic schemas and problematic motivations are frequently obscure in emotionally unresponsive clients. Also, emotional expression helps to reveal the things that distress clients so that coping skills can be developed to reduce distress that may otherwise initiate the chain of events leading to offending.

There can be no doubt that sexual sadists have deviant sexual fantasies. Whether they enjoy these fantasies as persistent and preferred sexual interests, or whether the fantasies occur only under stressful or other problematic circumstances, does not matter. These sexual fantasies involve the control of, as well as the physical and psychological suffering of, their victims. Clearly, even occasional fantasies of this kind, in someone who has committed a serious sexual offense, need to be eliminated. We can expect antiandrogens to reduce the frequency and intensity of deviant sexual fantasies (Bradford, 2000), but behavioral procedures should also be employed to reduce the possibility of these fantasies recurring in the future. Marshall et al. (in press) provide detailed descriptions of appropriate behavioral strategies to achieve this goal. Our preference is to employ the combination of deliberately masturbating to appropriate fantasies (which we help the client construct) until orgasm and then shifting (during the refractory period—see Masters & Johnson [1966] for a description) to articulating all possible variants of the deviant themes for a further ten minutes. This latter aspect of the procedure is called "satiation." This combination of masturbating to orgasm while fantasizing appropriate sex and then engaging the satiation procedure has been shown to be effective across a range of deviant sexual fantasies and behavior (Johnston, Hudson & Marshall, 1992; Marshall, 1979; Marshall, in press).

Finally, the sadist, like all other sexual offenders in treatment, must formulate plans for the future that he will implement after discharge from the program. These plans include some limited avoidance strategies (i.e., what have been called "relapse prevention plans") meant to reduce contact with potential victims or to prevent the reemergence of risk factors, but they should emphasize the development of what Ward (2002; Ward & Marshall, 2004) calls a "good life plan" designed specifically for, and with, the client. This good life plan is meant to encourage the offender to build a new life that will prove to be more fulfilling across various domains of functioning such as health, knowledge, work and leisure, creativity, and relationships. Associated with these plans, the client's plans for accommodation, work, and friendships need to developed, and he needs to identify support groups who will help him with both the transition back to the community and with his attempts to remain offense-free.

Pharmacological Treatment

There has been a wide range of medical intervention used to treat sexual offenders, from psychosurgery at one end of the body to castration at the other. Clearly, the motivations for their use can be considered as either punitive or therapeutic depending on one's point of view. The scientific grounds for operating on an otherwise healthy brain are highly suspect and the evidence for so doing in terms of control of sexually deviant behaviors is questionable (e.g., Rieber & Sigush, 1979) such that the procedure has not been used for many years (Pfäfflin, 1995). Physical castration is no less controversial (Berlin, 2005; Weinberger, Sreenivasan, Garrick, & Osran, 2005) and in most Western countries it is not a practical consideration. As a result, since World War II, pharmacological approaches have been explored.

In the 1970s the antipsychotic drug benperidol was tested a number of times in sexually deviant individuals. It was found to reduce sexual desire but not sexual behavior when compared with chlorpromazine and placebo in a double-blind trial (Tennant, Bancroft, & Cass, 1974). Subsequently, other antipsychotics, including thioridazine and haloperidol, enjoyed a vogue, as did the anticonvulsant carbemazepine. However, they lacked demonstrable effect on sexual behavior, other than what could be accounted for by overall sedation. In addition to unwanted side effects, the availability of hormonal alternatives led to the eventual abandonment of antipsychotics and anticonvulsants.

Hormonal compounds were the most frequently used medical treatment for sexual offenders in the latter half of the twentieth century. The rationale for their use is to imitate the effect of physical castration, which lowers levels of circulating testosterone and thereby reduces sexual arousability. The female hormone, estrogen, was found effective in lowering male sex drive (Foote, 1944; Golla & Hodge, 1949) but was soon abandoned as it was found to cause severe side effects such as nausea, vomiting, feminization, and thrombosis (Gijs & Gooren, 1996). Two substances in particular replaced it in common use. In Europe, cyproterone acetate (CPA, Androcur) became the standard and is still in common use, whereas in North America, following its introduction by Money (1968) at Johns Hopkins Hospital, medroxyprogesterone acetate (MPA, Provera) was the alternative, as CPA was not available.

Cyproterone acetate has its principal mode of action on androgen receptors and is therefore a true antiandrogen. This term is often misapplied to sex-drive-reducing hormones as a group, even those, like MPA, that do not act by blocking androgen receptors. Over the years since its introduction, a wide variety of sexual offenders and paraphiliacs have been treated with CPA and the studies reported have included double-blind controlled trials (e.g., Bancroft, Tennant, Loucas, & Cass, 1974; Bradford & Pawlak, 1993; Cooper, Sandhu, Losztyn, & Cernovsky, 1992), which confirm the drug's efficacy in reducing sexual activity and arousability. Side effects experienced include fatigue, hypersomnia, depression, and weight gain, feminization, breast enlargement, reduction in body hair, and increase in scalp hair. At the same time, reduction in sexual fantasies and drive, as well as reduced erections and ejaculate volume, are usually noted (Bradford, 2000).

Experience with MPA has been similar, and in clinical practice there is little to choose between the two drugs (Gijs & Gooren, 1996). MPA is not, however, an antiandrogen, and reduces testosterone levels mainly by increasing testosterone metabolism. There have been double-blind controlled studies confirming the effectiveness of the drug in suppressing sexual behavior and arousal compared with placebo (Hucker, Langevin, & Bain, 1988; Langevin et al., 1979; McConaghy, Blaszcznski, & Kidson, 1988; Wincze, Bansal, & Malamud, 1986). The side-effect profile of MPA is similar to CPA. Rare but serious side effects of both drugs include thrombo-embolic disorders, hypertension, gallstones, hyperglycemia, and bone demineralization (Grasswick &

Bradford, 2003). These effects are more likely to occur with prolonged usage (Gijs & Gooren, 1996).

Both MPA and CPA are artificial steroid hormones chemically related to the sex steroid hormones that occur naturally in the body. More recently, interest has focused on a different class of drug, a nonsteroid, which lowers the blood testosterone levels even more dramatically than MPA and CPA. This type of drug, known as a luteinizing hormone releasing hormone (LHRH) agonist, is a peptide or protein substance similar to a naturally occurring hormone that is released from the hypothalamus. This LHRH agonist mimics this naturally occurring hormone and stimulates the anterior pituitary at the base of the brain to produce luteinizing hormone (LH), which, in turn, acts on the testes to stimulate release of testosterone. After injecting the LHRH agonist, by a feedback loop the initially increased testosterone levels circulating in the blood quickly cause the hypothalamus to cease producing LHRH and testosterone levels then fall.

The LHRH agonists have to be administered by injection, as they would, like any other protein, be digested in the stomach if taken by mouth. Two special precautions have to be taken with these drugs. First, a small test dose has to be given with the first injection to ensure that the patient is not allergic to the foreign protein that the drug constitutes. Second, to combat the potential increase in libido that the initial surge of testosterone might cause, it is important to concurrently administer an anti-androgen, such as CPA, for about the first two weeks. Longer-term side effects with LHRH agonists include hot and cold flashes, loss of facial and body hair, asthenia, diffuse muscle pain, and loss of bone density (Briken, Nika, & Berner, 2001; Grasswick & Bradford, 2003). Unlike CPA and MPA, LHRH agonists have not yet been subjected to the same degree of scrutiny. Briken, Hill, and Berner (2003) reported that there had been only four case reports, one single-case controlled study, seven open uncontrolled studies, and one study comparing an LHRH agonist with CPA. Nonetheless, it appears that this type of drug is a safer alternative to CPA and MPA and likely to be more effective as testosterone suppression is more complete (Briken et al., 2003, 2001; Dickey, 1992). However, more research is needed (Briken et al., 2003) and the issue of bone loss as a potentially serious side effect needs further exploration, especially with respect to preventative measures (Grasswick & Bradford, 2003).

In the face of such potentially serious side effects as have been described above in connection with hormonal treatments, it is not surprising that interest has been shown in more common psychotropic drugs, such as antidepressants, as well as the antipsychotics already described. The possible benefits of the traditional antidepressants and lithium carbonate were explored a number of years ago (e.g., Snaith & Collins, 1981; Ward, 1975), but it was not until the introduction of the specific serotonin reuptake inhibitors (SSRIs) that their utility as sex-drive suppressants became fully exploited. These drugs, of which Prozac is one major type, have a high incidence of sexual side effects. In fact, hypotheses have been elaborated to explain sexually anomalous behaviors, as well as other obsessive-compulsive behaviors, in terms of cerebral serotonin dysfunction (Kafka & Coleman, 1991; Pearson, 1990).

Unlike hormonal agents, SSRIs are not associated with thrombotic disorders and have no deleterious effects on the bones. However, there appear to be other troublesome, though comparatively mild, side effects, including nervousness, irritability, nausea, diarrhea, constipation, headaches, and insomnia. Evidence for the effectiveness of antidepressant drugs on sexual behavior and arousability appears impressive although it has been observed that there are many methodological problems with nearly all the published studies of drug treatments with sexual offenders (Gijs & Gooren, 1996). Most of the studies include a variety of offenders so that the groups treated are not homogeneous either in terms of diagnosis or, more importantly, with respect to the type and frequency of the subject's sexual urges and fantasies. Review of the published studies suggests that the types of paraphilia represented in them include the more common ones such as exhibitionism, pedophilia, voyeurism, and frotteurism. Specific mention of cases of rape or sadism is quite rare (e.g., Bradford & Pawlak, 1987).

Several authors have attempted to develop protocols for the use of hormonal treatments (Reilly, Delva, & Hudson, 2000), while Bradford (2000, 2001) has outlined an algorithm to assist in the selection of the most appropriate medication. Bradford suggests a classification scheme based on the three levels of severity of paraphilia included in *DSM-III-R* (American Psychiatric Association, 1987): mild, moderate, and severe, to which Bradford has added an additional category of "catastrophic." He links his treatment algorithm with this classification. Thus, for any paraphilia, regardless of severity, he believes, as we would, that cognitive behavioral/relapse prevention treatment is essential. However, Bradford also believes, unlike us, that all paraphilias also need pharmacological interventions.

For all cases of mild paraphilia, Bradford recommends starting treatment with an SSRI, and for mild to moderate paraphilias, if the SSRI is not effective after adequate dosage for four to six weeks, he recommends adding a small dose of an anti-androgen. For most moderate and some severe cases, he suggests that a full dose of oral anti-androgen therapy is indicated. For severe cases, and some catastrophic cases, Bradford suggests that CPA or MPA be given intramuscularly. Bradford's final category describes a regimen for some severe cases and is his preferred treatment for catastrophic cases. This approach entails complete testosterone suppression with CPA, MPA, or an LHRH agonist. In contrast, Briken et al. (2003) describe only three levels of severity (mild, moderate, and severe). In agreement with Bradford, they recommend that mild cases be treated with SSRIs, especially for those clients with concomitant depressive or obsessive-compulsive symptoms. For moderate cases, Briken et al. suggest the use of CPA or MPA employing the intramuscular mode of administration if compliance is problematic. If the patient does not

improve, or if there are medical complications such as liver disease that pre-
clude treatment with CPA or MPA, Briken et al. switch to an LHRH agonist,
which is the treatment they recommend for all severe cases. Briken et al. also
recommend that all sexual offenders should receive psychotherapy together
with pharmacotherapy for comorbid disorders.

Properly identified sexual sadists would fit into Bradford's classification as
at least severe, and more likely catastrophic, cases, and would be included in
Brinker et al.'s severe cases. Thus, sexual sadists would appear to warrant both
extensive psychological treatment, either cognitive behavioral/relapse prevention or some other form of psychotherapy, as well as either CPA, MPA, or
an LHRH agonist. Whether it is necessary with sexual sadists to apply a dosage
that would completely suppress testosterone production, as Bradford recommends, remains to be seen. However, when sexual sadists are released to
the community, it would seem prudent, given the threat for harm that they
pose, to aim for complete suppression as the first step in a process of careful
monitoring of their functioning and behavior.

So far, no research has demonstrated the effectiveness of treatment with
sexual sadists, although, as we have seen, there is evidence of its effectiveness
with other sexual offenders. It will be difficult to evaluate treatment for these
individuals because (fortunately) they constitute a small proportion of sexual
offenders and thus there are rarely enough available to justify an outcome
study. In addition, quite a number of sexual sadists are incarcerated indefinitely, further reducing the number available for an outcome study. However,
the following case description illustrates the potential benefits of combining
medications and psychological treatment.

A CASE STUDY

Donald, now in his 30s, is currently free of any legal constraints and living and
working in the community with periodic visits to his psychiatrist and a relapse
prevention group. He rarely experiences sadistic fantasies but has them well under
control, thanks to many years of combined psychological therapy and pharmacological treatment. However, Donald's early offense history was truly alarming.

Donald had his first and only girlfriend, who was a year younger than
himself, at age 14 years. They had enjoyed sexual contacts short of intercourse
over a fifteen-month period before her parents found them in bed together
and terminated their relationship. This experience left Donald feeling angry
and frustrated.

Donald's first sexual assault occurred at the age of fifteen when he attacked
a 10-year-old girl. He maintained that this was a spontaneous act and that he
experienced "raw" feelings of "anger, fear, and rejection" at the time, accompanied by the urge to hurt her. Using a knife he used to carry to fix his
bike, Donald coerced the girl into removing her clothing and then tied her feet
and hands with her shoelaces. She became uncooperative, which increased

Donald's anger. He slapped her face and buttocks, forced her to fellate him, and attempted anal and vaginal intercourse but was only able to manage digital penetration. He held her captive for a short period and then allowed her to dress and leave.

Within the next three days, Donald committed two other similar sexual attacks on girls of a similar age. Shortly thereafter, Donald was apprehended. He received a twelve-month sentence followed by two years' probation. During his incarceration Donald ruminated on his offenses, and his fantasies of kidnapping, raping, and bondage became more intense. Before the end of his sentence, Donald was transferred to a psychiatric facility, but he was afraid to disclose the extent of his fantasies to clinicians and was not motivated to seek treatment.

Within four months of his discharge from the hospital, Donald was working in the community. Although he was on probation, Donald's sexual fantasies of kidnapping and raping young girls, and his feelings of revenge against females who had spurned or ridiculed him, were beginning to preoccupy him. He also engaged in voyeurism and cross-dressing at that time and started breaking into houses.

Donald was laid off from work and as a result had more time to fantasize. Shortly after becoming unemployed, Donald broke into a home he had been observing voyeuristically. After entering the house, Donald discovered the young woman he had been watching. Using scissors he had taken with him, Donald forced her to perform fellatio. He was unable to complete sexual intercourse, but he cut up her clothes and hair in order to frighten her; then he left.

A few days later Donald broke into another home of a victim he knew who had once refused to date him. Donald was very resentful and angry toward her. This victim was humiliated by having kitchen refuse smeared on her. Unfortunately for Donald, she recognized him as he ran off. Donald turned himself in shortly afterward.

Donald was found "not guilty by reason of insanity" (NGRI), though he has never shown any signs of major mental illness. This verdict reflects the somewhat idiosyncratic way the insanity defense was applied at the time in Canada. His clinical diagnoses have included sexual sadism together with various combinations of personality disorder, though he has never been considered psychopathic or antisocial.

As was typical at that time, Donald began his treatment in a maximum-security forensic facility. There he eventually elaborated his sexual fantasies to his therapists. He admitted to having intense and frequent sadistic sexual fantasies involving tormenting females, though not involving cutting or stabbing them, but sometimes breaking their fingers while raping them. Donald expressed a strong interest in pornography, especially bondage, as well as fetishism for female clothing and transvestic fetishism, which he had practiced on a number of occasions. His stated interest at that time was in females aged 12–16 years. Phallometric testing demonstrated a clear sexual preference for pubescent females and he responded to both rape and nonsexual violence. It was noted that Donald was introverted, egocentric, and emotionally constricted, had great difficulty forming relationships with others, and spent much of his time sexually fantasizing. His primary treatment was in a social therapy program and also a variety of behavioral treatments, but he made little headway in controlling his fantasies.

Eventually, Donald was transferred to a medium-security facility where he participated voluntarily in a research study of cyproterone acetate (CPA). However, this produced only a limited reduction in his arousal to violent themes. Although Donald remained a loner in most of his interpersonal relations on the unit, he did become attracted to a female copatient. Donald's fantasies about her quickly became sadistic in nature and he admitted to entering her dormitory at night to watch her sleep.

Another attempt was made a few years later at suppressing Donald's deviant fantasies with CPA. At this time he responded better to an increased oral dose of 200 mg daily. Donald's interpersonal behavior also began to improve and there was noticeable increase in his self-confidence and socialization. About seven years after his NGRI finding, he was enjoying an open ward in the hospital and was able to have access to the hospital grounds in the company of staff.

Donald began a cognitive behavioral relapse prevention (CBT/RP) program at this time, during which he admitted that he was spending several evenings a week writing out his sexual fantasies and pornographic letters. He showed his therapist a large pile of these writings that he had collected. Donald willingly allowed nursing staff to confiscate these and any others that were later found in his possession. He also indicated that he felt depressed and overwhelmed at times, so he was given antidepressant medication, which he said elevated his mood and controlled his deviant thoughts.

Donald's progress was such that he was transferred to another psychiatric facility with a minimum-security forensic unit. He began attending an upgrading course in the community and did very well. Meanwhile, Donald continued with individual psychological counseling aimed at improving his relapse prevention strategies.

Phallometric testing was repeated ten years after his index offense. Unfortunately, this demonstrated that Donald's maximum response was still to pubescent females and he continued to be aroused by sadistic/bondage stimuli despite his claim that CPA had effectively suppressed his arousal. The results of the assessment and pressures of his schoolwork increased Donald's depression and he was given an increase in antidepressant medication (Fluvoxamine 300 mg per day). On this regimen, combined with psychotherapy, Donald stabilized over the following year. He began attending a regular CBT/RP group and he functioned extremely well in that program. His compliance and attendance were excellent. However, a random check of Donald's computer revealed a number of sadistic images. As a result, his medication was switched to medroxyprogesterone acetate, but this was discontinued because of lack of efficacy and it was decided to change to leuprolide acetate (an LHRH agonist), which can only be given by injection. Donald felt that this was much more successful in curbing his paraphilic desires than his previous medications had been.

Since beginning treatment with leuprolide acetate nearly ten years ago, Donald has been regularly monitored by an endocrinologist with annual bone scans. He takes supplementary calcium and vitamin D but has not so far suffered any significant bone loss or other serious side effects from the medication. He discontinued the antidepressant medication two years ago with no relapse into depression.

After nearly twenty-five years of progressive treatment in the forensic system, Donald was given an absolute discharge, which means that he is no longer subject to legal restrictions of any kind. He is free in the community and working at a job that gives him satisfaction, and he is no longer tormented by the sadistic and pedophilic fantasies that caused suffering in himself and others. Donald appears to have been successfully rehabilitated through a combination of psychological and pharmacological approaches.

REFERENCES

American Educational Research Foundation. (1999). *Standards for educational and psychological testing*. Washington, DC: American Psychological Association.

American Psychiatric Association. (1980). *Diagnostic and statistical manual of mental disorders* (3rd ed.). Washington, DC: Author.

American Psychiatric Association. (1987). *Diagnostic and statistical manual of mental disorders* (3rd ed., Rev.). Washington, DC: Author.

American Psychiatric Association. (2000). *Diagnostic and statistical manual of mental disorders* (4th ed., Text rev.). Washington, DC: Author.

Andrews, D. A., & Bonta, J. (1998). *The psychology of criminal conduct* (2nd ed.). Cincinnati, OH: Anderson.

Apsche, J. A. (1993). *Probing the mind of a serial killer*. Morrisville, PA: International Information Associates.

Bancroft, J., Tennant, G., Loucas, K., & Cass, J. (1974). The control of deviant sexual behaviour by drugs: Behavioural changes following oestrogens and anti-androgens. *British Journal of Psychiatry, 125,* 310–315.

Barbaree, H. E., Seto, M. C., Serin, R. C., Amos, N. L., & Preston, D. L. (1994). Comparisons between sexual and nonsexual subtypes: Sexual arousal to rape, offense precursors, and offense characteristics. *Criminal Justice and Behavior, 21,* 94–114.

Baumeister, R. F., & Vohs, K. D. (Eds.). (2004). *Handbook of self-regulation: Research, theory, and applications*. New York: Guilford.

Berlin, F. (2005). Commentary: The impact of surgical castration on sexual recidivism risk among civilly committed sexual offenders. *Bulletin of the
American Academy of Psychiatry and Law, 33,* 37–41.

Bradford, J. M. W. (2000). The treatment of sexual deviation using a pharmacological approach. *Journal of Sex Research, 37,* 248–257.

Bradford, J. M. W. (2001). The neurobiology, neuropharmacology, and pharmacological treatment of paraphilias and compulsive sexual behaviour.
Canadian Journal of Psychiatry, 46, 26–34.

Bradford, J. M. W., & Pawlak, A. (1987). Sadistic homosexual pedophilia:
Treatment with cyproterone acetate. A single case study. *Canadian Journal
of Psychiatry, 32,* 22–31.

Bradford, J. M. W., & Pawlak, A. (1993). A double-blind placebo cross-over
study of cyproterone acetate in the treatment of the paraphilias. *Archives of
Sexual Behavior, 22,* 383–402.

Briken, P., Hill, A., & Berner, W. (2003). Pharmacotherapy of paraphilias with
long-acting agonists of luteinizing hormone-releasing hormone: A systematic review. *Journal of Clinical Psychiatry, 64,* 890–897.

Briken, P., Nika, E., & Berner, W. (2001). Treatment of paraphilia with luteinizing hormone-releasing hormone agonists. *Journal of Sex & Marital
Therapy, 27,* 45–55.

Brittain, R. (1970). The sadistic murderer. *Medicine, Science, and the Law, 10,* 198–207.

Cooper, A., Sandhu, S., Losztyn, S., & Cernovsky, Z. (1992). A double-blind
placebo-controlled trial of medroxyprogesterone acetate and cyproterone
acetate with 7 pedophiles. *Canadian Journal of Psychiatry, 37,* 687–693.

Dickey, R. (1992). The management of a case of treatment-resistant paraphilia with
long-acting LHRH agonists. *Canadian Journal of Psychiatry, 37,* 567–569.

Dietz, P. E., Hazelwood, R. R., & Warren, J. (1990). The sexually sadistic
criminal and his offenses. *Bulletin of the American Academy of Psychiatry and
the Law, 18,* 163–178.

Doren, D. M. (2002). *Evaluating sex offenders: A manual for civil commitments and
beyond.* Thousand Oaks, CA: Sage.

Egger, S. A. (1998). *The killers among us: An examination of serial murder and its
investigation.* New York: Prentice Hall.

Foote, R. M. (1944). Diethylstilboestrol in the management of psychopathological
states in males. *Journal of Nervous and Mental Diseases, 99,* 928–935.

Fromm, E. (1973). *The anatomy of human destructiveness.* New York: Holt.

Giannangelo, S. J. (1996). *The psychopathology of serial murder: A theory of violence.*
Westport, CT: Praeger.

Gijs, L., & Gooren, L. (1996). Hormonal and psychopharmacological interventions in
the treatment of paraphilias: An update. *Journal of Sex Research, 33,* 273–290.

Golla, F. L., & Hodge, S. R. (1949). Hormonal treatment of sexual offenders.
Lancet, 1, 1006–1007.

Grasswick, L., & Bradford, J. M. W. (2003). Osteoporosis associated with the
treatment of paraphilias: A clinical review of seven reports. *Journal of
Forensic Sciences, 48,* 1–7.

Gratzer, T., & Bradford, J. M. W. (1995). Offender and offense characteristics of sexual sadists: A comparative study. *Journal of Forensic Sciences, 40,* 450–455.

Grubin, D. (1994). Sexual murder. *British Journal of Psychiatry, 165,* 524–629.

Hucker, S., Langevin, R., & Bain, J. (1988). A double-blind trial of sex drive reducing medication in pedophiles. *Annals of Sex Research, 1,* 227–242.

Johnston, P., Hudson, S. M., & Marshall, W. L. (1992). The effects of masturbatory reconditioning with nonfamilial child molesters. *Behaviour Research and Therapy, 30,* 559–561.

Kafka, M., & Coleman, E. (1991). Serotonin and paraphilias: The convergence of mood, impulse and compulsive disorders. *Journal of Clinical Psychopharmacology, 11,* 223–224.

Kennedy-Moore, E., & Watson, J. C. (1999). *Expressing emotion: Myths, realities, and therapeutic strategies.* New York: Guilford.

Krafft-Ebing, R. von (1886). *Psychopathia sexualis.* Philadelphia: F. A. Davis.

Langevin, R., Bain, J., Ben-Aron, M. H., Coulthard, R., Day, D., Handy, L., et al. (1985). Sexual aggression: Constructing a predictive equation: A controlled pilot study. In R. Langevin (Ed.), *Erotic preference, gender identity, and aggression in men: New research studies* (pp. 39–76). Hillsdale, NJ: Lawrence Erlbaum.

Langevin, R., Ben-Aron, M. H., Wright, P., Marchese, V., & Handy, L. (1988). The sex killer. *Annals of Sex Research, 1,* 263–301.

Langevin, R., Paitich, D., Hucker, S., Newman, S., Ramsay, G., Pope, S., et al. (1979). The effect of assertiveness training, Provera, and sex of therapist in the treatment of genital exhibitionism. *Journal of Behavior Therapy and Experimental Psychiatry, 10,* 275–282.

Levenson, J. S. (2004). Reliability of sexually violent predator civil commitment criteria. *Law & Human Behavior, 28,* 357–368.

Levin, J., & Fox, J. A. (1985). *Mass murder: America's growing menace.* New York: Plenum Press.

Marshall, W. L. (1979). Satiation therapy: A procedure for reducing deviant sexual arousal. *Journal of Applied Behavior Analysis, 12,* 10–22.

Marshall, W. L. (in press). Olfactory aversion and directed masturbation in the modification of deviant preferences: A case study of a child molester. *Clinical Case Studies.*

Marshall, W. L., Anderson, D., & Fernandez, Y. M. (1999). *Cognitive behavioural treatment of sexual offenders.* Chichester, UK: Wiley.

Marshall, W. L., & Fernandez, Y. M. (2003). *Phallometric testing with sexual offenders: Theory, research, and practice.* Brandon, VT: Safer Society Press.

Marshall, W. L., & Kennedy, P. (2003). Sexual sadism in sexual offenders: An elusive diagnosis. *Aggression and Violent Behavior: A Review Journal, 8,* 1–22.

Marshall, W. L., Kennedy, P., & Yates, P. (2002). Issues concerning the reliability and validity of the diagnosis of sexual sadism applied in prison settings. *Sexual Abuse: A Journal of Research and Treatment, 14,* 310–311.

Marshall, W. L., Kennedy, P., Yates, P., & Serran, G. A. (2002). Diagnosing sexual sadism in sexual offenders: Rehability across diagnosticians. *International Journal of Offender Therapy and Comparative Criminology, 46,* 668–676.

Marshall, W. L., Marshall, L. E., Serran, G. A., & Fernandez, Y. M. (in press). *Treating sexual offenders: An integrated approach.* New York: Routledge.

Masters, W., & Johnson, V. (1966). *Human sexual response.* Boston: Little, Brown.

McConaghy, N., Blaszcznski, A., & Kidson, W. (1988). Treatment of sex offenders with imaginal desensitization and/or medroxyprogesterone. *Acta Psychiatrica Scandinavica, 77,* 199–206.

Money, J. H. (1968). Discussion of the hormonal inhibition of libido in male sex offenders. In R. Michael (Ed.), *Endocrinology and human behavior* (p. 169). London: Oxford University Press.

Myers, W. C., Burgess, A. W., Burgess, A. G., & Douglas, J. E. (1999). Serial murder and homicide. In V. Van Hasselt & M. E. Hersen (Eds.), *Handbook of psychological approaches with violent offenders* (pp. 153–172). New York: Kluwer Academic/Plenum.

Myers, W. C., Scott, K. I., Burgess, A. W., & Burgess, A. G. (1995). Psychopathology, biopsychosocial factors, crime characteristics and classification of 25 homicidal youths. *Journal of the American Academy of Child and Adolescent Psychiatry, 36,* 1483–1489.

Pearson, H. J. (1990). Paraphilias, impulse control and serotonin (letter). *Journal of Clinical Psychopharmacology, 10,* 233.

Pfäfflin, F. (1995, September). *Issues, incidence and treatment of sex offenders in Germany.* Paper presented at the International Expert Conference on Sex Offenders, Utrecht, Netherlands.

Proulx, J., Blais, E., & Beauregard, E. (2005). Sadistic sexual aggressors. In W. L. Marshall, Y. M. Fernandez, L. E. Marshall, & G. A. Serran (Eds.), *Sexual offender treatment: Controversial issues* (pp. 61–77). Chichester, UK: Wiley.

Reilly, D., Delva, N., & Hudson, R. W. (2000). Protocols for the use of cyproterone, medroxyprogesterone and leuprolide in the treatment of paraphilia. *Canadian Journal of Psychiatry, 45,* 559–563.

Ressler, R. K., Burgess, A. W., & Douglas, J. E. (1988). *Sexual homicide: Patterns and motives.* New York: Free Press.

Rice, M. E., Chaplin, T. C., Harris, G. T., & Coutts, J. (1994). Empathy for the victim and sexual arousal among rapists and nonrapists. *Journal of Interpersonal Violence, 9,* 435–449.

Rieber, I., & Sigush, V. (1979). Psychosurgery on sex offenders and sex deviants in West Germany. *Archives of Sexual Behavior, 8,* 523–527.

Seto, M. C., & Kuban, M. (1996). Criterion-related validity of a phallometric test for paraphilic rape and sadism. *Behaviour Research and Therapy, 34,* 175–183.

Snaith, R. P., & Collins, S. A. (1981). Five exhibitionists and a method of treatment. *British Journal of Psychiatry, 132,* 126–130.

Stekel, W. (1929). *Sadism and masochism: The psychology of hatred and cruelty* (L. Brink, Trans.). New York: Horace Liveright.

Tennant, G., Bancroft, J., & Cass, J. (1974). The control of deviant sexual behaviour by drugs: A double-blind controlled study of benperidol, chlorpromazine and placebo. *Archives of Sexual Behavior, 3,* 261–271.

Ward, N. (1975). Successful lithium treatment of transvestism associated with manic depression. *Journal of Nervous and Mental Diseases, 161,* 204–206.

Ward, T. (2002). Good lives and the rehabilitation of offenders: Promises and problems. *Aggression and Violent Behavior: A Review Journal, 7,* 513–528.

Ward, T., & Marshall, W. L. (2004). Good lives, aetiology and the rehabilitation of sex offenders: A bridging theory. *Journal of Sexual Aggression, 10,* 153–169.

Weinberger, L. E., Sreenivasan, S., Garrick, T., & Osran, H. (2005). The impact of surgical castration on sexual recidivism risk among civilly committed sexual offenders. *Bulletin of the American Academy of Psychiatry and Law, 33,* 16–36.

Widiger, T. A., & Coker, L. A. (2003). Mental disorders as discrete clinical conditions: Dimensional versus categorical classification. In M. Hersen & S. M. Turner (Eds.), *Adult psychopathology and diagnosis* (4th ed., pp. 3–35). New York: Wiley.

Wincze, J., Bansal, S., & Malamud, S. (1986). Effects of medroxyprogesterone acetate on subjective arousal, arousal to erotic stimulation, and nocturnal penile tumescence in male sex offenders. *Archives of Sexual Behavior, 15,* 293–305.

11

Violent Sex Crimes

Lester W. Wright, Jr., Angela P. Hatcher,
and Matthew S. Willerick

INTRODUCTION

Most of us fear being the victims of violent crimes, particularly ones that are sexual in nature. It is horrific enough to lose one's life to criminal behavior, but to be captured and tortured sexually prior to being killed is beyond comprehension. Violent sex crimes often get sensationalized in the media and then take on lives of their own. The hype associated with these cases leads to inaccurate information and heightened fears, many of which are unfounded. Additionally, there have been many movies, novels, and works of fiction about violent sexual crimes that are often confused with actual cases. What follows is a review of the literature regarding violent sex crimes. The focus of this chapter will be on the act of sexual homicide, on the individuals who commit these crimes, and on how sexual homicide is investigated.

Sexual homicide has been defined as the killing of another person in the context of power, sexuality, and brutality (Ressler, Burgess, & Douglas, 1996). A murder may be classified as a sexual homicide when the evidence or observations at the crime scene indicate that the murder was sexual in nature. The evidence or observations could include the attire or lack of attire of the victim; exposure of the sexual organs of the victim; sexual positioning of the victim's body; the insertion of foreign objects into the victim's body cavities; evidence of oral, anal, or vaginal sexual intercourse; and/or evidence of substitute sexual activity, interest, or sadistic fantasy (Ressler et al., 1996).

Individuals who commit this type of crime derive some sort of sexual satisfaction from committing the crime, either as a result of a connection between sexual satisfaction and violence or as the result of dominating the victim.

It is difficult to assess the number of sexual homicides for several reasons. For instance, many crimes get reported as ordinary or motiveless homicides even when it is obvious that the crimes were sexual in nature (Ressler et al., 1996). Additionally, the evidence may have been inadequate to state conclusively that the crime was sexual in nature (Groth & Burgess, 1977), the investigators at the scene may not have been trained to detect the underlying sexual dynamics of the crime scene (Cormier & Simon, 1969; Revitch, 1965), or the investigators may not have shared their findings (Ressler, Douglas, Groth, & Burgess, 1980). It is largely agreed upon that the majority of serial murders are sexual in nature (Lunde, 1976; Ressler, 1985; Ressler et al., 1996; Revitch, 1965).

Hickey (2002) suggested that while serial murder is rare, the number of serial killers surged between the years 1950 and 1995, and since 1975 the rise has been even more dramatic. Similarly, Jenkins (1992) suggested that the number of serial murders in American society is increasing. Schlesinger (2001) argued that this increase in serial homicide may be an artifact of the increase in contract killings; thus, while the rate of serial murder may have increased, the rate of sexual homicide may not have increased. According to Hickey, the FBI estimates that there are between 35 and 100 serial killers active in the United States at any one time; however, Holmes and Holmes (1998) estimated that there are as many as 200 serial killers at large. Regardless of the actual number of serial killers at large, the odds of becoming a victim of a serial killer are minuscule when one takes into account the size of the population as a whole (Hickey, 2002). Serial killing does appear to be correlated with population density, that is, states with the largest populations and large metropolitan areas are most likely to report cases of serial murder; however, Hickey pointed out that researchers have not been able to find any regional subcultural variables, that is, poverty or race, that correlate with serial violence.

TYPES OF MULTIPLE KILLERS

The term "serial killer" encompasses several types of murderers, but is sometimes mistakenly applied. It is important to realize that serial murder is different from mass murder or spree murder; the distinction between these types of crimes will be described below. Specific types of serial killers will also be described.

Mass Murderer

Mass murder is a situation in which several victims are killed within a few moments or hours of each other (Hickey, 2002) and in one place (Holmes &

Holmes, 1998). Mass murderers, except those who kill their own families, will usually commit their crimes in public places (Hickey, 2002). Douglas and Olshaker (1999) reported that a mass murderer often kills in a place that is familiar to him, a place where he feels comfortable. The victims of mass murderers are often intentionally selected, such as a former boss, ex-wife, or friend, but other people who happen to be in the vicinity may also be killed. Sometimes, however, an offender gets so frustrated that he lashes out at groups of people who have no relationship to him. When an offender is angry at society in general, the best way to get even is to kill innocent children, perhaps in a schoolyard (Hickey, 2002).

Spree Killer

The spree killer kills a number of victims, usually at least three, at different locations in a short period of hours or days (Douglas & Olshaker, 1999; Hickey, 2002), and the killings are usually accompanied by the commission of another felony (Holmes & Holmes, 1998). Hickey noted that spree killers "often act in a frenzy, make little effort to avoid detection, and kill in several sequences" (p. 16). There appears to be no cooling-off period even though the murders occur at different places over what may be several hours or days (Greswell & Hollin, 1994; Hickey, 2002). Fox and Levin (2005) explained that the short amount of time between murders for a spree killer is spent planning and executing his crimes or evading the police.

Serial Killer

A serial killer is an individual who kills three or more people over a period of more than thirty days with a "cooling-off" period between killings (Holmes & Holmes, 1998). This is a person who hunts human beings for the sexual thrill it gives him, and he will do it over and over again. The serial killer individualizes his murders and often continues to kill over a longer period of time than the types of killers described above (Hickey, 2002). During the cooling-off periods the serial killer may continue about a daily routine that could include going to work and spending time with friends and family (Fox & Levin, 2005). He believes he can outwit and outmaneuver the police, sometimes posing as a police officer, and never expects to get caught (Douglas & Olshaker, 1999; Fox & Levin, 2005). If a serial killer is apprehended, it is typically only after he has eluded detection for weeks, months, or even years (Hickey, 2002). In some instances a serial killer will appear to stop killing; however, it is not known if the killer was jailed for another offense, that is, a single murder or another crime not linked to the other murders, died due to an illness or an accident, changed his modus operandi (method of operation), moved to a new location, or simply decided to stop killing. A serial killer is capable of producing quite a bit of fear since he is often thought to be killing for sport and is able to blend in with others, making him difficult to detect. Hickey noted that he may be one of the nicest people by day and a killer by night. Serial killers are often described as charming, ordinary, are often loners or asocial, and may have a good relationship with a wife or a girlfriend; likewise, it has been noted that when a serial killer does get apprehended, neighbors, acquaintances, or co-workers will often express shock and report that he was the last person they would have suspected of being a vicious murderer (Douglas & Olshaker, 1999). Fox and Levin (2005) noted that the typical serial killer does not "look or act like the strangers that our mothers always warned us about" (p. 36). They added that many serial killers are clever, inventive, and project a "nice guy" image that makes them so difficult to apprehend.

Within serial murder, it is frequently noted that there are different categories. Hickey (2002) distinguished between the visionary, mission-oriented, hedonistic, and power/control-oriented serial killers. According to Hickey's classification system, a visionary serial killer is an individual who murders at the command of voices that he hears or visions that he sees; a missionary-oriented serial killer is an individual who murders because it is his mission to get rid of certain groups of people; a hedonistic serial killer is an individual who obtains some sort of pleasure from the murders that he commits; and a power/control-oriented serial killer is an individual who obtains pleasure by exerting control over others. A sexual homicide might fall into either the hedonistic type or power/control-oriented type of serial killing.

From a psychological perspective, the evidence at crime scenes seems to indicate that there are two types of sexual murderers: the rape or displaced anger murderer (Cohen, Garofalo, Boucher, & Seghorn, 1971; Groth, Burgess, & Holmstrom, 1977; Prentky, Burgess, & Carter, 1986; Rada, 1978), and the sadistic or lust murderer (Becker & Abel, 1978; Bromberg & Coyle, 1974; Cohen et al., 1971; Groth, et al., 1977; Guttmacher & Weihofen, 1952; Podolsky, 1966; Prentky et al., 1986; Rada, 1978; Ressler, 1985; Scully & Marolla, 1985). The rape or displaced anger murderer kills his victim after committing the rape to avoid getting caught (Podolsky, 1966). It has been noted (Rada, 1978) that these murderers rarely report sexual satisfaction from their murders and do not perform postmortem sexual acts with their victims. The sadistic murderer, however, kills as part of a ritualized, sadistic fantasy (Groth et al., 1977). As Ressler et al. (1996) explained, for the sadistic murderer, "aggression and sexuality become fused into a single psychological experience—sadism—in which aggression is eroticized" (p. 6). Additionally, Brittain (1970) pointed out that the subjugation of the victim is important to the sadistic murderer, and cruelty and infliction of pain are merely the means by which this subjugation is achieved.

SOLO VERSUS TEAM KILLERS

Serial killings are often masterminded by one person, but may have one or more individuals who play subservient roles, as in the case of team killers

(Hickey, 2002). Team killers, that is, dyads, triads, or even larger groupings, are thought to be less common than solo killers (Hickey, 2002). With regard to relationship, Hickey noted that sometimes the members of a team are related, either legally (for example, spouses or stepsiblings) or by blood (for example, siblings or parent-child combinations). However, members of a team may also be intimately involved with each other but not related, acquaintances, or even strangers. As with solo serial killers, team killers are likely to have had a sexual motivation for committing their murders (Hickey, 2002). An example of team sexual serial killers is Kenneth Bianchi and Angelo Buono, better known as the Hillside Stranglers, who were adoptive cousins.

It has been noted (Hickey, 2002) that within teams there is always one person who maintains psychological control over the other member(s) of the team. Likewise, Kelleher and Kelleher (1998) noted that while the dynamics of team killers are frequently volatile, these teams will be dominated by a single individual who attempts to organize the criminal activities of the team, taking a leadership role in most of the homicides. Sometimes the control seems mystical, as in the case of Charles Manson; however, in other cases the control may take the form of coercion, intimidation, and persuasion (Hickey, 2002). Some leaders have reported experiencing a sense of power and gratification, not only through the deaths of their victims, but from getting others to do the killing for them. If caught, the leader of the team will usually turn on the other member(s) of the team and blame them for the murders (Hickey, 2002). Hickey also pointed out that not all members of the team share equally in the thrill of the kill; although, for some, killing not only becomes acceptable, but desirable.

Kelleher and Kelleher (1998) noted that the primary criminal activity of serial-killing teams that include one male and one female is sexual homicide. Kelleher and Kelleher stated, "male/female teams that specialize in sexual homicide are maintained by the synergy of the sexual relationship between the partners and their combined pathological obsession with sexual domination and control" (p. 121). While a majority of the female serial killers are part of a male-dominated team, there have been a number of cases in which the female member is very active in murders and whose magnitude of sexual psychopathic killing rivals that of her male counterpart (Kelleher & Kelleher, 1998).

Hickey (2002) determined that among nonrelative team killers, a man almost exclusively assumed leadership; in fact, very few cases have been documented in which a woman masterminded multiple homicides, was the main decision maker, or was the main enforcer. Kelleher and Kelleher (1998) noted that while the male partner of a serial-killing team was usually the dominant partner, a man was often a solo sexual serial killer as well. Hickey noted that some women who were followers went on to become " 'equal partners in the killing' and participated directly in some of the bloodiest murder cases ever chronicled" (p. 187).

Team killers, according to Hickey (2002), are not responsible for as many victims as solo killers. Specifically, he noted that on average team killers were responsible for four to five killings per offender whereas solo killers had a slightly higher average number of victims. He also noted that team killers were most likely to remain in local proximity to their killing sites and were not as mobile as other types of offenders (Hickey, 2002).

Team killers were similar to their solo counterparts on many background variables. However, some of the dissimilarities are that team offenders had a slightly higher rate of psychiatric problems, were less likely to have criminal records for sex-related crimes, and seemed more interested in financial gain than solo killers (Hickey, 2002). Solo killers, however, were more likely to report feelings of rejection in childhood, remember more beatings as a child, report having been adopted, and report parents dying or being an orphan. Team killers, for the most part, did not receive college educations and few received postsecondary training, such as vocational training. Most were employed in blue-collar work (Hickey, 2002).

FEMALE KILLERS

It is commonly thought that most women who kill do so in domestic situations and, thus, are not multiple killers (Hickey, 2002). However, some of these women go on to remarry and kill again. The notion of women as mass murders or serial killers goes against some long-held, and perhaps sexist, views of women, and is still quite controversial. These beliefs, held by mainstream society, as well as those of the courts, about female killers make it less likely that a woman will come under suspicion for multiple killings. According to Hickey, in 1991 the FBI labeled Aileen Wuornos the nation's first female serial killer basically because she was the first woman to kill like a man. She was not, however, the first female serial killer. It has been noted that there have been approximately fifty-six female serial killers since 1900; however, statistics have shown that the number of women who kill is relatively low in comparison to the number of men (Hickey, 2002).

One facet that sets female serial killers apart from male killers is their preferred choice of weapon—more specifically, poison; however, other female killers, particularly those with an accomplice, may also resort to more violent methods, such as shooting, bludgeoning, or stabbing (Hickey, 2002). According to the data in the Hickey study, female offenders differed from their male counterparts in several ways. Female offenders, in general, selected less-violent methods of killing, did not sexually attack the victim, did not mutilate the corpse, and were generally not sexually involved with their victims. Kelleher and Kelleher (1998) pointed out that the "female serial murderer was most successful when motivated by reasons other than sex and when operating alone" (p. 15). They also found that compared to the male serial killer, who frequently attacks strangers, the female serial killer's victim of choice is usually someone who depends on her for care or a person with whom she has some type of relationship. Hickey pointed out that the motives for female serial crimes are largely unknown, but financial security, revenge, enjoyment, and sexual stimulation have been identified as reasons for killing. However, as previously mentioned, women who commit serial murder are less likely to commit sexual homicide (Keeney & Heide, 1994; Kelleher & Kelleher, 1998).

MOTIVATIONAL FACTORS

Serial killers have frequently reported experiencing trauma during their formative years (Hickey, 2002). This trauma often took the form of instability in the home and included such things as alcoholic parents, prostitution by mother, incarceration of parent(s), periodic separation from parents due to trouble at home, and psychiatric problems involving the parents (Hickey, 2002). Many childhood factors, such as experiencing a trauma, and family of origin variables for sexual murderers have been examined in order to determine what motivated their acts. Several characteristics have been identified and include childhood abuse, neglect, poverty, violence in the home, violence in the media, exposure to pornography, genetics, cognitive disabilities, insanity, PMS, blood sugar imbalance, and/or substance abuse. However, these variables either singularly or in combination have been identified in the backgrounds of many individuals who do not grow up to be serial killers. While these variables have been identified in, and seem to be correlated with deviant offenders, these variables are not causal, that is, possessing these characteristics does not cause an individual to commit serial murder.

Development of Deviant Fantasies

Hazelwood and Michaud (2001) stated that aberrant sexual fantasies play a central role in the planning and the enactment of violent sexual offenses. They also pointed out that only a small minority of fantasies actually led to sexual crimes. Salter (2003) added that aberrant fantasies play an enormous role in the development of compulsive rapists, yet she cautioned that not every person who may have rape fantasies will turn into a rapist. Hazelwood and Michaud defined fantasy as "a mental rehearsal of a desired event" but noted that it may also include behaviors that the individual has no desire or intention of actually engaging in (p. 18). This continual mental rehearsal serves as a kind of editing mechanism that allows the offender to focus on the details of the crime that are uniquely arousing to him (Hazelwood & Michaud, 2001). He can rearrange the parts of his fantasy to his liking and mentally practice his crime with no negative consequences; thus, the fantasy ultimately becomes a template or map for the offender to follow when he commits the crime and, once the offender has a fully developed fantasy, he is ready to search for a victim to live out the fantasy (Hazelwood & Michaud, 2001). Salter stated that this process may take months or even years as these fantasies often start very early and continue for years before the assaults begin.

Hazelwood and Michaud (2001) have noted two disturbing trends with regard to sexual fantasies: (1) "Offenders today are conceptualizing their crimes at a much earlier age than their predecessors did," and (2) "Their fantasies are growing more complex and, in some cases, deadlier over time" (p. 19). As previously mentioned, Hazelwood and Michaud noted that an individual might fantasize about engaging in sexual murder but will not actually engage in the behavior. The distinction between individuals who only fantasize about committing a sexual murder and those who actually commit a sexual murder is that the latter actually made the choice to cross over from fantasy to reality. Salter (2003) stated that individuals who actually commit rape differ from those who only fantasize about rape in that the rape fantasies are more prevalent, are more obsessive, and are more important to the rapist.

It is not enough to know that deviant fantasies are part of the motivation for committing a sexual homicide; it is also important to examine what actually motivates an individual to act out his aberrant sexual fantasies. It is sometimes mistakenly believed that rape is a sexually motivated act and that the offender committed the crime because he was "horny" (Hazelwood & Michaud, 2001); however, sexual assault is an act of aggression, an assertion of power, an expression of anger, or some combination thereof. The rapist achieves gratification, not from the sexual release, but from the result of having power, exerting aggression, and expressing anger, while gaining the thrill of domination and control. Rapists are basically using sex as a tool of aggression as it serves nonsexual needs (Hazelwood & Michaud, 2001). Hickey (2002) stated that sexual assault appears to be the method of gaining control over the victims, which is very similar to an individual who commits sexual homicide for which he might receive sexual gratification from the power, control, or domination that he has over his victim.

The Role of Paraphilias

Paraphilias may also play a large role in the fantasies of serial killers. The *Diagnostic and Statistical Manual of Mental Disorders* (*DSM-IV-TR*; American Psychiatric Association, 2000) describes paraphilias as recurrent, intense sexually arousing fantasies, urges, or behaviors that generally involve nonhuman objects, the suffering or humiliation of one's partner or children or other non-consenting persons that occur over a period of at least six months. The *DSM-IV-TR* includes nine categories of paraphilias and it has been noted (Abel, Becker, Cunningham-Rathner, Mittelman, & Rouleau, 1988) that individuals typically have more than one paraphilia, although one paraphilia may be dominant over the others. The paraphilias that are most relevant to sexual homicide are sexual sadism and necrophilia.

Sexual sadism involves real, not simulated acts in which the individual derives sexual excitement from the psychological or physical suffering of his or her partner (American Psychiatric Association, 2000). This suffering may include humiliation and the partner may or may not consent to the activity. What is important is the suffering of the partner; this is the stimulus that elicits sexual arousal in these individuals. Sadistic fantasies or behaviors may include activities that indicate the dominance of the sadist over the partner, such as being forced to engage in submissive behavior and restraints, bondage, beating, burning, rape, cutting, stabbing, strangulation, torture, and/or mutilation. Killing of the partner may also occur.

Necrophilia, a sexual attraction to corpses, may take a variety of forms. Rosman and Resnick (1989) distinguished between three forms of genuine necrophilia—necrophilic homicide, the commission of murder in order to obtain a corpse for sexual purposes; regular necrophilia, the use of already dead bodies for sexual purposes; and necrophilic fantasy, the fantasizing about sexual activity with a corpse without actually engaging in necrophilic behavior. In examining the motivations behind necrophilia, it was noted that 68 percent of the individuals in their sample ($n = 34$) engaged in necrophilia in order to have an unresisting and unrejecting partner, and 12 percent of the sample engaged in necrophilia in an "attempt to gain self-esteem by the expression of power over homicide victims" (p. 159). Other reasons for engaging in necrophilia included reunion with a romantic partner (21 percent), conscious sexual attraction to corpses (15 percent), and attempting to gain comfort or overcome feelings of isolation (15 percent).

Committing Murder and the Escalation to Increased or Repeated Violence

There are a number of circumstances that might lead an individual to commit sexual homicide. As previously mentioned, perpetrators of this crime enjoy the power, control, and/or domination that they exert over their victim; likewise, if the individual feels as if he has no control over his life, he might commit murder in order to gain some form of control. Ressler et al. (1996) noted that an individual might commit a sexual homicide following a conflict, with either a woman, another man, parents, or a spouse; if the individual is under financial stress; is having marital, legal, or employment problems; after the birth of a child; or if there has been stress due to a death.

Douglas and Olshaker (1999), as well as Holmes and Holmes (2002), noted that as a serial killer progresses in his criminal career, there is sometimes an increase in violence, less planning, and less time between murders. For example, before he was apprehended, Ted Bundy escalated his rate of murder and engaged in very little planning.

PROFILING

The examination of criminal behavior, particularly sexual homicide, is multidisciplinary with fields such as psychology, sociology, geography, biology, and law enforcement making important contributions (Hickey, 2002; Ressler et al., 1996). The field of psychology offers assistance by providing diagnoses of the offenders, examining the childhood antecedents to criminal behavior, assessing the development of criminal behavior as a result of learned responses to particular stimuli, and implementing techniques for treating offenders (Ressler et al., 1996). Sociology helps to explain the actions of a murderer as a social phenomenon, examining murder within the larger social context in which it occurs (Ressler et al., 1996). Spatial mapping is a technique that combines geography with environmental criminology in order to connect crime scenes to offender habitats and hunting grounds (Hickey, 2002). Geographic profiling allows investigators to determine if various crime scenes are related to one another by location, which aides in finding a relational pattern to the crime scenes in order to pinpoint an offender's zone of familiarity—for example, where he lives or works (McCrary & Ramsland, 2003). Biology has contributed techniques such as DNA analysis to link perpetrators to specific crimes (Hickey, 2002). The primary objective of law enforcement is to determine the identity of the offender and apprehend him as soon as possible in order to prevent future victims (Ressler et al., 1996). The synergy of these fields working together makes it possible to accomplish more than they could working alone. While there are many types of profiling, the focus of this chapter will be on offender (criminal) profiling, victim profiling, equivocal death profiling, and crime scene profiling.

History of Profiling

Attempts at profiling prior to the 1970s were basically composite construction of murderers, which described the "typical murderer" (Palmer, 1960; Rizzo, 1982). Criminal profiling, as we now think of it, began informally in the early 1970s by using crime scene information to infer various offender characteristics to help in the apprehension of the criminal (Ressler et al., 1996). During the early days, criminal profiling was referred to as "psychological profiling" or "criminal personality profiling" and was a little-known and spare-time service that was provided to local law enforcement officers if requested (Hazelwood & Michaud, 2001). These newer criminal profile analyses conducted by the FBI proved useful in identifying offenders and, due to the requests of local authorities, were then made available to all law enforcement agencies (Ressler et al., 1996). Within a span of a decade, criminal profiling became very popular. The results of a 1981 evaluation questionnaire revealed that criminal profiling had helped to focus 77 percent of the cases in which the subjects were later identified (Ressler et al., 1996). Today, criminal profiling is just part of a more comprehensive behavioral assessment program called criminal investigative analysis (McCrary & Ramsland, 2003). For more information on criminal investigative analysis, see McCrary and Ramsland, *The Unknown Darkness* (2003).

What Profilers Do

Criminal profilers examine crime scenes for clues that reveal behaviors that are characteristic of, and perhaps unique to, the offender. Hazelwood and Michaud (2001) stated that although investigators can find patterns and common elements among offenders, no two offenders ever commit the exact same sexual crime. "The crime scene may be the point of abduction, a location where the victim was held, the murder scene, and/or the final body location" (Ressler et al., 1996, p. xiii). Crime scene characteristics, as described by Ressler et al., include "those elements of physical evidence found at the crime scene that may reveal behavioral traits of the murderer" (p. xiii). This could include a variety of physical remnants of the crime, including a weapon, tools used in the crime, positioning of the victim, and evidence of various acts committed against the victim, just to name a few. Ressler et al. defined profile characteristics as "those variables that identify the offender as an individual and together form a composite picture of the suspect" (p. xxii). Profile characteristics may consist of any defining feature about an individual, including the perpetrator's sex, age, occupation, level of intelligence, acquaintance with the victim, residence, and mode of transportation. According to Hazelwood and Michaud, the most difficult crimes to profile are those in which there is no known cause of death, an unidentified victim, and/or a lack of behavior to study and analyze.

Criminal profilers assist with investigations by describing the type of individual who committed a crime (Douglas & Olshaker, 1999). A major fallacy that exists is that profilers can identify a specific person as the individual who committed a crime. Ressler et al. (1996) pointed out that rather than providing the identity of the offender, a criminal profile indicates the kind of person who is most likely to have committed a crime based on observation of the characteristics at the crime scene. Thus, criminal profilers can help law enforcement narrow its field of investigation and concentrate its efforts in a particular area, but cannot tell the law enforcement personnel who is responsible for the crime, (Ressler et al., 1996; Hazelwood & Michaud, 2001; see also Chapter 9 in this volume).

Criminal investigative analysis has been shown to be especially useful in solving cases of sexual homicide (Ressler et al., 1996). To an untrained investigator, many of these crimes appear to be motiveless and the crime scenes seem to offer few obvious clues about the killer's identity, which may often be the case in many sexual homicide crime scenes. Since obvious as well as implied clues are pieced together to form leads that contribute to the killer's profile, attention to detail is extremely important when profiling crime scenes (Ressler et al., 1996). Hazelwood and Michaud (2001) stated that when creating a profile for any type of crime, it is very important for the profiler to maintain an open mind and not lock in on only one possibility. Victims of a killer often share common characteristics that may or may not, at first, be obvious. Analyzing the similarities and differences among the victims of a particular murderer can provide information about the motive for the crime as well as information about the perpetrator himself (Ressler et al., 1996).

In addition to sexual homicide, criminal profiling has also proven to be useful in solving such crimes as hijacking of aircrafts, drug trafficking, anonymous letter-writing, spoken threats of violence, arson, and rape, to name a few (Ressler et al., 1996; Casey-Owens, 1984; Hazelwood, 1983; Miron & Douglas, 1979).

The FBI, in order to manage their workload, will now only get involved in cases that meet the following three criteria: (1) the crime must be violent or potentially violent; (2) the crime must be unsolved; and (3) all major leads must be exhausted (Hazelwood & Michaud, 2001).

Crime Scene Profiling

In crime scene profiling, investigators rely on information from the crime scene to construct a profile of potential perpetrator characteristics. A classification system for serial killers that was developed by the FBI classifies perpetrators of sexual homicide as organized, disorganized, or mixed. This classification system denotes how much planning and how much control the offender had over the victim during the commission of the crime (Ressler et al., 1996).

An organized perpetrator is deliberate in his actions, methodical, premeditated, mature, and resourceful, which denotes more experience (Hazelwood & Michaud, 2001; Hickey, 2002). An organized offender usually brings his preferred weapon and whatever else he needs with him to commit the crime and will leave as little evidence of his identity as possible (Hazelwood & Michaud, 2001). Organized killers most often select total strangers as victims, and they tend to hunt outside their neighborhood (Hazelwood & Michaud, 2001). They are also more likely to engage in sexual perversions (Hickey, 2002).

A disorganized offender appears to act more randomly or opportunistically, as if he was in a rush, careless, or sloppy (Hazelwood & Michaud, 2001; Hickey, 2002). A disorganized offender has not thought ahead; he acts impulsively, using any available weapon. He may "leave both his victim and ample evidence of his own identity, i.e., fingerprints or blood, where they can be readily discovered" (Hazelwood & Michaud, 2001, p. 127). For a complete list of variables that distinguish between organized and disorganized offenders, see Hickey (2002) and Ressler et al. (1996).

Criminal/Offender Profiling

Criminal profiling is the way in which law enforcement has sought to combine the information from research in other disciplines with more traditional investigative techniques in an effort to combat violent crime (Ressler et al., 1996). Various other authors have described profiling as a collection of leads (Rossi, 1982), an educated attempt to provide specific information about a certain type of criminal (Geberth, 1981), thinking about a case in a way in which no one else has (Hazelwood & Michaud, 2001), and a biographical sketch of behavioral patterns, trends, and tendencies (Vorpagel, 1982; Ressler et al., 1996). The process of criminal profiling is more of an art than a science; it is subjective rather than objective. However, it does not involve psychic powers, such as ESP, second sight, intuition, or voodoo (Hazelwood & Michaud, 2001). It should be viewed as an investigative tool rather than a magical solution to a crime (Hazelwood & Michaud, 2001; see Chapter 9 in this volume).

A profile of an UNSUB, that is, an unidentified subject, according to the Behavioral Science Unit of the FBI is "a listing of the characteristics and traits of an unidentified person" (Hazelwood & Michaud, 2001, p. 133); those characteristics and traits are the variables that together form a behavioral composite of the unknown offender (Ressler et al., 1996; McCrary & Ramsland, 2003). When completed, "a profile is a detailed analysis that reveals and interprets significant features of a crime that previously had escaped notice or understanding" (Hazelwood & Michaud, 2001, p. 123).

Victim Profiling

In order for a profiler to assist in identifying an offender, he or she must understand the motive for the crime, and, according to Douglas and Olshaker (1999), the key to understanding motive is in the victimology. Specifically, the profiler wants to know who the offender has chosen as his victim and why (that is, if it was a victim of opportunity or if a careful and deliberate choice was made). This is based on the assumption that behavior reflects personality and, even though every crime is unique, behavior fits into certain patterns (Douglas & Olshaker, 1999). Identifying significant pieces of the crime pattern enables the profiler to determine why the offender committed the crime, which will aid in answering the ultimate question of who committed the crime. For example, when examining a break-in, it is important to know what items were taken because this can provide valuable information as to what type of perpetrator you should be looking for and what his motive was for committing the crime (Douglas & Olshaker, 1999). Specifically, if the property taken was valuable and could be sold for cash, you will have one type of offender; however, if the property taken was some personal item of little value, such as women's underwear, then you have a very different type of offender. The offender who stole the women's underwear had a very different motive than the offender looking for valuable property to sell. Knowing the motive helps the officials know the dangerousness of the offender. A panty thief does not take women's underwear because he cannot afford to buy them; the theft is motivated by the sexual images related to the items, the fantasy, and the associated sexual arousal (Douglas & Olshaker, 1999). Based on experience from other crimes, profilers know that fetish burglars are not likely to stop on their own; however, criminals who commit crimes for different motives, that is, for money or for drugs, may stop when they gain employment or enter rehab (Douglas & Olshaker, 1999).

An examination of the victim in relation to the offender helps us to understand the social dynamics of serial murder (Hickey, 2002). It allows investigators to clarify the victim side of the killer-victim relationship and to measure, in part, the degree of vulnerability and culpability of some victims. Research on victims of serial killers has shown that they were more likely to be killed away from their homes, which means that they may have been in areas of the community where their assailants had easy access. Three categories of potential victims—family, acquaintances, and strangers—have been identified. Research has demonstrated that serial killers most often kill strangers, whereas with homicide in general, relatives and close friends are most often the victims (Hickey, 2002).

Various reasons have been offered as to why the majority of serial killers focus on strangers. It may be easier to dehumanize a stranger, which enables the killer to view the victims as objects of hatred and lust; the offender likely perceives that killing strangers provides some level of safety from detection (Hickey, 2002); and the offender might get a thrill from seeking out unsuspecting strangers (Leyton, 1986). Most homicides are committed by an individual with whom the victim had a relationship, and, as a result, the focus of the investigation will be on the victim's friends and family members until the death is linked to a serial killer.

With regard to victim selection, some victims are chosen because they match the killer's paraphilic fantasy; some murderers engage in proxy killings in which they focus on individuals who remind them of someone, perhaps their mother (Hickey, 2002); and there have been victims who have just been at the wrong place at the wrong time. Some offenders are drawn to victims who represent what they want for themselves, such as beauty, wealth, or assertiveness; other offenders destroy those who symbolize what they fear or loathe, such as gay individuals, the homeless, the elderly, and the infirm (Hickey, 2002). The latter groups of individuals represent what Egger (2003) calls the "less dead," or the "devalued stratum of humanity" (p. 48). He refers to these groups—gays, homeless, prostitutes, migrant workers, runaways, elderly, infirm—as "less dead" because they were "less alive" before their violent deaths. In other words, these groups were marginalized and devalued members of the community who were seen as vulnerable and powerless by the perpetrator. There is, unfortunately, support for Egger's proposition that marginalized groups are viewed as being "less alive" and that their deaths will not cause a public outcry. For example, the task force for the Green River serial killer was disbanded prior to the conclusion of their work due to lack of public support and dwindling leads even though the investigation produced over fifty verifiable victims, most of whom were prostitutes (Egger, 2003).

The degree of power and control the killer is able to exert over the victim is another factor influencing victim selection (Hickey, 2002). Serial killers seem to carefully target and prey upon individuals whom they perceive as less physically and intellectually capable than themselves. These categories of strangers, while not mutually exclusive, were reportedly the most frequently sought after by serial killers: young women alone, including female college students and prostitutes; children, both boys and girls; and travelers, including hitchhikers. On the one hand, when acquaintances were killed, the top three categories that represent the majority of victims were friends and neighbors, children, and women alone; on the other hand, when the victims were family members, children, husbands, and wives were the top three categories. When the three categories of victims (strangers, acquaintances, and family) were combined, women and children made up the majority of the victims, which makes sense if these offenders prey on those they perceive as weaker, helpless, or as having less power and control. This statistic is in sharp contrast to homicide in general, in which 78 percent of the victims were men. Another difference between the types of homicide is that the majority of victims of serial killers are Caucasian, whereas overall, the majority of general homicide victims are African American. Young and middle-aged adults and teens were the most likely targets of serial killers, but the very young and the elderly were also represented. Hickey has noted that since 1975, there has been an increase in those offenders who target only the elderly. Hickey suggested that with the aging of the population in the United States, nursing homes and hospitals may need to pay close attention to employees to prevent individuals from living out their "angel of death" fantasies.

Victim facilitation, or the degree to which victims make themselves accessible or vulnerable to attack, is another factor that needs to be considered (Hickey, 2002). Most serial killers murder strangers and their victimization may be determined by the degree to which the victim placed him- or herself in a vulnerable situation (Hickey, 2002). Reiss (1980) determined that victims who had been multiply victimized were more likely to experience the same form of victimization than be subject to two different criminal acts. McDonald (as cited in Hickey, 2002) determined that victim-prone individuals developed certain attitudes and lifestyle choices that increased their vulnerability. People who hitchhike or prostitute themselves, as well as individuals who pick up hitchhikers and prostitutes, are considered high facilitators. Low-facilitation victims can be thought of as sharing little or no responsibility for victimization, such as when a stranger kidnaps a child playing in a yard or when a nurse poisons a patient in a nursing home. The risk of being a victim of a serial killer is small and most victims are considered low facilitation, but there are those who are at greater risk as a result of their age, gender, place of residence, or lifestyle, and the number of these individuals is increasing (Hickey, 2002).

Children are more likely to die in domestic homicide than at the hands of a serial killer, but they can be at risk both in and out of the home (Hickey, 2002). Female serial killers of children are more likely to murder either their own children or those of relatives, whereas male offenders were seven times more likely to be strangers to their victims. The primary motives for female offenders of children from highest to lowest were financial, to collect insurance money; to exert control; enjoyment; and sexual gratification (the last two were tied at 8 percent). The primary motives of male offenders of children in order from highest to lowest were sexual gratification, to exert control, enjoyment, and financial reasons; however, the majority of men reported having a combination of reasons for why they murdered children. Serial killers who kill children engage in a variety of methods to lure children. They will sometimes ask for the child's assistance, perhaps in looking for a lost puppy; they will sometimes tell the children that there has been an emergency and that they are there to escort them home; they will sometimes use a badge to look as if they are an authority figure; or they may sometimes appeal to the child's ego by telling the child that he or she should be in a beauty contest or in a television commercial (Wooden, 1984; Hickey, 2002). As is true with those who kill adults, the offender is usually a psychopath and will use a combination of techniques that begin with charisma or manipulation, move to intimidation, and, ultimately, become brutal (Hickey, 2002).

Linkage Analysis

Criminal investigative analysts use a different profiling procedure called linkage analysis to determine if a murder is linked to other murders and to help the investigators determine if the same killer is responsible for multiple homicides (Hazelwood & Michaud, 2001). Investigators using linkage analysis look for a particular modus operandi and ritual behaviors, that is, type of weapon used, age and gender of victim, performance of sexual acts, amount of violence used, etc. They also look to see if the murders were grouped together, both geographically and chronologically. According to Hazelwood and Michaud, in addition to examining the similarities in the crime scenes, it is also important to look at the differences, as dissimilarities in crime scenes do not necessarily mean that different people committed the crimes. Dissimilarities in various aspects of two crime scenes could merely mean that as the killer committed more murders, he altered his preferred method of killing (that is, changed type of weapon, acted alone rather than as part of a team, chose a different type of victim, used a different method to dispose of the body, etc.) (Hazelwood & Michaud, 2001). Differences or inconsistencies in crime scenes could also be due to variables such as the specific crime scene circumstances, victim behavior, the amount of time the offender has, and even the killer's mood. Linkage analysis can be a valuable tool to link cases together in situations where there are no reliable witnesses or physical evidence (Hazelwood & Michaud, 2001).

Equivocal Death Analysis

Equivocal death analysis, or what is sometimes referred to as a psychological autopsy, is another facet of the criminal investigative analyst's work (Hazelwood & Michaud, 2001). The goal for someone conducting an equivocal death analysis is to verify what happened when the way in which a person died is unclear or in dispute; the analyst attempts to determine whether the death was an accident, suicide, or homicide (Hazelwood & Michaud, 2001). Rather than answering the question of who committed the murder, an equivocal death analyst's task is to answer the question of what happened to the victim. Knowing what happened to a loved one can be very important to the victim's family, as well as having ramifications regarding insurance payment and burial rights in a church-sanctioned facility. In order to determine what happened to the victim, the equivocal death analyst needs to have a lot of information about the victim and the circumstances surrounding his or her demise. The analyst attempts to identify and list every material fact or instance of behavior that is consistent, or inconsistent, with homicide, suicide, or an accident. The result is an evidence tally sheet of all the relevant data pointing toward a manner of death (Hazelwood & Michaud, 2001). It might be necessary for the analyst to interview family, friends, coworkers, neighbors, teachers, acquaintances, etc., in order to obtain as much information as possible regarding the individual's personality and behavior. Hazelwood and Michaud stated that they interview each person on two different occasions from three to six months apart since most people will not speak ill of someone shortly after his or her death. Letting time lapse between interviews allows people to provide contrasting views of the deceased, which results in a well-balanced description of the victim (Hazelwood & Michaud, 2001). The investigator will want to obtain answers to such questions as: Who might have benefited from the victim's death? Was the victim suicidal or depressed? Did the victim engage in behaviors that might have led to an accidental death? Based on this information and evidence from the crime scene, the equivocal death analyst can provide a determination as to the manner of death.

Problems in Profiling

Profiling should be considered one tool that can assist in the investigation of criminal behavior. It is often, as stated earlier, a technique that is employed as a last resort, when all other leads have been exhausted. When using profiling as a tool in investigations, one has to always consider that the profile could lead investigators in the wrong direction, which is a waste of resources and could facilitate the loss of additional lives (Hickey, 2002). Even if the profile is based on the best crime scene evidence and employs the most precise attention to detail, it is rarely 100 percent accurate, which, again, may cause investigators to ignore other leads that do not match the information in the profile (Goodroe, 1987; Hickey, 2002). Additionally, some investigators may not understand how to properly use the information in the profile. They may base their conclusions about the identity of a suspect or whether two cases can be linked to a common suspect on one piece of physical evidence from the crime scene(s) that was mentioned in the report (Hickey, 2002). In conclusion, it takes experienced investigators to thoroughly investigate a crime and create a profile, and it takes investigators trained in their use to properly use profiles once they are obtained (see Chapter 9 in this volume).

REFERENCES

Abel, G. G., Becker, J. V., Cunningham-Rathner, J., Mittelman, M., & Rouleau, J. L. (1988). Multiple paraphilic diagnoses among sex offenders. *Bulletin of the American Academy of Psychiatry and the Law, 16,* 153–168.

American Psychiatric Association. (2000). *Diagnostic and statistical manual of mental disorders* (4th ed., Text Rev.). Washington, DC: Author.

Becker, J. V., & Abel, G. G. (1978). Men and the victimization of women. In J. R. Chapman & M. R. Gates (Eds.), *Victimization of women.* Beverly Hills, CA: Sage.

Brittain, R. P. (1970). The sadistic murderer. *Medical Science and the Law, 10,* 198–207.

Bromberg, W., & Coyle, E. (1974). Rape! A compulsion to destroy. *Medical Insight,* April, 21–22, 24–25.

Casey-Owens, M. (1984). The anonymous letter-writer—a psychological profile? *Journal of Forensic Sciences, 29,* 816–819.

Cohen, M. L., Garofalo, R. F., Boucher, R., & Seghorn, T. (1971). The psychology of rapists. *Seminars in Psychiatry, 3,* 307–327.

Cormier, B. S., & Simon, S. P. (1969). The problem of the dangerous sexual offender. *Canadian Psychiatric Association, 14,* 329–334.

Douglas, J., & Olshaker, M. (1999). *The anatomy of motive.* New York: Pocket Books.

Egger, S. (2003). *The need to kill: Inside the world of the serial killer.* Upper Saddle River, NJ: Prentice Hall.

Fox, J. A., & Levin, J. (2005). *Extreme killing: Understanding serial and mass murder.* Thousand Oaks, CA: Sage.

Geberth, V. J. (1981). Psychological profiling. *Law and Order, 29,* 46–49.

Goodroe, C. (1987). Tracking the serial offender. *Law and Order, 35,* 29–33.

Gresswell, D. M., & Hollin, C. R. (1994). Multiple murder: A review. *British Journal of Criminology, 34,* 1–13.

Groth, A. N., & Burgess, A. W. (1977). Sexual dysfunction during rape. *New England Journal of Medicine, 297,* 764–766.

Groth, A. N., Burgess, A. W., & Holmstrom, L. L. (1977). Rape: power, anger and sexuality. *American Journal of Psychiatry, 134*, 1239–1243.

Guttmacher, M. S., & Weihofen, H. (1952). *Psychiatry and the law.* New York: Norton.

Hazelwood, R. R. (1983). The behavior oriented interview of rape victims: The key to profiling. *FBI Law Enforcement Bulletin, 52*, 8–15.

Hazelwood, R., & Michaud, S. G. (2001). *Dark dreams: Sexual violence, homicide, and the criminal mind.* New York: St. Martin's Press.

Hickey, E. W. (2002). *Serial murderers and their victims* (3rd ed.). Belmont, CA: Wadsworth.

Holmes, R. M., & Holmes, S. T. (1998). *Serial murder* (2nd ed.). Thousand Oaks, CA: Sage.

Holmes, R. M., & Holmes, S. T. (2002). *Profiling violent crimes: An investigative tool* (3rd ed.). Thousand Oaks, CA: Sage.

Jenkins, P. (1992). A murder "wave?" Trends in American serial homicide 1940–1990. *Criminal Justice Review, 17*, 1–19.

Keeney, B. T., & Heide, K. M. (1994). Gender differences in serial murderers: A preliminary analysis. *Journal of Interpersonal Violence, 9*, 383–398.

Kelleher, M. D., & Kelleher, C. L. (1998). *Murder most rare: The female serial killer.* Westport, CT: Praeger.

Leyton, E. (1986). *Hunting humans: Inside the minds of mass murderers.* New York: Pocket Books.

Lunde, D. T. (1976). *Murder and madness.* San Francisco: San Francisco Books.

McCrary, G. O., & Ramsland, K. (2003). *The unknown darkness: Profiling the predators among us.* New York: HarperCollins.

Miron, M. S., & Douglas, J. E. (1979). Threat analysis: The psycholinguistic approach. *FBI Law Enforcement Bulletin, 48*, 5–9.

Palmer, S. (1960). *A study of murder.* New York: Thomas Crowell.

Podolsky, E. (1966). Sexual violence. *Medical Digest, 34*, 60–63.

Prentky, R. A., Burgess, A. W., & Carter, D. L. (1986). Victim responses by rapist type: An empirical and clinical analysis. *Journal of Interpersonal Violence, 1*, 73–98.

Rada, R. T. (1978). *Clinical aspects of the rapist.* New York: Grune & Stratton.

Reiss, A., Jr. (1980). Victim proneness in repeat victimization by type of crime. In S. Fineberg & A. Reiss, Jr. (Eds.), *Indicators of crime and criminal justice: Quantitative studies* (pp. 41–54). Washington, DC: U.S. Department of Justice.

Ressler, R. K. (1985). Violent crimes. *FBI Law Enforcement Bulletin, 54*, 1–31.

Ressler, R. K., Burgess, A. W., & Douglas, J. E. (1996). *Sexual homicide: Patterns and motives.* New York: The Free Press.

Ressler, R. K., Douglas, J. E., Groth, A. N., & Burgess, A. W. (1980). Offender profiling: A multidisciplinary approach. *FBI Law Enforcement Bulletin, 49*, 16–20.

Revitch, E. (1965). Sex murderer and the potential sex murderer. *Diseases of the Nervous System, 26*, 640–648.

Rizzo, N. D. (1982). Murder in Boston: Killers and their victims. *International Journal of Offender Therapy & Comparative Criminology, 26*, 36–42.

Rosman, J. P., & Resnick, P. J. (1989). Sexual attraction to corpses: A psychiatric review of necrophilia. *Bulletin of the American Academy of Psychiatry and the Law, 17*, 153–163.

Rossi, D. (1982). Crime scene behavioral analysis: Another tool for the law enforcement investigator. *Police Chief, 3*, 152–155.

Salter, A. C. (2003). *Predators: Pedophiles, rapists, and other sex offenders: Who they are, how they operate, and how we can protect ourselves and our children.* New York: Basic Books.

Schlesinger, L. B. (2001). Is serial homicide really increasing? *Journal of the American Academy of Psychiatry and the Law, 29*, 294–297.

Scully, D., & Marolla, J. (1985). "Riding the bull at Gilley's": Convicted rapists describe the rewards of rape. *Social Problems, 32*, 251–263.

Vorpagel, R. E. (1982). Painting psychological profiles: Charlatanism, charisma, or a new science? *Police Chief, 3*, 156–159.

Wooden, K. (1984). *Child lures.* Shelburne, VT: National Coalition for Children's Justice, Child Lures.

Index

abuse. *See also* alcohol abuse; child sexual abuse; childhood abuse; childhood sexual abuse; drug/alcohol abuse; sexual abuse; substance abuse: exploration/exploitation and, 60; by female babysitters, 60

abuse reenactment, by juvenile female sex offenders, 73

abused-abuser hypothesis, of pedophilia, 89

acceptance-based therapy, 170

adolescence. *See also* juvenile female sex offenders: bestiality in, 35; incest impact during, 143

adolescent sexual abuse victims, 136; eating disorders among, 137; substance abuse by, 137; suicide and, 136

adult male incest offenders, 144–145

adult on adult assault, by female sex offenders, 65

aggression: among homosexual offenders, 67; among pedophiles, 89; sexuality and, 89, 167; treatment of, 167

AIDS. *See* HIV/AIDS

alcohol abuse: approach goal programs for, 199; among female sexual offenders, 52; myopia theory and, 113; sexual assault and, 105–106, 111–112, 114

American Psychiatric Association (APA), 1; sexual deviation according to, 82

American Psychological Association (APA) Ethical Guidelines, 221

anger management training, 167

antiandrogen treatment: cyproterone acetate, 163, 240, 245; medroxyprogesterone acetate, 163, 240, 246; for sex offenders, 163–164; for sexual sadists, 239

anxiety management training, for sexual assault victims, 122–123

APA. *See* American Psychiatric Association

About the Editors
and Contributors

M. MICHELE BURNETTE holds a doctorate in clinical psychology and a Master of Public Health in epidemiology. Dr. Burnette was formerly a psychology professor at Western Michigan University, during which time she taught courses in human sexuality and conducted research on sexual function and health. She has also taught at the community college level and at the University of Pittsburgh. She is currently in private practice in Columbia, South Carolina, where she specializes in therapy for sexual problems. She has coauthored two textbooks with Richard D. McAnulty, *Human Sexuality: Making Healthy Decisions* (2004) and *Fundamentals in Human Sexuality: Making Healthy Decisions* (2003). She is also coeditor of this set.

RICHARD D. McANULTY is an associate professor of psychology at the University of North Carolina at Charlotte. He earned his Ph.D. in clinical psychology from the University of Georgia under the late Henry E. Adams. His research interests broadly encompass human sexuality and its problems. His books include *The Psychology of Sexual Orientation, Behavior, and Identity: A Handbook*, edited with Louis Diamant (Greenwood Press, 1994), and *Human Sexuality: Making Healthy Decisions* (2004, with M. Michele Burnette). He has served on the board of several journals, including the *Journal of Sex Research*.

LAURENCE J. ALISON is professor of forensic psychology at the University of Liverpool, director of the Centre for Critical Incident Research, and codirector of the Centre for the Study of Critical Incident Decision Making (www.incscid.org). His work involves training and evaluating responses to high-profile incidents, including security planning, siege, anticorruption investigations, and most recently, debriefing international negotiating teams. His work has attracted the attention of the United Kingdom police, the fire service, specialist operations, the intelligence services and, more recently, the United Nations in New York. Professor Alison has published widely on offender profiling and psychological contributions to law enforcement practice in major incidents. His current research focuses on decision-making and leadership qualities in critical incident management. He has provided psychological advice in armed robbery, murder, rape, and child abduction cases. He has presented his work in several international journals and recently published *The Forensic Psychologists Casebook: Psychological Profiling and Criminal Investigation.*

KAREN S. CALHOUN, Ph.D., is professor of psychology at the University of Georgia. She is a fellow of the American Psychological Association and a past president of the Southeastern Psychological Association as well as the Society of Clinical Psychology (Division 12 of APA). She has been associate editor of the *Journal of Consulting and Clinical Psychology* and the *Psychology of Women Quarterly.* Her research into the consequences, causes, and prevention of sexual assault has been funded by the NIMH, the CDC, and National Institute of Justice. She is director of the University of Georgia's Center for Research on Violence and Aggression. Her research has been honored by the university with the award of its Creative Research Medal and the William A. Owens Award for Creative Research, the university's highest research honor for the social sciences.

RACHAEL M. COLLIE, M.A., Dip.Clin.Psyc., is a clinical psychologist who has worked in the clinical forensic field since 1996. She currently teaches clinical forensic psychology at Victoria University of Wellington, New Zealand. She is completing her Ph.D. on personality processes in violent offenders.

MEGAN E. CRAWFORD is a doctoral student in clinical psychology at the University of Georgia in Athens, Georgia. Her primary research interests center on understanding the factors and mechanisms responsible for sexual revictimization among women, with a particular emphasis on interpersonal processes that impact risk. Additional research interests include prevention of sexual assault and the relationship between personal narratives and psychosocial adjustment.

THERESA A. GANNON is lecturer in forensic psychology at the University of Kent, United Kingdom. She earned her D.Phil. in forensic psychology from the University of Sussex in 2003, and her major research interest is in the cognition of sexual offenders.

ANGELA P. HATCHER is a graduate student in clinical psychology at Western Michigan University under the supervision of Lester W. Wright, Jr. She is interested in studying sexual behavior, criminal behavior, and offender treatment programs. Her thesis project involved the examination of sexual functioning in college students. She has been involved in research examining individual versus group substance abuse treatment in individuals on probation, parole, supervised release, or pretrial. Most recently, she has been accepted into the Federal Bureau of Investigation Behavioral Science Unit's Research Internship program.

STEPHEN J. HUCKER, M.B., B.S., FRCP(C), FRCPsych., is a professor of psychiatry in the Law and Mental Health Program at the University of Toronto and a member of the medical staff at the Centre for Addictions and Mental Health, in addition to his independent forensic consulting practice. The author of over eighty publications, his research interests include sexual offending, risk assessment, and sexual deviations. His recent books include *Release Decision-making*, coauthored with Dr. Chris Webster in 2004, and the edited book *Handbook of Psychiatry and the Law in Canada* (in press).

RITA KENYON-JUMP, Ph.D., is a clinical psychologist with the Department of Veterans Affairs in Battle Creek, Michigan. She has provided extensive inpatient and outpatient group and individual psychotherapy to male and female veterans who have experienced sexual trauma in childhood and as adults. She is the Military Sexual Trauma Coordinator for seven Veterans Affairs (VA) Medical Centers in Michigan, Illinois, and Indiana, and currently serves on a National Committee for Women Veterans Mental Health.

WILLIAM L. MARSHALL, Ph.D., FRSC, is professor emeritus of psychology and Psychiatry at Queen's University, Canada, and director of Rockwood Psychological Services, Kingston, Ontario, which provides sexual offender treatment in two Canadian federal penitentiaries. Dr. Marshall has thirty-five years of experience in assessment, treatment, and research with sexual offenders. He has over 300 publications, including sixteen books. He was president of the Association for the Treatment of Sexual Abusers from 2000 to 2001, and he was granted the Significant Achievement Award of that association in 1993. In 1999, Dr. Marshall received the Santiago Grisolia Prize from the Queen Sophia Centre in Spain for his worldwide contributions to the reduction of violence, and he was elected a fellow of the Royal Society of Canada in 2000. In 2003, Dr. Marshall was one of six invited experts who were asked to advise the Vatican on how best to deal with sexual abuse in the Catholic Church.

JENNA McCAULEY is a graduate student at the University of Georgia. Her work, under the supervision of Dr. Karen Calhoun, focuses on sexual assault and revictimization. Her more specific research interests address the role of alcohol and other risk factors in impacting women's risk for assault with the ultimate aim of integrating this information into intervention programs aimed at victims of sexual assault.

WILLIAM D. MURPHY, Ph.D., is a professor in the Department of Psychiatry, Division of Clinical Psychology, at the University of Tennessee, Memphis. He serves as director of the Special Problems Unit, an evaluation, treatment, and research program for sexual offenders, and is the director of the APA-approved University of Tennessee Professional Psychology Internship Consortium. He is a past president of the Association for the Treatment of Sexual Abusers. He is on the editorial boards of *Sexual Abuse: A Journal of Research and Treatment* and *Child Maltreatment*.

NIKLAS NORDLING is a researcher in the Department of Psychology at the Åbo Akademi University in Finland. His research has concentrated on sadomasochistic sexuality.

JONATHAN S. OGAN is a Ph.D. student at the Centre for Investigative Psychology, based in the University of Liverpool, England. His interest is in victimology, especially with regard to vulnerable victims, which was the subject of his master's degree. He has given a presentation at the Investigative Psychology Conference (2002) on victim characteristics as basis for offender profiling. He has cowritten a chapter with Professor Laurence Alison on the Jack the Ripper killings as the archetypical high-profile, serious investigation. His current research, under the supervision of Professor David Canter, is on elderly victims of homicide.

I. JACQUELINE PAGE, Psy.D., is a clinical psychologist and associate professor in the Department of Psychiatry at the University of Tennessee Health Science Center. She specializes in working with adolescent male and female sexual offenders, children with sexual behavior problems, and sexual abuse victims.

N. KENNETH SANDNABBA is professor of applied psychology at the Åbo Akademi University in Finland. He has written widely on aggression and sexual behavior. He is also a registered clinical sexologist and psychoanalytic psychotherapist.

PEKKA SANTTILA is professor of psychology at the Åbo Akademi University in Finland. His research has mainly concentrated on forensic psychological issues as well as sexual behavior, including sexual behavior of children and sadomasochism.

DONNA M. VANDIVER, Ph.D., is an assistant professor at Illinois State University, Department of Criminal Justice Sciences. Her research interests include sex offender classification, female sex offenders, and juvenile sex offenders. Her work has been published in *Sexual Abuse: A Journal of Research and Treatment, Criminal Justice Review, International Journal of Offender Therapy and Comparative Criminology,* and *Journal of Interpersonal Violence.*

TONY WARD, Ph.D., Dip.Clin.Psyc., is professor of clinical psychology at Victoria University of Wellington, New Zealand. Professor Ward's research interests fall into five main areas: rehabilitation models and issues; cognition and sex offenders; the problem behavior process in offenders; the implications of naturalism for theory construction and clinical practice; and assessment. He has over 160 research publications. His two most recent books are *Theories of Sexual Offending* (coauthored with Devon Polaschek and Tony Beech) and *Culture and Child Protection: Reflexive Responses* (coauthored with Marie Connolly and Yvonne Crichton-Hill).

MATTHEW S. WILLERICK is a graduate student at Western Michigan University working toward his Ph.D in clinical psychology. His main areas of interest involve the study of sex offenders and the treatment of sexual dysfunctions. His secondary interests lie in the sexual education of children and adolescents. He is currently working on several projects under Lester W. Wright, Jr., in the areas of sexual scripts and courtship disorders.

LESTER W. WRIGHT, JR., is an associate professor of psychology and directs the Clinical Studies Laboratory at Western Michigan University. His areas of interest are in human sexual behavior, particularly deviant sexual behavior and criminal behavior. His current research focuses on sexual scripts, hypermasculinity, empathy in sex offenders, the effects of mood disorders on sexual functioning, and negative and positive gender roles. He is the past president of the Western Michigan Psychological Association.